S0-AEK-997

CONSUMER RITES

SANTA CLAUS
HEADQUARTERS
MERRY CHRISTMAS

CONSUMER RITES

The Buying & Selling of American Holidays

LEIGH ERIC SCHMIDT

PRINCETON UNIVERSITY PRESS

PRINCETON, NEW JERSEY

Published by Princeton University Press, 41 William Street,
Princeton, New Jersey 08540
In the United Kingdom: Princeton University Press,
Chichester, West Sussex

Library of Congress Cataloging-in-Publication Data

Schmidt, Leigh Eric.
Consumer rites : the buying and selling of American holidays /
Leigh Eric Schmidt
p. cm.
Includes bibliographical references (p.) and index.
ISBN 0-691-02980-6 (cloth : alk. paper)
1. Holidays—Economic aspects—United States. 2. United States—
Religious life and customs. 3. United States—Economic conditions. I. Title.
GT4986.A1S35 1995
394.2'6973—dc20 95-10604

This book has been composed in Berkeley Book

Princeton University Press books are
printed on acid-free paper and meet the guidelines
for permanence and durability of the Committee
on Production Guidelines for Book Longevity
of the Council on Library Resources

Printed in the United States of America by Princeton Academic Press

1 3 5 7 9 10 8 6 4 2

TO MY PARENTS

ROGER AND ANN SCHMIDT

A HOLIDAY GIFT

BOOK

CONTENTS

Illustrations

CONSUMER RITES

INTRODUCTION

In a *Family Circus* cartoon that a colleague passed along to me a couple of years ago, two little boys are in a shopping mall surveying various Easter commodities—baskets, candies, rabbits, eggs, and other novelties of the season. The slightly older boy says to his little brother, "This may be Good Friday, but Sunday's gonna be even gooder." Underlining the consumer-oriented nature of the occasion, their mother stands behind them, her arms full with two loaded bags of merchandise. Admittedly it was a bit disconcerting to discover that a *Family Circus* cartoon illuminated my research (how much lower, after all, can one sink in that putative hierarchy of cultural texts than this campy little strip?). But I had learned long ago to look in the miscellaneous nooks of popular culture for materials, and here was another find, however modest: Commerce and religion, celebration and consumption, commingle in a one-ring cartoon in what is a curious, if familiar, mix. Two of the great festivals of Christianity, Good Friday and Easter, are overshadowed in these little boys' minds by their wide-eyed anticipation of candy and other treats. The mall, not the church, is the venue for their fascination with Easter. The marketplace serves, in this cartoon and in the culture, as an obvious arena of holiday preparation, observance, and enthrallment—a central location for the commemoration of Christianity's most important holy days as well as for the enactment of America's most prominent civic holidays.

This book is a historical exploration of how these now taken-for-granted connections in American culture between commerce and celebration were forged. It examines the evolving relationships between what Jacques Le Goff called, for the medieval world, "the church's time" and "the merchant's time," between America's religious culture and its consumer culture, between holidays and the market. In a word, it is a history of that old bugbear, commercialization. The book focuses on St. Valentine's Day, Christmas, Easter, and Mother's Day (a distinctly Protestant feast day at its founding), but also roams more widely across the American calendar, pausing to scrutinize other events such as New Year's, the Fourth of July, and Father's Day. It explores the widening influence of the commercial culture on the way Americans celebrate, on the gifts they exchange, on the holiday rituals and liturgies they enact. But it is a book, too, about "devout consumption" (in Thorstein Veblen's sardonic phrase), about the ways in which religious folks embraced and helped foster a new consumer culture, about how such high holy days as Christmas and

Easter came to provide the occasion, timing, and inspiration for shopping and merchandising. In its broadest intent the book offers a religious and cultural history of American holidays centered on the themes of commerce, Christianity, and consumption. In chronological scope it ranges over a wide sweep of American time from the colonial period into the twentieth century.[1]

So deeply enmeshed are commerce and the calendar in American culture that most holidays would be scarcely recognizable without the trappings of the market. Christmas stands out as the grand "festival of consumption," with a significant segment of American retailing living or dying on profits connected with the Yuletide season. Indeed, many department stores as well as smaller retailers count on Christmas for a quarter of their annual sales and, because of higher margins in pricing, half of their annual profits. And sometimes the percentages for Yuletide earnings run even higher—up to 70 percent of the year's profits. In all, according to one recent estimate, Christmas gift giving is worth some $37 billion to the nation's economy. (One commentator has wryly pointed out that this makes the American Christmas bigger than the gross national product of Ireland.) In the United States, Christmas would simply not be Christmas without its commercial forms—without the department-store Santa Clauses, without the mall wonderlands of seasonal decorations and festive cheer, without Yuletide promotions and advertisements in the mass media, without Christmas clubs at the bank, without gifts, cards, ribbons, wrapping, and tinsel. The festival is such a pervasive and inescapable part of the culture that it all but consumes the calendar from Thanksgiving to New Year's, and businesses now make a year-round trade of preparing for the holiday, often beginning to plan the next Christmas before the one preceding it has even been celebrated. If an anthropologist were to draw up a "temporal map" of American culture, Christmas would have to be inscribed in giant red letters.[2]

Christmas unquestionably stands out as the country's peak consumer fête, but the holiday is surrounded by a series of foothills that merchants and advertisers have long striven to raise to its heights. Calendrical festivities and commercial objectives have been brought into alignment at nearly every turn in American culture. Sales are announced around the various holidays from Washington's Birthday and Memorial Day to Labor Day and Veterans Day. A seemingly simple and age-old folk holiday, St. Valentine's Day, is hailed for the "orgy of spending" it produces. Some merchants have even begun to recast Halloween, a rising star in the firmament of commercial holidays, as "Malloween," where trick-or-treaters are removed from the dark dangers of the streets to the safe haven of the shopping center. At the Fourth of July, advertisements urge people to declare their independence from high prices or limited selection and proclaim that freedom is the luxury of choice. At Father's Day, Bloomingdale's, under the slogan "EVERY DAD'S A HERO," offers assistance in celebrating the "special spirit of fatherhood."[3]

The list goes on and is more than a matter of holiday advertisements. At Thanksgiving, department stores such as Macy's harness the popular, often carnivalesque medium of the street parade for huge, televised fêtes to kick off the Christmas shopping season. In a more modest vein, at Halloween, local businesses regularly sponsor parades to channel the celebration away from youthful pranks into civic boosterism. Even the folklore of modern holidays is often the product of the "fakelore" or "folklure" of American business, evident in Montgomery Ward's Rudolph the Red-Nosed Reindeer and in the familiar images of Santa Claus created for Coca-Cola in the 1920s and 1930s. Whole industries—for example, those of florists, confectioners, and greeting-card manufacturers—have been built around times of celebration, special occasions, and life passages. Indeed, the goods that these merchants provide have come to stand among the chief artifacts of modern American festivals. Where religious, civic, or folk rituals commemorated such solemn celebrations and transitions in the past, twentieth-century Americans, following a trend that was already gathering momentum in the nineteenth century, have turned more and more habitually to the commercial culture to bless these ceremonial moments. In the words of a television advertising campaign for Korbel champagne that aired in the wake of the Gulf War, "We have so much to celebrate." One editorial cartoon about the Columbus quincentenary wittily captured this American predilection for turning any holiday or celebration into a commercial event: A sign in a show window at "Jack's department store" reads, "COLUMBUS DAY * Sale * ALL MERCHANDISE MARKED UP 200% BECAUSE, LET'S FACE IT, COLUMBUS WAS A GREEDY LITTLE OPPORTUNIST JUST LIKE JACK IS."[4]

As this barbed cartoon suggests, commercialization is a topic on which one has come to expect a certain amount of disapprobation, cynicism, and even moralizing. Protests in Christian circles about the commercialization of Christmas, for example, are familiar and recurrent; shibboleths like "Put Christ Back into Christmas" or "Jesus Is the Reason for the Season" are annually repeated in tones of both annoyance and despair. (The irony that such slogans themselves have become marketable in Christian bookstores—appearing on cards, sweatshirts, and coffee mugs—suggests the way in which commercialization often subsumes even the resistance to it. That the Knights of Columbus have chosen billboards, a quintessential modern advertising form, as the medium for their ongoing campaign to "keep Christ in Christmas" only underlines the power of the commercial culture.) But, despite the ease of co-optation, various church groups and pastors have kept up a drumbeat of protest from one year to the next against "the delirium" of the commercial Christmas and "the advertising lords of Madison Avenue," who have reduced "the true glory of Christmas" to "a crass marketing ploy." The lament over the blitz and glitz of Christmas is one of the culture's fondest, most pervasive jeremiads.[5]

The critique of the commercial exploitation of the holidays has not been confined to church folk. Scholars, social critics, and secularists have often joined the refrain. Alienated from a commodity-driven mass culture, commentators have rued the diminution of play, fantasy, and misrule in a society of commercialized leisure. In this vein of criticism, the philosopher Josef Pieper decried the "sham festivals" of modernity and the market's desolation of "true festivity": "The real festival is almost disappearing behind the commercialized folderol that has come to the fore." Other, more accommodating pundits have still recognized this fundamental alienation from modern forms of holiday observance. One pair of counselors, for example, advised Americans on how to "unplug the Christmas machine" and how to restore love, spontaneity, and simplicity to the holidays. "The one concern that unites virtually all the people we've talked to," these ritual therapists noted, "is a yearning for a simpler, less commercial, more soul-satisfying celebration. . . . We want to ward off the commercial excesses of the season and create an authentic, joyful celebration in tune with our unique needs and desires." To the weary and the estranged, commercialization has come to pose a redoubtable challenge to the sacredness and authenticity of the holidays—even somehow to their very reality.[6]

From the vantage point of its antagonists, the modern commercial culture is viewed as intrinsically profaning: The boundaries that mark out holy time are overwhelmed by advertising and merchandising, by the rationalistic calculation and hard-bitten secularism of business. The machinations of the marketplace are seen as subverting free participation in the effervescent gaiety of a festival; manipulation and obligation displace spontaneity and sincerity. Both the profit making of merchants and the gift seeking of individuals are viewed as supplanting community celebration; the integrative, unifying powers of festivity are lost in the impersonal world of malls and the private, fragmented dreams of consumers. More than that, the homogeneity of mass-produced gifts and goods is seen as shearing celebration of imagination, originality, and self-expression. This concern plays on an essential nostalgia in modern industrialized societies for the genuine, the handcrafted, the authentic, or the real. Modern holidays and their rituals are often thought to be sadly insubstantial, ersatz, or hollow; they are never so good, genuine, joyous, or fulfilling as they used to be. The suspicion that the holidays have somehow been worked up by Hallmark or Macy's, that the holidays are not our own, hangs like a shadow over modern American celebrations.

Perhaps most insistently, the fundamental religious meanings of Christmas and Easter are seen as being lost in a sea of goods. Spiritual, nonmaterialistic, and eternal verities are thought to be seriously subverted in a consumer culture enthralled by abundance, self-gratification, and novelty. In this view, the transcendent claims of Christian time, the revelatory power of the Incarnation and the Resurrection, are dwarfed by the mundane claims of merchant's time, which are puffed up in modern American culture like a big balloon in a Macy's Thanksgiving Day parade. Moreover, feasts celebrating affluence and indulgence are seen as standing the liberating message of Christianity—good news for the poor and the downtrodden—on its head: The corpulent figure of Santa Claus and the promise of material reward, not the Christ child and the divine humility of the manger, become the ultimate symbolic measure of American time. From this critical vantage point, the American versions of Christmas and Easter manage to consecrate consumption, even as the feasts themselves are desecrated and distorted. Much the same has been said, too, about the American version of Chanukah as it has become increasingly engulfed in and enlarged by the merchandising réclame of the American Christmas: The light of religious miracle is said to be obscured in the glare of modern Hellenizers.[7] Commercial contrivance, in short, is thought to erode the religious significance of the holidays, disconnecting them from the transcendent and displacing their "true" meaning.

This book is only a partial heir to these venerable traditions of social and religious criticism. (It is hard to imagine that one would choose to write—or read—a book like this one without sharing at least some of these critical concerns.) Yet throughout I have sought historical perspective and insight first; even where I have found the critics to be most on the mark, I have put balance before judgment. Only in the acknowledgments at the end of this book do I make more "confessions" of my own slippery positioning in these ongoing cultural contests. As a historian, what I have consistently attempted to do is to set the very tradition of the jeremiad against festal indulgence and holiday consumption in dense historical context: for example, to see its Puritan and evangelical sources, to probe its expression in the liberal Protestant tradition of the social gospel, and to explore its wider dimensions in diverse forms of cultural criticism. It would be ingenuous, in any case, to think that a work of historical scholarship would somehow redeem American time or recapture "genuine" festivity. On the whole, historians make poor prophets: With their archival hoe in hand, they are still doing spadework when reform-minded religious leaders, cultural critics, and popular writers have already moved on to the harvest.

But my wariness of conjoining history and social criticism in this book arises from sources other than simply a lack of clear-eyed commitment or a nostalgia for the vanished dream of historical objectivity. One reason is a premise based in the anthropology of festival and celebration: A common feature of festivity is to overindulge, to eat, drink, or spend to excess, lavishly to use up resources otherwise diligently saved. The surfeit of gifts and spending associated especially with Christmas, but also with other holidays, gives expression to a kind of festal excess that is often fundamental to celebrations. In other words, festive behavior is built in large part on wastrel prodigality, on surplus and abundance, on conspicuous consumption.[8] The critique of American holidays as consumer fêtes is often an attack on festival itself, a repudiation of celebratory indulgence and dissipation out of adherence to puritanical or republican values emphasizing hard work, self-control, frugality, and simplicity. To put this in concrete terms, much the same ascetic logic that condemned the potlatch in the nineteenth century condemns the modern Christmas. The contemporary contest stands as another battle between the heirs of the Puritans and the perennial bacchanalians of popular culture. The contention also suggests the ongoing struggle between republican, producer values and therapeutic, consumer ones—a conflict that has been fought out in the United States with particular intensity in the realm of ritual and holiday observance. For my part, instead of quickly taking sides in these long-standing contests, I have tried to fathom the power of consumer-oriented versions of celebration, their emergence and standing as "genuine" festivals, and the process by which they have been vested with significant cultural authority and legitimacy. Conversely, I have also sought to understand how it is that the commercial renderings of the holidays came to be viewed as "a cold, lifeless business" (in Emerson's estimation of shopworn gifts), poor facsimiles of lost originals.[9]

A second reason for my hesitancy in throwing my lot in with the critics derives from the anthropology and sociology not of festival, but of consumption and gift exchange. Like any number of other scholars, I am interested in the meanings with which people imbue material things—that is, how people construct, design, and order their physical world through goods and gifts. I am thus concerned with explicating the expressive significance of objects, the symbolic power of commodities, the meaning-laden quality of goods. As a sizable cohort of anthropologists, historians, and sociologists has pointed out, social critics have all too often succumbed to the temptation of seeing gifts and goods in terms of simplicities: hierarchic display, status competition, consumer manipulation, capitalist hegemony, mass-cultural banality, and the like. Lost in such interpretations are the miscellany of cultural meanings and the array of intimate relationships that various possessions and presents embody. This loss would be particularly grave with holiday gifts, goods, and decorations; these things involve an intricate web of familial ties, cherished memories, and treasured associations. People have regularly invested the presents they give, seek, long for, and receive with considerable importance. Recognizing the puissance of commercial institutions to refashion the holidays and to mold gift-giving customs is no substitute for seeing these braided threads of meaning and relationship. In this book I try to comprehend both the power of market forces and the semiotics of gifts; the very ability of commerce to reshape the calendar would have remained superficial without the deep reservoirs of religious and cultural meaning from which holiday keepsakes took their varied significance. This, in short, is an attempt to synthesize two strands of contemporary scholarship that too often go their separate ways.[10]

A third reason for my reluctance to hop on the critics' train arises from my interest in the history of popular religion and popular culture. The history of popular culture, especially the history of popular festivals, is full of reform-minded stratagems to purify, streamline, or correct the perceived excesses and deficiencies of plebeian celebrations. At one level, the lament over modern versions of Christmas or such modern inventions as Mother's Day is yet another highbrow indictment of popular culture and its feast days. The critique displays an enlightened disdain for the supposed gullibility of people as they marvel at Christmas windows or buy yet another bouquet for Mom. If only they could see through the manipulation—the logic seems to go—they would be freer, better human beings, socially and religiously more aware. Whether commercial versions of festivals can really be said to be "popular" or are actually another "elite" bid for control over popular forms of leisure and celebration is an open question. The dialectics between "popular" and "elite," between improvisation and orchestration, between buying and selling, recur throughout this book, but it is important to underline at the outset that modern commercialized forms of holiday observance remained popular in crucial ways. Consumers embraced, "bought," and helped create the market versions of St. Valentine's Day, Christmas, Easter, New Year's, Mother's Day, and other holidays, imbuing these rites with their own hopes and desires, recognizing in them resonant and fluid symbols of love, family, faith, prosperity, and well-being. Even as modern celebrations were given shape and structure in and through the marketplace, their varied enactments need to be seen simultaneously as vibrant and creative. These new rituals, then, were "regulated improvisations" (to borrow a phrase from Pierre Bourdieu), and the old dualisms—of agency and determinism, individual consciousness and economic materialism—simply do not make sense of them. The popularity of modern holidays is to be understood through the dense interplay of cultural production and consumption, in the powerful dynamism of "cultural creation and cultural reception."[11]

A fourth and final reason for not joining the critics' parade concerns issues of gender. These festivals of home and marketplace were in good measure women's rituals and celebrations, and cultural critics have often shown a distinct disdain for mass-cultural forms—whether sentimental fiction, domestic periodicals, or millinery fashions—associated predominantly with women. In the seasoned Protestant and republican rhetoric against luxury and consumption, women, in particular, were seen as especially vulnerable to fashion—a disease that was feared to be highly communicable, spreading effeminacy and foppery among men and endangering civic virtue and male solvency. In these cultural markings of gender, women were associated especially with fashions in dress, home decoration, shopping, and gift giving, all sharply removed from male realms of work and leisure. Also, historians have tended to take more seriously "public" versions of the holidays, whether Puritan sermons for fast and thanksgiving days, Fourth of July spectacles, St. Patrick's Day parades, or street festivals among the working classes. Though in the nineteenth century women sometimes found space in the "public" enactments of the holidays, usually they were edged as spectators to the periphery of official ceremonies, or they simply stayed inside, distanced from the riotous street carnivals in which rowdy male celebrants fired guns, banged kettles, fought, drank, and pillaged. Together critics and historians have often slighted what Louisa May Alcott fondly called "home-festivals," those rituals centered on domestic gift giving and orchestrated almost exclusively by women. Middle-class women were actively engaged in the reconstruction of celebration in ways that tamed the riotous, carnivalesque, and frequently misogynistic street versions of festival. This was evident in the varied efforts to refine or domesticate Christmas, New Year's, and St. Valentine's Day as well as in the attempts to lift up that new triumvirate of festivities dedicated to the Christian home—Children's Day, Mother's Day, and Father's Day. In short, the twin feminization of consumption and festivity in American culture requires careful consideration, not wry dismissal.[12]

Winding my way through the thicket of debate on the blessings and banes of commercialized holidays—through those who condemn, those who celebrate, those who calculate, and those who do not think twice about the matter—has been one of the more difficult tasks to which this book has summoned me. I have struggled to find the right voice, one of keen participation in the tensile ambiguities of the subject—the satisfactions and dissatisfactions of consumers, the piety and ingenuity of merchants, the anger and acquiescence of critics, the devotion and distraction of churchgoers. The right voice, in this case, then, is hardly univocal or final; indeed, I have sought to make this a work of many voices, competing, interacting, equivocating, and pronouncing in a conversation without closure.[13]

It is a standard scholarly pose to claim that not enough has been said or written about whatever one happens to be talking or writing about at the moment. But it is hard to say this about the holidays, ever awash as they are in coverage from the popular media and garnering as they have growing attention from scholars in various disciplines. The holidays have long had more than their share of chroniclers. This attention has especially been embodied in the venerable "Book of Days" genre. From Henry Bourne's *Antiquitates Vulgares* (1725) to Robert Chambers's *Book of Days* (1863–64) to Edward Deems's *Holy-Days and Holidays* (1902) to Robert Haven Schauffler's expansive series *Our American Holidays* (1907–47) to Jane Hatch's *American Book of Days* (1978) to Jack Santino's *All Around the Year* (1994), a distinctive genre devoted to British and American calendrical traditions was forged and continues to thrive. This genre, usually moving in encyclopedic fashion through the calendar from New Year's to Christmas, has amassed (and often repeated) a vast assemblage of folklore about a wide range of holidays. Deeply rooted in their own historical worlds, these holiday books have served a variety of purposes over the long period of their flourishing: Bourne's antiquarian curiosity about the "superstitions" of the common people and his desire to abolish any "sinful and wicked" customs that persisted; Chambers's romantic nostalgia for fading calendrical traditions and his hope to save them; Schauffler's progressive, Americanizing emphasis on the moral, educational, and assimilative value of holidays for school, church, and community. These works also testify to the expansive reach of modern historicism. With the advent of this genre, the holidays were made the object of extensive historical rationalization and explanation. Rituals were collectible, like museum specimens of bones and butterflies, and, even more, they were typeset, a matter of literary romance and printed commodity. Performance became text.[14]

The "Book of Days" genre, in reflecting the changing contours of British and American calendars, also exhibited the impact of merchandising, often becoming part of the marketing apparatus of modern holiday observance. No text displayed this turn more clearly than Harry Spencer Stuff's *Book of Holidays*, published in 1926. Though heavily indebted to earlier works in the genre, Stuff's slim volume gave a distinctly modern rationale for attending to the holidays. "This is an age of commercialism," he announced, "and lest the advantage of this *The* BOOK *of* HOLIDAYS be overlooked commercially, merchants, window dressers, advertising agents and publicity men are invited to note the many suggestions offered herein." In this vein Stuff provided, for example, a special section called "Greeting Card Days" and included a list of monthly birthstones being promoted by the American Jewelers' Association. In his entry on Mother's Day, he said simply that it is "a day particularly sponsored by the Florists and the Greeting Card dealers of the United States." Commerce was the central theme in Stuff's book; unlike earlier works in the genre, its own value was conceived not in antiquarian, but in market terms. Holidays were interesting as much for their merchandising potential as for their folkloristic curiosity, religious solemnity, or civic pageantry. Where Edward Deems conceived the "inestimable value" of holidays in didactic terms, Stuff saw their value in the quite estimable terms of a dollar sign. With Stuff, the "Book of Days" genre was brought to bear on the very construction of market-centered, sales-driven, consumer-oriented celebrations.[15]

Holiday books in this genre—from those of Henry Bourne, John Brand, and Robert Chambers onward—have served as the standard sources of reference about British and American calendrical customs. In their extensive compilation of folk beliefs and rites, these works have been the most enduring and common way in which the holidays have been addressed. In the last decade or so, however, historians have increasingly broken the hold of this genre on the calendar. Questions about how cultures structure time and celebration have long been recognized as crucial ones in the anthropology and sociology of religions, and historians of American religion and culture have, for their part, increasingly engaged these questions of ceremony and festival. Scholars have turned to ritual—whether the fervent worship practices of evangelical Protestants or the grand spectacles of civic pageants and street festivals—to understand more deeply the diverse patterns and rhythms of American culture, to see the round of events that gives form and tempo to the day-to-day lives of people.

The holidays have been beneficiaries of this turn to ritual. Recent discussions of American feast days have been multifarious. Attention has been paid, for example, to the Puritan calendar in seventeenth-century New England, to slave holidays in the antebellum South, to African American Emancipation Day celebrations, to working-class versions of Christmas and the Fourth of July, to the multicultural energies of Mardi Gras, to Roman Catholic festivals dedicated to the Virgin Mary, and to the broad-ranging place of the holidays in civic ritual.[16] In some cases, notably in Daniel Boorstin's *Americans: The*

Democratic Experience and Andrew Heinze's *Adapting to Abundance*, commerce has already proven a prominent thread in the skein of holiday interpretation. For obvious reasons, this has been particularly true in examinations of Christmas, such as in James Barnett's pioneering work *The American Christmas* and William Waits's *Modern Christmas in America*.[17] *Consumer Rites* builds on these solid foundations, even as it offers the first sustained interpretation of American holidays and the consumer culture.

In focusing on the interplay of commerce, Christianity, and consumption in the holidays, this book elaborates on a variety of themes in American religious and cultural history. It suggests the impact of national markets on local traditions and ethnic customs as commerce has tended to homogenize the images and forms of holiday celebration—that is, to mass-produce and mass-market holiday materials, whether valentines or Easter novelties. In important and substantial ways, commercial institutions helped lift up and standardize a set of national holiday symbols out of a welter of local, regional, and ethnic traditions. Merchants also tended to offer safe, respectable, civic-minded versions of the holidays that centered on the carefully controlled environs of stores, not on the festive disorder of the streets. Retailers were interested in sales, not subversion; they wanted to absorb carnivalesque play for their own ends, not generate topsy-turvy license (and its associated vandalisms). Yet the well-worn motifs of homogenization, disciplined control, and Weberian rationality are hardly adequate handles for the complexity of this story. New forms of magic, improvisation, charivari, enchantment, and trickery were also prevalent in the modern rituals of holiday observance and gift giving. In the nineteenth and early twentieth centuries, the carnivalesque energies of popular festivity among the middle classes were not so much repressed as diluted, diffused among the diversions of St. Valentine's Day, the tricks of April Fools' Day, the summer amusements of revival meetings and Chautauquas, the reinvention of Halloween games and Maypoles, the marvels of Easter parades, and the reimagined excesses of Christmas and New Year's. The nineteenth-century marketplace provided a fertile domain for eclecticism and play, and bourgeois forms of ritual and celebration remained remarkably intricate and full of life.[18]

The book uncovers as well the links between consumer-oriented and family-centered celebrations—connections that focus especially on the combined roles of women as shoppers, gift givers, and superintendents of the holidays. Wanamaker's version of Christmas or the florists' vision of Mother's Day dovetailed with the growing emphasis on domestic and familial forms of celebration. Women became the primary movers behind many of the holidays (and the actual founders of several, such as Mother's Day and Father's Day), and merchants encouraged and sponsored this female initiative and inventiveness.

Through expanding rituals of shopping and gift giving, holidays became an integral part of women's work and their familial obligations.[19] This book also attempts to bridge the chronological gap in the history of consumer culture in the United States. Much of the literature in this field has focused on the period after 1880, while a burgeoning scholarship has begun exploring eighteenth-century antecedents in America's widening emulation of the aristocratic culture of gentility and in the deepening involvement of the colonies in London's commercial revolution. This work spans that temporal divide, tracking the unfolding impact of the commercial culture on ritual and celebration across the early modern world to the edges of postmodernity.

Perhaps most consistently, the book ponders the complex, hybrid relationship between Christianity and the consumer culture—a relationship that was, by turns, symbiotic and conflictual, complementary and contested. At one level, American churches happily participated in the advent of the consumer culture, and their own modes of festival often encouraged and even celebrated the new patterns of display and the new therapeutic values of relaxation and self-fulfillment. At the same time, the churches repeatedly produced steely, sharp-tongued prophets, advocates of simplicity and enemies of indulgence, who regularly critiqued the commercial exploitation of the holidays. The churches clearly profited to some degree from the new cultural prominence that the market gave Christmas and Easter; the commercial culture, after all, helped make them pervasive, almost obligatory observances and provided the relatively austere liturgical culture of evangelical Protestantism with lush new corporeal forms for celebration. Still, this dalliance with the marketplace was always problematic. The commercial culture sought to redefine Christianity and its feasts in its own promotional image. Old Christian rituals were refashioned into new liturgical forms that provided the rubrics for a consumerist gospel of prosperity and abundance. As the *Millinery Trade Review*, which had no small stake in the celebration of Easter, observed approvingly in a "sermonette" in 1886, "We suit our religion to our business, not our business to our religion." Yet such singular redefinition was never the whole story, and certainly there was no sweeping march of secularization, but instead a dance of the sacred and the secular, sometimes graceful, sometimes awkward. Often, the story circles back to Reinhold Niebuhr's "paradox" of the thriving coexistence of "traditional piety" and "modern secularism," the irony that Christianization and commercialization have regularly processed together in American culture, that the two have frequently blended with little sense of contradiction or need for distinction.[20]

Perhaps most pointedly, this book is another subversion of the elitist dimensions of modernist aesthetics, a blurring of those hierarchies—long etched with such solemn assurance—that placed high art over popular art, avant-garde over kitsch, highbrow over middlebrow over lowbrow. In *Kitsch: The World of Bad Taste*, Gillo Dorfles fumed with typical exasperation over the banal, sentimental rituals of mass culture; Mother's Day and St. Valentine's Day, weddings and anniversaries, were all celebrated with a flood of the tacky and the maudlin. "It is hard to believe that men have been able to wrap their most sacred relationships in such a thick veil of bad taste, dragging them down to the level of perverted rituals," Dorfles harangued. "From the Christmas tree to the Nativity, from Santa Claus to Hallowe'en and Twelfth Night, it is a long chain of festivities linked to a trail of images which seldom escape the mark of kitsch." The "aesthetic populism" of postmodernism and the eclecticism of cultural studies serve as solvents for such sharp hierarchies, and, as the boundaries blur, the material forms of popular ritual—the kitsch, schlock, and camp of modern holidays—can be taken with both a new seriousness and a new playfulness. From valentines to Easter bonnets, these popular holiday tokens possess a mirthfulness and imaginative possibility long obscured through modernist, highbrow forms of elitism and corresponding interpretive constructs such as the culture industry. And this aesthetic subversion can occur, I am convinced, while continuing to preserve room for critical perspectives on the expansive reach and power of consumer capitalism.[21]

The book broaches such issues over the course of five chapters. In the first, I survey the evolving relationship between holidays and commerce from late medieval Christianity through the end of the nineteenth century. I emphasize, in particular, the modern reconfiguration of Sabbatarian and Enlightenment convictions about the economic bane of festal observance, and stress how the romantic longing for a rebirth of holiday insouciance fed the commercial appropriation of celebration. In the second chapter, I look at St. Valentine's Day, especially at its refashioning in the 1840s and 1850s and the emergence of the valentine vogue. In many ways St. Valentine's Day led the way as a commercialized holiday, serving as a locus for new merchandising experiments and for the incipient cultural debate about the fate of celebration, ritual, and gift giving in a market economy. In the third chapter, I explore the Victorian transformation of the American Christmas into both a commercial and a familial fête, its emergence from the shadows of Puritan contumely into the bright light of the department store and the glowing warmth of the home. I preface the discussion of Christmas with a consideration of the rituals of New Year's, the presents for which helped lay the foundation for the contested gift-giving observances of Christmas Day.

In the cycle of Christian time, Easter follows Christmas, and it followed, too, in the process of commercialization. In the fourth chapter, I examine the interweaving of this paschal feast and the consumer culture—for example, the interplay of emergent patterns of church decoration with burgeoning practices of merchandising display. In particular, the chapter looks at the Easter parade and its extravaganza of fashion; it explores, too, the proliferation of Easter gifts and goods—cards and confectionery, for example—and probes as well the exasperation of critics with all this Easter fanfare. In the fifth chapter, I investigate the invention of Mother's Day in the early twentieth century and ponder particularly its zealous founder, Anna Jarvis, who became outraged at the floral industry for its systematic commercial promotion of her new holiday. I suggest how Mother's Day served as a model for the further commercialization of the calendar, inspiring a series of spin-offs—Father's Day most evidently.

All this is a lot to promise. In an eighteenth-century English translation of one of the classic handbooks on military and festal fireworks, *The Great Art of Artillery of Casimir Simienowicz*, an introductory note contained the observation "that Prefaces to Books, as well as their Title-Pages, are too often guilty of promising much more than ever the *Readers* can discover in them." It went on to predict boldly: "But this shall not be the case here."[22] Who would quarrel with such a claim for a book that diagramed numberless weapons of war as well as designed the materials with which to celebrate after the victory—flaming fountains, fire wheels, and triumphal arches? The substance of this book is admittedly less incendiary, but I hope that it too will be found equal to its opening promises.

1

Time is Money

N FEBRUARY 1900 one of the nation's leading trade papers, the *Dry Goods Chronicle*, set out the modern vision of the commercial possibilities of holidays. "Easter, in common with the other great festivals of the year," the trade journal related, "has already been recognized as a basis of trade attraction, and, while it commemorates an event which is sacred to many, yet there is no legitimate reason why it should not also be made an occasion for legitimate merchandizing." As diligently as Christian pilgrims absorbed in the preparatory disciplines of Lent, modern merchants were to ready themselves for the great feast. "Plan for it in your store, look far enough ahead, so that your special sale or window display need not be hurried. . . . Make much of these things. They are the life and stimulus of trade." Two months later the *Dry Goods Chronicle* further generalized the commercial interest in such festivals: "Never let a holiday . . . escape your attention, provided it is capable of making your store better known or increasing the value of its merchandise." The modern, up-to-date businessperson realized the economic potential in holidays, exploited them through sales and advertising, and took the lead in promoting them. Whether the occasion was Easter or the Fourth of July, Thanksgiving or Memorial Day, "wide-awake" retailers were to conjure up "the spirit of hearty celebration" for the purposes of merchandising and consumption.[1]

Envisioning holidays in this way represented a striking transformation of festival—a compelling linkage of religious, civic, and folk celebration to modern forms of display and retailing. For the *Dry Goods Chronicle* and the great company of American retailers it represented, Easter, like Christmas, was one more trick of the trade, one more occasion to exhibit a mastery of merchandising techniques. This brazenly commercial conception of festival on the part of modern merchants needs to be situated within the context of long-standing debates in Western culture about the religious and economic significance of holidays. In some ways, the modern perspective looked backward to the traditional merger of fair and festival in popular religion—that is, to a world of hawkers and vendors who provisioned pilgrims and who magically turned holy days into alluring bazaars and shrines into open-air marts. As John Bunyan remarked of the mythic Vanity Fair in *Pilgrim's Progress*, it was "no new-erected business, but a thing of ancient standing." Offering all sorts of merchandise, delights, and amusements, the "lusty fair" had been set up in that place—by Beelzebub, Bunyan declared—precisely because of all the Christian pilgrims passing through on their journey.[2] If "ancient" in their fair-like hybridity of festival and marketplace, the modern retailer's holiday dreams also represented a distinctly new commercial fantasy. The merchandising vision of the *Dry Goods Chronicle* (and its various precursors and confederates) sharply diverged from much of the received wisdom of Protestantism and the Enlightenment about the social and economic drain of extensive holiday observance. Between the late eighteenth century and the early twentieth, American merchants fashioned a new economy of celebration out of a potpourri of romantic, genteel, consumerist, domestic, religious, and civic sensibilities.

CHURCH FESTIVALS AND COMMERCIAL FAIRS: THE PEDDLING OF FESTIVITY

Jacques Le Goff, writing of time and work in the Middle Ages, observed that "against the merchant's time, the Church sets up its own time, which is supposed to belong to God alone and which cannot be an object of lucre." In theory and in ideal, "the time of business" and "the time of salvation" were in medieval Christianity counterpoised worlds.[3] Christian worship envisioned a time apart, a time distinct from worldly business, a time of the soul; it created its own calendar, rhythms, and cycles. Sundays and other holy days were, by theological definition, separate from workaday time. As a sixteenth-century Catholic bishop instructed, on holy days people "must utterly withdraw themselves from all worldly and fleshly business and occupations, and houses of games and plays, specially from all sin, and entirely and wholly employ themselves to ghostly works behovable for man's soul."[4] Carefully differentiated from the time of business, labor, trade, court, and government, the liturgical time of the church was intended to point believers to the transcendent timelessness of God in Christ, the realm of the unchanging and everlasting in a world of flux and contingency. The seasons and feasts of the church year reenacted the sacred history of Christianity through devotion to the saints and the Virgin Mary and through the ritual representation of Jesus' life and ministry. The Christian year moved from the Savior's advent and incarnation through his death and resurrection to his ascension and his sending of the Holy Spirit, cycling back again to his advent and the anticipation of history's culmination in Christ's return to judge the quick and the dead.

Those were the familiar theological and liturgical ideals. In practice, the drawing of a sharp line around Sundays and holy days in order to insulate them from economic pursuits and to ensure their solemnity was invariably hard to achieve, and neat boundaries between the sacred and the profane were in the quotidian world of lived religion hard to come by. When Constantine took the momentous step in the early fourth century of instituting Sunday observance in the Roman Empire, the edict created a day of rest in the cities, halting urban commerce and government, but it exempted outright the countryside and those engaged in agricultural labor. Likewise the medieval church found it expedient to allow various exemptions for holiday labor, and the rules were of necessity quite detailed. In matters of exigency and commonweal, such as the repair of bridges and dikes, the building of fortifications, and the harvesting of crops threatened by storm, labor on holy days was permitted. In some cases, buying and selling were allowed, even encouraged; this included, for example, the vending of candles for religious devotions, souvenirs for pilgrims, and medicines for the ill. Small domestic chores tended to be countenanced, and religious work, such as helping the poor or showing hospitality to strangers, was wholly meritorious.[5] The very detail of the official distinctions and exemptions suggested how complex the negotiations were between the church's time and more-mundane times. Between church holy days and economic activities always ran a border that allowed multiple crossings.

What blurred the boundary more than official qualifications were the rich, festive practices of the popular marketplace. Fairs, markets, and amusements regularly cropped up on Sundays and on other important feast days, sometimes competing with divine worship in frank disregard of ecclesiastical admonitions, often simply complementing church life with a dense play of trade and diversion. As the anthropologist Alessandro Falassi points out, across Europe the etymologies of the terms for fair and festival crisscross one another; indeed, the Latin *feria*, a word originally denoting abstinence from work for religious observance, was transmogrified into "a term for market and exposition of commercial produce" in Spanish, Portuguese, Italian, Old French, and Old English. Time and again, the confluence of people for church festivals provided an ideal occasion for haggling and trade, and often wares were peddled in the churchyard or even at the church door. As one fourteenth-century French writer lamented:

> In many districts of the kingdom of France there has grown up an irreligious custom, nay rather an abominable abuse, namely that on Sundays and the other important festivals of the year, dedicated to the Majesty of the Most High, when Christian people should cease from servile work, come to church, spend their time in divine service, and receive the food of the Word of God, which they sorely need, from prelates and other authorized preachers—at such times they hold markets and fairs, pleas and assizes. . . . Whence it comes to pass that on those holy days on which God ought to be worshipped above all, the devil is worshipped.[6]

In some sense, medieval and early modern peddlers, victualers, and innkeepers long grasped what modern merchants were to discover for their own purposes in the nineteenth century: Holidays and festivals were superb commercial opportunities. As John Bunyan well knew, the predilection for turning holy days into market days and for transforming places of pilgrimage into festive marts had ancient roots in popular Christianity. Equally deep-rooted were official critiques of that predilection.[7]

That hawkers at local fairs and festivals perhaps prefigure the holiday mass markets of an Adam Gimbel or a Joyce Hall may not be so unlikely a historical leap as it first seems. The chapman has drifted into recent studies of consumption as an important transitional figure in the commercial transformation of eighteenth- and nineteenth-century America (Gimbel and Hall are exemplars in this regard: both started as peddlers on their way to becoming corporate titans).[8] Pushing at the geographical bounds of the market, the peddler was the wayfaring counterpart to the itinerant preacher—the latter expanding the market for evangelical Christianity, the former for consumer goods. The itinerant evangelist helped democratize religion, the roving chapman consumption. The two figures, peddler and preacher, converged at camp meetings, those great feast days of American evangelicalism. The prevalence of hucksters around the edges of the gatherings, proffering their wares and diverting people from the revivalist's message of salvation, was a common complaint and even, in some cases, a matter of legal regulation. To weary pilgrims and camp-following sinners, hawkers offered food, liquor, patent medicines, books, ballads, shoe polish, and daguerreotypes, or even such services as shaves, haircuts, and tooth pulling. As one revival-meeting veteran from the 1840s complained, "I have myself seen as many as fourteen huckster wagons at one camp meeting, and perhaps one-fourth as many boys, and lads, and young men, and even middle-aged, and old men about them, as were on the camp ground to attend religious service."[9]

Other convergences of fair and festival were evident in the American landscape. For example, in Albany, New York, in the late eighteenth and early nineteenth centuries, Pinkster, the Dutch Whitsuntide, was transformed into a slave-led street celebration, replete with the temporary booths and stalls of hawkers, who vended various spirituous liquors, meats, and cakes, among other goods.[10] Likewise, in nineteenth-century New Orleans, the "festive marketplace" of Bakhtin's carnival was reinvented and made indigenous; masked revelers and latter-day barkers jostled in a Rabelaisian world of inversion, mixture, and monstrosity.[11] In a parallel vein, during the Jewish feast of Sukkot, peddlers with their pushcarts crowded the streets of the East Side in turn-of-the-century New York: "At these holy days," a writer for the *Independent* noted in 1906, "the number of the carts increases marvelously. . . . Every conceivable plan is adopted to display goods."[12] The persistent presence of peddlers at times of festival was given visual form in the illustration of a Christmas market in *Harper's Bazaar* in 1884. Hawkers, along with the women and children who admire their trinkets, dominate the street scene. As these

1. “Christmas Shopping,” *Harper’s Bazaar*, 20 December 1884, 817.

Christmas chapmen suggest, the entrepreneurial cultivation of religious festivals was a familiar, even hoary, pursuit. In bustling scenes of booths, stalls, packs, and carts, peddlers trafficked in the marvelous and the mundane, in charms and aphrodisiacs, in the spirits and souvenirs of festival. From the hawkers of valentines to the street vendors of Easter flowers to that archetypal peddler, Santa Claus, the new commodities of American holidays would find powerful agents in these colporteurs of celebration.

In the nineteenth-century United States, as in early modern Europe, festival crossed easily into fair. The modern conjunctions of holy day and holiday, festival and market, have important roots in these ancient blendings and jumblings. The visionaries of the modern consumer culture—from P. T. Barnum to R. H. Macy—mastered the exotic excitements of the fair, packaging and refining them for middle-class consumers. The retailing of modern celebrations continually built on this antecedent peddling of festivity. With its carnivalesque edges, the festive marketplace of the premodern world lingered in various guises, always providing a powerful repertory for appropriation and refashioning.

"ENTERPRISE HOLDS CARNIVAL, WHILE POETRY KEEPS LENT": FROM SABBATARIAN DISCIPLINE TO ROMANTIC LONGING

The selling of American holidays represented far more than the simple extension of age-old fairs and markets, the predictable outgrowth of the venerable folkways of peddlers and chapmen. In many ways, the modern entrepreneurial embrace of holidays was discontinuous with what had gone before, and this was not just a matter of degree or magnitude. Instead, the shift suggested a reevaluation of the basic economic and religious convictions that underpinned the advance of industrialization and modernity. In the face of the economic and industrial rationalization that transformed early modern Europe and America, holidays looked decidedly backward. The great round of saints' days, the festivals of the Virgin, the processions of Corpus Christi, the extended holiday seasons of Christmas and Easter, the convivial frolics of church ales and harvests, and the topsy-turvy energies of the Feast of Fools and Mardi Gras—all such festivities were increasingly viewed as terrible impediments to work discipline and economic growth, clear occasions for idleness, dissipation, and immorality. The sooner such festivals and holy days were brought under control and reduced in number, the better for commerce, civic prosperity, and genuine piety.

This line of thought, which proved highly influential in early America, had various sources. Among the most important was Protestant Sabbatarianism. Protestants everywhere had sought to streamline the medieval calendar and to reduce to varying degrees the great number of Catholic holy days, which potentially took up more than half the year. Luther, though willing to recognize more holy days than many subsequent Protestant reformers, pointed the way: "With our present abuses of drinking, gambling, idling, and all manner of sin," he concluded, "we vex God more on holy days than on others. . . . Besides these spiritual evils, these saints' days inflict bodily injury on the common man in two ways: he loses a day's work and he spends more than usual, besides weakening his body and making himself unfit for labor, as we see every day."[13] Such sentiments became an essential plank in the Protestant platform. An English reformer, John Northbrooke, remarked in 1577 that the pope, "not God in his word," had appointed holy days in order "to traine up the people in ignorance and ydlenesse, whereby halfe of the year, and more, was overpassed (by their ydle holy-dayes) in loytering and vaine pastimes, &c., in restrayning men from their handy labors and occupations."[14] With the floodgates of reform lifted in the sixteenth century, holidays were a consistent focal point for criticism and conflict as Protestants worked out new versions of time, celebration, worship, and labor. Nowhere would the welter of Protestant opinion and the strenuous vigor of Sabbatarianism be more fully displayed than in early America.

In Sabbatarian ardor, New England set a mean standard. The streamlined calendar of the Puritans was a model of liturgical austerity, spiritual discipline, and theological rigor. Firm in their biblical conviction that six days thou shalt labor, the Puritans focused their church year on the Sabbath. Only occasionally would this weekly round of labor and devotion be broken with special days of fasting and thanksgiving. Civic and religious solemnities gradually emerged in election days, militia musters, public executions, and the Harvard commencement, but the dominant rhythm of the Puritan calendar remained the weekly cycle of the Sabbath.[15] The festivities of Christmas, Easter, and Whitsuntide were all rejected, as were other popular occasions such as midsummer bonfires on the eve of the feast of St. John the Baptist or perambulations of the parish during Rogationtide, the week before the feast of the Ascension. In a notorious incident in Massachusetts in 1627, the old English customs of May Day confronted the calendrical severity of Puritanism. With an eighty-foot-high Maypole topped with deer antlers and with the concomitant dancing, drinking, and singing, Thomas Morton and his fellow "Madd Bacchinalians" at Merrymount outraged the settlers at Plymouth. William Bradford expressed his disdain in a pun, attacking "this idle or idoll May polle," which the devout soon vanquished.[16] The play on words captured Puritan opposition to popular holidays and festivals: They encouraged both idolatry and idleness. They were both religious and social evils.

The Puritans, in their assault on the traditional calendar, showed their contempt for Catholic and Anglican holy days by profaning them. They toiled in their fields or shops; they bought and sold; they recognized no distinction between these days and any other times of labor; they desacralized them by secularizing them. But these studied acts of profanation did not mean that the Puritans had abandoned the church's traditional concern with safeguarding holy time.[17] Instead they focused that concern with renewed intensity on the Sabbath and on occasional days of fasting and thanksgiving. The New England divine Thomas Shepard insisted that on the Sabbath "we are to abstain from all servile work," so that "having no work of our own to mind or do, we might be wholly taken up with God's work." Worldly thoughts and labors—"the noise and crowd of all worldly occasions and things"—were to give way to devotional absorption in prayer, meditation, self-examination, familial catechesis, and public worship.[18] Issues of profit and gain, occasions of market and trade, were sharply divided from holy time. The Puritans' demarcation of the church's time from the merchant's time was scrupulous and exacting, but this line no longer extended to saints' days and other holy days: People were not only free to labor at these times, they were positively expected to keep their shops open, to plow their fields, and to stay at their regular employments.

The liturgical razor of plainness, simplicity, and discipline was whetted not only in New England; it was sharpened to similarly acute form among Baptists, Presbyterians, and various other Sabbatarians in one settlement after another throughout the colonies. For their part, Quakers in Pennsylvania and elsewhere went even further, not only rejecting the whole of the Christian year, but questioning the notion of any and all holy time, including days of fasting and thanksgiving and even the Sabbath itself. To underline their iconoclastic cleansing of the calendar, the Quakers replaced all the "pagan" names of the days and months—Sunday, Monday, January, February, and so on—with simple numerical references.[19] Theirs was the temporal equivalent of a blank slate on which one could inscribe a whole new mapping of Christian time. With the Quakers the Protestant dictum on the liberty of the Christian was pushed perhaps to its logical conclusion: Ideally there were to be no guiding forms for worship, no sacraments, no special times or days whatsoever; each Christian was to follow the internal promptings of the Holy Spirit. Yet despite their disagreements with other Protestants over how clean-swept the calendar should be, Quakers were in accord with Puritans and other Sabbatarians on the larger point: They, too, were to concentrate on redeeming time, on the disciplined use of their resources, rather than squandering time, money, and their souls on idolatrous holy days and popular celebrations.[20]

There were always various dissenters to these grand projects of calendrical purification. Colonial Anglicans, for example, tried to preserve their Old World via media between Puritan Sabbatarianism and the Roman Catholic calendar, but this often proved difficult to achieve. A report from Virginia in 1719 noted that the unsettled conditions made holiday observance burdensome and impractical. Hard-pressed to subsist, colonists reportedly kept "no Holydays, except those of Christmas day and good Friday, being unwilling to loose their dayly labour."[21] Even those communions that defended the traditional church year often felt the sharp pinch of austerity. Lutherans, Moravians, and the small Anglo-Catholic presence in Maryland added to the calendrical diversity of the colonies, holding off the levelers from complete triumph. Still, those hoping to truncate traditional festivals and holidays clearly had the upper hand. Sabbatarianism was the regnant religious perspective in the colonies.[22]

The Enlightenment gave a new turn to the assault on popular holidays and festivals. Where Protestant reformers asked in zealous conviction what configuration of time conformed to the truth made manifest in Christ and revealed in Scripture, Enlightenment rationalists made the question one of simple economic calculation: What configuration of Christian time was best for business, commerce, and civic prosperity? The Puritans had formulated a view of time based fundamentally on theological conviction and biblical foundation that then carried economic consequences. Enlightenment thinkers increasingly bypassed theological and scriptural concerns and concentrated on the social, ethical, and economic implications of festival and holy day. Suggestive of this shift was Montesquieu's laconic conclusion in his *Spirit of Laws* (1748): "In a country supported by commerce, the number of festivals ought to be relative to this very commerce." If economic demands required "the suppression of festivals," then religion should oblige those requirements.[23] Just as Enlightenment thinkers subjected Christian beliefs about eternal rewards and punishments to the gauge of social utility, so too Christian worship and holy days were measured in terms of civic welfare.

The economic argument against holidays was given extensive formulation and calculation in the thought of English mercantilists. Exemplifying this rationalistic line of thought, John Pollexfen in his *Discourse of Trade* (1697) gave hard specificity to the economic drawbacks of holiday observance in a mode of computation that became a staple of Enlightenment critics: "Whether the many Holydayes kept now be not a great load upon the Nation, may be Consider'd; for if but 2 Millions of working people at 6d. *per* day comes to 50000£. which upon a due Inquiry from whence our Riches must arise, will appear to be so much Lost to the Nation, by every Holyday that is kept."[24] Benjamin Franklin's subsequent maxim, offered in *Poor Richard's Almanack*, crystallized the creed that was behind all such calculations: Tradespeople were always to remember that "*Time is Money*." "He that is a prodigal of his Hours," Franklin insisted, "is, in Effect, a Squanderer of Money." Such wisdom cut against festivals and holidays at every turn. The way to wealth and prosperity was to rationalize time, to save it and spend it wisely, to make good use of it. The time of the merchant and the shopkeeper, the time of the wage laborer and the manager, the time of the factory and the clock, and eventually the standardized time of the railroads—these emerged as the quintessential modern timekeepers. The agrarian rhythms of seasonal festivals and the religious rhythms of church holy days would have little place or utility in modern economic thought and in the labor structures of industrial capitalism.[25]

A classic example of Enlightenment opposition to church holy days is found in an eighteenth-century tract on Scottish worship in which the assault on popular festivity was ironically turned on the revivalistic jubilees of evangelical Protestantism. The tract, entitled *A Letter from a Blacksmith to the Ministers and Elders of the Church of Scotland*, went through multiple editions in Scotland, England, Ireland, and America and became a standard text in the Enlightenment's critique of the enthusiastic excesses of Protestant piety. To the pseudonymous Blacksmith, the thronged revivals and lengthy sacramental occasions of the evangelicals hindered the Scottish economy as much as Catholic festivals slowed the economies of Italy and France. "The people lose many labouring days by them," he said, "and the country is deprived of the fruit of their industry." These holy days, or, as the Blacksmith preferred to label them, "idle days," were a massive hindrance to Scottish commerce:

> I have seen above three thousand people at one of these *occasions*. But supposing that one with another, there are only fifteen hundred, and that each of them, one with another, might earn 6d. a day. Every sacrament, by its three idle days, will cost the country much about 112£. 10s. sterling, not including the days that they who live at a great distance must lose in coming and going, nor the losses the farmer must sustain when *occasions* happen in the hay, harvest or seed times; the man of business, when they chance to fall upon market days; or the tradesman, when any particular piece of work is in hand that requires dispatch. . . . These *occasions*, as they are managed at present, will cost Scotland at least 235,000£. sterling; an immense sum for sermons![26]

Popular holidays and religious festivals were hardly considered economic opportunities, but instead were understood to be in clear opposition to the interests of merchants and tradespeople.

This kind of economic slide rule was explicitly extended to the United

States in commercial critiques of the camp meetings. An article in the *Wesleyan Repository* in 1822, appearing under the pen name Scrutator, sounded the same alarm as had the work of the Blacksmith. "Hundreds and perhaps thousands of the spectators," the author observed, "who attend these occasions day after day, *losing their time, spending their money, and acquiring, or indulging in habits of dissipation*, would be *much better* employed in pursuing their respective occupations at home, for the support of their families." Scrutator went on to make the point explicitly in terms of cash, subjecting the camp meetings to an audit as vigorous as the Blacksmith's:

> If "*time* is money," and "*labor* is the wealth of the community," as is granted by all, it must be admitted that camp meetings . . . [are] one of the most expensive measures to the community where they prevail, that could be devised. It could be easily demonstrated, that at any given camp meeting, where the totality of persons, at any given time, was equal to 5000 persons, with the horses and carriages, night and day, for one week, it is attended, at a moderate computation, with a loss of productive labor and expense for diet, drink, &c. of 25,000 dollars—exclusive of cost of tents, furniture, congregation benches, and pulpits, and the time employed in preparation for camp, and for return.[27]

Submitting American revivals to this kind of economic reckoning became a commonplace—one that professional evangelists increasingly obliged in streamlined lunchtime or evening meetings and in statistics that demonstrated their cost-effectiveness in saving souls.

The relationship between disciplined enterprise and festal observance was thus routinely conceived in oppositional terms. Among the best embodiments of this widespread assumption is the fabled figure of Ebenezer Scrooge. No text was more influential in the sentimental recovery of Christmas in the nineteenth century than Charles Dickens's *Christmas Carol* (1843), and few exclamations were more memorable than Scrooge's holiday dismissal, "Bah, humbug!" Scrooge stood as an archetype of those modern merchants who always "hurried up and down, and chinked money in their pockets, . . . and looked at their watches"; for Scrooge and his ilk, time was most assuredly money. His business and his ledgers occupied him "constantly"; long into the evening, he pored over his accounts. Scrooge saw no need for any holidays whatsoever and upbraided his clerk for wanting the full day off for Christmas. "A squeezing, wrenching, grasping, scraping, clutching, covetous old sinner," Scrooge had to be converted to holiday observance. Indeed, the story was cast in the classic form of a conversion narrative: The hard-hearted Scrooge (the name *Ebenezer* derives from a Hebrew word for stone) must repent for his calculating ways and be reborn to the cheer, charity, and plenty of Christmas.[28]

By the 1840s, a number of American merchants had already come to share in Scrooge's conversion to holiday observance, and certainly Scrooge's transformation offered a model for additional enlistments. (Dickens's enactments of the *Carol* in his tour of the United States in 1867–68 were wildly popular and often resembled revival meetings more than dramatic readings. People wept and swooned and pledged hearty Christmas observance; they included the occasional industrialist who promised to close his factory for the holiday.)[29] Still, for many American merchants, as had been the case for the unregenerate Scrooge, what remained most compelling were the routine rhythms of capitalist discipline and hard work. This can be seen, for example, in the diary of C. W. Moore, a New York dry-goods merchant, who paid little attention to any holidays in his diary in the 1840s. On Christmas, he often worked at least half the day and made no particular note of its observance as a religious or commercial event. On 22 December 1842 he commented that there was "very little doing" at his store and expressed no sense of this as a season of special opportunity for him as a merchant. As for Scrooge, so too for Moore: The holidays were not the object of commercial ballyhoo; instead, their indulgent celebration was the humbug, a dangerous seduction for driven tradespeople.[30]

Even when merchants came around to the observance and commercial promotion of holidays, modern work discipline still remained paramount. The motto that George Whitney, one of the leading nineteenth-century producers of valentines and other holiday cards, took for his company was typical: "Industry, Punctuality, and Christianity." In recognizing the potential in holidays for the evocation of consumer fantasies, American merchants hardly abandoned the rhythms of Yankee enterprise and Sabbatarian discipline. Scrooge's newfound insouciance was an optimistic and sentimental solution. More often, when merchants rediscovered the holidays, the former transformed the latter, not vice versa, as merchants systematically extended the apparatus of the market into the realm of celebration. As John Wanamaker, the Presbyterian impresario of the carnivalized theater of the department store, exhorted, "'Time is money,' and it's much *more* than money." He scorned "wishy-washy amusements" and "dawdling"; like Whitney's, Wanamaker's business entailed a regimen of holiday goodwill, a rigorous system of merchandised celebration.[31]

The rationalization of time, the reform of holidays, and the streamlining of popular celebrations were standard items on the industrial and managerial agenda by the nineteenth century. These processes, with a long and uneven history in Western culture, were by the 1800s in full swing. The confluence of Protestant Sabbatarianism, Enlightenment rationalism, industrial work discipline, and commercial capitalism had forged a consensus: Popular forms of celebration, plebeian patterns of leisure, and the bountiful round of holy days were bad for business. This basic drive for calendrical restraint continued unabated into the late nineteenth and twentieth centuries—for example, in Britain, the license of St. Monday was tamed, and the dissolute energies of Harvest Home were largely domesticated. Likewise in the United States, efforts at holiday reform were apparent in pressures to make the Fourth of July safe, sane, and sober and in attempts to make Halloween a home-centered party rather than a night of pranks and property damage.[32] Still more recently, the charged debates about Martin Luther King, Jr., Day revealed the deep hold of economic considerations on public discourse about holidays. Opposition to the occasion took varied forms, but economic costs and the loss of productivity were among the primary arguments advanced against the day. (Ronald Reagan regularly invoked these issues.) The holiday's projected cost was consistently presented, however disingenuously, as among its principal drawbacks.[33]

As the eventual success of the King holiday suggests, commerce did not invariably triumph. Preindustrial and agrarian rhythms persisted alongside the modern timekeepers; ethnic and working-class traditions refused to yield to the dictates of moral reform and the homogenizing force of industrialization; Christians often continued to go about their celebrations with the leisurely exuberance of the spirit-filled at a camp meeting or with the patient solemnity of Lenten devotees. But certainly the pressures of reform took their toll. In England, for example, there had been forty-seven bank holidays in 1761; by 1834 there were only four.[34] The precipitous decline of holidays was felt across the board, but with special keenness among those who most internalized the demands and ideals of Sabbatarianism and industrial capitalism—namely, middle-class Protestants.

A perspicacious article in the *North American Review* in 1857 suggested the extent to which these reform pressures had affected American holidays, particularly for those New England Protestants for whom and about whom the unnamed author wrote. Holidays in the United States, in this author's view, were sadly deficient. For one thing, there were not many of them. This, the author admitted, was "consistent with the industrious habits and the civic prosperity of the land," but perhaps such virtues had been pressed too far to the detriment of "the boon of leisure, the amenities of social intercourse, the sacredness and the humors of old-fashioned holidays." The devotion to thrift and enterprise, "the absorption in business and the dominion of practical habits," seemed to shroud even those few holidays that were celebrated. To this writer, the typical American festival had been the celebration at the opening of the

Erie Canal, a fête for a commercial and technological feat. "Our festivals," the author concluded, "are chiefly on occasions of economical interest. Daily toil is suspended and gala assemblies convene to rejoice over the completion of an aqueduct or a railroad, or the launching of an ocean-steamer. . . . Too many of our so-called holidays are tricks of trade, too many are exclusively utilitarian, too many consecrate external success and material well-being, and too few are based on sentiment, taste, and good-fellowship." From this New England perspective, the classic American pageant was not a mystery play or Mardi Gras, but "a fleet of steamers." "Enterprise holds carnival," the author aphorized, "while Poetry keeps lent."[35]

The romantic nostalgia for festivity and the lament concerning its loss were important themes among middle-class Victorians. This author fittingly invoked Charles Lamb's despondent complaint that "the *red-letter days*, now become, to all intents and purposes, *dead-letter days*," a nearly habitual expression of romantic despair that functioned in itself as a call for revival. Like Lamb and other romantics, the essayist for the *North American Review* championed the recovery of various holiday observances in sociable, sentimental forms. This nostalgic yearning for renewed holiday celebration, for "those *consolatory interstices*, and *sprinklings of freedom*," proved a crucial underpinning for the commercial refashioning of celebrations in the nineteenth century. Merchants rushed in to satisfy this romantic longing for "old-fashioned holidays," for the "hearty sentiment of festivity." If the commercial pressures of thrift, industry, and productivity threatened to destroy these holiday genialities, the fantasies, dreams, and wonders of the marketplace were an apparent source of salvation. Not that this romantic critic (and others) found in this prospect a wholly satisfying solution. As the author bitterly observed, "capital is made of amusement as of every other conceivable element of our national life," and making capital of the holidays was fraught not only with sentimental possibility, but also with the peril of further romantic estrangement.[36] By the 1850s the Victorian revival of Christmas and St. Valentine's Day had already proceeded fairly far, and the dramaturgy of merchants would greatly assist the jovial, sentimental rebirth of both. As the sociologist Colin Campbell has argued, the "romantic ethic" of feeling, sentiment, and imagination did much to inspire modern forms of consumerism, and this link certainly also held in the realm of holiday observance.[37] Ironically, the romantic alienation from bourgeois disciplines and Enlightenment rationality—the quixotic longing for festival and play, the renewed yearning for freedom, license, and imagination—invited new market experiments with the holidays: Merchants could both stir and satisfy these romantic cravings for sentiment, fantasy, and celebration.

A COMMERCIAL REVOLUTION: NATIONAL HOLIDAYS AND THE CONSUMER CULTURE

Romanticism, with its deeply felt longing for the "recreative zest" of festivity, provided a crucial basis for the modern recalculation of the economic benefits of holiday observance. But this refiguring also looked back to aristocratic, courtly sources, which have long been recognized as foundational for the rise of the consumer culture. Patrician forms of celebration often entailed elaborate rituals of gift giving, and these genteel ceremonies, particularly on New Year's and St. Valentine's Day, served as models for more-democratic versions of holiday consumption. In the eighteenth-century colonies, merchants were already encouraging and facilitating the widening reach of this culture of refinement, and, as was the case with the modish emulation of aristocratic furnishings among the rising bourgeoisie, courtly versions of holiday observance proved quite amenable to middle-class translation. The ceremonies of genteel gift giving percolated downward, and merchants promoted (and assisted) the popular emulation of the fashionable rituals of the polite and cosmopolitan. The spreading holiday gift culture of the nineteenth century was thus not only one of romance and sentiment, but also one of respectability and sophistication. As a repertory of celebration, the genteel forms were orderly, refined, and decorous; they were often depicted in explicit contrast to the carnivalesque revels and drunken binges of street celebrations, the "relics of barbarous usages." To middle-class celebrants, the "innocent" amusements of holiday gift giving within the "domestic circle" represented "the progress of refinement."[38]

What made the emulation and democratization of genteel observance possible was the ever-widening scope of the commercial revolution of the eighteenth and nineteenth centuries. A vast consumer culture was already flourishing in late-eighteenth-century London, and the spreading of that culture in North America was a matter of both immediate and prolonged enterprise. This "empire of goods" was built on an array of new industries that made commodities of everything from pottery to pets, from clocks to cutlery, from leisure and entertainment to shaving and soap. With the need to match the rising levels of industrial production with comparable boosts in demand, the burgeoning consumer culture was founded as well on ever-expanding forms of advertising, marketing, and promotion—newspaper puffs, bow-window displays, handbills, fashion magazines, and fashion dolls. Novelty and abundance, not the old bugaboos of scarcity and necessity, were at the heart of the new culture: the frequent changing of styles, the rapid obsolescence of goods, the endless profusion of consumer choices, the fantastic play of dreams and passions. In the increasingly democratic world of consumption, luxury and self-fulfillment countered thrift and frugality, and protean self-fashioning subverted the fixedness of hierarchy.[39]

From the late eighteenth century into the twentieth, this expanding world of goods shaped more and more aspects of American social life, and its hand would be felt with particular weight in the realm of ritual, festival, and celebration. The posh visits of New Year's, the toy-laden joys of Christmas, the lace-paper missives of St. Valentine's Day, and the plumes of Easter millinery vied effectively with Sabbatarian austerity and republican simplicity. Easy Enlightenment tallies of the economic cost of holiday observance seemed to pale beside the radiant illuminations and grand spectacles of the consumer culture. From the perspective of modern merchandising, holidays were fraught with possibility and allure, a temporal cycle that could provide rhythm and ritual for the unfolding culture of consumption. *Time is money*. The consumer revolution gave new meaning to Poor Richard's adage.

In addition to satisfying romantic, genteel, and consumerist sensibilities, the staged rites of the nineteenth-century marketplace offered potential solace for those who desired national, unifying, and patriotic observances. As the market widened its reach, it brought not only ready-made goods, but also common rituals, such as the little exchanges of holiday greetings or the grander scenes of firework displays. For the civic-minded, the new republic seemed distressingly short on shared national traditions; among the things about American celebrations that troubled the *North American Review*'s essayist the most was their consistently "local character." Ethnic particularity, eclecticism, and localism seemed to impede national observances at every turn. The "partial and isolated festivals of every race and country" found performance in America—"harvest-songs among the German settlers of Pennsylvania, here a 'golden wedding,' there a private grape-feast; in the South a tournament, at Hoboken a cricket-match, . . . a Vienna lager-bier dance in New York, or a vinedressers' merry-making in Ohio."[40]

When the writer for the *North American Review* turned to view the formal civic holidays, things seemed all the more local and confused. Evacuation Day, celebrated in New York City on 25 November to commemorate the removal of British military forces from the city in 1783, flourished as a republican festival there, but was little seen elsewhere. The processions on St. Patrick's Day, with "green sprigs and uncouth garments," were the alarming peculiarity of Irish Catholics (and even these parades remained under the charge of local clubs and boosters). In a parallel vein, St. Andrew's Day was the toast of Scots gentlemen in scattered antebellum fraternities, and St. Nicholas's Day had long been under the patronage of patrician Knickerbockers. In this local welter, the holiday celebrations of New Englanders simply added to the provincial amalgam. Pilgrim Day or Forefathers' Day, a feast of Puritan ancestral devotion, had little appeal outside New England or even beyond Plymouth. Bunker Hill Day was observed in Charlestown, and Patriots' Day served as a heyday in Lexington. Also, Thanksgiving itself was not much more than a regional New England tradition before the mid–nineteenth century. (It was Sarah Josepha Hale, editor of *Godey's Magazine and Lady's Book*, who gave the holiday growing publicity in the 1850s and 1860s in hopes of fostering a healing national tradition in the face of sectional strife.) In the twin centrifuges of democratization and immigration, localism and heterogeneity reigned as guiding spirits of antebellum celebrations.[41]

Even as the civic-minded from Washington Irving to Sarah Hale lamented the lack of shared celebrations, centripetal forces were emerging that would effectively counter, though never override, the ethnic particularity and localism of American holiday observances. National holiday traditions gained increasing sway over the course of the nineteenth century, and this was in part the result of mounting commercial patronage. Sponsorship of the holidays by retailers and trades, already incipient in the antebellum period, became a foregone conclusion in the half century after the Civil War. In this regard, the Easter preparations and holiday wisdom of the *Dry Goods Chronicle* were standard fare. Any number of trade publications from the *American Florist* to the *Confectioners' and Bakers' Gazette* to the *Dry Goods Economist* to *Geyer's Stationer* saw the merchants' role in the observance of national festivals in much the same way: Holidays were a great store attraction, and merchants should take the lead in hearty commemoration. In carefully staging holiday celebrations from one year to the next, merchants helped lift certain observances and symbols into national prominence. Cupids, hearts, Santa Clauses, stockings, cards, Christmas trees, Easter eggs, rabbits, bonnets, shamrocks, cornucopias, turkeys, pumpkins, and the silhouettes of Lincoln and Washington—these were hardly "local" holiday symbols by the end of the century, and commercial institutions played an important role in the nationalization of these holiday emblems and customs.[42] Through advertisements, show windows, trade cards, circulars, interior displays, trade-journal campaigns, and store-sponsored parades and floats, nineteenth-century merchants developed an influential and lasting repertory of celebration.

However, for those patriots who were looking for national, unifying celebrations—for a common culture—in the face of the fearsome anarchy of localism, the market did not always deliver the goods. To the essayist in the *North American Review*, the best hope that Americans had for a genuinely national observance was the Fourth of July. In the antebellum period the celebration of independence was torn between official observances that were long on military processions, windy orations, and partisan toasts, and popular enactments that were long on drunkenness, rowdiness, and noisemaking. Though firecrackers for the occasion were regularly sold (and sometimes advertised) in the early republic, shooting guns, pealing bells, and firing cannons provided most of the hoopla and fanfare. (Much the same pattern of celebration can be seen in the only other early republican tradition with national pretenses, Washington's Birthday.) Fireworks, the Fourth's quintessential commodity, were not yet goods for widespread sale or consumption. Large firework displays were primarily produced for civic exhibitions; with an aristocratic lineage of royal weddings, visits, and coronations, fireworks had long been emblems of monarchical and military power. This connection was underlined in firework manuals in the juxtaposition of chapters on military pyrotechnics (bombs, shells, grenades, and rockets) with chapters on recreational fireworks (Roman candles, flying dragons, sun wheels, blazing ships, and prismatic fountains). Fireworks were an extravagant theater of military and national prowess; they were an artifice of war and statecraft. Boys might play with firecrackers, but the elaborate display of fireworks was a far more serious business, a grand staging of power and polity, a public exhibition of considerable civic consequence.[43]

Commerce took a good deal of the civic and martial bang out of fireworks. In 1870 the pioneering firm of Masten and Wells in Boston began to market special "Box Assortments of Fire-Works for PRIVATE USE"—that is, for domestic consumption. Other American pyrotechnics companies soon followed suit, offering all kinds of exploding devices that were "just the thing for private parties." By 1887 the Masten and Wells Company was offering twelve different boxed collections of fireworks for "private exhibition," ranging in price from fifty cents to one hundred dollars. (At the turn of the century, the fireworks industry, or "the Fourth of July trade," as E. Bennett and Company dubbed it, had grown into a $10 million enterprise in the United States.) All this was a happy democratization of a once aristocratic, monarchical medium, but it was also a notably privatizing shift, the very antithesis of a public-minded, unifying ritual. Private fireworks displays helped middle-class Victorians reshape the contours of celebration and withdraw from the raucous tomfoolery of the streets. It allowed them to see the holiday as more of a domestic affair, a lawn party, in which families and friends set off their own fireworks at private retreats. This tendency can be seen clearly in the *Harper's Weekly* engraving from July 1871 in which fireworks, far from being associated with civic engagement or military display, have been snugly domesticated, translated into a middle-class medium of family-centered entertainment. For commercial purposes,

2. "The Glorious Fourth," *Harper's Weekly*, 8 July 1871, cover.

the freedoms of Independence Day were easily translated into the idiom of consumer choices. (The Fourth of July slogan that the journal *Advertising World* tendered in 1899 epitomized this predilection: "1776 rang liberty to America. 1899 rings your liberty from high prices.") The extension of the market into the realm of celebration often served to privatize and domesticate holiday rituals; only as an adjunct to consumption did it nationalize traditions. In the nineteenth-century search for civic celebrations of national consequence, retailers regularly ended up patriots of domestic consumption and bourgeois family life.[44]

By the end of the nineteenth century, modern merchants had largely put the image of Scrooge behind them. Just how much this was the case can be seen in a little article on the Fourth of July that the *Dry Goods Economist* published in 1897. The paper simply mocked those of steady habits who still looked "upon holidays as . . . an interruption of business," rather than as an opportunity for "special sales and attractive displays." Such "hard workers" were hopelessly behind the times; they had lost "all claims to leadership," conducting their businesses "much in the same way" they would have "a century ago." In sharp contrast to such misguided, puritanical shopkeepers, the forward-looking merchant stood out as "a leader . . . in the matter of observing holidays." Indeed, the modern retailer knew that there was "never a holiday" that did not make for "increased business" when "used to good advantage." Holidays, rather than being impediments to disciplined economic advancement, were seen as critical for consumption and profit.[45] Or, as the director of publicity for the National Confectioners' Association concluded in still bolder terms in 1924: "What we want [are] ways and means of increasing the consumption of candy and the Holidays offer these means."[46] Over the course of little more than a century, the commercial estimation of the economic import of the holidays had been transformed in the whirl of the consumer revolution. In the process, the very rituals and materials of modern American celebrations—both religious and civic—would be dramatically refashioned.

2
St. Valentine's Day Greeting

N FEBRUARY 1841, *Godey's Magazine and Lady's Book*, that great repository of Victorian fashion and fiction, gave barely a mention to St. Valentine's Day and concentrated editorial attention instead on the patriotic feast of Washington's Birthday. A mere eight years later, the magazine was scrambling to keep up with the "New Fashion for Valentines," publishing a delicate frontispiece with Cupid, flowers, and cooing doves as "GODEY'S VALENTINE" to its readers and trying, self-servingly enough, to promote a subscription to the *Lady's Book* as an appropriate gift for the holiday. The next year the magazine displayed added interest in the old saint's day with a holiday short story in which the young female protagonist was swept up in the raging "Valentine epidemic." The character's new fondness for these holiday tokens personified how the ritual of exchanging valentines had suddenly become "so popular," how indeed the celebration had attained faddish acclamation.[1]

In the 1840s St. Valentine's Day in the United States was rejuvenated, almost reinvented: It went from being an often forgotten, easily neglected Old World saint's day to being an indigenous, not-to-be-missed American holiday. As a writer for *Graham's American Monthly*, one of *Godey's* estimable counterparts, proclaimed in 1849, "St. Valentine's day . . . is becoming, nay, it has become, a national holyday." "We shall think better of the age in which we live," the essayist eulogized, "for the restoration to homage and joyful devotion of good old St. Valentine of blessed memory." Over the course of little more than a decade, this centuries-old folk observance was refashioned into a modern American holiday, and fashion it was. Valentines became all the mode; people spoke of a valentine mania, craze, rage, or epidemic—a "social disease" that seemed to recrudesce each year with ever-heightening interest and anticipation. In early February as the seasonal displays went up, people crowded into the stores of booksellers, printers, stationers, and fancy-goods merchants, lingering outside shop windows and gazing at the huge variety of sentimental and comic valentines. With great suddenness and thoroughness, the commercial revolution loosened St. Valentine's Day from its early modern moorings and redirected it into little-charted waters. The holiday stood as a harbinger of the new possibilities and strange sardonicism that inhered in allying commerce and celebration, mass production and deeply felt sentiment.[2]

The transformation of St. Valentine's Day into a modern American holiday makes for a complicated bit of cultural history, one that entails a rich interplay of commerce, gender, ritual, and material culture. It is a story with roots in the medieval and early modern cult of St. Valentine, in a medley of long-standing religious, folk, and aristocratic customs. More-immediate inspiration for the nineteenth-century version of the holiday was found in the middle-class enshrinement of romantic love, sentimentalism, and fashion. But inspiration came from more-popular or plebeian sources as well: the carnivalesque world of the charivari, the charms of conjurers, the barking of chapmen, and the ballyhoo of promoters. As an early exemplar of how the emergent consumer culture transformed traditional holidays, the reconfiguration of St. Valentine's Day suggests the modern reshaping of popular ritual in terms of vast markets, private exchanges, and standardized commodities. The proliferation of mass-produced, shrewdly marketed valentine greetings increasingly raised worries about the loss of sincerity, authenticity, and self-expression, and in this, St. Valentine's Day provided an augury of the peculiar dilemmas of modern celebrations. The commercial appropriation of the festival by booksellers, stationers, and printers in the 1840s and 1850s also pointed ahead to the systematic envelopment of the holidays in the world of business and enterprise after the Civil War. The greeting-card industry, in particular, would take its cue from this earlier valentine vogue, and confectioners and florists, among other merchants, would soon learn the value of the St. Valentine's Day trade.[3]

ST. VALENTINE'S PILGRIMAGE FROM CHRISTIAN MARTYR TO PATRON OF LOVE

Until the late fourteenth century, the era of Geoffrey Chaucer and Oton de Grandson, St. Valentine was remembered, like any number of other saints, for his steadfastness in the face of a torturous martyrdom and for miraculous cures, not for any special affinities with the lovelorn. While dozens of Christians named Valentine were martyred and attained sainthood in the early church, two third-century martyrs by this name, a bishop in Terni and a priest in Rome, were especially lifted up in the early medieval hagiography. Each was putatively executed on 14 February, and hagiographic accounts of their martyrdom—their perseverance in the faith, their conversion of pagans, their successful prayers for miraculous healing, and their arrest and execution—served as the essential body of legends behind the saint's day. As an elaboration and composite of these hagiographic traditions, St. Valentine became the focus of devotion in several locales throughout Europe. Churches, shrines, and basilicas were dedicated to him. His relics, real or supposed, were widely dispersed; a number of different shrines, for example, claimed possession of his skull (both the bishop in Terni and the priest in Rome were said to have been decapitated by their persecutors).[4]

In the medieval world, St. Valentine, like other saints, was a model of holiness and divine accessibility, an intercessory to be called on in times of scarcity or exigency, drought or disease. Like other saints, he was an ambassador who helped link the remote, unseen, and numinous expanses of heaven with the material, humble, and local corners of earth. In twelfth-century Jumièges in Normandy, for example, St. Valentine was responsible for several instances of divine intervention in the day-to-day affairs of the local community; he healed the afflicted and freed the fields of a plague of rodents. In fourteenth-century Paris, he was the subject of an elaborate miracle play: Based on the hagiography of the bishop of Terni, it was a sanguinary drama in which the saint was beaten, bloodied, and beheaded before angels transported him to glory, and in which the unbelieving emperor choked to death at the table before demons snatched him away to hell. As one historian concluded, this performative retelling of the saint's story combined "two typical features" of medieval hagiography, "violence and religious teaching."[5] For centuries such dramatic stories of miracles and martyrdom were the prevailing ones by which St. Valentine was known. Through the mid–fourteenth century, the cult of St. Valentine was fully enmeshed in the wider devotional and liturgical traditions surrounding the veneration of the martyrs and saints of the church.[6]

The axial shift of St. Valentine from Christian martyr to front man for Cupid occurred in the late fourteenth and early fifteenth centuries. Popular historical accounts of St. Valentine's Day, beginning in the eighteenth century and repeated regularly thereafter, have often concocted classical or pagan sources for this confluence of the saint's day and courtship, especially presenting a Roman feast of fertility and purification, the Lupercalia, as the root of popular valentine customs. But, as the medievalists Henry Ansgar Kelly and Jack B. Oruch have demonstrated, no solid historical evidence exists for this link.[7] Nor, they point out, is there any evidence before the end of the fourteenth century for folk or literary traditions that treat St. Valentine's Day as a time of coupling birds and pining lovers. Instead, this transformed imagery is first discernible in the poetry of Chaucer, his contemporaries, and his heirs.

In his *Parliament of Fowls* Chaucer convened a vast assembly of birds that were said to choose their mates each year on the holiday:

> For this was on seynt Valentynes day,
> Whan every foul cometh there to chese his make.[8]

Repeating such allusions to matchmaking and waxing amorousness in a number of additional works that addressed the holiday, Chaucer helped lay the foundation for St. Valentine's transformation. Other poets, such as Oton de Grandson, John Gower, John Clanvowe, Christine de Pizan, and Charles

D'Orléans, made similar associations of the saint with amatory scenes of courtship, spring festivities, floral rebirth, and cooing birds—a dreamlike world long conjured up by the troubadours, but now specifically and lastingly joined to St. Valentine. By the early decades of the fifteenth century, connecting the holiday to courtly conventions of "mannered love" had become a literary commonplace, so much so that the monk John Lydgate could use the term *valentine* as shorthand for one's fairest love, and others simply used it as a synonym for sweetheart. For Lydgate, though, the valentine relationship, like the ardor of the Song of Songs, remained suggestive of spiritual more than sexual longing. Still, Lydgate's imagistic associations for the holiday—the heart burning out of love for Christ, the Virgin Mary, or the saints—easily translated into a more elementary idiom of amorous passion.[9]

Joining the saint to coupling birds, springtime, and lovers was a striking innovation, and why Chaucer and his compeers should have done this remains something of a literary mystery. Henry Ansgar Kelly suggests that Chaucer may have actually had another Valentine in mind, a local saint in Genoa, whose commemoration fell in early May and whose celebration blended there into Maytime festivities and rites of spring. Indicating how Chaucer may have come to know the Genoese St. Valentine through various Italian connections, Kelly argues that the poet was creatively playing on this particular conjunction of saint's day and springtime in his work. In turn, Kelly posits that this connection was then picked up by Chaucer's various imitators, who, unfamiliar with the Genoese St. Valentine, adapted these vernal and amatory images to the more widely known saint's day of 14 February. For his part, Jack B. Oruch suggests a less elaborate hypothesis, concentrating on medieval datings of the beginning of spring in February and the poetic possibilities of connecting love with this time of year. Whatever the explanation, Oruch and Kelly are in agreement on the importance of Chaucer and his circle in remaking the saint into a patron of lovers and a sponsor of matchmaking. To the traditional hagiography of St. Valentine was added a fresh fount of myth and ritual that gradually recast the saint's day into a new kind of holiday focused on coupling and love poetry. The saint might still be an intermediary and an ambassador, but now he would intercede between young men and women more than between humanity and God. Not until the early decades of the nineteenth century would St. Valentine's Day again undergo such extensive revision.

In early modern Britain, the immediate cultural source for much of the American inheritance of the holiday, the traditions of St. Valentine's Day were carried forward from the era of Chaucer and Charles D'Orléans on three distinctive, if interrelated, paths—one religious or ecclesiastical, another popular or folk, and a third aristocratic or courtly. The new prominence given St. Valentine as a patron of lovers did not fully eclipse the saint's liturgical place in the cycle of the Christian year. Though sharing in Protestantism's sharp truncation of the devotional role of the saints, the Church of England remained committed to the early Christian martyrs as holy examples. The fabled lives of the saints were still frequently recounted, and some writers even rued the irony that carnality and self-indulgence were usurping the ascetic example of an ancient martyr. Playing liberally with the conventional hagiography, Ben Jonson had one of his characters complain in *A Tale of a Tub* (1633) that Bishop Valentine had

> Left us example to do deeds of charity;
> To feed the hungry; clothe the naked; visit
> The weak, and sick; to entertain the poor;
> And give the dead a Christian funeral;
> These were the works of piety he did practise,
> And bade us imitate; not look for lovers,
> Or handsome images to please our senses.[10]

Not surprisingly, such calls for good works and disciplined austerity were invariably hard-pressed to compete with holiday insouciance and sensuality.

Some ambitious interpreters tried to salvage the church's martyr by merging him with the lover's saint. One popular eighteenth-century commentary on the *Book of Common Prayer* fancifully suggested that the third-century bishop was "a man of most admirable parts, and so famous for his love and charity, that the custom of *choosing Valentines* upon his festival . . . took its rise from thence."[11] Still more oddly, a nineteenth-century antiquarian hypothesized out of thin air that St. Valentine was a suitable patron for lovers because he was "the only one among the fathers of the church who contemned celibacy."[12] Even with such embellishments of the hagiography, it was hard to hold on to the religious example of the saint amid the ever-growing attention given to sociability and matchmaking. The ancient religious strand in St. Valentine's Day continued to attenuate, and this would be all the more true in North America, where Puritan, Quaker, and evangelical antipathy to the observance of saints' days ran deep. In the end, the hagiographer's saint would have little place in the American appropriation of the holiday.

While the religious aspects of the saint's celebration were increasingly lost, the holiday throve at the level of popular culture. Although local and regional variation had always characterized the holiday's folk observances, one of the occasion's most widely reported activities was drawing lots to choose a valentine. This custom could act as both a type of nuptial divination and a frolicsome form of youthful entertainment. The collector and clergyman Henry Bourne explained in 1725: "IT is a *Ceremony*, never omitted among the Vulgar, to draw Lots, which they Term *Valentines*, on the *Eve* before *Valentine-day*. The Names of a select Number of one Sex, are by an equal Number of the other put into some Vessel; and after that, every one draws a Name, which for the present is called their *Valentine*, and is also look'd upon as a good Omen of their being Man and Wife afterwards."[13] Though for his part Bourne thought that such divinatory practices were best laid aside, these sorts of folk customs were commonplace in early modern Britain. Like the notable days that were believed to carry omens or portents about the weather, special days for fortune-telling to discern one's future spouse were sundry. St. Agnes's Eve (20 January), St. David's Day (1 March), May Eve and May Day, St. Anne's Eve (25 July), St. Faith's Day (6 October), Halloween, St. Thomas's Eve (20 December), and New Year's Eve, among other occasions, all served in one place or another as times for love charms and matrimonial divinations.[14] The folk customs of St. Valentine's Day were thus situated in a much wider framework of youthful conjuration and pairing games. In popular Protestant cultures, this was one of the last functions left to the saints—not miraculous intercession, but divinatory matchmaking.

The young, especially young women, turned to divination on St. Valentine's Day (and at other times) in hopes of gaining, as a traveler in Scotland noted in 1769, some hint of their "future fortune in the nuptial state."[15] Drawing lots was apparently the most common practice, but, depending on the region or the locale, a young person might resort to the churchyard at midnight to seek an omen about a future mate, or might place hemp seed or bay leaves in his or her own bed to help induce dreams or premonitions of the beloved. Then again, the young person might recite one of various incantations—in one case, over a bowl of water with pieces of paper in it that contained the letters of the alphabet. If the divination worked, the initials of the future spouse would be revealed in the bowl. Children and young people might go around singing and doling, expecting small gifts of coins or food from those they visited.[16]

Like other popular celebrations, the festivities of St. Valentine's Day courted license. A poem called "The Drawing of Valentines" from *Westminster Drollery* (1671) captured a scene of raucous sociability:

> There was, and there was, and I marry was there,
> A crew on S. Valentines Eve did meet together,
> And every lad had his particular lass there,
> And drawing of *Valentines* caused their coming thither.

After much tomfoolery, sly exchanges, and the suspenseful drawing of valentines, the versifier concluded:

> Then ev'ry one i' th' Tavern cry amain, Sir,
> And staid till drawing there had filled their brain, Sir.[17]

Tinged with festive indulgence and sexual license or, as Bourne moaned, "with Scandal, and sometimes with Ruin," St. Valentine's Day was a mottled and mirthful celebration in the popular culture of early modern Britain.[18]

In addition to its folk expressions, the holiday also throve at an aristocratic or courtly level, and it is in this context that seventeenth- and eighteenth-century renderings of the celebration most clearly prefigured the modern consumer-oriented version of the holiday. The courtly traditions of love poetry for St. Valentine's Day, epitomized especially by the fifteenth-century musings of Charles D'Orléans for the occasion, long flourished. For example, the seventeenth-century Anglican vicar and royalist poet Robert Herrick employed the familiar valentine imagery as a commonplace:

> Oft have I heard both youths and virgins say,
> Birds choose their mates, and couples too, this day.

Similarly, John Donne celebrated the royal wedding of Princess Elizabeth, daughter of James I, on 14 February 1613 in an epithalamium that hailed Bishop Valentine once again as matchmaker of "all the chirping Choristers":

> This day more cheerfully than ever shine,
> This day, which might inflame thyself, old Valentine.

Such courtly conventions suggested the holiday's enshrinement as a time for the formal offering of compliments in rhyme and verse. These literary forms, if monarchical or aristocratic in their underpinning, nonetheless pointed the way toward the wider circulation of holiday greetings and love poems.[19]

Courtly influences on St. Valentine's Day did not end with poetic forms. In patterns of gift giving, too, "the courtly model of consumption" shaped the holiday. In the narrow but splendid confines of European courts, Renaissance aristocrats and Elizabethan nobles gave paradigmatic expression to fashion, taste, and etiquette. With "elaborate ceremonies of consumption," the courts exhibited styles and furnishings that were emulated, in turn, by the emergent middle classes—merchants, tradespeople, and professionals. In historian Rosalind Williams's phrase, the courts were "the cradles of consumption"; their refined rituals of consuming, acquiring, doting, and gift giving served as prototypes for the more democratized patterns of consumption that would succeed this "closed world of courtly consumption."[20] In the lurching and long, drawn-out transition from courtly to mass consumption, the rituals of St. Valentine's Day were pitched along. Here, as was the case with New Year's Day, aristocratic customs of gift exchange would eventually be popularized.

This courtly influence on St. Valentine's Day can be nicely seen in the mid-seventeenth-century diary of Samuel Pepys, the son of a tailor who rose to the level of court insider as a naval official. Pepys regularly commented on the gift-giving obligations that came with St. Valentine's Day and the costs of supplying his wife and anyone else he might draw as a valentine with suitable presents. While he often gave small gifts of embroidered gloves and silk stockings, these paled before the sumptuous display at the highest levels of the court. Of the duchess of Richmond, Pepys remarked in 1667, "The Duke of York, being once her Valentine, did give her a jewell of about 800£; and my Lord Mandeville, her valentine this year, a ring of about 300£." The next year at St. Valentine's Day Pepys tellingly suggested the pressures and pleasures of emulation. Having given his wife a ring that cost him five pounds, he noted, "This evening, my wife did with great pleasure show me her stock of Jewells, encreased by . . . my Valentine's gift this year, a Turkey-stone set with Diamonds."[21] Below these elite echelons, gift exchanges during the holiday were necessarily a far more modest enterprise, when they existed at all. Gloves, for instance, were sometimes offered as tokens of courtship, being given on St. Valentine's Day and then worn as new clothes for Easter, but a custom like this received far less mention than other folk practices such as drawing lots or divination.[22] The courtly model, in sum, most clearly pointed the way toward the modern version of the holiday as a time to exchange substantial gifts and refined poetic compliments. The commercial revolution made it possible to democratize and popularize courtly patterns of consumption and gift giving, and made it easier for more folks like Samuel Pepys to gratify their spouses, lovers, and friends.

In outline, then, this is the convoluted history of St. Valentine's Day before it was taken up by American printers, booksellers, and lithographers, before valentines became an epidemic or craze, before confectioners offered heart-shaped boxes of candy as a more delectable holiday greeting. From an early medieval saint's day brimming with stories of martyrdom and miraculous intercession, the holiday became through poetic invention and elaboration a day of matchmaking and conviviality. Though not wholly shorn of his religious roots, St. Valentine flourished in both court and countryside as a patron of sociability and pairing games. Folk customs of drawing lots, fortune-telling, drinking, and doling existed alongside elite traditions of courtly poetry and gift giving. The commercial culture would play on various dimensions of this diverse heritage even as it transformed the holiday. From a youthful folk gathering with ample carousing and local variety, St. Valentine's Day would emerge as an occasion for the private exchange of mass-produced greetings. The new ceremonies would be the intimate, personal transactions of relatively autonomous couples, not a community activity; the great themes of the new rituals would be fashion and romance rather than fate or tradition; the sovereign choices of consumers would replace the blind luck of village fortunes.

THE HANDMADE AND THE READY-MADE: OF PUZZLE PURSES, CHAPBOOKS, AND THE VALENTINE VOGUE

Before the 1840s, St. Valentine's Day was not much of a holiday in the United States. Within the month of February, that leading saint's day of the American Revolution, Washington's Birthday, had dwarfed the old saint's day in stature and importance. The transatlantic crossing had diluted most British saints' days, and there was no reason to think that St. Valentine would not fade with other champions of the faith who had likewise become notable mostly for folk divination, love charms, or doling—St. Agnes, St. Anne, St. Faith, St. Simon, and St. Thomas. Under the disciplined rigors of industrial and Protestant timekeepers, St. Valentine's Day, like so many other saints' days that had dotted medieval and early modern calendars, seemed doomed to desuetude. The calendar in the new United States would not be a web of church holy days, craft ceremonies, and monarchical commemorations, as it was in early modern England, but would be characterized instead by a pastiche of republican rituals, immigrant customs, evangelical revivals, and the Sabbath.[23] Like St. Patrick's Day, St. Valentine's Day would prove an exception; unlike with St. Patrick's Day, commerce rather than ethnicity would be the creative and guiding hand in the holiday's American rebirth.

Certainly some of the folk beliefs surrounding St. Valentine's Day were preserved all along in early America. Almanacs, for example, often made note of the holiday, sometimes including a rhyme or two about the occasion. Typical of the persistence of the holiday's conventional imagery, a St. Valentine's Day poem published in Burlington, New Jersey, in 1811 evoked the traditional Chaucerian world of courtship, springtime, and billing birds: Robins, blackbirds, wrens, hedge-sparrows, starlings, and jays all "assemble in flocks on this festival day" in order to "court their coy loves in the sun's early ray."[24] Still, mention of St. Valentine's Day in the press in the early decades of the nineteenth century was scarce, and those writers who did comment upon the holiday treated it as an almost exclusively British observance, especially popu-

Valentine's Day.

"Love calls the Birds to the Altar of Hymen."

3. *The Butterfly's Birth Day, St. Valentine's Day, and Madam Whale's Ball: Poems, to Instruct and Amuse the Rising Generation* (Burlington, N.J.: D. Allinson, 1811), facing 11.

lar in London but without notable appeal or acclaim in the United States.[25] The novelist Samuel Woodworth, one of the earliest chroniclers of American calendrical traditions, went so far as to conclude in 1832 that the "English custom of sending *valentines*, and drawing lots for husbands and spouses, on the 14th of February, was never much practised by the people of the United States, and is now almost unknown." In 1858 *Harper's Weekly* reported that when valentine dealers first began to send out "traveling agents" with samples of their product around 1840, these salespeople were actually "forced, in a majority of cases, to explain . . . the use to be made of the curious missives, and to make a minute of the particular season for which they were prepared." Before the 1840s the holiday was thus of little moment in American popular culture, and it could easily pass unnoticed.[26]

The holiday's lot improved dramatically in the 1840s and 1850s. "A few years ago, and we read that this Saint's day was observed in Europe, but we did not observe it here," the *Philadelphia Public Ledger* commented in 1845. "But now things have changed. St. Valentine's letters and hearts and darts, &c., are domesticated among us. Especially in New York city is the fashion of half-serious, half-comic love-making, and humbug amorous declarations, made on paper through the Post, on this day. Thousands on thousands of such missives are sent. . . . Even in sober Philadelphia the Saint's day is at a premium." The *Public Ledger* saw in the rekindling of this holiday only hopeful signs. With more than a little romantic longing for lost folk traditions and festivities, the newspaper praised this recovery. "We have grown so common-sensical, that all the old feast, or holi, or holy-days are nearly blotted off from the calendar. . . . We all calculate too much." What the country needed was "more soul-play and less head-work," more times that allowed for "an *abandon* of feeling," more occasions that laid aside "business cares and thoughts," and a revitalized St. Valentine's Day—a respite for whimsy and caprice—fit the bill. Hidden in this quixotic relish of the holiday's rebirth was a precious irony: It would be precisely the infusion of business concerns into the calendar that facilitated the romantic revival of "this blessed day."[27]

What made St. Valentine's Day a fashion in New York, Philadelphia, and an ever-widening circle of places were valentines.[28] In this vogue Americans looked initially to London for inspiration; from the turn of the century, printers and booksellers there had been developing a market for commercially produced valentine greetings. By the mid-1820s, estimates put the number of valentines circulating annually in London at two hundred thousand. By the late 1840s yearly exchanges there had reportedly doubled, and by 1867 the figure had climbed to more than a million for that metropolis alone.[29] In 1843 a writer in the *Boston Daily Evening Transcript* regretted that the burgeoning valentine business in England was "not half understood in the United States, by which misunderstanding, *Uncle Sam*, we fear, is defrauded of a rightful increase in his revenue." In their initial cultivation of St. Valentine's Day, American firms relied heavily on British imports and technology—in lace paper production, for example—often boasting that they carried the best lines that London had to offer. By 1848, however, a large Philadelphia establishment could confidently declare that "these tasteful and classical effusions" were becoming "as popular on this, as on the other side of the Atlantic." By then at least eleven American businesses had begun to produce their own valentines; numberless shops were retailing these British and American goods; and droves of peddlers and traveling agents were taking these holiday wares into town and countryside.[30]

American interest in this London fashion was, indeed, rapidly accelerating in the 1840s. A Yale student spoke of a "general mania" for valentines in New Haven already in 1842, though he himself tried to affect dispassion about the hubbub. "A thousand notes," he heard, had passed through the local post. One estimate put the number of valentines going through the New York mail in 1843 at fifteen thousand; the next year a calculation for that city stood at twenty-one thousand; and in 1847 the estimated number was up to thirty thousand. Similarly, in Boston one express company alone in 1847 reportedly delivered eight thousand of these holiday greetings.[31] Despairing of offering any firm estimates of the dimensions of the valentine vogue in Philadelphia, the *Public Ledger* seemed almost dumbfounded in the face of the growing hoopla: "There were so many modes of conveyance by the Post Office and Despatch Post, that it is impossible to ascertain the number of missives which were sent out yesterday. It is believed that the number was considerably greater than was delivered last year. We, ourselves, saw a postman staggering under a huge market basket filled with the dainty epistles, and we have heard that Blood's Despatch sent them out by the wheelbarrow load."[32] Though the ardor of this craze inevitably cooled in ensuing decades, a new, deeply etched ritual of greeting, compliment, and jest remained. Between the 1840s and the 1860s, exchanging valentines was established as an enduring American holiday custom.

The new rituals were built largely on a commercial medium, on the understanding of the valentine as a commodity. Reflecting this basic refashioning of the holiday, the meaning of the word *valentine* itself shifted in the middle decades of the nineteenth century. The word's early modern meaning focused on a person or a relationship—that is, one drew lots to establish who was one's valentine for the occasion or one used the term to refer to one's sweetheart or betrothed. By contrast, in the nineteenth century the word came to mean preeminently an object of exchange—a fancy lace-paper missive or colorful lithographed sheet for which one went shopping. A valentine, in short, became a commercial product, a piece of merchandise to be marketed and consumed like any other line of goods. The very etymology of the term suggested this fundamental change.[33]

The relationship of this new commodity to folk traditions of handcrafted love tokens and hand-scrawled love poems was complicated. In the seventeenth and eighteenth centuries, poetic verses or epigrams were at times part of courtly and folk customs of drawing lots for valentines. People selected verses or mottoes by chance, which they then used to address their chosen valentines, or they wrote their own poems in response to the fateful pairing. As one man versified in 1788 in a manuscript poem to his valentine:

You are my right, for yesternight,
With scrips of paper rolled;
I drew your name which made my flame,
Too high to be controlled.

. . . .

Grant then, dear miss, some hopes of bliss,
If I deserve your notice;
If not be free, and let me see
My chance not worth a groat is.[34]

Besides such homespun poetic come-ons, people had begun by the end of the eighteenth century to make more-substantial love tokens, sometimes of filigreed intricacy, for the holiday. Using puzzle purses, love knots, fancy cutwork, and charming designs of hearts, birds, and flowers, people created elaborate handmade love tokens and forget-me-nots. These, too, were often given as emblems of entreaty and endearment in response to having drawn someone as a valentine by lot:

Lots was cast and you I drew
Kind fortune favoured me with you
Sure as the grape grows on the vine
I choos'd you for my valentine.

Surviving examples from the late eighteenth and early nineteenth centuries testify to the richness of this folk art. The very complexity of the puzzle purses—the layers, folds, and multiple scenes—suggested something of the intricacy of courtship itself, a folk expression of the convoluted social rituals of attaining intimacy. The commercial valentine built on these popular customs of poetic compliments and love tokens, even as it displaced these preindustrial forms.[35]

The displacement was not unilinear, however. From all indications the commercial promotion of the holiday initially increased the popularity of exchanging valentines of all kinds, handmade as well as commercially produced. Archival holdings of valentines bear out this point. In the Hallmark Historical Collection, with its remarkably extensive holdings of nineteenth-century handmade and manufactured valentines, the preponderance of hand-scribbled missives that carry specific dates are from the 1840s and 1850s, precisely when the commercially produced valentines were first coming into vogue. For example, in one box of manuscript valentines at Hallmark, thirty-two of the sixty-eight valentines are dated, and twenty-six of these carry dates between 1845 and 1859. The earliest is from 1823, another is from 1837, and there is

4. Handmade puzzle-purse love token (folded), 1797.

5. Handmade puzzle-purse love token (unfolded), 1797.

one for each of the last four decades of the century. In another box of hand-scrawled missives all twenty-seven of those that are dated fall between the years 1839 and 1864. This essential pattern holds for the hundreds of handmade valentines at Hallmark and is borne out as well by the substantial holdings at the Smithsonian and the American Antiquarian Society. For example, in the latter's collection of valentines no handmade emblem is dated before 1839, while there are dozens of manuscript missives from the 1840s and 1850s. What this suggests is that the commercial revolution helped stimulate and give shape to a largely new custom. Playing upon various strands within

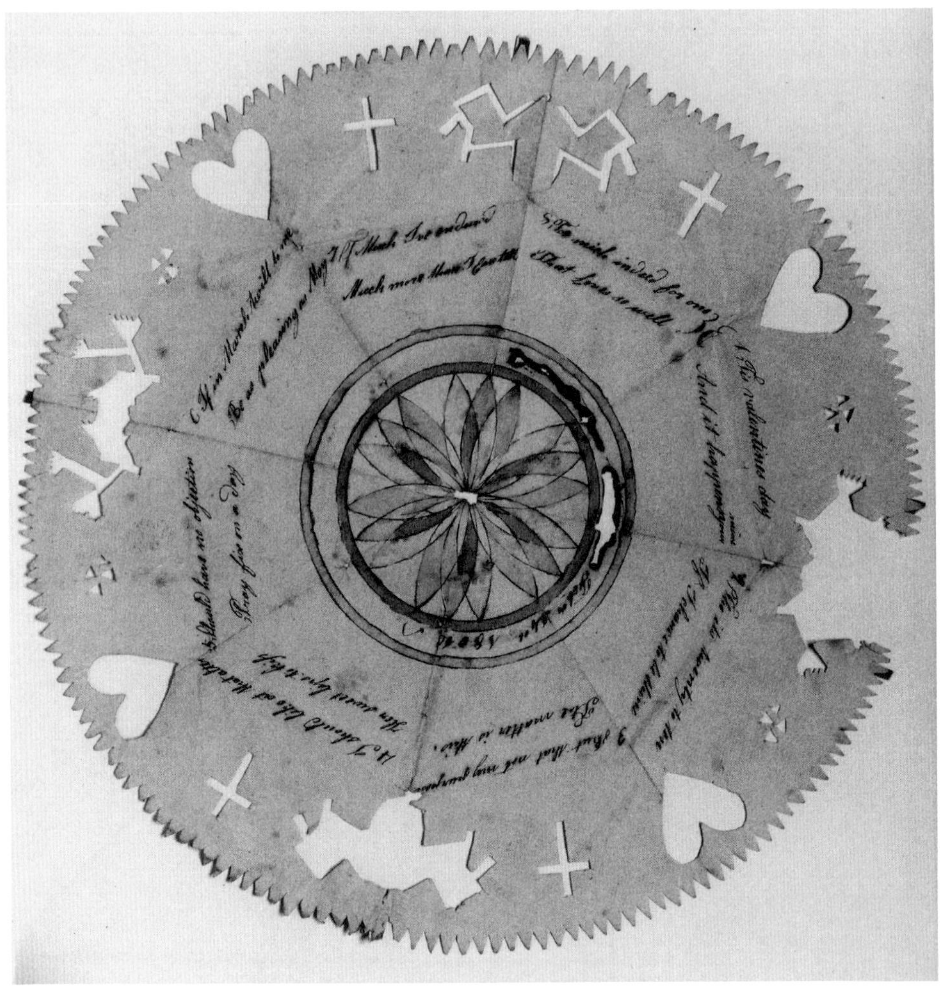

6. Cutwork love token, 1810.

the folk tradition, merchants refocused the holiday on a freshly minted love token, the valentine. Handmade valentines were thus as much a spin-off of commercially produced valentines as vice versa. As the latter proliferated, so did the former.[36]

A story published in *Godey's Magazine and Lady's Book* in 1852 nicely illustrates this reverse relationship between handmade and ready-made valentines. On a trip into Philadelphia from the farm, the youthful and callow Jason Thompkins arrives during "St. Valentine's week," and it is "the Valentine shops" that most attract his attention. Tellingly he is initially "at a loss" as to

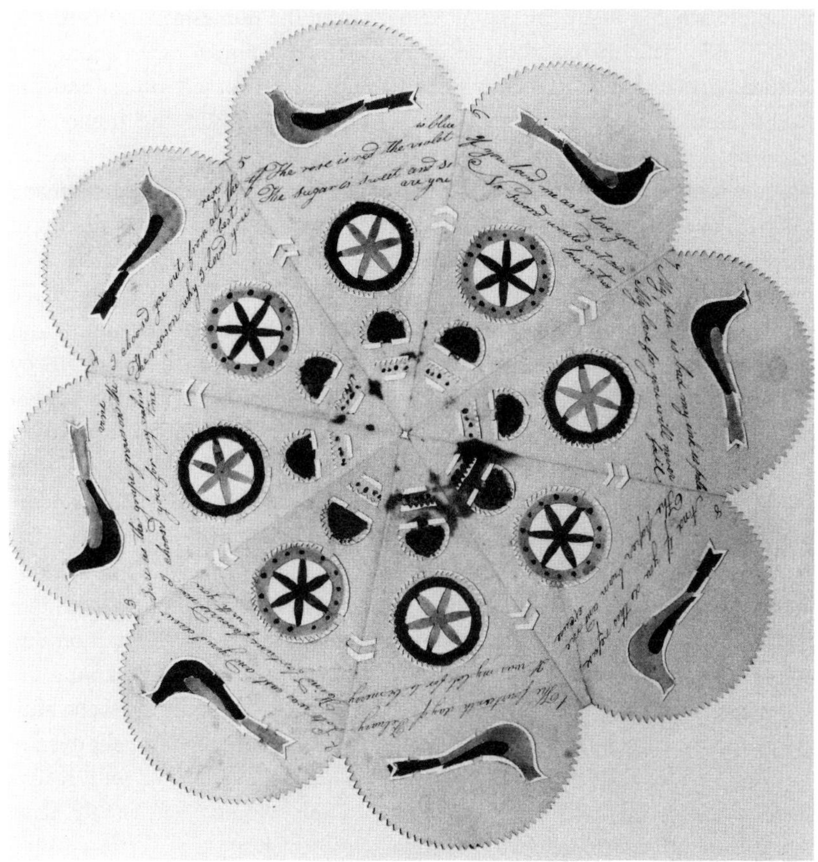

7. Cutwork love token, ca. 1830.

what these elaborate, frilly "monstrosities" are, but he soon discovers their application. Though "the great display of Valentines at Zieber's had taken a firm hold upon [his] imagination," Jason is without the financial resources to purchase one for a would-be sweetheart. Upon his return to the country, he tells a pal of his desire to send "a Voluntine," and the friend responds quizzically, "What's that?" Jason's explanation is that "it's a sheet of paper all pictered over with love fixins, with love verses underneath." His solution is not to return to the city, but to make a valentine himself, which he and his friend accomplish with some ordinary paper and a heart-shaped cake-cutter. The story is a suggestive one: The commercial valentines introduce Jason and his friend to unfamiliar goods and newfangled rituals, but their response is to make a handcrafted love token. In this story the commercial medium actually gives rise to the folk artifact. Thus in the material culture of St. Valentine's Day no simple schema that depicts a movement from the homespun to the ready-made is adequate. In the short term, at least, exposure to new commercial products sparked the imaginative engagement in unwonted rituals and the proliferation, even invention, of a new-fashioned artifact, the homemade valentine.[37]

In the long run, though, ready-made valentines clearly swamped handmade missives, and this inundation is important to recognize. Archival holdings of hand-scrawled, homespun valentines decline precipitously for the decades after 1860. Likewise, elaborate puzzle purses and cutwork love tokens made for the occasion all but disappear. By contrast, mass-produced valentines from the late nineteenth and early twentieth centuries are housed in collections by the tens of thousands and were sent by the tens of millions. Manufactured valentines with commercially created sentiments simply flooded the market and had by the 1870s largely overwhelmed hand-scribbled, hand-cut, and hand-painted valentines. Thus with these holiday goods as with so many other commodities in the nineteenth century, industrialization ultimately dwarfed the homemade and the handcrafted. Not that people were unable to individualize mass-produced greetings or tailor them to their own liking. This is quite evident from the hand-scrawled sentiments inscribed under the flap on one nuptial valentine: In vowing her love to Johnny and in actually naming the figures on the commercial valentine, Flora took a generic wedding scene and, quite literally, personalized it. Like a palimpsest, the handmade might overlay the ready-made. Still, the overarching shift remained evident. As with ready-made clothing or ready-made furniture, people would increasingly have ready-made holiday merchandise with which to celebrate.

The gradual transition to commercially produced valentines was clearly discernible in the appearance of "valentine writers," affordable chapbooks of comical and serious verses from which appropriate sentiments could be chosen for copying out onto a sheet of paper to create a valentine. Within a long lineage of books on courtship, courtesy, etiquette, and letter writing, valentine writers developed into a distinctive genre of their own in late-eighteenth- and early-nineteenth-century Britain. Among the earliest was *The Complete Valentine Writer; or, The Young Men and Maidens Best Assistant* published in London about 1783 by Thomas Sabine—a work that proved popular "so much beyond his Expectation" that Sabine was quick to see the possibilities of an annual market and had a new "Book of VALENTINE" ready for 1784. He also embellished his work with an engraved frontispiece of an elaborate courtship scene, and these kinds of engravings became a common feature in the valentine writers.[38] It was a only small step for producers to detach these frontispieces from the covers of the valentine writers to create freestanding engraved or lithographed valentines. By the early decades of the nineteenth century, a wide

8. "Believe I Love Thee," personalized manufactured valentine, ca. 1845.

variety of these valentine writers was available in London, and the titles they carried were always alluring, such as *The Turtle Dove; or, Cupid's Artillery Levelled against Human Hearts*, *Hymen's Revenge against Old Maids, Old Bachelors, and Impertinent Coxcombs*, and *Cupid's Annual Charter; or, St. Valentine's Festival*. With prices ranging typically from one pence to six, these chapbooks throve as an inexpensive medium of holiday expression.[39]

American booksellers and stationers were always able to import such works, and eventually they spun off their own. In 1823, in what appears to

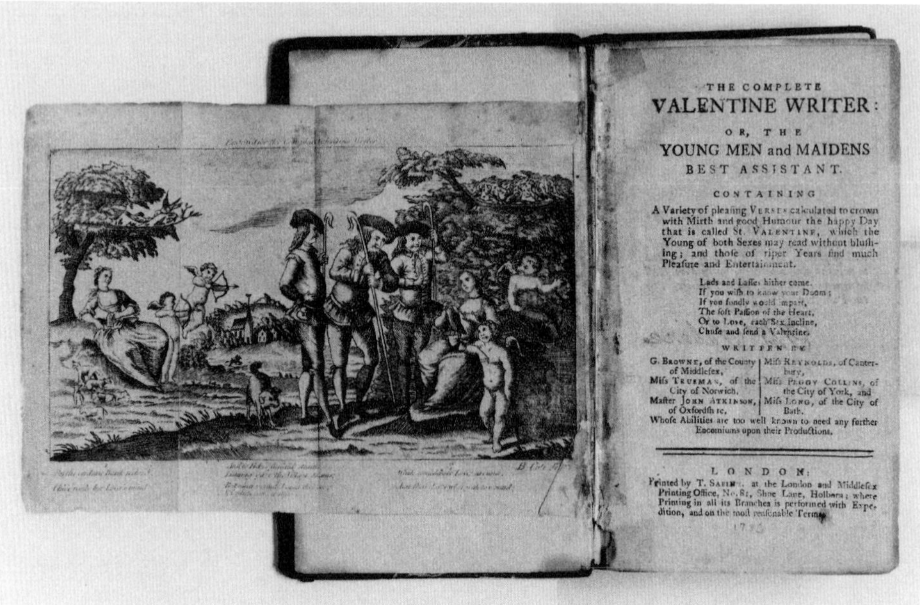
THE COMPLETE
VALENTINE WRITER:
OR, THE
YOUNG MEN and MAIDENS
BEST ASSISTANT.

CONTAINING

A Variety of pleasing VERSES calculated to crown with Mirth and good Humour the happy Day that is called St. VALENTINE, which the Young of both Sexes may read without blushing; and those of riper Years find much Pleasure and Entertainment.

Lads and Lasses hither come,
If you wish to know your Doom;
If you fondly would impart,
The soft Passion of the Heart,
Or to Love, each Sex incline,
Chuse and send a Valentine.

WRITTEN BY

G. BROWNE, of the County of Middlesex,
Miss TRUEMAN, of the City of Norwich,
Master JOHN ATKINSON, of Oxfordshire,
Miss REYNOLDS, of Canterbury,
Miss PEGGY COLLINS, of the City of York, and
Miss LONG, of the City of Bath.

Whose Abilities are too well known to need any further Encomiums upon their Productions.

LONDON:
Printed by T. SABINE, at the London and Middlesex Printing Office, No. 81, Shoe Lane, Holborn; where Printing in all its Branches is performed with Expedition, and on the most reasonable Terms.

9. *The Complete Valentine Writer; or, The Young Men and Maidens Best Assistant* (London: T. Sabine, [1783]), frontispiece.

have been the first valentine writer published in the United States, a New York printer simply pirated material from British valentine writers, republishing these well-worn verses under the title *The New Quizzical Valentine Writer*. In turn, another New York printer pirated this work, reissuing it under his own imprint and again proclaiming it to be new.[40] Borrowing and close imitation were standard procedures: The valentine writers were invariably promoted for their newness and originality, and this claim was made even when there was little new about a given valentine writer. Indeed, including words such as *new*, *original*, *fashionable*, *annual*, or *for the present year* in the titles of these chapbooks was among the most common ways of promoting them. This tendency was epitomized in one title that claimed just about all of these things at once: *The Beauties of Hymen; or, A New Valentine Writer for the Present Year, Being a Choice Collection of Original Valentines, Sentimental and Pleasing; Written Expressly for this Work*. It became common in the consumer culture to advertise essentially unchanged products as new, original, improved, or modishly seasonable, and the valentine writers were an early exemplar of this frame of mind. In their titles and on their covers, they tried to accent novelty, fashion, and innovation, even when the verses inside often went unchanged from one year to another. With the valentine writers, as with today's new and improved

10. *Hymen's Revenge against Old Maids, Old Bachelors, and Impertinent Coxcombs* (London: J. Dean, [1805?]), frontispiece.

versions of breakfast cereals or detergents, people were offered the veneer of novelty more than novelty itself. By the 1840s, a number of American printers were issuing these motley, if not-so-original, chapbooks in various editions and permutations. They even made such stock valentine verses available in the form of broadsides, which peddlers and criers then hawked in the streets.[41]

Like earlier letter writers or advice books on courtship, the valentine writers provided forms of expression for wooing, eloquent verses for those who lacked the resolve or wherewithal to come up with their own loving sentiments. Conversely, these chapbooks also provided witticisms and barbs to discourage unappealing suitors or simply to insult the unattractive and the déclassé. Typical of the "serious" rather than "satirical" side of the genre was the thirty-two-page *Sentimental Valentine Writer, for Both Sexes*, published by a Philadelphia stationer and engraver in 1845. In its pages could be found such charming and saccharine verses as:

Oh! come my love, my own delight,
My joy by day, my dream by night,
And both our hearts shall close entwine,
A blessing from St. Valentine.

Or, one could thumb a few pages further and choose option number 47:

Fly Cupid, fly, and wing thy way,
  To the youth, (maid,) I long have given my heart,
Show him (her) how in wreaths of flowrets gay,
  United—we could never part.[42]

Rather than struggling to produce original verses, the lovelorn could turn to the valentine writers for just the right sentiment or, in opposite cases, just the right insult or rebuke.

If hackneyed and formulaic, these inexpensive little books nonetheless proved popular and useful. People turned to them for assistance in articulating difficult feelings and emotions, for help with rhymes and bon mots. They were a Cyrano de Bergerac for the coat pocket. In one of the chapbooks that survive at the American Antiquarian Society, it is evident that a would-be valentine thumbed through the dozens of options in T. W. Strong's *St. Valentine's Budget* marking the suitable verses for her friends and suitors. One she singled out for Jack, another for Willie, and others of interest she noted with check marks.[43] Similarly, a dog-eared copy of *Strong's Universal Valentine Writer* at the Smithsonian shows again the uses to which these chapbooks were put: Pieces of paper marked promising pages; the corners of other pages were folded down; and inked brackets enclosed chosen verses. A couple of verses proved especially serviceable, the owner annotating them with the names of both Miss Angelia Miller and Miss Caroline Crawford. Both women evidently received the same heartfelt effusion from this prospective valentine:

Doubt not—believe each word you see,
  And treasure up each sacred line,—
Deep from my heart they come to thee,
  Then oh! be thou my Valentine.[44]

Professions of sincerity, ardor, and truthfulness tripped off the pages of valentine writers and onto valentines, and people clearly found these standardized words of homage useful and versatile.

The valentine writers did not skirt issues of self-expression, originality, and genuineness, but instead flaunted them. These chapbooks accentuated their wide expressive freedom; a selling point for the valentine writers was always the wealth of verses of varying sentiments that they offered. Their design was "to suit all classes and reach every case, for we should be pained, if, by our neglect, two young hearts, under the witching influence of love, should fail to make known their sentiments to each other." Printers of the valentine writers regularly accented the flexibility and comprehensiveness of their verses. For example, J. M. Fletcher in Nashua, New Hampshire, stressed that his *Ladies' and Gentlemen's New and Original Valentine Writer* was

> capable of a great number of modifications, alterations and amendments, which might give it a personal character, and thereby adapt it to numberless cases; for instance, the line reading,
>
> And offer unto thee my love,
>
> may be written,
>
> And offer sweetest Nell my love,
>
> or,—
>
> And offer Adaline my love,
>
> or,—
>
> And offer Mary all my love,
>
> and so on through the book.

Others made more-direct pleas for personalizing valentines, even for originality. "See to it that your 'Love Knot' does not lose its distinctive character—its highest charm—and become love *not*," the New York printer T. W. Strong often admonished in prefaces to his assorted valentine writers. One "mercenary bard" in London went further still, suggesting that his valentine writer was no substitute for creativity. "In writing a Valentine, the very best way of all is to *write an original one*. . . . Nothing can be so telling or so pungent as an immediate emanation from your own heart, or a direct inspiration of your own brain." By romantic ideal, people would use a valentine writer as they would a rhyming dictionary, something to rouse or assist their muse, not as something procrustean or formulaic. Thus the publishers of valentine writers, with not a little Barnumesque gall, effectively grasped the sentimental values of romantic love—the commitments to self-disclosure and imagination—and turned them into a commodity.[45]

It is important not to romanticize or overemphasize the place of self-expression and originality in folk versions of the holiday. Even when people eschewed valentine writers and wrote their own verses, they tended to tread well-worn poetic paths. Valentine verses about roses being red, violets blue, and sugar sweet were commonplace, cropping up time and again on handmade valentines. Even the elaborate and beautiful handmade love tokens—the puzzle purses and the cutwork pieces—were regularly inscribed with oft-repeated verses of ritualized familiarity; for example, the same rhyme of *vine* and *valentine* was used repeatedly. That is not to say that inventive handmade valentines were lacking. One, for example, cleverly strung together a series of scriptural citations to produce a valentine cryptogram that could then be decoded by turning to the Bible. Another sketched portraits of a sympathetic heart, a sentimental heart, a scornful heart, and a poetic heart, declaring of the last "That's Us!!!!"[46] Others were similarly creative and resourceful. Nonetheless, it is important to recognize that St. Valentine's Day, like other holidays, was a structured ritual event, and that people, when left to their own devices for valentine utterances, often held fast to the conventional, the customary, and the traditional. It was, after all, the emergent consumer culture (and its romantic analogue), not folk cultures, that enshrined variety and novelty as unassailable values. The ever-growing abundance of sentiments available in the marketplace—rhymes to cover an expanding range of romantic feelings—often made the homespun verses seem quaint, predictable, unimaginative, or perhaps even obsolete.[47]

Still, the valentine writers represent a significant step in the commercialization of the holiday. Even given the holiday's already conventional poetic images, as well as the nods within these chapbooks to flexibility and originality, the valentine writers remained in uneasy tension with romantic ideals of self-expression and self-disclosure.[48] Like letter writers and etiquette books, valentine writers offered to speak for people; they tendered eloquence and taste in the place of the anxious unknowns of self-giving or self-revelation. The historian Ann Douglas, with little affection for her object of study, has seen the sentimental fiction of this period as contributing to "a commercialization of the inner life," and the valentine writers with their simple formulas and their standardized words for wooing certainly participated in this packaging and selling of human feeling.[49] However useful or pliant they proved, these little books edged the holiday along the path of commercial transformation. Soon handwritten or hand-copied verses, even from valentine writers, were rare in comparison to the prevalence of preprinted sentiments and images.

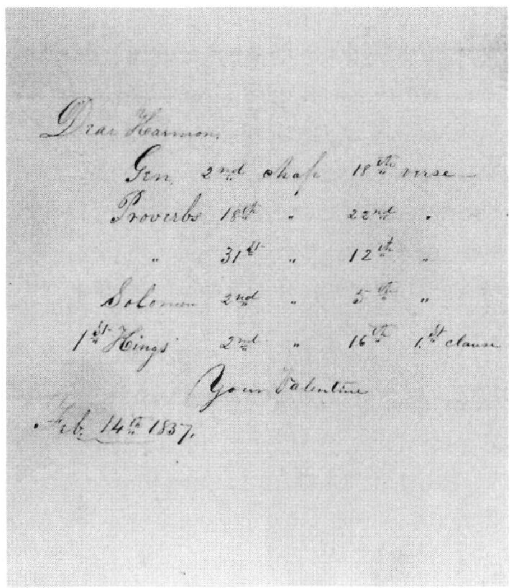

Dear Harmon,

Gen. 2nd chap. 18th verse

Proverbs 18th " 22nd "

" 31st " 12th "

Solomon 2nd " 5th "

1st Kings 2nd " 16th 1st clause

Your Valentine

Feb. 14th 1837.

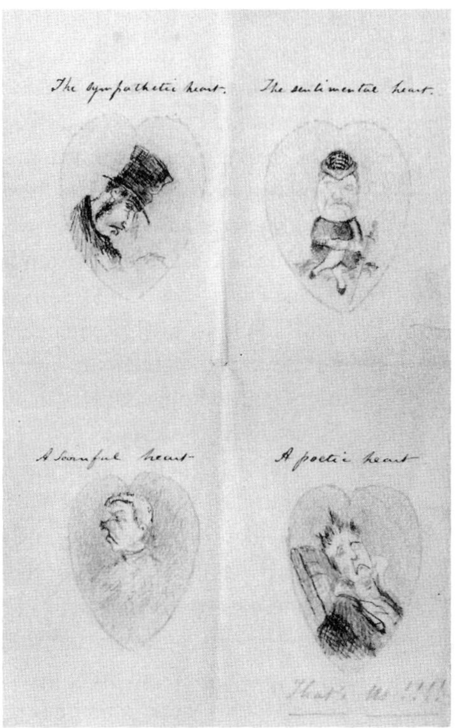

11. *(Left)* Bible verse cryptogram, handmade valentine, 1837.
12. *(Right)* "The Sympathetic Heart," handmade valentine, 1846.

REMAKING THE HOLIDAY'S RITUALS: THE MARKETING OF VALENTINES, 1840–1860

For printers, booksellers, and stationers, valentine writers were only one part of an enlarging market for products connected with St. Valentine's Day. Considerable marketing and entrepreneurial ingenuity went into the holiday's promotion, and the advertising often broke new ground. With the massive market for Christmas presents still in its infancy (in the 1840s lingering Puritan and evangelical suspicions continued to slow Christmas's middle-class ascendancy), the ballyhoo surrounding valentines was all the more striking. In effective and often innovative ways, merchants dramatized these new holiday goods as objects of allure, taste, romance, fantasy, and magic. The successful merchandising of valentines pointed to the incipient power of advertising and the spreading authority of fashion in American culture. Advertising, perhaps the cornerstone of the consumer culture, would expand into a vast industry after the Civil War, advancing from a $9.5 million business in 1865 to a $1.1 billion enterprise in 1929. It would develop its own corps of trade journals, such as *Printers'*

Ink(1888–) and *Signs of the Times* (1906–), and would form elaborate systems of management. But the massive, enterprising presence that advertising occupied in American culture by the turn of the twentieth century was built on the dramatic rehearsals of antebellum merchants. As one episode in the long history of advertising, the marketing of valentines was a portentous experiment.[50]

Newspaper advertising was a primary conduit for the promotion of valentines and an essential means by which the holiday was refashioned in the 1840s and 1850s. The growing number of advertisements for valentines in the *Philadelphia Public Ledger* in these years serves as a good case in point. Between 1840 and 1843, no advertisements for valentines were run, but after that, the amount steadily increased. In the issue immediately preceding the holiday, the number of valentine advertisements went from one in 1844 to five in 1845 to eight in 1846 to thirteen in 1847 to nineteen in 1848 to twenty-four in 1851. From there the numbers leveled off again as two large firms—Magee's and Fisher and Brother's—came to dominate the Philadelphia market and as the new holiday rituals became institutionalized and routinized, part of the familiar and accepted customs of the culture.

Valentine advertisements were filled with creative pufferies that called attention to the new products and to the specific firms that were vying for the holiday's business. Poems were popular for this rhyme-filled holiday, and the advertising ditties were sometimes crassly (even humorously) commercial, as was the case with Graham's, a New York bookseller:

> VALENTINES! VALENTINES!!—
> Come ye Lovers, one and all,
> Be ye great or be ye small,
> Into Graham's make a dash,
> There's the place to spend your cash.
> Every Lover there will find
> Valentines to suit his mind.
> From high to low his prices range,
> To suit the quantity of change,
> Which in your pocket so loosely jingles,
> To Graham's ears so sweetly tinkles.

Peterson's, a Philadelphia establishment that styled itself Cupid's Headquarters, likewise waxed poetic about its valentines:

> And those you buy at other places
> Will never win the ladies' graces;
> For Peterson has all the best—
> Don't give a penny for the rest!

In the 1840s and 1850s in one newspaper after another, dozens of firms puffed their valentine inventory along these lines.[51]

Aside from newspaper advertising, retailers of valentines touted their wares through specially decorated shop windows and other imaginative contrivances. One Philadelphia merchant, for example, linked an age-old advertising device to the holiday, making known that his valentines could be found on North Eighth Street "at the sign of the HEART." Others went farther and turned their shop windows or stores into small theaters of holiday fun and excitement. Turner and Fisher in New York, for example, had "Cupid, as large as life," in their store window in 1846. That same year T. W. Strong concocted a "dazzling," "brilliant," and "glorious" hundred-dollar valentine as a centerpiece of curiosity and captivation for his "Valentine Window." In 1847 the Philadelphia merchant George W. Adriance offered a still more ambitious decorative scheme, effectively recasting the traditional rites of St. Valentine's Eve into a shopping excursion. "THE CASTLE OF ST. VALENTINE," he reported, "will be brilliantly illuminated, THIS EVENING, and kept open till 12 o'clock. Don't fail to pay a visit." In 1850 Fisher and Brother's proclaimed its store to be "ST. VALENTINE'S THEATRE" and even pronounced that it had established a "ST. VALENTINE MUSEUM." Perhaps most grandly, Zieber and Co., a prominent Philadelphia firm, claimed to have St. Valentine himself "on hand" personally to "distribute his favors of every description."[52] With such eye-catching holiday attractions, shops were being transformed from places of grubby market exchanges to realms of fantasy, imagination, and exoticism—castles, theaters, and museums with mythic saints and Roman gods. Behind the spirit of modern consumerism, the sociologist Colin Campbell has glimpsed "a castle of romantic dreams," a sentimental ethic of feeling, longing, and reverie.[53] In the 1840s and 1850s retailers of valentines forwarded this confluence of romantic sentimentalism and modern consumerism, and, in doing so, they helped lay the foundation for still grander castles of desire.

All this inventive advertising and decoration suggested the emergence of a new holiday drama centered on shopping. This was a new kind of festival; "CUPID'S GRAND CARNIVAL" was one not of the streets, but of stores—a consumer celebration in which merchants took the lead in staging the fête. The responsibility that retailers assumed for promulgating this feast day was evident in an advertisement of Fisher and Brother's in 1850. Employing the diction of a fast or thanksgiving day proclamation, the promotional pitch took on the language of religious ritual and civic celebration for comic and commercial ends: "CUPID, *Governor* of the Commonwealth," set apart and ordained 14 February as a "FAST DAY OF LOVE AND MATRIMONY," and all citizens were enjoined "to fast for fast partners, for a fast life," and to go "fast unto FISHER & BROTHER'S Fast Temple of Heart Fastenings." The burlesque play on the word *fast* suggested

13. "Strong's Grand Valentine Depot," T. W. Strong advertisement, ca. 1848.

in miniature the changing contours of American celebration: It evoked the larger transition from a Puritan world where a fast meant repentance, abstinence, and discipline to a consumer world where fast meant dissipation, prodigality, and speed. The "new secular carnivalesque" that the historian William Leach has found in the department stores and show windows of the early twentieth century had an important antecedent in Cupid's fast-and-loose commercial carnival of the 1840s and 1850s.[54]

The promotions for St. Valentine's Day did not simply point ahead to the grander holiday spectacles of the department stores. Valentine advertisements also pointed back to folk uses of divination and love charms—that is, to the popular world of magic. This was quite clear in a Turner and Fisher advertisement in 1849 depicting valentines as amulets or potions that worked like "an 'Open Sesame'" upon the heart and that rendered "courting easy." "No one makes love," Turner and Fisher counseled, "without sending one as a pioneer." Merchants thus presented themselves as conjurers or wizards in the art of love; they offered valentine charms that contained the "wonderful power" to make people susceptible to passion and affection. Like the "recipes for love" of peddlers and quacks, valentines were offered as talismanic cure-alls: As

Turner and Fisher proclaimed, "COQUETRY cured in ten minutes. PROUD MAIDENS rendered soft and tender on reasonable terms. . . . VIRAGOS mollified cheap. . . . OLD BACHELORS entrapped." Like the magical aphrodisiacs of fortune-tellers and chapmen, valentines were presented as fast, affordable, and unfailing; like Cupid's magical arrows, they were sure to hit their mark. Maybe all this hocus-pocus about valentines was so much humbug, but it remains profoundly evocative of the homologies between the old magic of bewitchment and the new "magic system" of advertising, between the charms of conjuring and the fetishism of modern commodities. (The common inclusion of ringlets of hair in valentines—some were produced with actual slots for inserting a curl or two—suggests something of the tangible link between these new goods and traditional forms of conjuring in which a lock of hair from the beloved might be used to cast a favorably seductive spell.) In sum, much of the glamour of these new goods was built on the absorption of traditional forms of love magic—charms, potions, and aphrodisiacs.[55]

Thomas W. Strong, a wholesale and retail printer and stationer who went into business in New York City in 1842, exemplifies the promotional developments that helped catapult St. Valentine's Day into its status as a major American holiday in the 1840s and 1850s. A publisher of almanacs, songbooks, and lithographs (including, fittingly, a series of prints on P. T. Barnum), Strong took a leading role in the refashioning of St. Valentine's Day, soon becoming one of the country's largest producers and promoters of valentines. Exploiting all the forms he had at his disposal, Strong published valentine handbills, circulars, and catalogues and ran advertisements in newspapers, almanacs, and periodicals. His own monthly, *Yankee Notions*, regularly carried full-page notices about his valentines, laden with grand claims about their magical power to smite people, as well as panoramic visions of a vast market of international reach. The monthly also ran inventive articles and editorials about the history and customs of St. Valentine's Day, thus allowing Strong to put forth promotional material under the guise of journalistic stories.[56]

Strong also diligently sought out agents and retailers in town and countryside to extend the market for his products, calling "BOOKSELLERS, FANCY GOODS DEALERS, Postmasters, Pedlars, and enterprising young men who wish to make money" to join his valentine enterprise. Indeed, in one ad in January 1856 he announced his desire to recruit three thousand agents. He customarily bragged about his immense inventory at the New York store, what he liked to call his "VALENTINE EMPORIUM" or "GRAND VALENTINE DEPOT," boasting of "$75,000 Stock of VALENTINES" in 1858.[57] He also ingeniously played on the romantic yearning to recover lost holiday traditions—since "we have so few Holidays," he surmised, we need to celebrate this one "with the more ardor"—

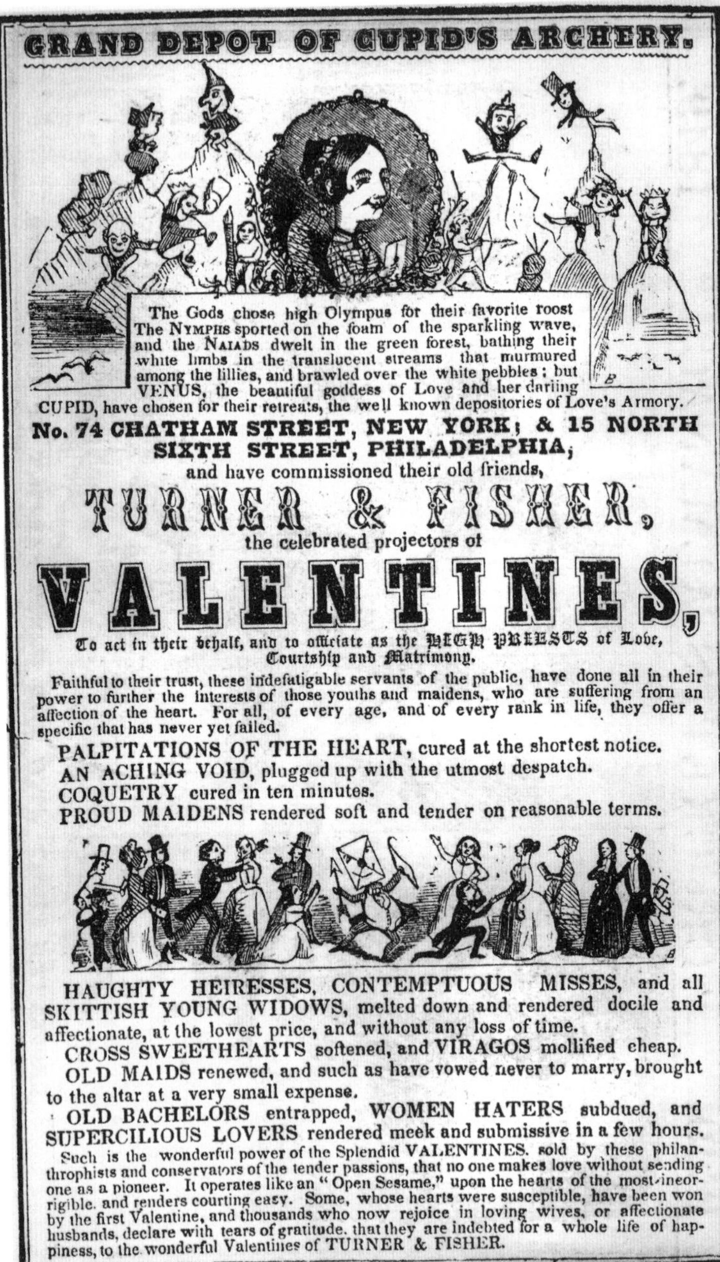

14. "Grand Depot of Cupid's Archery," Turner and Fisher advertisement, from *Crockett's Almanac, 1849* (Boston: James Fisher, 1849).

64 YANKEE NOTIONS.

Hurrah for the Valentines ! !

Now, all you that wants to get married, boys or gals, or old maids or old bachelors, all the way from the old "Deestrict of Maine" away down East, to the new "Deestrict of Californy" away out West, now's your chance! Jest send to STRONG's everlastin' great Valentine "Dépot," 98 Nassau Street, N. Y., and you'll find lots of amminition that'll be sure to do execution. Pick out anybody in this world that you are a mind to, and send 'em one of Strong's Valentines, and they are gone, they are nailed, hooked, done brown, and your'n forever!

I've been all over his establishment, seven stories high, and seen all hands to work, nigh about a hundred of 'em. And it beat all nater to see how they turned out the Valentines and Courting Picters, and Ornaments—and they was the most finest and the most takin things tu that ever I laid my eyes on. All sorts and sizes, and all sorts of prices, from a penny apiece up to fifty dollars—and ali sure to kill, hit or miss. So now come on, and ketch 'em while you can, for they are goin off like hot cakes. Strong has got the greatest pile of 'em that ever was made or imported in one establishment in America; but I'll bet my hat they'll every one be gone smack smooth before Valentine's day.

JONATHAN.

The New Stock for 1853

Is now ready, and far exceeds, in novelty of design and beauty of finish, any heretofore offered. It comprises the following assortment:

1 Cent Valentines, - - -	24 kinds,
3 " " - - - -	36 "
6 " " - - - -	48 "
12 " " - - - -	72 "
25 " " - - - -	72 "
37 " " - - - -	144 "
50 " " - - - -	288 "
100 " " - - - -	72 "
200 " " - - - -	72 "

$5, $10, and $25 Valentines, of various and elegant designs.

Over 1000 kinds of Comic Valentines,

THE BEST IN THE MARKET,

$1 50 PER GROSS,

Also on hand a large stock of

FANCY AND LACED PAPERS AND ENVELOPES

AND

VALENTINE ORNAMENTS,

IN GREAT VARIETY.

This Establishment being the largest and most celebrated **Valentine Manufactory and Importing House** in this Country, offers advantages to dealers and others, not to be found elsewhere.

Orders by mail or otherwise, promptly attended to.

N. B.—**Agents** and **Valentine Companies** supplied with **Stock** from **$50** to **$1,000.**

☞ A Liberal Discount to the Trade. ☜

T. W. STRONG, 98 Nassau Street, N. Y.

15. T. W. Strong advertisement, *Yankee Notions* 2 (February 1853): 64.

and lifted up the holiday as a rare opportunity in a hard-boiled world for dalliance, innocent mischief, and fond conceits. He relished the spectacle of his shop window bedecked for the holiday and prided himself on the numbers that came to gaze at his costliest and most fashionable specimens, "the very rarest gems of the art." Typically, in his *Annual Valentine Advertiser* for 1847, itself an eight-page pamphlet, Strong boasted of his success: "Last year, for two weeks, crowds filled the Valentine warehouse at 98 Nassau-street, above and below, and even blocked up the doors and sidewalks."[58]

In that same advertising circular Strong commented that "of late" the observance of St. Valentine's Day had been "steadily increasing throughout the United States."[59] He and other merchants like him could take much of the credit for this ascendancy. Zieber's, Magee's, Fisher and Brother's, Elton's, George Cottrell, Esther Howland, Fred Turner, P. J. Cozan, J. M. Fletcher, McLoughlin Bros., and James Wrigley all rose to commercial prominence with Strong in the 1840s or 1850s.[60] The holiday's approach came to be defined in terms of their shops, advertisements, display windows, and products; these things heralded and structured the holiday's celebration. The *Boston Daily Evening Transcript* suggested in 1845 the crucial role that merchants had come to play in signaling and framing the holiday: "TOMORROW is *St. Valentine's Day*—as the advertisements in the papers from the 'Court of Love' have duly informed us fourteen days in advance of the interesting anniversary!" Or, as the *New-York Tribune* indicated in 1848, "Our readers need no reminder concerning the festival of the tender saint. The hundreds of colored and gilded messages, fluttering in the [shop] windows, like the wings of the child-deity who inspired them, have for weeks past proclaimed its approach." With considerable entrepreneurial energy and foresight, merchants prepared people for the holiday's celebration and marked its approach through recurrent reminders the month before. As the sociologist Michael Schudson comments of advertising's influence, "Little is more important than naming, marking, and reminding," and such reminding—whether of St. Valentine's Day, Mother's Day, or Secretaries' Day—remains among the crucial pieces of cultural work that holiday advertising performs.[61]

The flurry of commercial activity that swirled around St. Valentine's Day in the 1840s and 1850s fundamentally refashioned the holiday's rituals and contours. For one thing, marketing expanded the festival's time frame. In the *Philadelphia Public Ledger* in the early 1850s, advertisements for valentines stretched from mid-January to late February. People began to speak of "Valentine week" or even "Valentine month" as the process of receiving valentines and then reciprocating with what the merchants labeled "return valentines" grew into a protracted period of exchange.[62] Advertising four days after

St. Valentine's Day itself, Fisher and Brother's suggested commercial interest in prolonging the holiday: "The gratified receivers of VALENTINES, and their name is legion, must not omit to send one in return to their best loved friend. . . . We shall keep up our assortment till March 1st. . . . Remember that old St. Valentine's reign lasts throughout February." Or, as J. M. Fletcher instructed the uninitiated in the etiquette of valentine greetings, "Valentines may properly be sent from the 14th of February to the first of March, and even later when answers are returned." Seeing the holiday more as a season than as a day had little or no precedent in the folklore of the occasion: It was a commercial contrivance—one that foreshadowed the eventual protraction of Christmas and Easter into long shopping seasons.[63]

Marketing also expanded the range of people who were to be included in valentine transactions. From an occasion that primarily involved marriageable young men and women, St. Valentine's Day was enlarged to embrace everyone. Valentines were not simply for lovers or would-be couples, but for any and all relations. "Remember that Valentines are appropriate," J. M. Fletcher advised, "for brothers, sisters, relatives and friends, as well as for sweethearts and lovers." Fisher and Brother's was still more expansive, pushing valiantly to widen the scope of relationships covered by valentines: "We conjure you, one and all, not to neglect this innocent festival. Brothers and sisters, come, Mothers and fathers, come, Lover and lady love, come, Uncles and aunts, come, Grandpa and grandma, come, Friend and stranger, come, Nephews and nieces, come, Wives and husbands, come, Mamma and the baby, come. COME! COME!! COME!!!" This was not mere merchandising bombast. As is evident in archival holdings of nineteenth-century valentines, these greetings were widely popularized as tokens of endearment for family and friends. Aunts and uncles presented them to nieces and nephews; mothers gave them to their children; siblings and friends exchanged them. Even adversarial relationships were included: Annoying neighbors, exacting bosses, harsh schoolmasters, unattractive suitors, and domineering wives, among others, could all be pilloried with comic or mock valentines. Merchants tried to enlarge St. Valentine's Day into a holiday that encompassed all the complex webs of social relationships, and they went a long way toward succeeding.[64]

While merchants were ready to involve anyone and everyone in the new holiday fashion, they especially linked valentines to women and children. Their marketing gave St. Valentine's Day a new feminized, domestic luster. Women were seen as the chief recipients, senders, and keepers of these fancy billets-doux, and certainly the most extravagant sentimental valentines with their layers of lace and ornament were aimed at them as the ultimate consumers of these gifts. Holiday illustrations from *Godey's* and *Harper's Weekly* in the

16. "Boarding-School on St. Valentine's Morning," *Harper's Weekly*, 13 February 1858, 105.

17. "Here's Another Valentine," *Godey's Lady's Book and Magazine* 58 (February 1859): 190.

18. *Strong's Annual Valentine Advertiser* (New York: T. W. Strong, 1847), cover.

1850s were filled with women and girls expectantly receiving these missives, and T. W. Strong tellingly emblazoned a woman on the cover of his *Annual Valentine Advertiser*. Merchants played up the popularity of valentines with women and saw these delicate missives as a way of getting women into their stores. An early Fisher and Brother's catalogue from about 1852 boasted to retail dealers that "Valentines will make your stores look lively, while the presence of the ladies will make them look lovely." Valentines were thus one product that helped mark the nineteenth-century shift from stores as an arena where men went to trade and fraternize to a place where women would go to shop and browse.[65]

In feminizing the holiday, merchants not only were recasting the gendered associations of their stores, but also were participating in a larger redefinition of middle-class womanhood in terms of fashion, sentiment, and consumer-

19. "Tuck's Valentines Welcomed Everywhere!" Raphael Tuck and Sons advertisement, ca. 1880.

ism. The involvement of the valentine vogue in this transformed construction of gender was evident in a short story published in *Godey's* in 1850 called "Kate's Valentine." As the holiday approached, so the story related, "the shop windows and counters began to be filled with emblematic love missives of all kinds." Having heretofore resisted this rampant fashion and these "costly, delicate, and refined" goods, Kate is this time caught up in the occasion after receiving an especially "handsome" missive containing a piece of jewelry. This unexpected valentine initiates her into the world of courtship and romance. Formerly clearheaded and unsentimental, she is brought under the sway of the new rituals and their emblems of tender feeling and expressive emotion. Through the new fashion in valentines, Kate is thus transformed; the novel rituals and their wares effect her identification with sentimentalism, romantic love, and consumerism.[66]

In their promotions, merchants also gave new emphasis to the role of children in the holiday. They created whole lines of "juvenile valentines," pointing the way toward one of the holiday's dominant modern forms—the exchange of valentines among schoolchildren. This juvenile turn was given pictorial

20. Prang's Valentine Cards, poster advertisement, ca. 1875.

expression in a show card for Raphael Tuck's valentines: Ambling, cavorting, innocent schoolchildren personified the holiday. This was very much a new image for the observance. A certain sentimental devotion to the child characterized middle-class Victorian culture, and St. Valentine's Day increasingly reflected the piety of the angelic youngster. In particular, the refashioned image of Cupid as an innocent cherub suggested the holiday's redirection toward children and familial devotion. On their valentines and in their advertisements, merchants helped create a darling infant Cupid who bore only a faint resemblance to the often capricious Roman Cupid, who was said, among other things, to have sharpened his arrows on a grindstone whetted with blood. One of Louis Prang's advertising posters suggested this new domesticated, desexualized form of Cupid imagery quite clearly: A dainty, adorable band of cherubs, happily tied to a young woman like a bunch of seraphic

VALENTINES

FOR THE

MILLION!

At 144 Merrimack St.

The subscriber has just received from New York and Boston, a general assortment of

VALENTINES,

Amusing and affecting; beautiful and bewitching; comical and capital; delicate and delightful; elegant and entertaining; fantastic and funny; grave and gay; handsome and humorous; incomparable and inexpressible; jocose and jovial; killing and knowing; lively and laughable; merry and magnificent; neat and nice; ornamental and overwhelming; panegyrical and pantomimical; queer and quizzical; refreshing and romantic; serious and sentimental; tender and tasteful; unique and utile; valuable and veritable; witty and wonderful; xtensive and xtraordinary, &c.

Also, VALENTINE WRITERS, ENVELOPES, LACE PAPERS, etc. etc.

☞Please call and examine.

JAMES P. WALKER,
144 *Merrimack St.*

B. H. PENHALLOW, PRINTER, Wyman's Exchange

21. "Valentines for the Million," handbill, ca. 1850.

balloons, evoke the pure delights of little children, not pagan eros. (In some sense, though, the old Cupid remained a fitting symbol of the modern commercial version of the holiday: In its Latin roots *Cupid* connotes passion, desire, and longing; it is closely connected to *cupiditas*—a craving for possessions, an acquisitive appetite.) In sum, the whirl of commercial promotion helped redefine the holiday in terms of women and children, giving the event a new domestic, feminized, and juvenile tenor.

Merchandising perhaps most clearly reshaped the holiday's contours in suffusing the occasion with the language of fashion, novelty, and consumer choice. The variety of valentines was dazzling, and every year there seemed to be a new fashion or style: satin, lace, perfumed, and gilt-edged valentines; painted and lithographed valentines; acrostic and arabesque valentines; cameo and box valentines; mechanical, cobweb, and banknote valentines; Leap Year valentines; California valentines for 1849; valentines with gold rings, small mirrors, or daguerreotypes; valentines with velvet, feather, and floral ornaments; and even exploding valentines (something akin to British Christmas crackers, first marketed by a London confectioner in 1846).[67] The enormous variety was portrayed as a consumer's dream: Every taste or whim could be satisfied; every income or class accommodated. At the same time, extravagantly expensive valentines continually raised the ceiling of fashion and elegance. With incredulity the *Boston Daily Evening Transcript* reported in 1845 on some white satin valentines "trimmed with Mecklin lace" that were priced at $80. Six years later the paper marveled at a $150 valentine that had "diamonds, pearls, rubies, and other precious stones, artistically displayed" on it. More modestly priced valentines, still rich in detail and embellishment, were themselves fraught with fashion, allure, and luxury. They were presented as objects of "indescribable elegance" and "exquisite taste"; they were lifted up as being among "the prettiest things in the world." "Nobody," the *Boston Daily Evening Transcript* concluded, "can look at those ornamental missives without being tempted." The Victorian vogue in valentines suggested the power of the consumer culture to remake an age-old folk holiday in its own image—one of annually changing styles, dainty frills, refined taste, and ardent desire.[68]

MOCK VALENTINES: A PRIVATE CHARIVARI

Underlying all the variety in nineteenth-century valentines was one basic distinction—the divide between sentimental and satiric valentines. Almost all the entrepreneurial energy was poured into the promotion of these two counterpoised product lines, one that was mushy and maudlin and another that was cutting and caustic. Sentimental missives tended to be more elaborate and costly, but comic valentines, cheap and crude, held a substantial part of the market. American manufacturers, *Harper's Weekly* reported in 1858, saw the market as "very evenly divided" between the two, sales for the prior year "being about one and a half millions of each kind." The valentine market was forged out of this basic dualism—a fundamental tension that energized valentine exchanges.[69]

The development of sentimental valentines is readily intelligible: They were a commercial elaboration of pairing games, youthful wooing, poetic compliments, and love tokens, all staples of the holiday. Hearts and hands, flowers and birds, bowers and churches, courtiers and ladies, Cupid and his arrows, Hymen and his torch—these were familiar romantic emblems that were predictably appropriated for the imagery of sentimental valentines. Within this common set of allusions, there remained plenty of room for whimsy and curiosity—a little Cupid hidden under a flower that pulled out from the lace paper or a miniature mirror tucked away beneath a pair of birds. Ample space was preserved, too, for genteel fantasy. Courtly scenes in which nineteenth-century democrats could imagine themselves as nobles and aristocrats were popular, for example. Perhaps the sentimental valentine's capacity for romantic phantasm was epitomized by one mythological rendezvous in which Hymen's reindeer-led chariot whisked the couple to the church for their nuptials—a conveyance suggestive of an overlap with Clement Moore's Santa Claus in "The Night before Christmas" (in the poem, one of Santa's reindeer is called Cupid). But to whatever dreams and fancies sentimental valentines beckoned, they were still predictable enough as a product line. Dainty and elegant, they were the very embodiment of romantic love, tastefulness, and fashion.

What to make of the comic valentines is another matter. As coarse as the sentimental ones were refined, mock valentines were caricatures, grotesques. They emerged as the carnivalesque underbelly of a holiday all too prone to mawkish sentimentality. Shot through with the rambunctious imagery of popular caricature and Rowlandsonian satire, the comic valentines were wholly a commercial invention. Little foundation in the folk traditions of St. Valentine's Day existed for turning the holiday into an occasion of ritualized mockery—a veritable charivari—but that is where the market took it. Merchants appropriated transgressive images of inversion, lewdness, and insult and gathered them in novel and popular ways around St. Valentine's Day. The producers of comic valentines effectively refashioned the carnivalesque tradition of the prank or practical joke into a commodity.[70]

From the turn of the nineteenth century, British publishers and engravers had experimented with satire and caricature in their valentine writers, and comic engravings to go with these mocking verses were soon developed. Like the valentine craze generally, the vogue for caricatures blossomed in the United States in the mid- to late 1840s. "The practice of sending comic Valentines," the *Philadelphia Public Ledger* complained in 1848, "is an innovation which has lately been introduced, and which tends to lessen the pleasures which ought legitimately to hallow the festival." In an early valentine advertisement in 1843, the New York merchant Robert Elton clearly subordinated comic valentines to sentimental ones, mentioning almost as an afterthought that he carried "a few comical Valentines to be sent to fusty old bachelors and sour old maids that are beyond cure." In 1847 Strong's *Annual Valentine Advertiser* went on for two pages describing his sentimental valentines, but covered satirical ones in a paragraph, the same space he gave to children's valentines. But by 1853 Strong was headlining his comics and the

22. *(Top left)* "All the World," sentimental valentine, 1864.
23. *(Top right)* "Receive This Tribute," sentimental valentine, ca. 1850.
24. *(Bottom left)* "My Dearest Girl," sentimental valentine, ca. 1850.

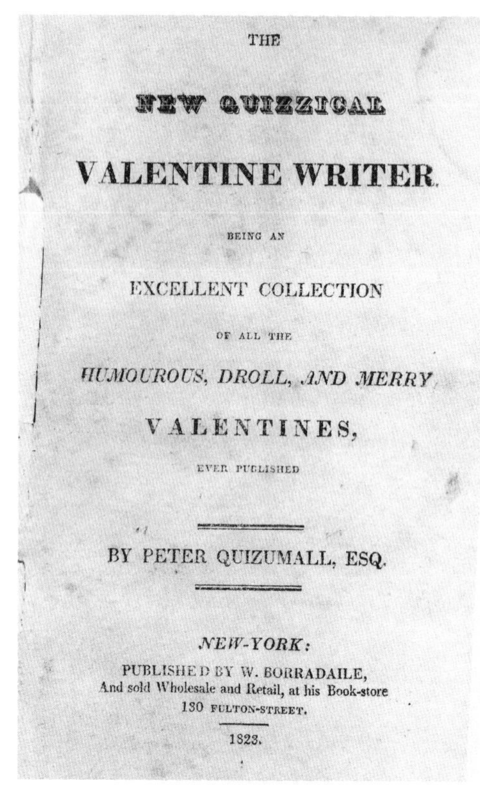

THE

NEW QUIZZICAL

VALENTINE WRITER.

BEING AN

EXCELLENT COLLECTION

OF ALL THE

HUMOUROUS, DROLL, AND MERRY

VALENTINES,

EVER PUBLISHED

BY PETER QUIZUMALL, ESQ.

NEW-YORK:

PUBLISHED BY W. BORRADAILE,
And sold Wholesale and Retail, at his Book-store
130 FULTON-STREET.

1823.

25. *The New Quizzical Valentine Writer* (New York: W. Borradaile, 1823), frontispiece.

thousand different types he offered, and other New York firms, especially McLoughlin Bros., made them their specialty. Some feared that the caricatures—"so gross and disgusting," *Godey's* said, "that it would seem only savages or brutes could have prepared them"—were taking over and ruining the holiday. Unexpectedly they had come to rival the sentimental valentines in numbers and popularity.[71]

The comic valentines took no prisoners. They lampooned people of all trades and professions; they stereotyped African Americans and the Irish; they mocked the ugly and the misshapen; they laid into the glutton, the drunkard, and the dandy; they heaped contumely on the greedy, the overbearing, the hypocritical, and the dim-witted. The comic valentines also teemed with ribaldry and phallic innuendo (men looking up women's skirts, firemen with their hoses, soldiers with their primed and loaded guns). While valentine caricatures are provocative at a number of levels, they are especially striking for

26. "Fireman," mock valentine, ca. 1850.

their carnivalesque mockery. They functioned, indeed, like some sort of private charivari. Whole groups of young men did not take up bells, horns, pots, kettles, and masks to make rough music in order to ridicule someone who had offended the norms of the community. Instead, under the anonymous cloak of the mail, individuals undertook rituals of insult that mirrored in modern guise long-standing communal forms of mockery.[72]

Elements of charivari were especially evident with those comic valentines devoted to disordered marital roles and relationships. For example, a scraggly bearded man with a baby in his arms was serenaded in derisive tones with the verse:

> You old henpicked wretch, you are quite a disgrace,
> Let your wife mind the baby and keep her own place,
> Be more of a man, dont allow her to roam,
> Make her leave off the breeches and keep her at home.[73]

27. "You Old Henpicked Wretch," mock valentine, ca. 1850.

In a similar vein, the picture of a "scolding wife" was used to chide an unmarried woman and dismiss her as a prospective valentine:

> Who will marry such a termagant wife,
> The plague of her own poor husband's life?
> Who distorts all her features with anger and rage,
>
> . . . .
>
> To others I such charms resign,
> You ne'er can be my Valentine.

As T. W. Strong boasted, comic valentines provided people with the opportunity to mock "queer kind of folks," those who did not conform to expected gender roles, those who were seen as marginal or different.[74]

Unruly and unwed women were the particular target of these attack valentines. Widows, old maids, loud and assertive women, flirts, and coquettes were standard objects of misogynistic derision, and the satiric valentines made a ritual sport of such ridicule. One of these grotesques, for example, showed

28. "The End of Old Maids," mock valentine, ca. 1850.

"the end of old maids": The devil impaled a woman on a fork and hoisted her over a fire; here the violence of demons, common enough in the holiday's medieval hagiography, resurfaced to torment ungoverned women. Similarly, another mock valentine pictured a man half prone at the feet of a woman with horns poking out of her head:

> You ugly, cross and wrinkled shrew,
> You advocate of woman's rights,
> No man on earth would live with you.
> For fear of endless fights.[75]

Intractable, willful, or publicly active women were portrayed as devils, snakes, tigers, or hissing cats; in posing a threat to prevailing cultural definitions of true womanhood, they were depicted in subhuman and bestial forms, recategorized in terms of the grotesque, the abominable, or the abject. Women's bodies were made the particular object of caricature, distortion, and rearrangement. In menacing images of unruliness, their tongues were regularly

29. "Corkscrew Tongue," mock valentine, ca. 1850.

elongated; one woman, for example, was depicted as having a "corkscrew tongue"—a comic valentine that served as an admonition:

> I send you this, as a warning, in time
> To unscrew your long tongue, if you'd have a Valentine.[76]

The voices of women were considered especially dangerous, and the grotesque images were aimed at silencing or "unscrewing" their tongues. In an ominous gender reversal, loud women with their protruding tongues threatened to "screw" men.

The intrusive, controlling roles that comic valentines were designed to play make them no laughing matter. These caricatures were a kind of extortion, especially when directed at women: Behave modestly and decorously or suffer the consequences of social rejection, ridicule, or even violence. In this regard, the comic valentines were transparent:

Among the women who in history brightest have shone
Are those who have left the men's affairs alone,
Who in their homes have found their proper places,
And sought not in crowds to show their faces;
We see you seek a different line—
You are too bold to be my Valentine.[77]

Coincident with the first wave of organized struggle for women's rights in the late 1840s and 1850s, this ritual of holiday caricature was wielded as another weapon of indignity and intimidation. Like the charivari itself, comic valentines used mockery for community regulation and social restraint. Here, however, the ritual was in a modern context in which the insults were more a matter of private exchange than public drama.

"A MEANER SORT OF MERCHANDIZE" OR "A PLEASURE WITHOUT ALLOY"? THE NEW FASHION CONTESTED AND CELEBRATED

Our tokens of compliment and love are for the most part barbarous. Rings and other jewels are not gifts, but apologies for gifts. The only gift is a portion of thyself. Thou must bleed for me. . . . It is a cold, lifeless business when you go to the shops to buy me something, which does not represent your life and talent.

Ralph Waldo Emerson, "Essay V: Gifts" (1844)[78]

The essence of the present, properly so-called, consists in the sentiment of the thing. . . . O! the sweetness of the real "present!" What wealth of love may be enwrapped in it—what mystic meaning—what vows of truth—what rich memories of the past—what promise of the future! What a glory envelops the simplest object the moment it takes that sacred character. . . . From whatever cause, presents, as we began to say, have almost lost their sweet significance, and become a meaner sort of merchandize.

C. M. Kirkland, A Book for the Home Circle (1853)[79]

The new fashion for valentines—comic and sentimental alike—did not go uncriticized. Many commentators who took stock of this "national whim" saw it in an unflattering light. Critics were indeed sundry, and they attacked the holiday, by turns, for its vulgarity, vengefulness, and irreligion. Most of all, they bemoaned its commercial trivialization and artificiality. As the epigraphs above suggest, the debate about the little gifts of St. Valentine's Day reveals a larger rift about the meaning of presents in a culture coming to terms simultaneously with romanticism and commodification, sentimentalism and consumption. The contest over these small tokens of love suggested a first wave of disaffection with the market's colonization of ritual, a swell that would roll into subsequent discussions of other holidays. Yet the critics were never so numerous as the celebrants, and the latter would ultimately carry the day.[80]

The invective of critics focused particularly on the comic valentines. With the flourishing of these caricatures, many came to see St. Valentine's Day as "a much degraded festival," a time of "low and foolish insult." This reproof often followed the fault lines of class—refined, upstanding middle-class sorts versus ignorant, vulgar plebeians. As the *New-York Tribune* viewed the matter, "the sweetness of St. Valentine's old, romantic associations" had been "nearly destroyed" by that "numerous class of individuals whose tastes take the lowest forms of all prevailing fancies." "The shocking attempts at low wit, and vulgar caricature," the paper continued, "alike disgraceful to those who make and those who send them, supply the wants of this class." But the critique of comic valentines was not only founded on class: Notions of the purity of womanhood clearly figured into Sarah Hale's editorial revulsion in *Godey's* from these indelicate and assaultive grotesques, and her call for their elimination was not simply repressive, but protective, an attempt to defend women from their aggressive misogyny. Also, the prominence of racist caricatures may well have factored into the general condemnation of mock valentines by the *Christian Recorder*, an African American Methodist publication. In its view the "rags and filth" of these satires so corrupted "the manners, and the morals of the people" that the holiday should, in good Puritan fashion, be abolished. Despite the outcry of critics, few merchants displayed many scruples about the caricatures: Most went on offering "rhymes of every degree of morality," along with comic images that were "decidedly vulgar." There was little incentive to stop selling satiric valentines, since "every one of them," the *New York Herald* moaned in 1855, "will be bought up." To critics, the very popularity of mock valentines suggested the degree to which the holiday had been sunk in immorality, even malevolence.[81]

As the concerns of the *Christian Recorder* suggest, the critique of this new fashion sometimes took a religious turn. Early on, Mary Lyon, founder of Mount Holyoke College, expressed an evangelical's suspicion of these new holiday customs, attempting without success to forbid her students—Emily Dickinson among them—from sending "any of those foolish notes called Valentines."[82] As a frivolity, these greetings pushed at the bounds of religious discipline and purity, a frilly and sensual indulgence that some considered to be in conflict with evangelical (and republican) notions of ascetic simplicity. Other commentators also registered a centuries-old discomfort with a Christian martyr being signalized as the patron of nubile youths and the sponsor of matchmaking. Like Ben Jonson before him, the Victorian writer Richard Le Gallienne found the ironies of St. Valentine's Day worthy of comment, if not redress. Contrasting "the grinding reality of that moment when the clubs descended on your frail ascetic frame" with the modern remembrance of the saint as "a sort of grandfather Cupid," Le Gallienne thought the modern holiday had degenerated into a bacchanal. "Time," he concluded, "makes a mock of your witness, and turns your agony into garlands." Le Gallienne had a point. As the modern version of the holiday developed, it tended to shunt aside the saint altogether, often dropping the *St.* from St. Valentine's Day, or, perhaps even more tellingly, remaking his image, like that of St. Nicholas, into a jolly, fun-loving old geezer. "We know he must have been an amiable, pleasant fellow, loving the pretty girls"; so read one newspaper's canard in 1845, "nothing improper, you know; all sentiment, and that sort of thing." With characterizations like these, it is no wonder that a few thought St. Valentine's Day had become "a silly sacrilegious jest" in which secular indulgence had utterly displaced religious example.[83]

What concerned observers most about the modern version of St. Valentine's Day was the feared loss of sincerity and authentic self-expression at the hands of industry, commerce, and mass production. It was in this context that the most far-reaching criticisms were leveled. Commentators wondered at those willing to accept prefabricated poems in the place of genuine gushings from the heart. "We are afraid," the *Boston Daily Evening Transcript* lamented in 1845, "there are many such, so poor in intellect that they must buy their verses ready made. For on that day every book store is turned into a Valentine slop-shop." From first to last, the critics were romantics and sentimentalists: They wanted heartfelt, earnest verses, not affected, stereotyped hack writing, real feelings, not simple formulas. As the *New-York Tribune* instructed succinctly in 1852, "One word only: Write your own poems to-day." Sincerity and social transparency, the historian Karen Halttunen has suggested, were the "sentimental antidote" to commercial artifice and the wiles of the confidence man, and in the contests over St. Valentine's Day critics likewise wanted to safeguard this social ritual from the cunning of the marketplace and the legerdemain of merchants. These critical concerns, as the musings of both Emerson and Kirkland suggest, had deep resonances in wider romantic understandings of the gift. Presents, fraught with profound relational possibility and emotional power, were being trivialized, turned into a commodity form, "a meaner sort of merchandize," mere "apologies for gifts."[84]

The *Philadelphia Public Ledger* presented the full thrust of such concerns about commodification in a sharp-edged riposte in 1848:

> We . . . think the entire tribe of engraved, painted, printed Valentines an abomination, invented by cunning stationers and booksellers for pecuniary profit, and a desecration of love's high festival. When we were young, they did these things differently; a Valentine was of no value then, unless it were original, for in that case there was some guarantee that the sentiments set down on the epistle shadowed forth the real feelings of the writer. But what satisfaction is it to a lady to receive a printed declaration, embossed and gilded according to a set pattern, and which is a precise facsimile of fifty thousand others which she knows to have been sent to half the young ladies in the town. Far better would be the most simple refrain from the pen of the loved one.

The sameness of mass-produced valentines was alienating. The most intimate feelings involved in love and romance were reduced to a pattern, a facsimile: How could such expressions possibly be genuine, sincere, and heartfelt? "The common gew-gaw affairs of the print shops" were unreal, artificial, ersatz; instead of bringing separate selves closer together, they distanced them, disconnecting people from their own emotions and from the feelings of those with whom they sought intimacy and familiarity. Where others saw elegance, the critics found only estrangement.[85]

So strongly did some critics feel about this that they appropriated, like the writer for the *Public Ledger*, the religious language of abomination and desecration. Sarah Hale expressed editorial displeasure with the new fashion in these terms: Most modern valentines were "stereotyped, miserable things," nothing more than "*printed* doggerel, bought in market and distributed through the penny post, with no more sentiment to consecrate the offering than though these Valentines were patented recipes for colds, or notices of a new milliner's shop." According to Hale, the market profaned the holiday. Commerce made these sentimental rituals little more than another nostrum of hucksters or another gimmick of Barnumesque promoters; boundaries had to be drawn. Festivals, if they were to remain consecrated, could not be the business of merchants and manufacturers. According to the critics, the unsentimental realities of small-scale factories and routinized production drained the holiday of mystery and charm. "Cupid's manufactory," one observer said of a valentine mill in 1864, was a "disenchanting" and "dingy" sight: pressmen and boys with ink-stained hands, women and girls working eleven-hour days at long tables repetitiously piecing together the layers of lace and ornament. Critics saw gifts that were purchased and exchanged in this context—one shaped by the cunning of business enterprise and the deadening routine of wage labor—as tainted and defiled.[86]

Nineteenth-century purists wanted their holidays free of the machine and the market, their gifts unspoiled by commercial manipulation and mere social obligation, their sentiments real and personal. What they got was something else. They were left to wonder about purer, truer times when "Valentine's Day meant something," when it was not a matter of "business fashion," but "real lovers." There had been a time, these romantics were sure, when people "entered into [the holiday's] celebration sincerely, joyously, spontaneously," but now all that had changed. "Modern commercialism" had sapped the holiday of its "real meaning." As one nostalgic critic sulked, "Ah me! the days of the troubadour are over—this *is* a 'bank-note world.'" Like the golden halo of community, the charged aura of holidays seemed always to be fading. The loss of community, the loss of tradition, and the loss of festivity were everywhere interrelated laments. Critics longed for a time when festivals built communities, not fortunes. As was the case with the Victorian nostalgia for the vanishing joys of Christmas past, the myth of a simpler, purer, better St. Valentine's Day found recurrent expression. Yet the critics' very celebration of such individualistic ideals as sincerity, spontaneity, and self-revelation made their hopes for the return of old-time village festivities all that much more forlorn. As often as not, the critique of the corrosive effects of modern commerce foundered on its own romantic individualism.[87]

Despite all their protestations and laments, the critics were overwhelmed. The enthusiasm for the new version of the holiday clearly outstripped any reservations. The British essayist and poet Charles Lamb captured the pleasure and excitement found in the new missives in his widely reprinted "Homily for the Fourteenth of February." He recalled the charm and expense of the "first valentine I ever opened," which he received from his sweetheart when he was seventeen. "The Valentine was radiant,—all gold and gay colours, red, and yellow, and blue, and embossed, and glittering with devices, all of love. It was like a dream, so fine. I had never seen any thing like it. . . . I was satisfied,—delighted—what is the word? *enchanted*!"[88] Or, as a twenty-eight-year-old Philadelphian rejoiced over a valentine greeting he received in 1847, "My little pet, Emily Lyman sent me a verse with a lock of her beautiful hair which has afforded me very great pleasure." The same sort of gleeful satisfaction was expressed in a letter from a Connecticut woman, Sophia Root, to her sister in 1861 about a valentine that the latter had sent to Sophia's young daughter Mary. "I cannot tell you how delighted Mary was with the valentine. . . . She jumped about and up and down in expression of joy. She has shown it to her schoolteacher and many other friends. It is a beautiful thing and she sends you many thanks for it." So treasured indeed was this valentine that the girl saved it along with the richly embossed envelope in which it had come. The beauty and radiance of new things, new commodities, new gifts captured the imagination.[89]

Like Mary Root, other women saved their valentines. Objects of reminiscence and memory, sentimental valentines were, as *Harper's Weekly* noted in 1858, often laid away among women's "hidden treasures," tied up with ribbons or cached in trunks. Frequently they were preserved, "uncreased and unsoiled," in elegant albums and scrapbooks as keepsakes. The Hallmark Historical Collection has amassed several dozen of these nineteenth-century albums, and in them one can see how valentines and other cards were prized. In mounting holiday greetings in these large, plush albums, women regularly wrote underneath the missives some identifying annotation—from cousin Elizabeth; Easter 1881; Helen's first valentine.[90] In this way a chronicle of friends, relatives, and important occasions could be maintained through albums filled with cards and other mementos. Sentimental valentines, like the Christmas and Easter cards that came into vogue a generation later, were thus cherished for the web of relationships, for the intimations of kinship and camaraderie, that they evoked. The little, formulaic, sentimental mottoes themselves consistently suggested this sense of lasting connection: "Yours forever"; "Think of me when far away"; "Fond remembrance." As these "ladies' albums" attest, the valuing of valentines and other cards for the attachments they represented was true of women in particular. The valentine vogue was crucial for establishing this "feminized" pattern of holiday remembrance and for forwarding the view that holidays were peculiarly part of the domestic, relational domain of women.[91] While the disaffection of critics would have nonplussed most celebrants, perhaps women especially would have found these concerns bewildering. Far from being alienating, sentimental valentines were expectantly received and highly esteemed; emblems to save and relish, they were "a pleasure without alloy." As Charles Lamb asked contentedly, "A Valentine—who would not have a Valentine?"[92]

These colorful missives proved popular, too, for the part they played in easing courtship, for providing a ritual medium through which delicate issues of affection could be broached in that widening, uncertain domain of romantic love. For young people who were timid or apprehensive, valentines offered a ceremonial means for expressing attachment or infatuation. As *Godey's* put it, "the ice of many a courtship" had been broken through "those emblematic pictures." In the place of drawing lots for valentines, which had formerly facilitated coupling, sending a dainty printed missive provided a new way of initi-

30. Mary Root's valentine, 1861.

ating or advancing courtship. One sentimental valentine, for example, admitted its sender's bashfulness and proffered a means to achieve candor:

> My falt'ring tongue has failed whene'er
> I've sought occasion to declare
> For you—my love concealed
> This day St. Valentine's affords
> Free scope to my imprison'd words
> And thus the truth's revealed.

Women, in particular, were given new freedom to make their affections known via the ritual exchange of valentines. This was especially true every four years with "Leap Year Valentines"; women were encouraged to take the initiative during this "privileged year," and men were expected to "submit" to this inversion. As T. W. Strong noted in 1856, "This being Leap Year, pretty girls will be freer / To tell their hearts' feelings in song." But in any given year, women might find a measure of liberty through these ceremonies to "speak out" to potential suitors as well as to pose otherwise ticklish questions.[93]

For their part, merchants recognized and accentuated the role their product could play as intermediary and solvent. An ad in the *Richmond Dispatch*, for example, said that valentines served as ambassadors between people; "where language fails they substitute." Likewise, Fisher and Brother's emphasized the usefulness of valentines in the "delicate ceremony" of broaching matrimony for those who "have not the courage to do it verbally." (Espousal and matrimonial valentines constituted a distinct line within the genre of sentimental valentines.) Valentines provided a ritualized exchange through which to negotiate awkward social situations, to help ease the transition from social distance to intimacy, and to minimize the social risks of rejection. They could also mediate the real distances of geographic separation. The soldier off at war and the lover back home were paradigmatic in this regard, and these missives offered a little bridge of connection and affection. Like St. Valentine of old, valentines served as an intercessory agent.[94]

Valentines were favored as well for the diversion they offered. No forbidding theories about social relationships and gift exchange, about the hegemony of commercial capitalism, about the pervasiveness of the market, about consumer manipulation and strategies of desire, or about romantic sensibilities and consumer longing are enough to explain the success of this new product. Valentines were, at bottom, a game, an amusement. They were fun. "I am sure I shall not very soon forget last Valentine week," the young Emily Dickinson wrote her brother in 1848, "nor any the sooner, the fun I had at that time." For Dickinson and her friends in Amherst, as for so many others, "Valentine's sun" with its "laughing beams" and "merry missives" was a bright spot of mirth in the winter calendar.[95] A large part of the merriment was that many, if not most, of these missives were sent anonymously, and considerable intrigue arose in trying to figure out who had sent them. People often used fanciful pen names—for example, "Hermit," "Dimple," "Ignotus," or even "Pharaoh's Toe Nail"—or simply left the valentines unsigned. "To my dear little Ella, who I love," one fancy missive read, "I shant tell my name."[96] Mistaken identities, suspenseful speculations, tentative responses, and practical jokes all followed. T. W. Strong recognized that this dimension of the valentine craze added immensely to it (and he was, of course, not loath to accentuate these little amusements in his advertising). Since valentines "are generally anonymous," he observed, "a great deal of the fun consists in the mistakes liable to occur,

31. "Valentine Packet," valentines for soldiers and sweethearts, promotional packaging, ca. 1863.

and in the means used afterwards to ascertain where the delightful missives come from."[97]

A Yale student gave a rich and revealing description of this valentine fun in a letter to his sister in 1842:

> I had a great deal of amusement from one [valentine] which I addressed to a lady, purporting to be "from the German." I heard of it indirectly several times, and shortly after she informed me, that *that* one had excited her curiosity very much, and she had been at a loss to whom she could attribute it: She had discovered however, by a resemblance pointed out to her in the writing, that it had come from a son of Dr Fitch's (a diffident young man, who though a good *German* scholar, would never have conceived the idea of translating a valentine.) With as grave a face as I could assume, under the circumstances, I read and praised the letter, and assented to the credibility of its coming from the supposed author. We also had a long conversation on the amusement to be derived from hearing a valentine you have written attributed to another, during which I assure you, I found it very difficult to restrain my laughter.[98]

Perhaps the woman was having her own fun with this young man: Who was really tricking whom in this conversation is unknown, but what is apparent is the sense of entertainment and farcical amusement. The deception kept getting more involved; this was, indeed, its own kind of "deep play" as valentine rituals offered layer upon layer of social trickery, one conspiratorial wink upon another.[99] These antics were a lot like April fooling, rituals of farce and pretense that sportively called attention to the fragile trust and complicated deceptions of human interaction.

All the trickery and bluff of St. Valentine's Day teasingly subverted the middle-class preoccupation with social transparency and sincerity. Romantic openness and self-revelation were prized, but only by way of this playful delight in masks and theatrical faces. The valentines themselves often reflected this fascination with deception and surprise—hidden mottoes, concealed mirrors, and mechanical devices that folded down or pulled out and that transformed one scene into something else (a volcano into a waterfall, a girl into an angel, a bouquet into a fan, a church into a wedding). The surfaces of these missives, like the masked self, concealed hidden depths that required unveiling. The cards were thus "animated," charged with masquerade, and these disguised effects mirrored the varied ruses that were at the heart of these social rituals.[100] As seventeen-year-old Calista Billings reported in her diary in 1849, "I had 2 Valentines[,] one from William[.] [H]e thinks I sent him one Monday night. . . . [H]e said when he first began reading it he did not suspect me but when he came to the end he knew it was me (I did not send it)." Still, a few days later, speculation and mystery continued: "William & Frank talked about Valentines[.] Mr Shumway told me he had sworn secrecy[.] He told me he had directed one to me but he wouldn't tell from who."[101] The fun of valentine games was embodied in this delicate dance of romantic self-disclosure and social masking—a frolic of candor and pretense, sincerity and secrecy.

EXPANDING HOLIDAY TRADE: FROM CONFECTIONERS' HEARTS TO HALLMARK CARDS

The critics of the modern version of St. Valentine's Day were not only overwhelmed by the stampede of consumers who rushed out and bought valentines because they found them charming, humorous, entertaining, or apt. They were also outflanked and overrun by a phalanx of merchants who diligently sought to establish the new commercial rendering of the holiday as the norm. Developing their own merchandising experiments, other trades soon began to widen the holiday's associations beyond printed greetings and fancy stationery. Though elaborate gift giving for St. Valentine's Day had precedent in early modern England, in the United States such customs were reinvented and popularized in the second half of the nineteenth century. Stray advertisements for other valentine presents had begun appearing by the early 1850s. "The most beautiful Valentine to send a Lady or Gentleman," a Philadelphia jeweler beckoned in 1850, "is a handsome Gold Breastpin, Finger ring, Gold Pen, Gold Pencil &c., or any article of Jewelry." Likewise, a farseeing florist in Boston offered this notice in 1853: "FLOWERS FOR VALENTINE PRESENTS. Rare Bouquets, Cut Flowers, Wreaths, Floral Baskets, &c." Evidence of just how far merchants tried to push this holiday association was one manufacturer's proposed gift in 1850 for the "cleanly housekeeper": "THE BEST VALENTINE YET—A Box of BURGESS & CO.'S ROACH, RAT AND MOUSE EXTERMINATOR." More typical was a holiday advertisement for daguerreotypes, declaring that "the surest way to gain a lover's heart is to present a PICTURE of yourself, taken in the inimitable style of MARSHAL & PORTER." Through such expanded merchandising, the valentine as a missive gradually became an adjunct to a larger gift rather than constituting the gift itself.[102]

Confectionery is perhaps the best example of the expanding repertoire of gifts for St. Valentine's Day. (Where, after all, would the modern holiday be without those ubiquitous heart-shaped boxes of candy?) The candy industry, like other trades, began to develop more systematic and aggressive retailing strategies in the late nineteenth and early twentieth centuries. And like other merchants, confectioners discovered the commercial possibilities of the holidays, turning to them as linchpins in an annual cycle of sales and trade. The flagship publication for the industry, the *Confectioners' Journal*, established in Philadelphia in 1874, only began taking notice of St. Valentine's Day in the early 1890s, by which time it was already well aware of the commercial benefits of New Year's, Christmas, and Easter. The author of an article in the *Confectioners' Journal* in 1892 marveled at the amount of money spent on valentines, which remained the holiday's most obvious material embodiment: "The sum annually expended for these pretty reminders of affection, to say nothing of the great snow storm of the cheap, grotesque sort, has never been computed, but it must be very great." Another article in the same issue mused that "if the confectioners would take up" St. Valentine's Day "and give some attention to it," the holiday could be given a new commercial twist "from which they would derive considerable profit."[103]

This new business turn was soon abundantly evident. In 1894 the *Confectioners' Journal* dismissed valentines as "relics of the middles ages" and assured its readers that "among the more refined classes" boxes of candy were now "being substituted" for those outmoded missives: "The custom is modern, but it is growing, and would soon become general if proper encouragement were given it by the trade. Pretty valentine boxes, filled with choice candies, would be a far more refined and welcome gift than the maudlin trash and sentimental nonsense sent as valentines in the present day, and they could be made as much of a feature of Valentine's Day as the most popular fancies associated by the trade with Christmas and Easter." A generation later the *Confectioners' Journal* was still waging this campaign against the venerable valentine, which invariably proved harder to displace or overtake than the trade imagined. "We do not want to disparage the old institution of the Valentine, but taking a more modern view of this holiday we cannot help but feel that the average individual would rather receive one gift of candy than several dozen Valentines." How, the writer wondered, could printed pieces of paper compete with candy for pleasure and delight? With confidence and fanfare the National Confectioners' Association in 1923 adopted the slogan "Make Candy Your Valentine"—a slogan thereafter repeated endlessly in trade publicity. In their drive to enlarge their share of the St. Valentine's Day market, confectioners were presented with the irony that cards had become traditional and theirs was the modern innovation. And with holidays nothing sells like tradition.[104]

But novelty sells, too, as the makers of valentines well knew, and the confectioners were able to exploit this approach. In 1895 the *Confectioners' Journal* shifted from exhorting the trade to take action to reporting on actual preparations and products. That year, the *Journal* observed approvingly, candy was available in "heart-shaped boxes of heavy cardboard," "hand-painted satin affairs," boxes with "dainty sprays of artificial flowers," boxes with "lace papers, roses, cupids, and verses pasted on the cover," boxes with gold lettering asking "Will You Be My Valentine?" and "beautiful glass-covered boxes of heart shape." Taken together, such devices constituted an explosion in holiday packaging. These fancy boxes and holiday novelties dovetailed with what Daniel Boorstin has called "the packaging revolution" in American retailing—a transmutation of commodities through whole new industries devoted to special boxes, bags, and wrappings. In this case, the same candies were given novel and elaborate coverings and thereby transformed into fitting holiday gifts. Confectioners, appropriating the symbols of sentiment and love long popular on valentines, were able to connect these emblems through packaging to their products. (What better present for a *sweetheart* was there, after all, than a heart-shaped box filled with sweets?) Soon enough heart-shaped, Cupid-embossed boxes were not so much novelties, but familiar or even traditional holiday symbols themselves.[105]

As the variety of gifts associated with St. Valentine's Day widened, valentine greetings did not so much decline in salience as diffuse in influence. The valentine craze of the 1840s and 1850s proved the rehearsal for that great fashion of the late 1870s and early 1880s, Christmas cards. Indeed, Yuletide greetings proliferated as a modish social custom in much the same manner

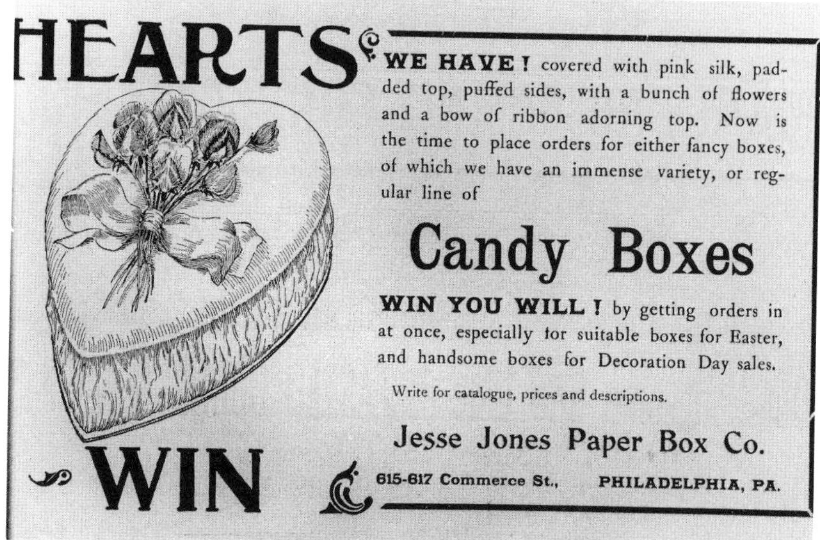

32. "Hearts Win," Jesse Jones Paper Box Co. advertisement, *Confectioners' Journal* 25 (February 1899): 23.

that valentine missives had a generation earlier. By 1880 manufacturers such as Louis Prang, Marcus Ward, Raphael Tuck, and George Whitney had also spun off cards for Easter, New Year's, and birthdays, among other special times. The valentine trade thus helped inspire a whole new holiday enterprise, the greeting-card industry, which took the lace-paper compliments of the valentine and turned them into a nearly universal holiday medium. By the 1920s, the trade had grown into a $60 million industry, and greeting cards had become the common accoutrement of almost any holiday or life passage. Put in the 1920s slogan of the Greeting Card Association: "Scatter Sunshine with Greeting Cards: There is one for EVERY occasion." (Or, as a 1990s press release from the same trade group observed on industry "trends," there are now greeting cards "for any occasion or non-occasion.")[106]

In 1910 a traveling salesman and native Nebraskan, Joyce C. Hall, launched the mail-order postcard business that would evolve into Hallmark Cards, and he stands as perhaps the culminating figure in a lineage that stretched back to such midcentury merchants as T. W. Strong, Robert Elton, and Esther Howland. Fittingly, when he added greeting cards to his wholesale line in 1912, he began with valentines, expanding to Christmas cards two years later. Hall's career serves as an illustrative capstone of the entrepreneurial and cultural forces that propelled holiday greetings into a massive trade in the late nine-

33. "Valentine Greetings," novelty, ca. 1880.

teenth and early twentieth centuries. Named after the Methodist Bishop Isaac Joyce by his mother (a literal feminizing of him by the church—Joyce was "a girl's name" that he was always trying to live down), Hall learned the habits of the peddling wayfarer from his father, a Methodist itinerant who was always on the road and who eventually deserted the family. The first thing Hall actually had to "peddle" as a boy were temperance handbills for his prohibitionist grandfather, who instructed him to take the fliers to every house in the small town of David City, Nebraska. By 1900, at age nine, Hall was going door to door for a perfume company, offering women "lemon extract, lilac cologne, soap and tooth powder." In his memoirs, small-town Nebraska seems an almost carnivalized world of touring circuses and week-long Chautauquas, Fourth of July pranks and fireworks, bare-knuckle fights and dice games, as well as stumping politicians and smooth-talking mountebanks. In this fluid mix of traveling salesmen and hucksters, itinerant evangelists "preaching

34. Joyce Hall, Kansas City, ca. 1910.

against sin" commingled in fairlike scenes with "military bands, choruses, quartets, comedians, [and] trained dogs." In Hall's memories of his boyhood, someone was always trying to sell someone something, and he took particular inspiration from the yarn-swapping drummers he encountered at nearly every turn. "I was convinced that salesmanship made the world go round," Hall said of himself after he had joined his older brother Rollie on a sales trip through South Dakota at age twelve, "and there was little doubt in my mind then that my future was in selling."[107]

Hall tried to push just about anything, and he had already learned something about holiday trade from helping out around a "notions store," selling fireworks for the Fourth and taking time off from school to assist with "the Christmas rush." He was already peddling postcards in 1905, along with a new sweeping compound, and five years later, urged on by a traveling cigar salesman, he gravitated to Kansas City, where he started up his mail-order postcard operation, initially running it out of his YMCA room. He soon signed up for courses at Spalding's Commercial College, the Franklinesque slogan of which was emblazoned on a tin sign: "Time is money—save time." Always a tireless systematizer and avid record keeper, Hall improved the maxim: "Time is everything—save time." As Hall built his business around holiday observances, adding cards for one occasion after another, he himself became all the more driven to "work around the clock," increasingly oblivious to festive time, except perhaps for Sunday baseball with the YMCA team: "We worked six days a week from seven in the morning until six at night," Hall insisted in tones that would make a Weberian proud. Indeed, his commercial success with postcards and greeting cards was emblematic in his own mind of the efficiency and energetic pace that modernity demanded. People simply did not have time any more "to write long thoughtful letters," and greeting cards were thus the right "social custom" for "our complex and mobile society." And Hall's commercial (and cultural) intuitions about modern ritual were clearly on the mark. His business grew phenomenally. By 1922 Hall Brothers had salespeople covering every state in the union, and by 1928 the company had begun national advertising in the *Ladies' Home Journal*. The empire that Hall built over the next half century was gargantuan. The company, twice the size of its closest competitor, holds more than 40 percent of the American market for greeting cards and had sales in 1993 of $3.4 billion.[108]

Despite Hall's unusual success, his marketing strategies were familiar enough. He attempted to differentiate his product from those of his competitors (and predecessors) through brand name and trademark: "So when you want to send the finest, look on the back for those three identifying words—A *HALLMARK* CARD." As other manufacturers also hoped to do, Hall wanted to distinguish his cards as the highest in taste, quality, sentiment, and refinement: Choosing a Hallmark card shows "you care enough to send the very best." (Conversely, of course, if one failed to send a Hallmark card, then one must not care all that much.) Underneath the familiar strategies of product differentiation lay fundamental similarities of message. In presenting his prod-

35. Hall Brothers advertisement, *Ladies' Home Journal* 45 (December 1928): 145.

uct as a true purveyor of human feeling and connectedness, Hall landed on the slogan "It's the Sentiment that Counts." It was a banner that the early valentine promoters, with their studied uses of romantic sentimentalism, would have readily recognized. Hall, and the industry he embodied, brought to full fruition the valentine vogue.[109]

By the time Hall's business was founded, St. Valentine's Day was clearly established as one of the high days in America's commercial calendar. It was a fixture in handbooks about show windows and a subject of annual attention in the trade journals of florists, confectioners, stationers, department-store retailers, and other merchants. Valentines, like Christmas cards, proved to be a fad that never went out of style—an enduring, even flourishing custom. Today the numbers for Cupid-inspired greetings are, if anything, more staggering than they were in the 1840s and 1850s. Industry estimates put the totals at more than one billion annually, second only to Christmas as a card-sending event. Hallmark alone offers more than two thousand different, annually changing valentine designs. Similarly, candy continues to stand out as a token of love and endearment; the National Confectioners' Association estimated sales at more than $600 million for St. Valentine's Day in 1990. The holiday is likewise a retailing bonanza for the floral industry: Approximately seventy million roses are purchased annually for the occasion. The nineteenth-century refashioning of St. Valentine's Day left an abiding impression on American rituals of celebration.[110]

What can be concluded about the modern fashioning of St. Valentine's Day? Certainly the holiday's history discloses much about the translation of a religious vernacular into secular idioms, the shifting patterns of early modern courtship, the complex sources of the consumer culture and modern forms of gift giving, the uneven altering of material culture through mass production, the distinctive interplay of consumer satisfaction and alienation in the face of modern commodities, the problems of artificiality and authenticity in a world of industrial facsimile, and the intricate interweaving of romantic sentimentalism, feminization, and consumerism in the nineteenth century. All these things bear emphasis, but perhaps what most warrants stressing is how the holiday's history illumines the changing contours of American ritual and celebration in the face of commercial revolution.

The course of St. Valentine's Day in the nineteenth century exemplifies the impact of expanding markets on holiday celebrations. A motley and localistic Old World folk occasion was refashioned and made indigenous as an American tradition of increasingly national scope through the widening reach of the market, mounting commercial sponsorship, and growing commodification. The historian T. H. Breen has argued in another context that the consumer culture provided a common idiom for transforming disparate, provincial folk customs into shared social rituals, and this old saint's day held out that promise.[111] As the *Boston Daily Evening Transcript* announced in 1845, St. Valentine's Day is "the best fete day we have," since its celebration is "general" rather than "sectional." Unlike other celebrations with their local or sectarian dimensions, this newly revived holiday presented the prospect of some common ground—a unity to be forged out of shared rituals of consumption and greeting that the marketplace facilitated. In this, the "restoration" of St. Valentine's Day was an important augury. The consumer culture provided a common currency for a growing number of American celebrations.[112]

The market did not simply standardize or domesticate the holiday, however. Where commercial forces would work to tame the street festivities of Christmas and New Year's as well as the destructive pranks of Halloween, in the case of St. Valentine's Day merchants imported ribaldry and mockery, printed it up, and sold it in the form of comic valentines.[113] This may have been a commercial containment or commodification of the dangerous energies of rough music; people bought insulting caricatures and secretly slipped them to the offending parties rather than engaging in derisive serenades or physical abuse. But in the context of St. Valentine's Day this still marked a transgressive turn. Entrepreneurial printers, booksellers, and stationers encouraged raucous insult and tomfoolery, not simply safe sentimentality and cozy affections. While merchants also promoted tenderness and refinement, with the jeering and even violent satire of the mock valentines retailers remained a long way from the touching, tasteful world of the Hallmark Hall of Fame.

In a sense, though, merchants did domesticate the holiday through their concentration on private exchanges. There was, to be sure, a new public or civic dimension of the holiday focused on shops and stores, but the ritual enactment of the holiday no longer centered on convivial groups of youths, but on the individual exchange of gifts and greetings. The commercial enlargement and redefinition of the holiday focused on personal relationships, especially on reciprocal exchanges among couples, friends, children, and relatives. This shift would prove characteristic of the commercial redefinition of the holidays as a whole—that is, the occasions would be seen more in terms of home and family than in terms of community, more in terms of personal greetings and private gifts than in terms of the open sociability of churchyards, fields, streets, and taverns. Stores and homes became primary staging areas for American celebrations, and the twin versions of the holidays that were performed in these two realms have long remained synergistic.

The centuries-long history of St. Valentine's Day has been filled with convolutions, but few turns have been as dramatic as that of its transformation in the mid-nineteenth-century United States. Out of Old World folk, religious, and courtly traditions largely moribund, the holiday was reinvented as a curiosity of the marketplace and a marvel of romantic fashion—a red-letter day for private exchanges, loving intimacies, and consumer pleasures. At the same time, it was recast as a ritualized parody of the very sentimentality, sincerity, and delicacy it enshrined—a carnival of taunting, lewdness, and trickery. The holiday's renewed popularity inspired a Boston writer in 1863 to proclaim that "with the exception of Christmas there is no festival throughout the year which is invested with half the interest belonging to this cherished anniversary."[114] Between the 1840s and 1860s, when St. Valentine's Day was at its most fashionable, some basis existed for comparing it with Christmas, but by the 1880s and 1890s, as the next chapter will show, the transformed Victorian Christmas would make the refurbished St. Valentine's Day look like child's play.

3
Christmas Bazaar

HE ENGLISH POET and essayist Leigh Hunt wrote a memorable meditation on Christmas for the *Monthly Repository* in 1837. Entitling the piece "The Inexhaustibility of the Subject of Christmas," Hunt opened his essay with a fitting sense of the depth and complexity of his topic. "So many things have been said of late years about Christmas," he confessed, "that it is supposed by some there is no saying more. Oh, they of little faith! What? do they suppose that everything has been said that *can* be said, about any one Christmas thing?" There followed a lengthy enumeration, longer than the most wishful Christmas list, and historians are well aware of the value of detailed lists: Hunt's serves as an inventory of holiday symbols, a catalogue of cultural traditions. "About beef, for instance?" Hunt began. "About plum-pudding? About mince-pie? About holly? About ivy? About rosemary? About mistletoe? (Good God! what an immense number of things remain to be said about mistletoe!) About Christmas Eve? About hunt-the-slipper? . . . About carols? About the fire? . . . About Christmas boxes? About turkeys? . . . About goose-pie? About mumming? About saluting the apple-trees? . . . About New Year's day? About gifts? About wassail? . . . About charity? . . . About the Greatest Plum-pudding for the Greatest number?" It was a long list, ironically exhaustive for a short essay on the inexhaustibility of Christmas. In all, it included sixty-one Christmas things.[1]

Leigh Hunt's list and his opening observation are striking in a number of ways. His comments highlight the intricacy of Christmas—a rich feast of food and song, games and greenery, drinking and revelry. Hunt sagely assures his readers that one does not get to the bottom of Christmas or even a single part of it, and cultural historians trying to fathom Christmas and its rituals would, I think, readily concur. To see the modern Christmas in the round would include—to make another partial list—folklore, religion, festival, art, music, literature, television, food, education, civic ceremony, gender, family, gift exchange, ethnicity, localism, race, class, and commerce. As in England, Christmas in the United States was and is a wonderfully variegated celebration. Reflecting the syncretic interplay of countless immigrant customs, the varying versions of the American Christmas are all the more elaborate and complex for this kaleidoscope of cultural traditions. (Already in 1855 the *Philadelphia Public Ledger* had hailed the "eclectic Christmas" that was emerging in the United States, a pastiche of "various customs and observances" from sundry countries and cultures.)[2] One can explore aspects of this eclectic Christmas, pieces in a changing mosaic, but one cannot survey the festival in its entirety. At best perhaps one can illuminate a few distinct facets, hoping to see in these particularities some shimmering, elusive reflections of the whole. The subject, as Hunt rightly observed, is inexhaustible. His is an important hermeneutic point to acknowledge at the outset. So while commerce, religion, and shopping are numbered among the Christmas things of this chapter, they are clearly not intended to circumscribe or consume this multivalent feast. Instead the aim is to evoke through the particularity of a John Wanamaker or a Clara Pardee or a Washington Gladden some of the inexhaustibility of Christmas things.

Also striking about Hunt's long list is the presence of so many items that are now rarely associated with the Christmas season at all. Indeed, much in the list is simply a mystery to the modern reader—for example, local customs such as saluting the apple trees for their fecundity or various folk pastimes such as hunt-the-slipper, forfeits, or thread-the-needle. Perhaps still more striking is the absence from Hunt's inventory of so much that is often taken to be the essence of the modern Christmas. In it we find no holiday shopping, no Christmas windows, no stockings, no Santa Claus, no reindeer or snowmen, no toys, no Christmas cards, no tree encircled by presents, no harried salesclerks, no obliging merchants, no Christmas club at the bank, and also, it should be noted, no Christmas Eve services, no Sunday school celebrations, no elaborate church decorations, no church bazaars, no Nativity scenes, no Wise Men, no angels. By both religious and secular measures, modern forms of observance are scarce in Hunt's tallying of Christmas.[3]

Not that the modern Christmas goes unpresaged. Gifts, for example, are mentioned in Hunt's inventory, but they immediately follow New Year's in the list, indicating their association with that part of the season rather than with Christmas Day itself. The allusion to Christmas boxes also suggested gift giving, but these were still largely associated with the slowly fading custom of doling, that is, with the young, the rowdy, and the poor who went about in groups, mumming and wassailing, demanding "gifts" of money and food from the wealthy and privileged. The mention of Christmas boxes pointed as well to small gratuities given by superiors to subordinates (such as to newsboys, apprentices, or servants) and to little tokens (such as candy or fruit) given by adults to children. In the 1820s and 1830s the English notion of Christmas boxes was merely a seed for the full flowering of the Victorian custom of Christmas presents. In all, Hunt's Christmas catalogue of 1837 suggested a popular festival only partially suffused with romantic nostalgia, only marginally Christianized, and only minimally aligned with commerce and consumerism. Written at the front edge of the Victorian transformation of Christmas (indeed, in the very year that Queen Victoria ascended to the British throne), Leigh Hunt's compendium evoked a popular celebration still dominated by food, drink, and carousing.

In the United States, as in England, Christmas in the 1830s was just beginning to show the signs of its modern transformation. In the next half century or so, Christmas would increasingly be recast in the crucibles of middle-class consumption, religion, and family life. That is, to put shorthand academic labels on these complex human experiences, the holiday was transformed through the intricately braided processes of domestication, Christianization, and commercialization. Sometimes complementary, sometimes tensile in their relationship, the churches and the consumer culture helped remake Christmas in the nineteenth century into a great familial fête. Enacted by turns in homes, stores, and churches, this modern Christmas in all its contradiction and capaciousness would be a location for conflict as much as for celebration. The contest between "pagan" festivity and Christian solemnity was age-old, but the modern commercial culture would give a new wrinkle to these encounters. Among the first battles in the modern skirmish would be those fought over the celebration of New Year's, as the refined visits and gift giving of the genteel would stand in sharp relief with the more plebeian observances of wassailers and the heady midnight meetings of evangelicals.

In the 1820s and 1830s Christmas emerged more clearly alongside New Year's as a distinct gift-giving occasion, and the market for Christmas goods grew correspondingly. The new Christmas bazaar found visual expression in special holiday decorations and illuminations, discovered a patron saint in Santa Claus, and reached an apotheosis in the department-store Christmas of the late nineteenth and early twentieth centuries. All along, people were both drawn to the Christmas rush and wary of it, caught up in the new spectacles of holiday shopping and the new joys of familial gifts, yet apprehensive about excessive consumption and commercialism and worn down by the busyness and the crowds. Religious reformers, in particular, sought ways to clear up this ambivalence, especially looking for new and more-thorough methods to Christianize the celebration. In the process, critics had forged by the early decades of this century an almost ritual critique of the modern Christmas that continues to resound in American public life. If a list comparable to Leigh Hunt's compendium had been drawn up a century later, it would have looked decidedly different; this chapter explores just how different as it ponders the sources, scope, and significance of Christmas's modern transformation.[4]

THE RITES OF THE NEW YEAR: REVELS, GIFTS, RESOLUTIONS, AND WATCH NIGHTS

In early modern Europe Christmas was a long season of festivities that reached a crescendo in the week between Christmas and New Year's and that often reverberated through Twelfth Night. The echoes of the Christmas season could be heard in some places right through Mardi Gras. Although this pattern of prolonged festivity was severely challenged in the British colonies by Puritans, Presbyterians, Quakers, and Baptists, the holiday jubilee was nonetheless widely replicated in North America, especially in the mid-Atlantic and the South. In the winter lull of agricultural and commercial calendars, the months of December and January gave license to several nights of holiday feasting, imbibing, dancing, masking, and gaming. Within this drawn-out period of celebration, the rites of the New Year were high points. Locations of conflicting popular, genteel, and evangelical celebrations, New Year's Eve and New Year's Day were lightning rods of cultural contest in the late eighteenth and early nineteenth centuries: The riotousness and violence of street celebrations were pitted against the fashion and ceremony of genteel gifts and gatherings, which were, in turn, matched against the fervor and gravity of evangelical meetings for "watching in" the New Year. The dramatic struggles over New Year observances were in many ways the precursors of subsequent controversies about the fate of Christmas in the marketplace; oddly enough, the commercialization of the Christmas season actually began not with Christmas Day, but with New Year's. Like St. Valentine's Day, New Year's was a bellwether of consumer-oriented holidays.

The most popular way of ushering in the New Year remained one of noisy revelry, openhanded eating, and bibulous drinking. The Christmas and New Year's doggerel of eighteenth-century almanacs regularly captured scenes of abundant joviality and sociability:

> Christmas is come, hang on the pot,
> Let spits turn round, and ovens be hot;
> Beef, pork, and poultry, now provide,
> To feast thy neighbours at this tide;
> Then wash it all down with good wine and beer,
> And so with mirth conclude the YEAR.[5]

Or, as the *Virginia Almanack* counseled for 1766, at this season of the year all "should feast and sing, and merry be."

> Keep open house, let fidlers play,
> A fig for cold, sing care away.

Like the rest of the Christmas season, New Year's Eve was a night for boisterous conviviality; it was a time for "strong ale, good fires, and noble cheer."[6]

New Year's merriment often grew to riotous and disorderly levels, especially in cities such as Philadelphia, New York, and Baltimore. A night of clamor and license, of shooting guns and rough music, New Year's was filled with youthful rowdiness that often edged into violence. An annoyed writer in the *New-York*

Journal complained in 1771 that "a Number of disorderly People, (whose Taste it seems is so strangely depraved, as to be delighted only in doing Mischief, and acting as Nusances to civil Society) celebrated the Night which ended the Old and began the New-Year, by a great variety of Acts of Malevolence—Such as disturbed the Repose of the Inhabitants, making all kinds of ridiculous and disagreeable noises, breaking Windows, &c. &c."[7] To an observer of New Year's festivities in New York in the 1820s, "these disgraceful saturnalia" had only gotten worse. Large groups of young men and boys paraded the streets, "shouting, singing, blowing penny-trumpets and long tin horns, beating on the kettles, firing crackers, hurling missiles, etc." These discordant rioters or "callithumpians" pelted houses, routed the night watchmen, disrupted fashionable balls, leveled gates and railings, and shattered windows. Sometimes they went still further, breaking into the homes of the well-to-do, demanding hospitality or money. The uproar kept the city in a mixed state of fear and excitement throughout the night. These popular street versions of New Year's festivities reveled in masquerade and inversion, license and mockery.[8]

Those respectable folks who found this New Year's revelry so fearful and threatening enacted various countervailing rituals of their own. On New Year's Eve in 1828, New York's callithumpians especially relished congregating "in front of the City Hotel" on Broadway, where "a festival Ball" for New York's polite sophisticates was in progress. The refined music and measured dancing within the hotel made for a marked contrast with "the music of cracked kettles" and the unconstrained gyrations of the plebeian celebration outside in the streets. Misrule reigned without, ceremony and fashion within.[9]

On New Year's Day itself, the contrasting ritual repertory of the genteel was further accentuated as decorous gentlemen called on finely apparelled ladies in a daylong series of urbane visits and formal receptions. This custom was especially associated with the well-to-do in New York City, but by the 1830s and 1840s these fashionable visits had become prevalent among the middle class in diverse cities and towns. The historian Mary Ryan has recently highlighted the "gender choreography" of these ceremonies as gentlemen poured forth to visit stylish women, who presided over these lavish home-centered festivities and who afterward counted up the number of their callers. It was "a set piece," Ryan concludes, "played out in public time, to celebrate women's private place." In a mirror reversal of the threatening and unpredictable visits of wassailers who exacted holiday munificence from the wealthy, these New Year's "calls from door to door" were noted for their decency and order. Gentlemen arrived with formal, engraved visiting cards or with other tokens of greeting; women arranged well-decorated tables, spread with "the luxuries of the season" and overflowing with libations, but these treats were for the "most fashionable," not for the rowdy, run-of-the-mill celebrants who had clamored through the streets the night before. Even these fancy spreads were subject to reform as middle-class advice literature increasingly extolled the holiday virtues of serving hot coffee to callers, instead of whiskey punch or other potables. In "civilizing" the festival, New Year's visits put a further mark of gentility and etiquette on traditional folk forms of celebration.[10]

Among the more prominent genteel rites of the New Year was gift giving. With origins stretching back to the rites of the Roman calendar (the *strenae* of the Latin New Year), the exchange of presents as "a Token and Omen of a good Year" was a custom with deep roots in Western culture.[11] Though it took various forms, the tradition of New Year's gifts had flourished in especially dramatic fashion in European courts and aristocratic culture. As with gift giving at St. Valentine's Day, nobles, courtiers, and monarchs cultivated elaborate patterns of exchange. Integral to monarchical display and the obeisances of court life, New Year's gifts were in these social echelons renowned for their "great pomp and show." These were rigorously hierarchical and carefully computed exchanges; gifts of silk finery, gilt cups and bowls, stupendous jewelry, and culinary delicacies moved with precision and splendor up and down the Tudor and Stuart courts. One colorful description of a gift from the earl of Leicester to Queen Elizabeth for New Year's in 1574 can stand for the whole. The present was "a splendid fan . . . being of white feathers, set in a handle of gold; one side of it garnished with two very fair emeralds, one of them especially fine, and garnished with diamonds and rubies; . . . and on each side a white bear and two pearls hanging, a lion rampant with a white muzzled bear at his foot."[12] As one English writer put it in 1692, New Year's was "the Festival of Gifts," and little expense was spared in their presentation among the courtly and the aristocratic.[13]

New Year's gift giving was not solely an elite tradition; it also found popular embodiment. Writing in 1725, the Anglican clergyman Henry Bourne, though ever wary of the "superstitious and sinful" customs of "the Vulgar," admitted that the common practice of sending "New-Year's-Gifts" to friends and acquaintances was not so bad. When shorn of pagan notions of fortune and luck, these "Tokens of mutual Affection and Love" were, in Bourne's estimation, acceptable emblems of friendship, gratitude, and charity. Bourne's need for such distinctions and rationalizations would have been lost on most people; "the Sending of Presents" was a plainly popular custom, widely regarded as essential to "Beginning well" the New Year. But these gifts among "the Common People" bore only a faint resemblance to the exchanges among the courtly and wellborn. Instead these were small tokens passed between friends who were relative social equals—holiday cakes, apples, meats, nutmegs, eggs, or oranges stuck with cloves—the chief purpose of which was to convey good wishes for health and prosperity in the coming year.[14] So familiar, even ordinary, were these seasonal compliments in eighteenth-century England and its colonies that the expression "a New-Year's Gift" was simply proverbial, a phrase that could be applied figuratively to a range of exchanges at that time of year—pastors' sermons to their people, petitioners' letters to their fellow freeholders, publishers' greetings to their readers.[15]

Illustrative of the simple, mundane exchanges that often made up New Year's gift giving were holiday gratuities for newspaper carriers. Printers had been making commodities of New Year's wishes from the first decades of the printing revolution in Europe, and the little broadsides of newsboys and criers in the colonies were a direct transplant of these European conventions. These broadside greetings, followed by holiday tips, were among the most common transactions of the festival. Indeed, so widespread and customary was this practice that it even managed to take firm hold in Calvinist New England, where Puritans had long weighed in against the paganism of New Year's observances. With clear affinities to older traditions of doling and begging, the seasonal solicitation of gratuities by newsboys was built around the carriers' first offering a New Year's compliment in verse to their customers and then having their efforts reciprocated with small amounts of money. After a year of hard work running "thro' winter's snow, and summer's shower," the newsboys and printers' lads expected some "small reward" from their patrons. This expectation resulted in hundreds of poems and broadsides—an abundance that makes these carrier addresses the most prevalent holiday artifact from the eighteenth and early nineteenth centuries.[16]

The toast offered by the carriers of the *Boston Evening-Post* to their customers for New Year's 1764 was representative of the basic themes sounded by these seasonal addresses:

> Your *News-Boy* humbly hopes to find,
> The Bounty of each generous Mind.
> *Christmas* and *New-Year*, Days of Joy,
> The Harvest of your Carrier Boy,
> He hopes you'll not his Hopes destroy.
> But cheer him as he trips along
> And kindly listen to his Song,
> Which runs so smooth in Rhime, ding, dong.
> . . . .
> And 'tis asserted by the Wise,
> That *Wealth* and *Spirits* sympathize,
> And with each other fall and rise.

If so, what pure poetic Fire
His generous Patrons may inspire,
By filling up his Pockets higher!
And, since they can, he hopes they will,
Inspiring Zeal to please, and Skill;
With *New-Year's Gifts* his Pockets fill.

Mostly solicitous and deferential, though sometimes tinged with a threat of poor service for those who failed to cough up some coins, these little exchanges typified an important dimension of traditional holiday gift giving—that is, the seasonal obligations of largess on the part of gentlemen and ladies to subalterns, servants, tenants, and slaves. As Bourne well knew, New Year's gifts were not only about the mutualities of friendship, but also about the maintenance of hierarchies through benefaction and patronage, about those in a "humble Sphere" looking for some token from their "Mistresses and Masters." These small gestures of holiday munificence recognized and underlined the tiered relations of the social order, the patterns of condescension and deference that governed social life.[17]

The commercial revolution of the late eighteenth and early nineteenth centuries had a pronounced effect on these varied traditions of New Year's gift giving. For one thing, the growing diffusion of goods through industrial production facilitated the democratization of the more elaborate forms of courtly exchange, a process that worked largely from the top down. As at St. Valentine's Day, it was the merchants, professionals, and other social climbers who were first able to afford to emulate the gift-giving customs of the aristocratic. In 1770 a New York merchant, James Rivington, ran an advertisement for New Year's presents in the *New-York Journal* that highlighted the social respectability and gentility of these exchanges: Necklaces, lockets, snuffboxes, toothpick cases, silver-plated tea urns and teapots, dress swords, pocket pistols, silk stockings, backgammon tables, chess sets, and other goods were all offered as "proper Presents to and from Ladies and Gentlemen at this Season, when the Heart is more peculiarly enlarged." Rivington's New York advertisement read like a catalogue of the booming consumerism of late-eighteenth-century London, and certainly England's commercial revolution made it possible for more and more people in the colonial provinces to style themselves gentlemen or ladies. Importantly, though, the advertisement was premised not on an appeal to republican virtue or democratic fluidity, but on an invocation of blue-blooded hauteur. The invitation to purchase these sophisticated New Year's gifts was founded on the hierarchic privileges of the wealthy, not on a new democracy of goods. To be sure, this was still gift giving for the sake of seasonal cheer and the hearty ties of friendship, but it was also for the sake of social distinction and aristocratic display. Silver-plated tea sets and dress swords were in the late eighteenth century clearly the things of genteel ceremony.[18]

Rivington's advertisement for New Year's gifts was still something of a rarity in the last decades of the eighteenth century, but by early in the next century such New Year's promotions were commonplace. To hail one's New Year's merchandise as "elegant" and "genteel" and thus to play on social aspiration and refinement as the basis of holiday purchases became stock commercial devices. By the 1810s and 1820s, long holiday wish lists of "Gold and Silver Fancy Articles"—rings, brooches, pens, and watches—often crowded New York and Philadelphia newspaper columns. Take one typical example: In 1816 the merchant Samuel Corkran, proprietor of the well-named Looking Glass Store, offered numerous possibilities for New Year's presents "TO THE LADIES OF NEW-YORK," among them "a great variety of elegant Pin Cushions of velvet, richly painted, with gilt mountings." Such bibelots became firmly established as part of the social rituals of New Year's as gentlemen were increasingly expected to present some token of refinement to the women they called on in their formal visits.[19]

These genteel New Year's gifts were often depicted as objects of London fashion and, even more, of Parisian high society. *Godey's Magazine and Lady's Book*, for example, seemed to relish telling its middle-class audience New Year's stories about Parisian self-indulgence in confectionery, jewelry, toys, and fancy goods, even picturing for its readers "New Year's Day in France" in a frontispiece in 1851—a giant spectacle of holiday shopping. The Parisian New Year, with its thronged stores along stately boulevards, was set up as a model of holiday consumption, thus imbuing the growing fondness for holiday gifts among middle-class Americans with an Old World cachet. Again the "wealth, refinement and taste" of New Year's gifts were accented—the Brussels lace, the fanciful dolls, the cashmere shawls, the delicate fans, and the choice bonbons. At New Year's, the fantasies of "Paris articles" danced like sugarplums before the eyes of the members of the American middle class as they were allowed to fashion themselves among *le beau monde*. The envious marveling of the *Album and Ladies' Weekly Gazette* over Paris's "Le Jour d'Etrennes" was palpable: "A pretty woman, respectably connected, may reckon her new year's presents at something considerable. Gowns, jewellery, gloves, stockings and artificial flowers, fill her drawing-room; for in Paris it is a custom to display all the gifts in order to excite emulation, and obtain as much as possible." The writer was obviously quite taken by these Parisian rituals and by the possibilities inhering in this new role for women as consumers: They could be the domestic stage managers of a modern celebration in which the novel bounties

36. "New Year's Day in France," *Godey's Magazine and Lady's Book* 42 (January 1851): frontispiece.

of the marketplace would be arrayed around them. With the American adoration of Parisian ceremony and fashion, the transit of New Year's gift giving from courtly obeisance to middle-class respectability was complete. Traditional republican fears of luxury and extravagance were all but lost amid wide-eyed wonder at Paris's holiday spectacle of style, display, and emulation.[20]

Another important effect of the commercial revolution on this "Festival of Presents" was that purchasing New Year's gifts for children became far more commonplace, and, in this, the holiday provided a crucial precursor for the subsequent emphasis on giving presents to children on Christmas morning. Advertisements for New Year's gifts for children burgeoned in American newspapers between 1800 and 1830, but there were already some occasional harbingers in eighteenth-century publications. For example, a very early holiday advertisement, appearing in the *Virginia Gazette* for 22–29 December 1738, offered a recently published Anglican catechism as a suitable New Year's token for children:

> Lately Published, (being very proper for a New-Year's Gift to Children,)
> *THE Church Catechism Explain'd; by Way of Question and Answer; and confirm'd by Scripture Proofs: Divided into Five Parts, and 12 Sections*
> Wherein a brief and plain Account is given of,

I. The Christian Covenant.
II. The Christian Faith.
III. The Christian Obedience.
IV. The Christian Prayer.
V. The Christian Sacraments.

Collected by John Lewis, Minister of Margate, in Kent. Printed, and Sold by William Parks. Price stitch'd 10d. bound 15d.[21]

What was parenthetic in this notice would eventually become the boldfaced convention of holiday advertising: Take an ordinary product and present it as somehow seasonable. It is also telling that this early New Year's advertisement featured a church catechism. Among the devout, the passing of another year was thought an especially appropriate time for clearheaded religious reflection, and children were the particular recipients of catechesis. The advertisement thus made the right religious connections. Devotional items eventually became typical holiday gifts: By the 1810s and 1820s handsome prayer books, elegant Bibles, engraved psalters, and finely bound hymnals were regularly featured as suitable New Year's presents. In the material culture of New Year's, books of religious advice and instruction, especially for the young, led the way as holiday gifts.[22]

Catechisms and other devotional books as New Year's gifts for children soon had plenty of competition from more-diverting and less-solemn reading. Already in 1784, Thomas Bradford, a Philadelphia bookseller, offered a huge variety of "little Books" as "proper NEW YEAR'S GIFTS, For Children." His list of thirty-nine titles in the *Pennsylvania Journal and Weekly Advertiser* was filled with such wonders as *Jack Horner's Toy*, *Christmas Rhymes for Mummers*, *Christmas Box*, *Lovechild's Present*, and *Lilliputian Auction*, though such works as *The Life of Christ* and *Spiritual Lessons* also made a strong showing.[23] Didactic tales of social etiquette and religious duty joined with the enchanted tales of Mother Goose to brighten a child's New Year with gifts from parents and relatives. Also by the late 1810s and 1820s, large assortments of "Interesting and Amusing TOYS" had been added to holiday books as appropriate New Year's gifts for children. In the calendar of the early republic, these rites of the New Year were precedent setting: The coddling of children, perhaps the quintessential characteristic of the modern Christmas, first appeared in the rites of the New Year.[24]

So prevalent were books as New Year's gifts that special annuals of stories, poetry, and engravings soon became holiday fixtures. In the second quarter of the nineteenth century, scores of annual gift books, intricately embossed and illustrated, emerged on the scene: *Atlantic Souvenir*, *Picturesque Annual*, *Christian Souvenir*, *Annualette*, *Forget-Me-Not*, *St. Nicholas Annual*, *The Catholic Keepsake*, *Friendship's Gift*, *The Boudoir Annual*, and *The Talisman*, among hundreds of others, flourished as New Year's and Christmas gifts. Some of these flowery keepsakes were designed for children, but the majority were patterned as gifts for women from callers, friends, or relatives. In the antebellum period no holiday gift was more typical than books, and these annuals, with their fine bindings, literary offerings, and pictorial embellishments, were among the most prominent seasonal mementos and the most successful holiday commodities. Even in a book market crowded with annuals, sales often ran into the thousands for the more popular volumes.[25]

New Year's advertisements had grown from being rare and infrequent reminders in the 1770s and 1780s to being numerous and recurrent promotions in the 1820s and 1830s. Some of the customary gifts such as cakes and candy remained prevalent in holiday notices, but even they showed signs of transformation through the theater of the marketplace, in the snobbery of French confections or in the showmanship of mammoth cakes that were claimed to weigh three hundred, five hundred, or even a thousand pounds and that were used as store attractions. Such grand exhibitions—a "LARGE FRUIT CAKE, WEIGHING MORE THAN 100 LBS" or a "MAMMOTH PLUMB CAKE, 16 feet in Circumference and Weighing 1000 lbs"—translated the Rabelaisian fascination with the gargantuan into a sumptuous commercial enticement.[26] A whole new gamut of appropriate New Year's gifts, ranging from ornamental books and annual souvenirs to toys and pincushions, had arisen and flourished. After 1820, New Year's gifts increasingly shared space with Christmas presents, and the latter would gradually eclipse the former in prominence and popularity. But the change was slow and incremental: New Year's gifts would shadow Christmas presents deep into the nineteenth century. Without the solid foundation of New Year's exchanges, the new Christmas emporium would have been a far less sturdy edifice.

All the thrill and tumult of New Year's celebrations did not go uncriticized. Puritans had long objected to the pagan frivolity of New Year's observances, and religious sorts across the denominational spectrum thought that mirthful revelers were missing the sobering questions at the heart of time's unyielding passage: Is your soul right with God? Are you ready to face the grand judgments of eternity? Among the devout, New Year's was invariably held up as a time for religious renewal and spiritual resolve, a time to move from irregular attendance on God's ordinances to disciplined, holy living. The young especially were exhorted to improve the time, not to while it away in vain and foolish amusements, to make New Year's the occasion of dramatic change or even conversion.

A Christian language of "pious resolution" haunted the holiday, a devotional rhetoric both solemn and routine. "As usual I have made fresh vows," one Baptist woman noted in her diary on 1 January 1846, "that this year shall be spent better than the last and more in the service of the Lord." A Massachusetts schoolteacher, Frances Quick, suggested something of the rich texture of these New Year's pledges:

> The last night and the last Sabbath of the year 1854. A year ago—what a conjurer that sound is—what thoughts spring up at its bidding! Like a wave sent back upon the shore, come dashing back tones, voices, forms, thoughts, aims and feelings upon the year's last day. . . . How shall we begin the New Year? As we should close the Old Year with prayers of praise, so we should begin the New Year with prayerful petitions. I feel firm, strong and resolute tonight. I will not seek to glean pleasure from the coming year, or reap selfish and mercenary advantage from it; but I will go forth in the strength of God to conquer my own weaknesses, improve the powers which he has given me, and make it my daily study to find some avenue of usefulness to others.

More-secular New Year's resolutions for therapeutic self-improvement and healthful living, which only came into vogue at the turn of the twentieth century, had their roots in these Christian practices of "pious resolution." (This overlap is apparent in one Christian's vow for New Year's in 1809 to "guard against all excess in eating and drinking" and to adhere throughout the coming year to an ethic of "strict moderation.") Rooted, too, in this language of "pious resolution" was a notion of human weakness that still shadows these vows, the knowledge that too many folks are incurable backsliders who will fail to uphold these pledges of reformation. As Frances Quick sadly noted the day after her solemn vows, "Resolutions are being tested." The troubled pursuit of self-improvement embodied in New Year's resolutions is a secularized version of the holiday's spiritual disciplines, which long served as milestones in the Christian journey toward holiness.[27]

Redeeming the time was a frequent concern of the devout, and so too were New Year's luxuries and gifts. Henry Bourne was one in a long line of churchmen from Tertullian and Augustine to William Perkins and Increase Mather who had worried, in varying degrees, about New Year's gift giving as a popular diversion susceptible to pagan superstition. For Puritans and evangelicals, holiday wastefulness and extravagance were as much a problem as festive rioting and reveling. Money spent on seasonal banquets and embellishments was money "mis-spent and lavished away in vain Prodigality and Luxury." Because it squandered resources, holiday consumption was in this view terribly immoderate and impeded real "Liberality to the Poor." The Puritan line of argument also found resonance in republican thought: The genteel opulence of New Year's munificence—the "luxurious dinners," "the largesses and banquets"—was corrupting and enervating, even "anti-democratick" in its hierarchic formalities and condescension. For the reformers, discipline and control were always major concerns, but so were social accountability and community. As one of the faithful devoutly resolved for New Year's in 1809, "I will watch against every rising of covetous desire, and while I carefully repress all tendency to improper expense, or the careless profusion of any of God's gifts, I will seek out proper objects with whom to share those good things of which God has made me the steward. . . . I will ask every night, whose distresses have I this day relieved?"[28]

Religious efforts to transform New Year's festivities gained consummate expression in the watch-night services of the evangelicals, especially those of the early Methodists. New modes of worship were clearly one of the distinguishing marks of the evangelical movement: love feasts, river baptisms, foot washings, covenant services, testimonials, outdoor revivals, field preaching, quarterly conferences, camp meetings, and sacramental seasons. To these popular evangelical solemnities was also added the watch night. Begun near Bristol, England, among Kingswood Methodists in the early 1740s as one more improvised gathering of the faithful for extended "prayer and praise and thanksgiving," watch-night services were initially held at various times throughout the year, especially timed to full moons for purposes of lighting people's way to and from these midnight vigils. Seeing great spiritual results in what he tellingly termed "the novelty of this *ancient* custom" of vigils, John Wesley quickly endorsed these meetings and encouraged their "more general use" among the Methodist societies.[29]

The preeminent occasion for the watch night soon emerged as New Year's Eve. For evangelicals, this timing was loaded with potential for pious practice as well as for countercultural resistance. Core evangelical beliefs found ready expression in watch-night hymns, exhortations, prayers, and testimonials. The end of another year added urgency to the evangelical call to repent, to turn to Christ before it was too late, to confirm one's commitment while there was yet time. Being vigilant until late into the night also placed the faithful, almost as a matter of course, in the eschatological framework of being ready for Christ's second coming. This was the Advent piety of evangelical Protestants: They were watchers in the night for the long-expected Jesus. Charles Wesley captured this motif in one of his many watch-night hymns:

Then let us wait to hear
The trumpet's welcome sound;
To see our Lord appear,
Watching let us be found;
When Jesus doth the heavens bow,
Be found—as Lord, thou finds us now.

Like the wise virgins with the oil in their lamps, the faithful were ready for "the midnight cry" of the Bridegroom. Such heartfelt piety galvanized these late-night meetings.[30]

Oppositional values and transformative visions loomed large in the watch nights. In these gatherings, the reborn visibly renounced the entrenched festivities of popular culture; they found new self-definition as well as community identity through their opposition to the familiar celebrations of the New Year. Charles Wesley sharply depicted this transformation in the opening stanza of another of his watch-night hymns:

OFT have we pass'd the guilty night,
In revellings and frantic mirth:
The creature was our sole delight,
Our happiness the things of earth;
But O! suffice the season past,
We choose the better part at last.[31]

The itinerant preacher Joseph Pilmore expressed similar sentiments in the journal covering his ministry in the colonies from 1769 to 1774. Participating in meetings for Christmas Eve, Christmas Day, and New Year's Eve in New York in 1770, he was struck by "how widely" these services diverged "from the feasting and entertainments of the wicked." For New Year's Eve, he observed specifically: "We had our Watch-Night. The Mob had threatened great things, but the terrors of the Lord made them afraid, and we continued till after midnight, that we might end the *old*, and begin the *New Year*, in the service of God." With the arrival of evangelical watch nights, New Year's Eve became an increasingly complicated cultural battleground. The joyful shouts of evangelicals in side-street chapels now challenged the boisterous noise of plebeian celebrants, and the evangelicals laid the gauntlet down directly on the turf of the common people—that is, they were more than happy to fight the contest in the vernacular of popular celebration.[32]

For the evangelicals, the cultural battleground at New Year's extended beyond the open conflict with "the slaves of excess" and "the drunkards" who, "in a circle of riot," threatened to break up their meetings. It also took in "the civiller crowd" with their masques, gifts, balls, visits, entertainments, and other pleasures and luxuries.[33] Here, too, the evangelicals were boldly subversive. In typical evangelical fashion George Whitefield centered a New Year's sermon on the need for immediate repentance: "A Penitent Heart" was "the best *New Year's Gift*." The solemnity, plainness, and otherworldliness of the Methodist watch nights (as well as their covenant services, which also were often timed to the New Year) stood in stark contrast to the New Year's rituals of the well-heeled. Fervent Methodists and other evangelicals who adopted the watch nights as their own long fought this battle over New Year's around the issues of "sobriety, economy, and gospel simplicity." In 1842 a Baptist congregation, for example, offered as its "HOLIDAY PRESENTS" to fellow Philadelphians a New Year's sermon for youth and a midnight "Watch Meeting," both under the banner "Silver and gold have I none, but such as I have give I thee." In 1862, a Methodist publication, *The Earnest Christian and Golden Rule*, exhorted the devout to give up the fashionable customs of "New Year's calls from house to house, where tables are spread with rich and costly viands, luxurious dainties, confectioneries, sparkling decanters, the intoxicating bowl!" "How much is squandered on lust on New Year's day," the *Earnest Christian* queried, "that might go to . . . supply the poor, the oppressed, the perishing?" The battle lines against the celebration of luxury, abundance, consumption, and gentility could hardly have been drawn more clearly. The *Earnest Christian* called the faithful back to the heartfelt moral seriousness of the watch night.[34]

The contests about New Year's adumbrated much that lay ahead in debates about Christmas Day. Evangelicals held up for emulation an expressive piety with a sober ethic of plainness and simplicity. In trying to redeem or Christianize New Year's celebrations and the wider festivities of winter, they raised anew long-standing conflicts about how to observe the Christmas season. These Protestants knew they wanted nothing to do with the carnival of the streets, and they were equally confident in their rejection of the mannered fashions of the genteel. But the holidays, like the consumer culture, were terribly alluring, and in combination they were doubly so. In the half century after 1820 many of the more strenuous Protestants made the requisite adjustments in their ritual life to include the holidays and to embrace the new Christmas bazaar. This growing alignment of evangelical Protestants behind the modern Christmas was integral to the holiday's cultural ascent. Though still alarmed by the ungoverned festivities of the streets, American Protestants seemed increasingly at home with Christmas and comfortable with all the familial gifts, the jollities of Santa Claus, and the allures of the holiday marketplace. But the old suspicions remained, sometimes tarrying just below the surface, and Christians (Protestants joined by Catholics) would regularly issue appeals for the hallowing of Christmas, just as the evangelicals had long pleaded for the solemnity of the New Year.

THE BIRTH OF THE CHRISTMAS MARKET, 1820–1900

The traditional liberality of the holiday season—the huge dinners and the hearty drinking—had long tied Christmas to the bustling energies of the marketplace. As a season of feasting, Christmas had always offered a good market for food and drink, and the holidays were especially kind to poulterers, butchers, bakers, vintners, distillers, and tavern keepers. The early modern Christmas market, with its stalls and booths, its chapmen and criers, its larder of foodstuffs, was both fair and festival; it was the very image of preindustrial abundance, a picture of near-utopian bounty set against the day-to-day realities of dearth and the fears of Malthusian scarcity. Well into the nineteenth century, newspaper accounts of the Christmas bazaar often turned as much on the cornucopia of poultry, turkey, beef, and wild game slaughtered for seasonal fare as on the display of toys, books, and fancy goods. Christmas consumption had long been conspicuous, and vendors had invariably clamored for a stake in the mart.

Beyond these customary holiday markets for food and drink, however, Christmas showed only limited signs of commercial aggrandizement before the 1820s and 1830s, especially lagging in comparison to New Year's. The relative sparseness of advertising for Christmas presents is one index of the holiday's modest commercialization through 1820. In good New England fashion, the *Connecticut Courant* made no mention of Christmas observance between 1779 and 1820 and carried no advertisements whatsoever for holiday gifts, whether for Christmas or New Year's. In Harrisburg, Pennsylvania, where German immigrants especially kept up Christmas festivities, the *Harrisburg Chronicle*'s main concern with the holidays well into the nineteenth century was an effort to keep legislators in session and hard at work, not letting them bilk the taxpayers by sneaking off for an extended holiday adjournment. Between 1813 and 1837 the paper ran only nine holiday advertisements, all for New Year's presents, none for Christmas. In *Poulson's American Daily Advertiser*, a Philadelphia newspaper, the occasional Christmas hymn or New Year's poem generally occupied more space from 1800 to 1820 than the handful of advertisements for holiday presents. Even in these notices, New Year's gifts again took precedence over those for Christmas.

In the 1820s and 1830s the gifts of New Year's—confections, cakes, devotional works, children's books, annual keepsakes, and toys—increasingly converged with Christmas. During this fluid holiday season of friendly compliments and good wishes, the preparations and purchases for Christmas and New Year's festivities easily flowed together. In the conflux of holiday parties, dinners, and visits, Christmas presents and New Year's gifts became all but interchangeable. Such holiday gift books as the *Atlantic Souvenir* and the *Picturesque Annual* moved back and forth between New Year's and Christmas without a change of cover. The earliest holiday advertisements had usually featured New Year's gifts without mention of Christmas; seasonal promotions in the 1820s and 1830s increasingly joined the holidays in an undifferentiated mix of gift giving. The growing prominence of generic or conjunctive phrases in newspaper advertisements, such as "NEW GOODS FOR THE HOLIDAYS" or "CHRISTMAS AND NEW YEAR'S PRESENTS," indicated this commingling.[35] Suggestive of this confluence were two poems for children, published respectively in 1821 and 1823. The first, *The Children's Friend*, known for its original depiction of Santa Claus in a reindeer-led sleigh, was yet another of those little books concocted as a New Year's gift for children. The second and more famous, Clement Moore's "Night before Christmas," though drawing on *The Children's Friend* in its depiction of Santa's reindeer, situated gift giving wholly in Christmas, not New Year's. In the antebellum period the relationship between New Year's and Christmas presents remained complementary: In this regard, *The Children's Friend* was perhaps a better social mirror than "The Night before Christmas," since it was packaged as a New Year's present, even as it told the story of Santa's Christmas visit, thus synthesizing the two holiday traditions.[36] But Moore's depiction was nonetheless fateful. His poem suggested the ultimate course of holiday exchanges in the United States as Christmas gradually emerged as the preeminent focus for both gift giving and merchandising.

Why gift giving, firmly established as a New Year's custom, slowly tilted more toward Christmas in the middle decades of the nineteenth century is something of a puzzle. Many of the dilemmas of the modern Christmas concerning the contested mixture of religion and market would have been avoided if the focus of holiday gift giving and commercial promotion had remained on New Year's, instead of being refocused on the celebration of Christ's nativity. That makes the question of why this shift took place all the more intriguing. The usual suspects of work discipline, middle-class reform, and modern timekeepers are no doubt a major part of the explanation. Shifting the bulk of gift giving from New Year's to Christmas helped further condense the holiday season and undercut the legitimacy of disorderly plebeian celebrations that often stretched out over a week or more. As class, ethnic, and racial divisions increasingly fractured urban street celebrations into occasions of violent confrontation, efforts at holiday constriction became all the more prevalent and imperative. For the sake of capitalist growth, industrial efficiency, and urban order, the drawn-out Christmas season of the early modern world needed to shrink, and what better way to do that than to focus most of the festivities on Christmas Eve and Christmas Day, gift giving included? In 1841, for example, the *Philadelphia Public Ledger* applauded the religious observance of Christmas, but discouraged the celebration of New Year's, saying of the latter that "the best way that it can be kept, is by setting an example of industry." From the perspective of reformers, the family-centered presents of Christmas set the right kind of example, helping locate the celebration within the bounds of the domestic circle and within tighter temporal parameters.[37]

Nineteenth-century middle-class folks were also clearly drawn to the familial intimacy and security that Christmas presents represented. This domestic appeal was evident in the growing fascination with the German observance of Christmas, which by midcentury rivaled the French celebration of New Year's for charm and enchantment in the pages of middle-class periodicals. Affectionate articles on the German Christmas tree and German gift giving at Christmas increasingly cropped up in such periodicals as *Godey's*, *Sartain's*, and *Peterson's* in the 1840s and 1850s. Warmhearted scenes of presents around a Christmas tree provided a clear familial cast to holiday gift giving; New Year's lacked this sort of symbolic center for the ritual exchange of familial gifts. With the implanting of the Christmas tree in American culture in the middle decades of the nineteenth century, Christmas had the perfect symbol for domestic celebration, hearthlike in its magnetic light and sparkling decorations. Americans found other sources of inspiration in addition to German customs in patching together their own traditions of Christmas gift giving. For example, the English notion of Christmas boxes was readily refashioned, and various Old World stories about St. Nicholas and his trinkets were easily enlarged and embellished. At bottom, Christmas presents and dinners, more clearly than New Year's gifts and visits, which fanned out into diffuse circles of friends and acquaintances, made home and family the heart of celebration. Christmas, the *Philadelphia Public Ledger* reported wistfully in 1844, "is religion in each man's house."[38]

Finally, Christmas's gradual eclipse of New Year's as a gift-giving occasion was built on its greater potential for consecration. For churchgoers, biblical stories about the gifts of the Wise Men, the baby Jesus, the Holy Family, and the benedictions of angels ultimately made for much more interesting and apt

37. "The Christmas Tree," *Godey's Magazine and Lady's Book* 41 (December 1850): frontispiece.

symbols around which to organize a great feast of familial gift giving than, say, Father Time or the Roman god Janus. For some Protestants, the exchange of gifts at New Year's, whatever the holiday's pagan associations, had been considered more acceptable than a similar observance of Christmas, with that holiday's dreaded Catholic connections. But as the theological precision and liturgical plainness that had long undergirded Calvinist opposition to Christ-

38. "A Fruitful Tree," *Sunday-School Advocate*, 28 December 1872, 24.

mas gave way to liberal flexibility and romantic sentimentalism, the way was clear for middle-class Protestants to lift up Christmas as a festival of home, church, Sunday school, and presents. By the 1850s and 1860s, fewer and fewer Protestants had scruples about Christmas, and most found Christmas presents well suited to religious reverence and domestic affection. In turn, this growing appreciation for the religious and domestic possibilities of Christmas made the celebration that much more interesting to merchants. The dense symbols of Christmas would ultimately play better in the marketplace than the thinner emblems of New Year's.

The heightening drama of the Christmas bazaar had already begun to display itself in cities such as New York and Philadelphia in the 1820s and 1830s. A wide-eyed account of the holiday marketplace in New York in 1832 suggested some of the dawning wonder of Christmas shopping:

> *Christmas-eve*, in the city of New-York, exhibits a spectacle, which, to a stranger, must be highly pleasing and effective. Whole rows of confectionary stores and toy shops, fancifully, and often splendidly, decorated with festoons of bright silk drapery, interspersed with flowers and evergreens, are brilliantly illuminated with gas-lights, arranged in every shape and figure that fancy can devise. During the evening, until midnight, these places are crowded with visiters of both sexes and

> all ages; some selecting toys and fruits for holyday presents; others merely lounging from shop to shop to enjoy the varied scene. But the most interesting, and, in our estimation, the most delightful sight of all, is the happy and animated countenances of children on this occasion.[39]

This description is suggestive of both the breadth and the borders of the Christmas marketplace in the 1820s and 1830s. Already stores are festooned with decorations; already children are at the center of things; already people take delight in the leisurely pursuit of holiday shopping. Still, in this depiction all the activity is confined to a small variety of stores, namely toy and confectionery establishments, and holiday shopping does not sprawl out over several weeks, but is largely limited to Christmas Eve.

Toy and confectionery shops may have taken the lead in staging this new Christmas pageant, but other entrepreneurs were certainly crowding into the performance. A New York coffeehouse, for example, beckoned people in 1827 with a fantastic array of "Holyday Decorations": There the visitor would find not simply holiday refreshment, but "a bower of evergreens and roses, and patriotic emblems arranged by the hand of taste and fancy—the thistle, the rose, and the shamrock, blended in harmony." And there was more. "A splendid Grecian cross is displayed in triumph against the Turkish crescent; the walls and canopy hung with festoons and stars, laurel and evergreen; the sides planted with olives, firs and shrubbery of every variety; and the American Eagle, with expanded wings, suspended over all."[40] It is not hard to see, in this hodgepodge of coffeehouse decorations in 1827, the mix of symbols—religious, patriotic, and ethnic—that would be enlarged to monumental scale in the department stores a half century later.

This kind of holiday display appeared in other venues of public amusement as well. Since more time was afforded for leisure during the Christmas season, theaters, music societies, circuses, and dance halls regularly offered one sort of Christmas gambol or another, and these holiday attractions were already promoted with considerable fanfare in the 1820s and 1830s. No antebellum institution, however, proved more adept at staging the Christmas festival for the purposes of commercial entertainment than the museum. Formerly the elite domain of America's few enlightened philosophes, the museum in the early republic went popular—a natural-history exhibit, curiosity shop, art gallery, theater, menagerie, and sideshow all rolled into one. Year-round fairs of science and illusion, Jacksonian-era museums became at the holidays even more of a jamboree of exotic entertainment. For example, the American Museum, founded in New York in 1810 by John Scudder and eventually taken over in 1841 by P. T. Barnum, was always "splendidly decorated" for the holidays. In typically dramatic fashion the front of the museum was "brilliantly illuminated" for the Christmas festival in 1827 "with nearly 200 gas jets."[41] The art of illumination, particularly lighting up the facades of buildings, was one of the great arts of celebration, used for such grand events as triumphal commemorations of the Fourth of July or imposing processions of heads of state and military heroes, but with the museums the form was taken over for the heraldic presentation of commercial entertainment.

In addition to illuminations, the museums had bands, paintings, wax figures, optical illusions, and the phantasmagoria of magic lanterns, all staged, it was claimed, with special care for the holidays. For example, on Christmas Eve in 1830 one New York wax museum, with little liturgical sensibility for the feast of Christ's birth, introduced a brand-new exhibit of "the Crucifixion of our Saviour on Mount Calvary, comprising about thirty figures." Not to be outdone, another New York museum for the same Christmas Eve put forth as its "GREAT NOVELTY" a display of "the Deities of Java." This was humbug at its most sensational and amusing, but it displayed a vernacular not only of artifice and hoax, but also of the grotesque and the colonizing. A few years earlier, for instance, still another museum had made a holiday exhibit of "the HEAD OF OHIBO, A NEW ZEALAND CHIEF," who had supposedly been killed in tribal battle and whose head, "beautifully tattooed," had been preserved as "a trophy." All too clearly the Christmas festival was already in the 1820s and 1830s the occasion of lurid commercial promotions—amusements that made a commodity out of the exoticism of the other. In this, the Christmas mart seemed an endless replaying of Shakespeare's *Tempest*, in which "holiday fools," as Trinculo remarks in thinking of Caliban's potential as a human commodity, "will not give a doit to relieve a lame beggar" but "will lay out ten to see a dead Indian." These early marvels of the holiday marketplace also absorbed energy from the outlandish, fantastical masking of the street celebrations; both were realms of disguise, chimera, and monstrosity. In the museums, the "startling Effects," the "singular Alteration[s]," and the "instantaneous Changes of Costume" were a circus spectacle, available for viewing for the price of admission. By contrast, in the streets, topsy-turvy and often fierce, the holiday carnival was participatory; it was, quite literally, a male free-for-all.[42]

The museums helped model a new kind of festivity, one of curiosities and novelties, consumption and spectacle, artifice and display. In the 1840s, when a Philadelphia store was grandly decked out for the holidays with "Camanchee Indian" beads and moccasins, evergreen festoons "in the good old Christmas style," and "a rich display of Toys of every kind," the *Public Ledger*, looking for the right analogy to describe the effect of this jumbled exhibition, did not have to reach far. It called the store a museum, and this similitude was suggestive.[43]

Critics have often lamented the semiotic confusion that the consumer culture creates, the endless changing of decorative motifs in the pursuit of novelty and effect, the surreal and disorienting juxtaposition of incongruous advertising images, and the slippery claims of commercial language that tend to drain signifiers of their meaning. The museum's cabinet of curiosities, with its enshrinement of humbug and hoax, offers an important source and metaphor for both the bewilderment and the attraction of the modern consumer culture. The store's combination of Indian art with Euro-American seasonal decorations to stage the sale of toys was an innovative (and colonizing) concatenation of symbols, but it had the familiar feel of the museum.

Just as holiday entertainments became ever more elaborate and flamboyant, so did the displays of Christmas merchandise, and, unlike the amusements of museums and theaters, the festal attractions of the stores carried no fee for admission. "As the Holiday season approaches," the *New York Evening Post* reported in 1839, "an unusual variety of tempting wares have been . . . arranged in the show windows of the brilliant shops of Broadway. . . . Book stores, print stands, confectionaries, and toy shops are filled with specimens of what are curious and amusing, adapted to every desire from that of the child to that of the philosopher." Holiday gifts were on display in bedazzling profusion—books, perfumes, dolls, writing desks, tortoise chessmen, "poodle dogs curiously made," "queer figures from Germany, queerer figures from Paris, and the queerest figures of all from China," plus "ten thousand other things no man could name, much less describe." In 1845 the *Public Ledger* was so moved by the plethora of Christmas and New Year's gifts in Philadelphia stores that the paper almost seemed ready to announce the descent of a millennial reign of abundance upon the city: "There is, indeed, every thing to find which can please the appetite, gratify the taste, add to the comfort, or contribute to the enjoyment of a Christian people." In the Christmas bazaar of the 1830s and 1840s, middle-class Americans already glimpsed a world of faith, freedom, and contentment that revolved around the plentiful choices of the marketplace. The Christmas fair was a grand theater for possibility and temptation, for the absorption of the strange and the new into the familiar and the tasteful.[44]

Soon, though, all this holiday abundance seemed at least to some like surfeit. In 1860 the *New York Evening Post* announced that Christmas in New York presented an embarrassment of riches that made holiday shopping increasingly difficult and time consuming: "The great trouble is to know *what to choose*." Things were so bad, the paper said, that "the bewildered gift-seeker" required a "classified manual" to make her or his way through the Christmas marketplace. The *Evening Post* did what it could to help; it systematically reviewed twenty-five different gift categories, from books and Bibles to soaps and wines, and mapped out the various establishments carrying these items. Other papers, such as the *New York Times*, joined in to offer their own guides in the perplexing "quest" for the right holiday goods. This search was becoming a new secular pilgrimage, fraught with its own perils. Unlike Vanity Fair in John Bunyan's tale of the pilgrim's journey heavenward, the marketplace was not to be feared as a source of temptation, but embraced—just so long as one had a good shopping guide. (That *Vanity Fair* could be latched onto as the title for a modish magazine of cosmopolitan fashions, several incarnations of which were launched between 1859 and 1896, suggests the changed view of the mart's allures.) By the 1850s and 1860s the Christmas market in urban centers, with an ever-expanding array of consumer choices, was commonly evoking expressions of awe and disorientation, amazement and stupefaction.[45]

The lively, magical scenes of the modern Christmas bazaar found a patron saint in Santa Claus, and his nineteenth-century ascent as a cultural icon offers a good symbol for the rise of the Christmas market and its significance. As a figure of hagiography, folklore, and legend, Santa Claus was a motley compound of European traditions and American embellishments.[46] Lifted up with romantic yearning and civic zeal by such New York writers as Washington Irving and James Paulding in the first decades of the nineteenth century, the European St. Nicholas was rapidly made indigenous as the American Santa Claus. But this reimagined holiday patron was hardly bound by the fancies of the Knickerbocker set, and depictions of Santa Claus before the Civil War displayed striking variety.

This diversity was conspicuous. In one of his first American incarnations in New York in 1809, St. Nicholas was toasted, ironically enough, as a sober republican, a patron of "virtuous habits and simple manners" that were endangered by "luxuries and refinements." In 1810 he was even pictured as a saintly bishop in episcopal regalia, flanked by a beehive symbolizing industry and a bulldog connoting fidelity. A benevolent gift giver and a friend of virtue, he brought toys and confections to good children, but he was also a figure of stern discipline who bore switches and rods for those children who had misbehaved.[47] The image of St. Nicholas as a righteous and virtuous patron of American republicanism was soon inverted by a more familiar embodiment—that is, Santa Claus as a puckish elf, treasure-laden and troll-like. He was often dressed in wild furs, as if he had walked somewhat uneasily out of a street masquerade and into a middle-class home, an awkward domestication of one of "the raging beasts of the mummers' world."[48] These versions of Santa Claus, suggesting something of the permeability of plebeian and bourgeois cultures, borrowed from European and African American traditions of the carni-

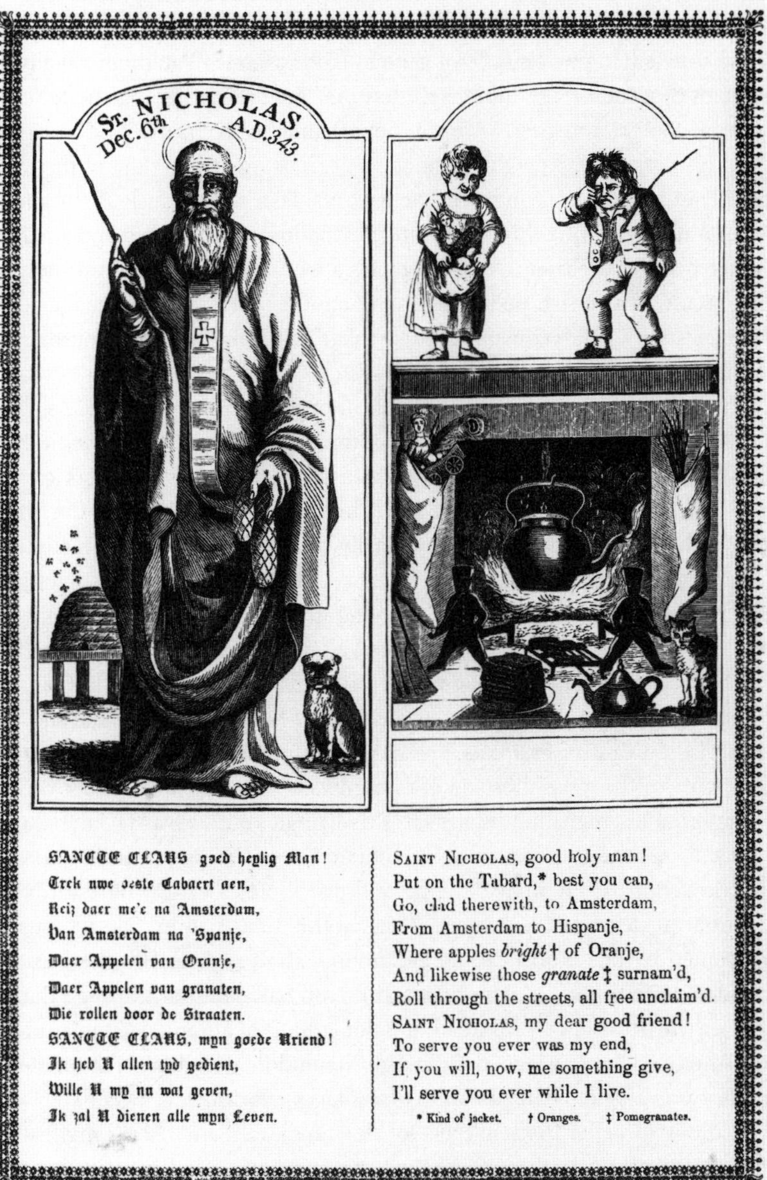

39. Alexander Anderson (engraver), St. Nicholas broadside (New York: n.p., 1810).

valesque in which it was common for people to costume themselves in furs and parade as beasts, even as the new images of St. Nick tamed these gargoyles of the streets. (In one episode of genteel fantasy, James Paulding actually had the saint descend on the "noisy splutterkins" and "roistering rogues" to rebuke them for their riotousness: "Are you not ashamed of yourselves . . . to set such a bad example to the neighbourhood, by carousing at this time of the morning?" Paulding's reform-minded Santa Claus asks censoriously.)[49] In another important variation in his American incarnation, Santa Claus appeared as a Yankee peddler, a roaming chapman with a wondrous pack who was now and then recast as a Jewish peddler.[50] In yet another form, he was imagined, "in German style," as a yeoman farmer, replete with his own farmhouse, cattle, and fowl.[51]

The diversity was more than a matter of profession and costume. As a magical visitor, this antebellum Santa Claus appeared in some homes on St. Nicholas Eve (5 December), in others on Christmas Eve, in still others on New Year's Eve, and in many on *both* Christmas Eve and New Year's Eve. In his rounds, he was accompanied occasionally by the Christ child, sometimes by a black assistant or servant named Peter, and at least once by the singer Jenny Lind, with whom he was pictured flying around on a winged broomstick, looking more the part of a patriot than of a saint or an elf. In another instance, in a comic proclamation in a New York newspaper in 1815, Santa Claus was even imagined as a woman, "the Queen . . . of handsome girls" and the "Empress of the Court of Fashions," perhaps a fitting inversion for a holiday long notorious for the cross-dressing of mummers.[52] Not only was gender bending a possibility in antebellum images of Kris Kringle, but so was racial inclusion. For example, one account in 1827 pictured Santa Claus as "a little old negro, who descends the chimney at night, and distributes a variety of rewards with impartial justice." Also a subject of the Gothic imagination, Santa Claus was envisioned by one North Carolinian around 1850 as "a fearful fire-breathing monster" with "big eyes" who breathed fire on bad children "through the keyhole on Christmas Eve." All in all, it is something of an understatement to say that American Santa Claus lore through the middle decades of the nineteenth century was a heterogeneous jumble of images, stories, and legends.[53]

In order to make profitable use of this tangle of Santa Claus myths, merchants, like others in the culture, had to draw quite selectively on this reservoir of images, folklore, and literary invention. Retailers obviously had little use for a frightening or judgmental figure. No monstrous or switch-wielding character need apply; an austere republican or self-sufficient farmer would have been quickly shown the door; and likewise, an early-fourth-century saint

40. *(Top left) Santa Claus; or, The Night before Christmas* (New York: Mathews and Clasback, 1856), frontispiece.

41. *(Top right) A Visit of St. Nicholas* (Philadelphia: Fisher and Brother, [1860?]), frontispiece.

42. *(Bottom left) Santa Claus and Jenny Lind* (New York: John R. M'Gown, 1850), frontispiece.

with miraculous powers or a Catholic bishop with episcopal vestments and a miter would not have been of much help around the store, since such images would have had highly negative associations for most American Protestants. Stories about Santa Claus having a black assistant, or even himself being black, also did not make the grade; such images were clearly out of harmony with the dominant white, middle-class market for Christmas presents. Indeed, by the end of the century Santa Claus's whiteness had become a cultural and commercial given, so much so that one early-twentieth-century Christmas play, entitled *A Department Store Santa Claus*, contained the telling line from a child that she "never saw no black Santa Claus. He's always white." Only in 1970 would major department stores such as Macy's begin to integrate their crew of Santa Clauses.[54]

For mid-nineteenth-century merchants, the Santa Claus who fit the bill was the jolly gift giver, the one who looked like a peddler with a magical and inexhaustible bag of presents or like an elfish gnome from an enchanted world of mysterious treasures. Clement Clarke Moore's version of St. Nicholas, with his sleigh full of presents and with his mission to transform ordinary stockings into cornucopias of novelties, was ideal: "A bundle of Toys he had flung on his back, / and he looked like a pedlar just opening his pack." With this sort of image, merchants would have a special claim on Santa Claus. He was one of them, a peddler who could produce toys and other goods in endless profusion, a magician whose theater of conjuring was the marketplace. At the same time, his magical travel over rooftops and his elusive movement up and down chimneys, "laden with toys, cakes, and books," made Christmas presents all the more fantastic, even mystical. Santa Claus lifted gifts out of the disenchanted realms of market exchange and industrial production and made them appear in a twinkling of an eye in the home. As with St. Valentine's Day, so with Santa Claus and Christmas: Old forms of magic and fable proved quite serviceable in the new "magic system" of advertising.[55]

Toy and confectionery shopkeepers, with their prime interest in children as a market, led the way in using Santa Claus or Kris Kringle as a drawing card for their establishments. The Philadelphia confectioner and caterer James Parkinson claimed to have been the first to employ Kris Kringle as an emblem for merchandising, turning the legendary gift giver into a piece of advertising art and setting him up as a giant sign over the door of his shop in 1840.[56] Parkinson's claim of originality, though, should be taken with a grain of salt: In the puffery of business promotion, no firm is ever second. A year earlier another Philadelphia store had tried to draw Christmas traffic by putting up a "BIG RED STOCKING" over its door, and a New York merchant, B. G. Jansen, already proclaimed himself in 1830 to be the duly appointed "Agent of St. Nicholas" and announced that his store, with its "very extensive assortment of Bibles, Prayer Books, Psalm Books, Hymn Books, Toy and Chap Books," was the veritable "Temple" of "*Santaclaus*." Like Washington Irving's historical fiction on New York's Dutch heritage, Jansen's advertisement was an act of mythic invention: Calling the descendants of New Amsterdam back to "the good ways of their fathers," he helped provide the new American Santa Claus with a fabled and largely fabricated past.[57]

If Jansen's proclamation was more a matter of words than of decorations, Parkinson's material contrivance of 1840 soon had plenty of company. On Christmas Eve in 1846 the *Public Ledger* reported crowds of "admiring gazers" in front of "our numerous fancy and confectionery stores," and the throngs seemed especially attracted to two establishments that boasted "representations of old Kriss Kringle." The previous year, the Philadelphia merchant William Maurice, proprietor of the Ladies' Favorite Store, had advertised the actual presence of Santa Claus *inside* his establishment, beckoning mothers and their children to "COME AND SEE KRISS KRINGLE" as well as the store's abundance of toys and confections. In this case, St. Nick had even been "fitted up" with his own "SALOON," from which he apparently held court for "the Gratification of the 'Little Ones.'"[58] Though it is impossible to know exactly what Maurice's creation entailed, Kris Kringle's saloon seems nonetheless a notable harbinger of Santa Claus's enthronement as a live presence in department-store Toylands a half century later. A more precise sense of Santa Claus's emergent image in the marketplace can be garnered from a surviving handbill from about 1846, distributed by Parkinson's partner and successor, Griffith Jones. Declaring the Chestnut Street store to be "KRISS KRINGLE'S HEAD QUARTERS," the handbill borrowed one of the most popular engravings of Santa Claus in the 1840s. Based on a sketch by the New York portrait painter Charles Ingham, the engraving pictures St. Nick descending a chimney with a pack of toys and other holiday treasures; standing nearby are his trusted reindeer. Once again, of the varied versions of Santa Claus, it was the magical peddler with whom the merchant chose to identify. In the 1840s, many urban merchants, like Jones and Maurice, had already made the shift in their Christmas dramaturgy "from the mechanics to the theatrics of commodity exchange"—a shift often attributed to their department-store counterparts of the 1880s and 1890s.[59]

After the Civil War, the stories and images of Santa Claus became increasingly standardized and nationalized. This was in part through the famed depictions of Santa Claus by Thomas Nast in *Harper's Weekly*, near-annual tributes from 1863 to 1886. Still clad in furs and still a peddler carrying his omnipresent pack, Nast's Santa Claus with his widened girth and his enlarged array of holiday presents improved on the holiday jollity and abundance of his

43. "Kris Kringle's Head Quarters," handbill, [1846?].

predecessors.[60] Likenesses in other media, such as those appearing on the booming number of Christmas cards in the late 1870s and 1880s, were also important in standardizing Kris Kringle's image. Santa Claus made an increasing number of appearances as well in Sunday school festivals and for charitable events. Religious-supply companies, like David C. Cook's in Chicago, offered appropriate Santa Claus masks with long white beards for such occasions at least as early as 1886, and these were necessarily standardized wares.[61] Supply houses for window trimmers and store decorators began to offer similar goods in the late 1880s and 1890s, increasingly providing the show-window and Toyland Santa Claus with an almost identical appearance from one place to another.[62] The Salvation Army Santa Claus with bells and a big kettle, making for a subdued echo of the callithumpians of a generation or two earlier, became ensconced on urban streets at the turn of the century, further fixing Santa Claus's public image.

44. Santa Claus as peddler, from Clement C. Moore, *A Visit from St. Nicholas* (New York: Henry M. Onderdonk, 1848), unpaginated.

Among the best sources for seeing the mature portrait of Santa Claus in the postbellum marketplace are holiday trade cards. Closely allied to the Christmas greetings exchanged among friends and relatives, holiday trade cards were given by merchants to customers as souvenir tokens. Like Victorian valentines and Christmas cards, holiday trade cards were not merely disposable or easily "discarded," but were often collected and valued. As "gifts" from merchants to patrons, holiday trade cards were more than another advertisement; they were a token of the merchant-customer relationship, a small reciprocation for valued patronage, an emblem of commercial trustworthiness and consumer loyalty. Cresting in popularity in the 1880s, when the chromolithography of Louis Prang and his competitors had attained considerable cachet among the members of the middle class, these fancy cards often found

45. "The Trojan Santa Claus," W. H. Frear advertisement, trade card, 1882.

their way onto Victorian Christmas trees as ornaments. Nada Gray in her study of nineteenth-century Christmas decorations found numerous instances in which trade-card images of angels, dolls, and Santa Claus were transformed into tree ornaments.[63] In this case, the boundary between the commercial culture and the domestic culture was quite permeable and comfortably negotiated, and trade cards, carried home from the stores and used as ornaments, were emblematic of this easy mediation. Often a far more innovative form of advertising than their printed, text-centered, black-and-white counterparts in newspapers, trade cards belonged to a colorful medium that performed varied cultural work in the late nineteenth century, especially at Christmas.[64]

No image was more popular on holiday trade cards than Santa Claus. As Griffith Jones had done in borrowing Ingham's sketch for a handbill, merchants of the 1870s and 1880s often relied on familiar images of Santa Claus from the wider culture for their holiday souvenirs. They regularly reprinted Clement Moore's "Night before Christmas" and commandeered the more recent works of Thomas Nast for their own trade cards, again effecting their identification with the magical peddler who, despite his growing paunch and expanding bag of toys, somehow still managed to slide down chimneys. Even more than they used visions of reindeer and rooftops, holiday trade cards combined images of Santa Claus and children, often bringing them into actual contact with each other. Instead of a mysterious figure, who usually got away unglimpsed, the store Santa Claus was there to be seen and hugged and to

46. "Toy Emporium," Richard Schwarz advertisement, trade card, ca. 1880.

imagine with the children all the good things Christmas might bring. The holiday trade cards of the 1870s and 1880s offered the very picture of Christmas plenty and visualized for parents and children the possibilities of Christmas morning—the entrancing variety of gifts and the dreams of fantastic toys.

On many of the cards, Christmas presents even took on a hallowed cast. They were God's blessings, the answer to children's prayers, and Santa Claus was God's peculiar messenger in these errands of bounty and grace. Indeed, St. Nicholas reemerged as a focus of real veneration; praying to him or through him became a recognized piety of Victorian childhood. For instance, on the front of one holiday souvenir, Kelly's emporium offered one of Nast's familiar pictures of Santa Claus (and also promoted its holiday payment plans), but on the back the store tendered the tearful story of "Annie and Willie's Prayer" in which Jesus and Santa Claus are mixed together in a jumble of successful petitions for Christmas toys. The children's invocation of a gentle Jesus and an indulgent Santa Claus breaks the "stern heart" of a cold, angry father who, softened, learns to purchase presents for his children with glad abandon. (This is a nice trade-card encapsulation of the larger shift from an austere Calvinist patriarchy to more-companionable forms of deity and family, with Santa Claus acting as the agent of theological transformation.) The new Santa Claus devotions also found expression through Christmas cards, Thomas Nast drawings, and other popular media. The prayerful posture of a little girl on one Prang card, for example, suggested the transfer of bedtime pieties from Jesus to Santa Claus at Christmas, and one of Nast's engravings made this translation explicit: A little boy kneels in prayer, seeking the material blessings that Santa Claus alone can magically bestow. The sense of religious waiting and preparation that surrounded Santa's visit on Christmas Eve was evident as well in the *Harper's Weekly* depiction of six African American children eagerly readying their stockings. These expectant preparations could even spill over into a kind of spiritual awe; in one picture from 1900 a little girl, barefoot and on bended knee, awaits the divine afflatus, an Advent mysticism explicitly turned toward Santa Claus. Holiday trade cards, along with various other cultural productions, helped situate Santa Claus within a marked devotional framework. The Victorian Santa Claus (and all he promised) roused the religious imagination. His superabundant bag of toys, something like the Christmas exhibition of F. A. O. Schwarz's Toy Bazaar condensed into an overflowing pack, was the embodiment of a blessed childhood.

Images of Santa Claus on trade cards overlapped with that great holiday contrivance of the late nineteenth century, the department-store Santa Claus, and pointed toward the new holiday ritual of children visiting St. Nick in gargantuan Toylands. Already a familiar presence in the grand Christmas windows of stores such as Macy's and Wanamaker's in the 1880s and 1890s, a live Santa Claus became a featured presence in toy departments in the same decades. In a holiday souvenir from 1888 entitled "Greetings from Santa Claus," one New York store cordially invited children "to come and see a real live Santa Claus," who was in residence at the store day and evening in his very own grotto.[65] By the turn of the century, these sorts of grottoes, thrones, cottages, and workshops for Santa Claus amounted to a store tradition, a Christmas rite all their own. The description in the *Dry Goods Reporter* of the getup at Siegel-Cooper in Chicago in 1901 was typical: "One of their attractions is a live Santa Claus right in the midst of the toy stock. He has all the regalia credited to the real Santa of story, and sits in a booth . . . from which he

47. "God Bless the Children," Sam M. Lederer Dry Goods advertisement, trade card, 1882.

distributes presents to the little folks. The booth is built so that a procession can pass through up the front steps past Santa Claus and out the back steps."[66]

Providing children with this encounter with Santa Claus was something the stores took with an almost religious seriousness. In 1909 *Playthings*, the leading trade journal of the American toy industry, pronounced in an article aptly entitled "The Mystic Spirit of Christmas" that "the presence of a flesh and blood Santa Claus" had become a requirement for any toy department. Climbing onto the lap of a flesh-and-blood Santa Claus in a department store was something of a sacrament for modern children, and merchants had the priestly responsibility of helping effect this transubstantiation of childhood fantasy. Santa's Toyland throne was a place of mysterious and sometimes frightening presence, a place of fantastic gifts, perhaps the closest thing for the modern child to a place of grace. But this was a mysticism that Marx would

Weekly Payments! Weekly Payments!

KELLY'S

S. E. Cor. Twelfth and Market Streets.

Improvements are all completed, and we are now ready to show to our patrons and others one of the largest and best selected stock of

DRY GOODS, CARPETS, FURNITURE, OIL CLOTHS, CLOTHING, HATS and CAPS, BOOTS and SHOES,

and novelties, ever before brought to the notice of the public

Make no mistake, it is the same corner, the same Kelly and the business is still conducted upon the same satisfactory plan that has characterized the firm for so many years.

Step in and examine before purchasing elsewhere, no trouble to show goods. Open until 10 P. M.

A. KELLY,

S. E. Corner Twelfth & Market Sts., & 1714 South St.

48. Kelly's store souvenir (front), ca. 1875.

THE CHILDREN PRAYING.

ANSWER TO PRAYER.

ANNIE AND WILLIE'S PRAYER.

A CHRISTMAS STORY.

[BY SOPHIA P. SNOW.]

'Twas the eve before Christmas; "Good-night" had been said,
And Annie and Willie had crept into bed:
There were tears on their pillows, and tears in their eyes,
And each little bosom was heavy with sighs,
For to-night their stern father's command had been given
That they must retire precisely at seven
Instead of eight for they troubled him more
With questions unheard of than ever before.
He told them he thought this delusion a sin,
No such a thing as "Santa Claus" ever had been,
And he hoped, after this, he should never more hear
How he scrambled down chimneys with presents each year.
And this is the reason why two little heads
So restlessly tossed on their soft, downy beds.

Eight, nine, and the clock on the steeple tolled ten—
Not a word had been spoken by either till then:
When Willie's sad face from the blanket did peep,
And whispered, "Dear Annie is you fast asleep?"
"Why, no, brother Willie," a sweet voice replies,
"I've tried in vain, but I can't shut my eyes;
For somehow it makes me so sorry because
Dear papa had said there is no 'Santa Claus;'
Now *we* know there is, and it can't be denied,
For he came every year before mamma died;
But then I've been thinking that she used to pray,
And God would hear everything mamma would say,
And perhaps she asked him to send Santa Claus here
With the sacks full of presents he brought every year."
"Well, why tan't we p'ay dest as mamma did then,
And ask him to send him with presents aden?"
"I've been thinking so, too," and without a word more
Four bare little feet bounded out on the floor,
And four little knees the soft carpet pressed,
And two tiny hands were clasped close to each breast.

"Now, Willie, you know we must firmly believe
That the presents we ask for we're sure to receive,
You must wait just as still till I say amen,
And by that you will know that your turn has come then.—
Dear Jesus, look down on my brother and me,
And grant us the favor we're asking of thee:
I want a nice book full of pictures, a ring,
A writing desk, too, that shuts with a spring.
Bless papa, dear Jesus, and cause him to see
That Santa Claus loves us as much even as he;
Don't let him get fretful and angry again
At dear brother Willie and Annie, amen!"
"Please, Desus, 'et Santa Taus tome down to-night,
And bring us some presents before it is 'ight.
I want he sould dive me a bright little box,
Full o' ac'obats, some other nice blocks,
And a bag full of tandy, a book, and a toy,
Amen, and then, Desus, I'll be a dood boy."
Their prayers being ended, they raised up their heads,
And with hearts light and cheerful again sought their beds;
They were soon lost in slumber—both peaceful and deep,
And with fairies in dream-land were roaming in sleep.

Eight, nine, and the little French clock had struck ten
Ere the father had thought of his children again:
He seems now to hear Annie's half-smothered sighs,
And to see the big tears standing in Willie's blue eyes.
"I was harsh with my darlings," he mentally said,
"And should I not have sent them so early to bed:
But when I was troubled—my feelings found vent,
For bank stock to-day has gone down ten per cent.
But of course they've forgot their troubles ere this,
But then I denied them the thrice asked-for kiss;
But just to make sure I'll steal up to their door,
For I never spoke harsh to my darlings before."

So saying he softly ascended the stairs,
And arriving at their door heard both of their prayers.
His Annie's "bless papa" draws forth the big tears,
And Willie's grave promise falls sweet on his ears.
"Strange, strange, I've forgotten," said he, with a sigh,
"How I longed when a child to have Christmas draw nigh.
I'll atone for my harshness," he inwardly said,
"By answering their prayers, ere I sleep in my bed."

Then he turned to the stairs and softly went down,
Threw off velvet slippers and silk dressing-gown,
Donned hat, coat, and boots, and was out in the street—
A millionaire facing the cold winter sleet;
He first went to a wonderful "Santa Claus" store
(He knew it, for he'd passed it the day before),
And there he found *crowds* on the same errand as he,
Making purchase of presents, with glad heart and free,
So, stepped he until he had bought everything
From a box full of candy to a tiny gold ring.
Indeed, he kept adding so much to his store
That the various presents outnumbered a score!
Then homeward he turned with his holiday load,
And with Aunt Mary's aid in the nursery 'twas stowed.
Miss Dolly was seated beneath a pine tree,
By the side of a table spread out for a tea;
A writing desk then in the centre was laid,
And on it a ring for which Annie had prayed;
Four acrobats painted in yellow and red
Stood with a block house on a beautiful sled;
There were balls, dogs and horses, books pleasing to see,
And birds of all colors were perched in the tree;
While Santa Claus, laughing, stood up in the top,
As if getting ready for more presents to drop;
And as the fond father the picture surveyed
He thought for his trouble he had amply been paid;
And he said to himself as he brushed off a tear,
"I'm happier to-night than I have been for a year.
I've enjoyed more true pleasure than ever before.
What care I if bank stock falls ten per cent. more?
Hereafter I'll make it a rule, I believe,
To have Santa Claus visit us each Christmas eve."

So thinking he gently extinguished the light,
And tripped down stairs to retire for the night.
As soon as the beams of the bright morning sun
Put the darkness to flight and the stars one by one,
Four little blue eyes out of sleep opened wide,
And at the same moment the presents espied.
Then out of their beds they sprang with a bound,
And the very gifts prayed for were all of them found;
They laughed and they cried in their innocent glee,
And shouted for papa to come quick and see
What presents old Santa Claus had brought in the night
(Just the things they had wanted) and left before light.

"And now," said Annie, in a voice soft and low,
"You'll believe there's a Santa Claus, papa, I know;"
While dear little Willie climbed up on his knee,
Determined no secret between them should be;
And told, in soft whispers, how Annie had said,
That their dear, blessed mamma, so long ago dead,
Used to kneel down and pray by the side of her chair,
And that God, up in heaven, had answered her prayer!
"Then we dot up and prayed dust as well as we tould,
And Dod answered our prayers: now wasn't he dood?"
"I should say that he was if he sent you all these,
And knew just what presents my children would please
(Well, well, let him think so, the dear little elf,
'Twould be cruel to tell him I did it myself)."

Blind father! who caused your stern heart to relent?
And the hasty word spoken so soon to repent?
'Twas the Being who bade you steal softly up-stairs,
And made you his agent to answer their prayers.

49. "Annie and Willie's Prayer," Kelly's store souvenir (back), ca. 1875.

50. "Dear Santa Claus," Louis Prang Christmas card, 1888.

51. "He Prayed," from Thomas Nast, *Thomas Nast's Christmas Drawings for the Human Race* (New York: Harper and Brothers, 1890), unpaginated.

52. "Christmas-Eve—Getting Ready for Santa Claus," *Harper's Weekly*, 30 December 1876, 1052.

53. "Where Santa Claus Lives," Christmas 1900.

have recognized; as *Playthings* confessed, Santa Claus was "the best advertised man in the whole world" and "to neglect this ready-at-hand advertising would be poor business anywhere." From the first uses of St. Nicholas and Kris Kringle as merchandising tools in the 1830s and 1840s, Santa Claus had become the guiding spirit of the Christmas bazaar, a stock device, who seemed no less alluring and enchanting for his tireless employment. From a figure of nearly endless variety and not a little monstrosity, he had become a tailored, predictable presence—a magical peddler who had pulled his superabundant cart into the department store, where he was enthroned and crowned.[67]

The modern Christmas bazaar continued to expand in the twentieth century, ceaselessly broadening its festal repertory. Santa Claus's presence in the marketplace, for example, would grow still larger as the marshal of innumerable department store–sponsored parades. Gimbel's famous holiday parade, with Santa Claus presiding, was inaugurated in Philadelphia in 1920, Hudson's in Detroit in 1923, and Macy's in New York in 1924, but there were a fair number of precursors and an even larger number of imitators. In this way, department stores increasingly took over the domain of the street festival and the street fair, colonizing the mummers' world and working-class celebrations with their own spectacles that were eventually staged more for the con-

54. Department-store Santa Claus, ca. 1930.

55. Robert L. May, *Rudolph the Red-Nosed Reindeer*, Montgomery Ward store souvenir, 1939.

sumption of television audiences than for the folks on the avenues.[68] St. Nick's image would continue to be standardized through special "schools" for department-store Santa Clauses, which began appearing in the 1930s, where everything about Santa would be subject to rationalization—the precise pattern of his costume, the correct application of prescribed cosmetics, the appropriate form for his gestures, and the etiquette of his interaction with children and parents.[69] In the Christmas emporium of the twentieth century, Santa Claus would also have increasing company from such new mythic creations as Rudolph the Red-Nosed Reindeer, introduced in a store souvenir from Montgomery Ward for the holidays in 1939. A whimsical children's story in the classic fairy-tale form of the ugly duckling, Rudolph took shape in the advertising studios of the commercial culture, but quickly moved out of them into the wider culture, becoming a popular emblem of the modern American Christmas. The story remains a prime example of the capacity of the commercial culture to generate modern folklore or "folklure."[70]

Still, whatever innovations came in the twentieth century, most of the pattern of the modern Christmas bazaar had been set by the end of the nineteenth century. That Rudolph began his career as a store souvenir in the tradition of holiday trade cards underlines this. By the turn of the century, Christmas already outstripped all other events as a time for merchandising. "On this occasion, above all others," *Advertising World* advised matter-of-factly in 1899, "do not stint the advertising appropriation."[71] Christmas promotions were everywhere evident—in show windows, mass periodicals, newspapers, and special holiday catalogues.[72] Indeed, Christmas advertising was so pervasive that *Advertising World* marveled that "there is scarcely any sort of store that does not make a special effort to capture Christmas trade." In a market philosophy organized on the guiding principle of growth, every year Christmas advertising was said to get "bigger and better," and seemingly the only question that remained was how early in November to begin the blitz. The *Dry Goods Economist* candidly noted in 1902 that many retailers considered 15 November or even 1 November "none too early" to open the "Holiday Campaign."[73] The *Merchants Record and Show Window* summed up commercial rejoicing over the celebration in 1908: "Christmas is the merchant's harvest time, and it is up to him to garner in as big a crop of dollars as he can." The new Christmas bazaar, born in the early decades of the nineteenth century, had reached a vigorous maturity by century's end. It had become "the great shopping carnival," a giant fair for commercial experimentation and contrivance.[74]

SHOPPING TOWARDS BETHLEHEM: WOMEN AND THE VICTORIAN CHRISTMAS

The new Christmas bazaar was a spectacle that drew people to its theatrical displays, festive excitement, and myriad gifts. Just as crowds of shoppers stop to admire Lord and Taylor's Christmas windows in New York City today, people flocked to see the urban Christmas a century ago—the holiday charm, mechanical sophistication, and sheer grandeur of the decorations as well as the plethora of gifts and goods. But one needs to go beneath this surface impression of allure, attraction, and enchantment to see how this new commercial Christmas played out in people's lives. The question is not only what merchants created through their displays and advertisements, but also how people responded to and received this new Christmas. Commercial efforts to expand the Christmas market and to reimagine the celebration are of obvious importance, but equally crucial are consumer perspectives. If harder to uncover than the public ballyhoo of merchants, these views, especially those of urban women who led the way as purchasers and preparers of Christmas gifts, must be sought out in the private recollections contained in diaries, letters, and family papers.

The diary of Elizabeth Powell is a good place to begin. She recorded in detail the holiday activities in which she participated in Louisiana in 1856 and then in the San Francisco area in 1868 and 1873, and something of the larger middle-class transformation of Christmas is helpfully condensed in these entries. Her first detailed account of Christmas, penned when she was working as a governess for a family near New Orleans, captured a jovial and raucous celebration, full of eating, dancing, and drinking. At a large outdoor feast on Christmas Day, celebrants sated themselves on hams, chicken pies, mince pies, biscuits, turnips, cakes, bread, and candy—all in "great abundance." The festivities continued on 26 December with a big dance, shared in by whites and blacks alike. She herself found the reels, jigs, and banjo music "so inspiring that it seemed as though I *must* get up and dance." The conviviality was patent: "After [Uncle Cooper] had had plenty of whiskey, he lost his religious scruples and made his feet fly as fast as any of them. Uncle Lorenzo also danced, and one of the men from Mr Metcalf's danced a jig with a tumbler of water on his head. The whole scene was very amusing and the way they bumped and thumped against each other was comical in the extreme." Gift exchanges, though confined mostly to little homemade presents, were not entirely absent from her account. For example, she received a stocking "full of candy and raisins," "a piece of patchwork," and rather inscrutably "three grains of corn" from Uncle Perry. Yet in comparison to the grandness of the feasting and the dancing, these were strikingly simple gifts.[75]

Christmas had changed for Powell by 1868; the gifts had become more elaborate, and the celebration had moved indoors to the parlor. Now living and teaching near San Francisco, Powell received on Christmas morning a "cornucopia" of presents—"a cross in a straw frame from Eddie, a wee needle-book from Leulu, and an ivory broach from them both; it is a sheaf of wheat most exquisitely carved and is very beautiful; it must be worth at least $12.00." Suggesting her enchantment with this new Christmas, she continued, "We were all up and down stairs before day-light to see the presents; the parlor was filled with beautiful things." What captured her imagination now was not dancing and singing, but a parlor resplendent with pretty gifts. Powell's third description of Christmas, this one from 1873, underlined her transition to a holiday focused on domestic, feminized gift giving: "My Christmas gift from Miss Baker was a lovely watch-case made of blue velvet and white-beads. Leulu Ogden gave me a glove box made of a rare and very fragrant wood which grows in some of the mountains of Mexico. Mrs Rutherford gave me a tattling collar; Miss Abby Hardwick, a pretty hair-pin cushion; and I am to have two other presents, but I don't know what they are." The sensuousness of the gifts—the appearance, the color, and the smell—was described in fond detail; before it, any other holiday activities seemed to pale. For Powell, Christmas had become a web of gifts, exchanged mostly with other women, a domestic event, a social ritual of the parlor, a potpourri of "beautiful things."[76]

While Powell's diary aptly captures both the changes and the satisfactions that this new Christmas entailed, it reveals little about the ritual that was the necessary prologue to all this domestic gift giving: shopping. As an activity, holiday shopping expanded dramatically after the middle of the century. Through the 1840s and 1850s the pleasures of the Christmas marketplace attracted people's attention for only a couple of days before the holiday. For example, the Philadelphian William Mactier found some time in the 1840s for Christmas shopping and browsing in the day or two before the holiday, even though in good Presbyterian fashion he regularly worked on Christmas morning itself before coming home to a large family dinner. It was only on Christmas Eve that the varied scenes of the holiday bazaar really caught his eye: "The streets are full of shoppers and pleasure-seekers," he fondly observed in his diary on Christmas Eve in 1847. "Every body appears in the *qui vive*." Similarly, Caroline Dunstan, a New York City woman, typically took care of her Christmas shopping in the 1850s in a trip or two on or around Christmas Eve. In 1856, she visited a toy shop on 23 December to buy "cups & saucers & table" for her daughter, and in the afternoon on 24 December she went to a religious bookstore or "Bible house" for one gift and to a dry-goods store for three final gifts—rubber boots, gloves, and some muslin. In 1860 she was at A. T. Stewart's giant emporium on 21 December and was out shopping again on Christmas Eve, but that was about the sum of her absorption. A number of gifts were exchanged in the Dunstan household, and stockings were filled, but Christmas shopping was not an activity of much note in itself, certainly not something that went on for most of the month.[77]

The late-nineteenth- and early-twentieth-century diaries of two New York City women, Clara Pardee and Elizabeth Merchant, are good places to see the expanding role of Christmas shopping in people's lives. Affluent and urban, both women participated wholeheartedly in the new Christmas, and both left extensive records over several decades of their day-to-day activities. After midcentury, women emerged more and more clearly as the superintendents of Christmas gift giving and the primary holiday shoppers, so the diaries of Clara Pardee and Elizabeth Merchant, far more than the diaries of their male counterparts in the same decades, help reveal the place of the Christmas bazaar within the bright fabric of popular holiday observance. Their diaries offer valuable glimpses into the female worlds of shopping and holidays—the pleasures and travails of these newly conjoined rituals of home and marketplace.

Elizabeth Merchant's diary spans the decades from 1863 to 1909. Begun two years after her marriage and the year her first child was born, the diary covers the full range of her family life. In the 1860s, Christmas was already an important occasion in the Merchant household. In 1864 Christmas shopping began for her on 19 December: "Alice and I went shopping for Christmas. Very busy! I shall be so all the week." By 23 December, she was almost ready for the big day: "About finished up the Christmas shopping. Have had a busy week of it." In 1868, she was out Christmas shopping by 14 December at A. T. Stewart's and also took daylong shopping trips downtown on 17, 19, 22, and 24 December. By 1872, she was already out "looking for Xmas presents" on 12 December and repeated the excursion four more times before the 25th. By 1883, she had moved the start of her Christmas shopping trips back to 3 December, and preparations in sending Christmas cards, shopping, decorating, and getting food and presents together went on for most of the month. Indeed, in 1883 she made specific mention of Christmas preparations in her generally spare diary entries on nine days between 3 and 24 December. In 1892, she again began Christmas shopping on 3 December, even though the family had left New York and relocated to Duluth, and she mentioned specific preparations on ten separate days leading up to Christmas.[78]

The holiday season had greatly expanded for Elizabeth Merchant between 1864 and 1892, but the development was not unilinear. In some years when the family's fortunes were down, such as in 1866 and 1873, there were few presents, and she curtailed almost all her shopping, buying only some small gifts for the children. The family's financial situation was troubled again in the mid-1890s, and after her husband's death in 1901 Christmases were modest affairs spent with her son Huntington, her daughter-in-law, and her grandchildren. Despite these vicissitudes and the clear fluctuations of the life cycle, the overall trend remained clear in Merchant's diary. The Christmas season lengthened over the course of her life. Shopping for presents grew in importance, becoming a more absorbing and time-consuming activity—one that she found both pleasurable and tiring.

The diary of Clara Pardee, while suggesting a similar pattern, reveals more expressly the joys a middle-class woman could find in Christmas shopping. Spanning the years from 1883 to 1938, the diary offers a helpful, if laconic, chronicle of Pardee's holiday rituals. There was a great deal of excitement and energy for her in the two weeks before Christmas as she went downtown repeatedly to shop, browse, and admire. For 15 December 1885, she commented: "Down town all the morning for Xmas . . . & went down town again in afternoon[,] a regular gad about all day." Though she often went home exhausted or felt "rushed to death," she was clearly pleased to be out of the house day after day and to be so engaged in holiday preparations. Her Christmas activities for 1893 were both typical and revealing:

> December 12 Went down town looking for Xmas
>
> December 13 Out to market & then down town & again in afternoon. everything is gay for Christmas.
>
> December 14 Out to market & down town until lunch time.
>
> December 18 Out to market & thence down town morning, afternoon & in evening to Bloomingdales.
>
> December 19 Out shopping to finish up in afternoon. . . . Am dead tired tonight.
>
> December 20 Out to market then took Harold, Gertrude & May down town to see Xmas. . . . Fixed my gifts in afternoon.
>
> December 21 Went out with sister "a Christmasing." Ensign [her husband] and I went up 8th Ave for stocking treasures.
>
> December 22 With sister down town for a few more errands.
>
> December 23 Out on errands until lunch time. . . . Out with Ensign in the evening for Christmas.
>
> December 24 Went to church after taking a short nap. Went to Sunday School in afternoon & trimmed tree, house &c &c in evening—dead tired but ready for Xmas.
>
> December 25 Had a royal good time all day especially the little ones. All had fine presents too. I got silver tea kettle & lovely sofa pillow & bureau set, gloves, after dinner coffees, powder box &c &c—the tree was fine, the dinner good & all happy.

This series of holiday rituals was repeated from year to year, and Christmas shopping was always an absorbing part of Clara Pardee's life.[79]

For Pardee, Christmas had become in many ways synonymous with shopping and presents. To go "a Christmasing" was in her diary an expression for going downtown to shop; for her, to take in all the "Xmas sights" meant to see all the festive decorations of the New York department stores. On 8 December 1894, for example, she noted with typical phrasing that she headed out "with the children for Macy's to see 'Christmas.'" The next year, when she took her son Harold shopping with her for Christmas presents, she noted that he "saw all the Christmas he could." Though a regular churchgoer (it was a matter of note to her when one of her children missed Sunday school for the first time in eight years), Pardee had come to experience the holiday largely in terms of shopping and gifts. At Christmas 1895, she commented with clear satisfaction on the Christmas she had orchestrated: "So many presents we could not count them & all so happy, so merry & so well. I had 13 presents & I cannot tell how many the Babes had." Pardee's Christmas took most of its form and meaning from the overlapping holiday rituals of home and marketplace.[80]

For Pardee and Merchant, as for so many others, Christmas shopping drew its power, warmth, and excitement from the Victorian enshrinement of the family at the center of the holiday's celebration. Christmas, as William Mactier noted in his diary in 1858, was "quite a family party." Time and again people recorded little scenes of domestic ritual at Christmas that were pleasing and sometimes poignant. One woman wrote in a memory book for her young son on Christmas Eve 1864: "'Tis the night before Christmas'—This favorite piece your Father reads to you every Christmas Eve and you enjoy it very much."[81] Another woman observed that her daughter was on Christmas Day "almost wild with joy and her presents."[82] Similarly, for Christmas 1867 Merchant said that the "children were crazy with delight" upon receiving their stockings and presents and that by the end of the day they were simply exhausted from "so much happiness." In 1885 Merchant's teenage son Huntington climbed into his parents' bed on Christmas morning and "opened his stocking"; in 1888, she observed with obvious warmth and affection that Huntington, home from Princeton for the holidays, "came down & opened his stocking on my bed, as he has always done."[83] These little moments of familial ritual and gift giving were at the heart of the middle-class Christmas. Nineteenth-century folks did not need anthropologists to make evident to them this special economy of gift exchange: The rituals of Christmas gift giving took their meaning from both the strength and the fragility of familial relationships, from both their durability and their impermanence.[84]

At the center of these new familial rituals stood the Christmas tree. With gifts sometimes hung on it and sometimes placed underneath, the Christmas tree flourished as a cherished emblem of seasonal cheer. As a focus for familial festivities and for the profuse display of ornaments and presents, the tree often stood out as the pièce de résistance in this domestic festival. A New York woman, Helen Grinnell, gave some sense of the wonder of the Victorian Christmas tree and its centrality to the familial ritual of giving and receiving presents in a diary entry for Christmas 1860:

> I have had the billiard room dressed with greens and a pretty tree placed in the bay window. . . . We hung all our gifts upon it accounting to about sixty, all labeled for distribution: the billiard table was covered with a fine white tablecloth and all the largest presents arranged on it; our friends arrived from town at three o'c at which time we collected them in the drawing room, and after turning the gas on suddenly at the metre, the darkened rooms were brilliantly lighted, the sliding

> doors thrown back, exposing to our view the lighted tree: it was certainly a beautiful sight, and a group of happy faces. The presents were passed around. The children were quiet, until they rec'd theirs, and then shouts of mirth, and glee filled the room.

In women's creative staging of the holiday drama in the home, the tree stood at the center as a unifying symbol of familial connection, happiness, and wholeness.[85]

Fundamental to these domestic rites were the affectionate, indulgent games parents and children shared. Tucked away in the back of Clara Pardee's diary for 1899 were her children's Christmas lists, addressed to Santa Claus at the North Pole. Gertrude's Christmas wishes ran through eighteen things, and Irving's through nineteen. Gertrude hoped for "a lot of little dolls," a ring, a bracelet, a sled, skates, pencils, and "a big, big box of candy," among other things. For his part, Irving wished for "a box of soldiers," a cap pistol, a train, a fishing rod, "Fun with magnetism," "Fun with soap bubbles," and also "a big, big box of candy." Their mother took obvious pleasure in drawing up these lists and in fulfilling her children's holiday fancies by playing the role of Santa Claus in their lives, a gift giver who provided presents without the expectation of material reciprocation. In her diary for 1899, Pardee delighted in her children's jubilation, especially her daughter's. "Children had *oceans*," she noted, "Gertrude 32 *dolls* and everything else in proportion." For Pardee, the Christmas bond remained particularly strong with her daughter; years later, with her grandchildren in mind, she would take great pleasure in shopping with Gertrude. They often went out together to see the "lovely stores" and "lots of Christmas," coming home with "bundles." These were the new Christmas rituals, shared in by parents and children, and passed especially from mother to daughter—the lists for Santa Claus, the trips to see him in the stores, the stuffed stockings, the carefully wrapped presents, and the culminating scenes of Christmas morning.[86]

In Pardee's diary, as in those of Grinnell and Merchant, the new pleasures and contentments of holiday shopping and gift giving—the allures of the Christmas marketplace and the fulfillments of Christmas Day—are quite evident. But a fair amount of ambivalence toward the new versions of the holiday was also apparent, and these qualms need to be considered. By the 1840s, William Mactier had already suggested this essential ambivalence. In 1847, he happily affirmed the importance of sacrificial giving and the meaningfulness of Christmas gifts: "I have spent a good deal of money this Season for gifts, but the pleasure it gives me to remember my family and friends, compensates me for any self-denial the indulgence of this desire may cost me." Yet the very next

56. Girl with her toys, Christmas morning 1902.

year he sounded as if he was still trying to convince himself of the wisdom of these expanding customs of gift exchange. Having again overspent, Mactier struck a strikingly modern chord in his estimation of the holiday season: "To give is a greater pleasure than to receive and while I welcome the return of the Season, I rejoice that it comes but once in a twelvemonth!"[87]

Others sounded graver notes of weariness and wariness. One New Yorker, Marguerite Du Bois, gave expression to her frustration over Christmas in her diary entries about the holiday in 1907. On 18 December she noted in her diary, "Went down town . . . Shopped all afternoon. Such a crush in the stores. home late tired." On the 21st her spirits had sunk even lower: "Worked hard all day. Oh! this silly Christmas trash makes me tired."[88] Even Clara Pardee sometimes expressed exasperation with all her Christmas preparations. Shopping often exhausted her; she would sometimes come home "*so* tired" that she felt "utterly used up," distressed with the seeming interminableness of her shopping. One time after a Christmas excursion to Macy's in early December she remarked bitterly: "How I hate to shop." "Still shopping all day long," she wrote on 21 December 1904, "seems I will never get through." Another day, shopping yet again, she noted: "Such a busy day & children all crazy too & Ensign too. We always get so at Christmas." Sometimes amid the holiday rush there seemed little solace or contentment for Pardee, only burdensome responsibilities, an oppressive routine, a dispiriting search for Christmas things. Some years later, in 1938, cynicism had even crept into her ritual of sending Christmas cards: "I sent out cards—such a job—must give it up—Don't think people care enough about receiving them."[89]

Weariness at Christmas was not simply a problem for middle-class women as they hurried to complete their holiday preparations. It was even more the plight of salesclerks, who worked long holiday hours in the stores and who had little of the time or money for the holiday shopping of the middle class. A clerk at Tiffany's in the early 1870s found the whole season draining. In 1873 Tiffany's began its extended holiday hours on 8 December, and from then until Christmas this young man had to work at the store "day and evening." On 19 December he entered a typical refrain in his diary; the holiday season made for "very tiresome work." There was evidently not much more to say; the dominant notes for him were simply ones of labor and fatigue. The holiday spectacles looked a lot less exciting from the other side of the counter. For overworked salesclerks, the Christmas season carried not so much ambivalence as simple exhaustion.[90]

Misgiving and foreboding even crept into the seemingly happy domestic scenes of Christmas morning. As the rush of holiday shopping and preparation was supposed to come to fulfillment in familial celebration, many grew melancholy. During the holidays in 1858, one woman noted in her diary that "as these days come round our hearts are made Sad[;] we miss our loved Mother, now gone to her rest."[91] At Christmas in 1872 Elizabeth Orr, a widow, could think of little else than her own loneliness and the loss of her "beloved husband." "It is four long sad years of my widowhood," she wrote on Christmas Eve that year. "These days are sad indeed to me. I try to conceal my feelings for the sake of those I am with. I do not want to be selfish and sadden them with my own thoughts and feelings." On Christmas Day, she was again "saddened by reminiscence." Looking around her at Christmas, she concluded, "There are many sad hearts, as well as merry ones."[92] After the death of her young son Charlie, Elizabeth Merchant found Christmas especially painful; often she simply went through the motions, with all delight vanished. "Am so thankful my Christmas work is over. It has become a duty now, instead of a pleasure; as it used to be when I had precious Charlie with me." On 26 December, she awoke "with the thought of our 'Merry Christmas' two years ago & the bright face & sweet voice of my darling."[93] Or, as another woman remarked succinctly in her diary in 1910: "What is Christmas without Grandma."[94] Having been recast as a festival of familial warmth and wholeness, the holiday became a painful reminder of familial loss and brokenness. This was the great and unsettling tragedy of the modern Christmas: It moved people away from the resources of community celebration and the raucous conviviality of the streets into the wonderful snugness of the home, but then when family ties failed or were broken by death, there was often little joy left in the festival, and much pain.

Another source of unhappiness at Christmas, the fitful dissatisfaction that often plagues the modern consumer, had more superficiality about it than poignancy. Take, for example, the holiday memory of Florence Peck, a schoolgirl from Rochester, New York, who wrote in her diary for Christmas 1898: "We always have a lovely Christmas. I don't think there is any use writting down all the things given me but just say that every body was lovely to me and I had everything I wanted except my gold watch."[95] The passage is suggestive. The only gift she specifically mentions is the one she did not receive. She takes much satisfaction in the things she did get, but perhaps more noteworthy is the tinge of disappointment, that tincture of unmet desire so characteristic of the consumer culture. Christmas lacks fulfillment because of a gold watch that eludes her. Similarly, another teenage girl, the highly affluent Grace Ashmore, displayed a similar attitude in her accustomed tallying of her presents. For Christmas 1901 she wrote, "All the children were delighted with their presents and so was I. . . . I got 23." As she enumerated one Christmas, "My presents were—a beautiful ring, five sapphires surrounded by diamond, a very pretty piece of Dutch silver in the shape of a heart. . . ." The list ran on and on. In 1899 she received a particularly large number of holiday gifts, which she listed at length in her diary, but her summary comment was most telling. "In all I got 30. Marie Van L. got over 70." Already somewhat jaded, Grace Ashmore sounds like Christopher Lasch's consumer in the making—"perpetually unsatisfied, restless, anxious, and bored." She is a child of Thorstein Veblen's leisure class in which goods, and even gifts, seem as much about social comparison as about cherished, meaning-laden exchanges among loving family members. At such moments, Lévi-Strauss's wry, sweeping remark that the contemporary Christmas was a modern version of the potlatch—that is, a system of hierarchic, competitive, conspicuous exchanges in the pursuit of prestige—actually finds some ethnographic resonance.[96]

Grace Ashmore's diary is revealing, too, for the place religion occupies in it. A Roman Catholic who regularly went to mass, she noted her church attendance at Christmas often as a brief appendage to her listing of presents. Phrases like "went to nine o'clock mass" or "went to high mass with Katie" follow seamlessly upon her compendiums of gifts.[97] Devotion was always part of the mix of her celebration, but its proportionate share in the holiday's concoction was hardly clear or straightforward. This tangled mix of piety and plenty was similarly apparent in Mary Knowlton's diary description of Christmas 1905. Her son John "took the part of S[an]ta Claus" and handed out the various presents from around the well-trimmed tree. "He acted his part well," she said, "and made the ceremony merry." Then she added without pause: "Christmas is the day, above every other day in the year to be celebrated, when Christ our blessed Saviour was born a babe in Bethlehem and knew all that was to come, to secure eternal life to a sinful world. Presents have been well distributed by the members of the different families."[98] A reiteration of Christian faith is sandwiched in the middle of her account of these cheery familial scenes of a Santa Claus masquerade. What is plain from the diaries of Ashmore, Knowlton, and others is that the relationship of Christianity to these new holiday rites of home and marketplace was intricate, woven one way and then another in an elaborate pastiche.

Of the various modalities in this relationship, one was clearly displacement. Often there seemed little room left for religious reflection or observance amid the bustle of holiday arrangements. For Clara Pardee, for example, the theater of the stores and the joy of familial gifts captured almost all her attention and imagination. Though she and her children were regularly drawn to the holiday festivities in the Sunday schools, these activities occasioned comparably small notations alongside the lists of stores she had visited, her cataloguing of holiday presents, and her close attention to her children's Christmas wishes. A

New York girl, Nellie Wetherbee, suggested in her diary entry for the holiday in 1860 how religious language could become little more than a benediction upon festal abundance: "Christmas day—My package came from home—how delighted I was. All so nice. & in my stocking came some diamonds. Helen & I got up in our nightys & looked in our stockings & had some fun. My set & all are *very* handsome, & I thank God for all His mercies."[99] A child's eager anticipation of gifts, along with the pleasures of holiday shopping, emerged as the greatest blessings the modern holiday could bestow. "The chief delight of Christmas is the happiness of the children," *Harper's* concluded in 1868; "the next is the Christmas shopping."[100] Holiday presents and packages were God's mercies, and Santa Claus, in particular, was the bearer and vehicle of these graces. Thus, one of the relationships of Christianity to the new Christmas bazaar was this: The rituals of home and marketplace competed with church-centered celebrations. Shopping and gift giving were, in fair measure, secular liturgies, representing a new kind of middle-class faith in family and abundance—a faith that showed a striking capacity both to absorb Christianity and to supplant it.

CHRISTMAS CATHEDRALS: WANAMAKER'S AND THE CONSECRATION OF THE MARKETPLACE

All was not displacement, competition, and secularism, however. Diaries, such as those of Grace Ashmore and Mary Knowlton, regularly offered religious notes. These cursory remarks did not have the system of a catechism or the order of a three-part sermon; they were instead religious fragments and traces from the quotidian experience of the holiday. Middle-class Victorian women regularly integrated Christian piety into the quite material world of the home and into holiday rituals that revolved around shopping and family. The Christmas emporium itself was not necessarily secular, and there emerged in the late nineteenth and early twentieth centuries an increasingly close fit, however incongruous and paradoxical, between Christmas shopping and Christian symbols. At Christmas (and also at Easter) there would be no clear line between church and mart, between the sacred and the secular. Indeed, the marketplace itself would often be stunningly consecrated, and nowhere would this hallowing be more evident than in the Christmas cathedrals of the department stores, especially those of John Wanamaker's Philadelphia store.[101]

The burgeoning department stores of the Gilded Age inherited from the museums, toy shops, coffeehouses, and confectionery establishments of ear-

57. "New York City—a Holiday Spectacle—the Show Window of Macy & Co., Corner of Sixth Avenue and Fourteenth Street," *Frank Leslie's Illustrated Newspaper*, 20 December 1884, 284.

lier decades a penchant for holiday spectacle, and soon learned to improve on antebellum experiments. Just as they took the embryonic experiments with Santa Claus and turned him into a sine qua non of Christmas Toylands, the department stores transformed the relatively small-scale decorations of antebellum shopkeepers into a monumental system of holiday exhibition. Of Lord and Taylor's Broadway store in 1874, the *New-York Tribune* commented, for example: "The store makes a great holiday display. Christmas trees, garlands of green and bunting adorn the spaces of which Santa Claus is patron saint, while music and pleasant scents fill the air." Similarly, Christmas for Macy's was a decorative marvel from the store's opening in 1858. By the mid-1870s, Macy's Christmas windows were "one of the 'institutions' of the season," attracting such a "throng of sightseers" that the surrounding sidewalks were often all but impassable. The store's holiday windows were especially famed for their "pretty *tableaux*" of dolls, with each year's display intended to outshine the previous year's exhibit. In one window in 1874, for instance, designers presented "a doll's croquet party," and all "the miniature men and women" were finely appointed to the last accessory. In another window the same year, Macy's decorators concocted "a sprightly masquerade," again with "marvelously attired" dolls serving, in effect, as mannequins. In 1883 the store added mechanical fascination to its Christmas windows, turning dolls and toys into "moving figures" through steam power. Department-store trade journals soon digested these decorative wonders into compact retailing advice for stores across the country. As the *Dry Goods Chronicle* exhorted for Christmas 1895, "Fit up your place as it was never fitted before. Dress it in evergreens and bright colors. Make your store such an inviting bower of Christmas loveliness that people cannot stay away."[102]

The department stores were always decidedly eclectic in their Christmas displays, creating an ever-shifting montage of holiday fantasies. In 1894, for example, Macy's created thirteen different tableaus, ranging from Gulliver's Travels to Sinbad the Sailor, from Jack and the Beanstalk to King Solomon and the Queen of Sheba.[103] As with the museums, a guiding principle of department-store display was the more exotic, the better. But at Christmas and Easter, traditionalism often matched exoticism. At these high days of the Christian year, the department stores regularly turned to Christianity for many of their grandest effects. With pipe organs, choirs, religious paintings and banners, statues of saints and angels, stained glass, floral emblems of anchors and crosses, miniature churches, and Nativity scenes, the stores often brimmed with Christian figures and symbols. *Printers' Ink*, for example, ran this telling evaluation, "New York Holiday Windows," in 1898:

> The prettiest and most dainty window display this season is in O'Neill's department store on Sixth Avenue. It is a model of a church and the title is "Christmas Eve." The church is probably ten feet long by four feet high, with a tower at either end and a large arched entrance in the center. The ground and the buildings are covered with snow, while the lights within stream through the stained glass windows and give a beautiful effect. But the wonderful part of the show is that the church is entirely built of lace handkerchiefs.

In such revealing juxtapositions—a church built out of a commodity to help sell it and other commodities at Christmas—one sees the subtle, evocative power of religious symbolism in the holiday marketplace. Religious symbols hallowed and mystified Christmas gift giving; such displays bathed both the stores and holiday shopping in the reflected glory of Christianity.[104]

With the hermeneutics of suspicion that operates among academics almost like a reflex, it would be easy to go about "unmasking" such displays. But these tantalizing shows deserve something more than a disbelieving glare, perhaps something more akin to the leisurely gaze of the window-shopper. And there is no better place to linger than in Wanamaker's in Philadelphia, where the celebration of Christmas long stood out as a revelatory mix of religion, community, and commerce. For John Wanamaker, Presbyterian builder of Sunday schools and bankroller of various Christian causes, his stores were simply his loftiest temples, the commercial counterpart of his longtime involvement in the Young Men's Christian Association. In a letter written in 1881, he referred to his stores as "a pulpit for me," and he would always see them as places of moral uplift and education as well as profit. Having gone into business in Philadelphia in 1861 as a clothier, Wanamaker opened his Grand Depot in 1876 and continued to expand his enterprise over the next several decades. He purchased A. T. Stewart's dry-goods palace in New York in 1896 and opened his new Philadelphia emporium in 1911—a twelve-story landmark with an immense Grand Court. As one of the most influential and powerful merchants of his day, Wanamaker was rarely outdone, and at Christmas he kept up a formidable flow of store souvenirs, gift catalogues, newspaper advertisements, trade cards, window decorations, musical concerts, Santa Claus stunts, and other holiday entertainments.[105]

But Wanamaker's Christmas really came together in the Grand Court of his Philadelphia store. At Christmas, he transformed this capacious interior into a church, establishing a tradition of religious celebration in his store in the 1910s and early 1920s that would long outlive him (he died in 1922). Graced with what was then the largest pipe organ in the world, the Grand Court had a head start on other stores in creating the ambience of a cathedral. Wanamaker's built on this advantage through the establishment of caroling and hymn-sings as a store tradition, sing-alongs that were usually conducted twice a day during the holiday season. (The store had its own musical director for planning its varied concert programs, including its Christmas performances.) To facilitate the carol singing, the store began in the late 1910s to print up its own Christmas hymnals for use by its customers, offering a new edition each year through at least the 1950s. Religious offerings—such as "O Come All Ye Faithful," "Hark! the Herald Angels Sing," and "All Hail the Power of Jesus' Name"—predominated over merely seasonal selections. The carol books often carried a prayerful message from John Wanamaker himself. (Two volumes of his religious writings were collected and published posthumously.) "No day ever equalled the birthday of Mary's Son in the stable of the little inn at Bethlehem," one of Wanamaker's typical Christmas messages read. "To get right with Christmas would make men right with one another, nation with nation, and put . . . right this old world, almost falling to pieces." During the holidays people did not just shop at Wanamaker's; they received devotional reminders and religious encouragement. And this was a congregation as large as any mega-church: as many as fourteen thousand people crowded into the Grand

58. John Wanamaker family, Christmas 1900.

Court and the galleries surrounding it to take in the biggest holiday programs on Christmas Eve.[106]

Beyond the caroling, the interior decorations of the Grand Court made for a spectacle of spirituality. To be certain that no one missed any of the layers of religious symbolism, the store always provided a detailed key to the decorations, and, given the intricacy of the pageant, the guide was something of a necessity. In 1925, for example, there were twelve-pointed stars symbolizing the apostles, golden candlesticks signifying the Seven Churches of Asia, flags of the Crusades, statues of heralding angels, and giant tapestries of the Three Wise Men and the Holy Family. In 1932, even more decorations had been added to the Grand Court, including wood carvings of the apostles, cathedral vaulting made of greenery, and a monumental re-creation of a rose window from Westminster Abbey. Almost always the Adoration of the Magi was a featured motif in a tapestry, painting, or banner; as the archetypal gift givers, the Wise Men offered crucial religious symbols for the marketplace. The Nativity itself, however, remained the centerpiece of Wanamaker's Christmas cathedral, often spotlighted with a beam of light that looked as if it had come shining down from the heavens. These manger scenes commemorated God's

59. Wanamaker's Grand Court, Christmas 1928.

60. Wanamaker's Grand Court, Christmas 1932.

61. Wanamaker's Grand Court, Christmas 1934.

exalted gift to humanity, his only-begotten Son, and again the interplay between the divine gift and human gifts energized these displays: Christmas gifts provided a tangible vehicle for connecting with this sacred drama. Combining, as a store souvenir said in 1926, "the pomp of pageantry, the magic of color, the marvels of modern art, [and] the lore of classic and medieval symbolism," Wanamaker's Christmas cathedral was, indeed, a stunning spectacle. It was the Gothic revival brought to bear on store decoration.[107]

Not surprisingly, people often found these Christmas decorations awe-inspiring. Far from viewing them with suspicion or cynicism, Philadelphians looked on Wanamaker's Christmas cathedrals with a fair bit of amazement and even gratitude. Like nineteenth-century farmers who wrote to Montgomery Ward as if the mail-order house were part of the family, twentieth-century urban shoppers wrote to Wanamaker's as if in the Grand Court they had discovered a religious shrine. "Dear Friends," one woman wrote on the back of a Christmas card to Wanamaker's in 1950, "I certainly want to congratulate you on your Christmas Decorations. It made me feel that Christ my Lord and Savior was in the midst of it all." Another patron found in the store's "beautiful decorations honoring Jesus Christ" a glimpse of the ineffable; they were "beyond human expression."[108] Indeed, upon entering the Grand Court at Christmas, many men reportedly removed their hats in a gesture of instinctive reverence.[109] As one woman concluded in a thank-you note to Wanamaker's, "You have taken a big step in dispelling the fear that so many of us have these days—that of a completely commercialized Christmas. You have shone that it is possible to combine merchandising with a religious background. I feel sure that your Christmas Sales will not suffer because of your effort to bring a feeling (if not a reality) of Peace into the hearts of those who gaze upwards from your Grand court." (This woman's experience suggests that Wanamaker's designer Howard L. Kratz may have been on the mark when he noted that the Christmas cathedrals were intended to present the store as "above commercialism," while at the same time winning big results for the business.)[110] In these testimonial letters, it is evident that Christmas shopping in Wanamaker's was hardly a secular surrogate for religious observance. Instead the marketplace itself took on sacral qualities that fed on and reinforced the churches' celebrations. In Wanamaker's, Christianity was brought into the marketplace for praise and homage, and in turn, the Philadelphia store took on a peculiarly hallowed aura.

For all its medieval and Gothic grandeur, Christmas in the Grand Court offered a distinctly modern experience of religious community. Consider the letter of one man who noted in 1949 how visiting the department store had restored "the glow of Christmas" for him. In Wesleyan diction, he said that he found his heart "strangely warmed" amid the "reverent throng" in Wanamaker's, the members of which, though "unknown to each other," lifted "their voices in the old familiar carols of Christmas" and shared "the tie of brotherhood." His was a peculiarly modern encounter with religious faith and Christian corporate action. Couching his experience in anonymous and impersonal terms, he described a feeling of electricity as if "Someone, whom I shall not name," had "turned a switch" and sent "the happy current of Christmas" through "this sea of faces." In the crowded interior of the urban department store, even God seemed a nameless Someone. For this man, the traditional evangelical language depicting a personal Savior and a close-knit body of believers faded into the nebulous glow of Wanamaker's Christmas cathedral.[111]

In these letters of thanks, one sees the ritual place that a Christmas visit to Wanamaker's had assumed in the lives of many Philadelphians. The store's holiday slogan in the 1950s was "Christmas Isn't Christmas without a Day at Wanamaker's," and the slogan contained a grain of ethnographic description along with its advertising hype. A Catholic nun and schoolteacher, for example, wrote warmly to the store in 1950: "I made a special trip, as many of us do, just to 'see Wanamaker's.'" These excursions to behold the Grand Court each year at the holidays had become, she said, part of her "Christmas ritual." "I loved it all," she wrote, "beginning with 'Christmas in Old Philadelphia' and ending—really not ending, for I can still see it all—with the lovely, lovely panels." As is the case today in Macy's claim "We're a Part of your Life," earlier department stores aspired to ritualized standing within urban communities, and in many instances they succeeded. Wanamaker's Christmas cathedral was perhaps the prime example, but others, such as Rich's Christmas celebration in Atlanta, with its "massed choirs" and popular tree-lighting ceremony, similarly prospered. In such cases, urban department stores created Christmas celebrations that transcended mere merchandising events, and instead took on the standing of civic solemnity or even religious ritual.[112]

Admittedly one would be hard-pressed to find such monumental and explicit interweavings of Christianity and commerce in a contemporary department store. These days in Wanamaker's Grand Court for Christmas no cathedral is erected; instead there is a "dancing water" show composed of colorfully lighted fountains, a device that was first introduced in 1956. ("A Snow Falling Lighting Effect," set to the score of "White Christmas," was added in 1962; Frosty the Snowman arrived in 1964; and Rudolph the Red-Nosed Reindeer landed in 1966. Such seasonal and folk symbols gradually took over the show at the expense of the store's long-standing religious embellishments.)[113] Perhaps the primary reminders of religion in most Christmas marts are outside on the sidewalks in the form of Salvation Army cadets, those sentinels of holiness amid the crowds of holiday shoppers. (In a suggestive overlay of Christian witness and commercial imagery, the Salvation Army's holiday publication in 1991, given free to interested shoppers, featured a bright cover depicting a show-window Nativity scene. Emblazoned over the window was the reminder that "Jesus is the Reason for the Season.") Perhaps, as is the case with public schools and public squares, religious symbols have been increasingly removed from the marketplace. But the marketplace is hardly naked. If rarely as grandly fused as they were in Wanamaker's Christmas cathedral, Christianity and commerce continue to merge at Christmas in subtle and not-so-subtle ways.

This continued confluence was evident in the famous legal example of the Pawtucket, Rhode Island, crèche in the early 1980s. When the American Civil Liberties Union challenged the constitutionality of the community's publicly financed Nativity scene, merchants in downtown Pawtucket were among the crèche's most consistent backers. The crèche, it was argued, was part of a much larger series of displays and decorations, all of which helped attract shoppers into the downtown district and contributed, in Mayor Dennis Lynch's words, to the overall "economic well-being of the city." The Christmas display was one part of the city's larger cooperation with the business community, a small piece of a redevelopment plan for the downtown area in which the municipal government coordinated its "Christmas observance with the activities of merchants." If not the focus of legal concern, the economic rationale was nonetheless an important subtext in the case. The market was offered as a legitimation for the use of religious symbols in public arenas. The Nativity scene, rather than being viewed as an anomaly in the marketplace or in a public park, was accepted as a vital cultural symbol in America's public celebration of Christmas.[114]

For more than a century, the American marketplace has displayed a striking capacity for consecration at Christmas. Christian symbols have been repeatedly brought into the public square and made a matter of public recognition through commercial institutions. Combined with all the other public ways Christmas was (and is) celebrated in the culture—in schools, in town parks, in the White House's national Christmas tree, in television specials, and in churches—the observance of Christmas in the marketplace has often helped give Christianity "official" or "established" standing in the American polity. At no other time in the year have the tensions over religious pluralism been more evident: Christmas has been set up as an all-embracing cultural celebration, often with only passing sensitivity to those whom the holiday marginalizes. Certainly the December dilemma for American Jews and American Muslims, among others, has been made all the more difficult because of the inescapable presence of Christmas in the marketplace. Wanamaker's Christmas cathedral, and those that emulated it around the country, created a seamless civic, religious, and commercial celebration that contained within it grand visions of peace, harmony, and goodwill. Yet this great fusion of commerce and Christianity was built on a foundation that was inevitably exclusive.

MAGI, MIRACLES, AND MACY'S: ENCHANTMENT AND DISENCHANTMENT IN THE MODERN CELEBRATION

In a chapter on the holidays in *The Color of a Great City* (1923), Theodore Dreiser confronted the fantasies and mirages of the modern Christmas. "The joys of the Christmas tide are no illusion with most of us, the strange exhibition of fancy, of which it is the name, no mockery of our dreams," he wrote, and the *us* and *our* here clearly meant the middle class and the affluent. "Rings and pins, the art of the jeweler and the skill of the dress-maker, pictures, books, ornaments and knickknacks—these with one great purpose are consecrated, and in the material lavishness of the season is seen the dreams of the world come true." After this short preface of dreams fulfilled, he turns his gaze on dreams deferred—that is, on Christmas among the working poor in the tenements. The Christmas market there bustles with carts of toys and candy, wagons of evergreens, Jewish peddlers with penny ornaments, and sidewalk vendors of meats. Factory workers, shopgirls, and sweatshop laborers throng the streets, patching together a Christmas from "the thinnest and most meager material forms." Children peer longingly into store windows, but for the poor, Dreiser surmises, the displays are a "world of make-believe and illusion." Workers and immigrants, going about Christmas with something of the energy of people at a street fair, seem to be doing better by the festival than Dreiser intuits. But his observations strike some of the principal chords of ambivalence in the modern celebration: namely, the incongruities of abundance and penury, fulfillment and longing, dream and illusion, enchantment and disenchantment.[115]

Ambivalence in various guises pervades the modern Christmas, and many of these tensions arise from the cloudy mix of commerce, consumption, and celebration. Two of the classic Christmas stories of the twentieth century, O. Henry's "Gift of the Magi" and Valentine Davies' *Miracle on Thirty-Fourth Street*, underline the paradox of attraction and alienation at the heart of the modern celebration. "The Gift of the Magi" suggests the tragic ironies and utopian longings that dwell in the merging of Christmas giving and consumer desire. Jim and Della Young, a New York City couple who are barely scraping by, face Christmas with little money for gifts for one another. Their most cherished possessions are Jim's gold watch, which is a family heirloom, and Della's cascading tresses of brown hair. Each wants to buy a gift for the other that will complement these treasures—namely, a platinum chain for Jim's watch and a set of combs for Della's hair. In self-sacrifice, Della sells her hair to a salon for money to buy Jim the watch fob, and Jim pawns his watch to buy Della the combs. These gifts, though they end up bringing sorrow as much as happiness, are depicted as the wisest of offerings; Jim and Della are pictured as being akin to the Magi, who, in their adoration of the Babe in the manger, are said to have "invented the art of giving Christmas presents."[116]

But these sacrifices for one another are prompted by consumer hopes that come with bitter cost to those like Della and Jim for whom affluence and middle-class status are a pipe dream. In the sharpness of winter Jim "needed a new overcoat and he was without gloves," but Christmas giving focused not on such necessities, but on luxuries, fancy goods, and special gifts. The couple's Christmas gifts were founded not only on self-sacrifice, but also on new desires, on the power and allure of the department store and the wider consumer culture. The description of the combs aptly captures this: "For there lay The Combs—the set of combs, side and back, that Della had worshipped for long in a Broadway window. Beautiful combs, pure tortoise shell, with jewelled rims—just the shade to wear in the beautiful vanished hair. They were expensive combs, she knew, and her heart had simply craved and yearned over them without the least hope of possession. And now, they were hers, but the tresses that should have adorned the coveted adornments were gone." Christmas giving was built on reciprocity, on a giving that was sometimes deeply sacrificial, but, as O. Henry's story captures with considerable poignancy, it was also a giving built on the new desires and possibilities of the consumer culture, in the worshipful longings of window-shopping.[117]

The couple's presents may have been the gifts of the Magi, given in wisdom and in love, but the pathos of these presents is also clear. Their tragic irony suggests a deep ambivalence toward a modern Christmas that tries to override the continuing realities of scarcity with visions of unbounded plenty and to satisfy yearnings for possession without recognition of the sacrifices of acquisition. As the poet W. R. Rodgers wrote, "at Christmas the soft plush of sentiment snows down, embosoms all," hiding "the shocking holes of this uneven world of want and wealth, . . . bleeding the world white." Like modern advertising itself, Christmas promises abundant life, often through a deceptive erasure of inequity. O. Henry's story surfaces those deceptions as well as the continually alluring fantasy of Christmas plenty.[118]

The second story, *Miracle on Thirty-Fourth Street* (1947), also suggests ambivalence, if not confusion. Written by Valentine Davies and made into an Oscar-winning movie, the story has emerged as an American Christmas classic, occupying a near-canonical place in the holiday season with its annual repetition on television. (The tale's cultural prominence was underlined by the new, closely imitative rendition by John Hughes in 1994.) The original movie is a rich text of popular culture that stands as both a condemnation and a celebration of the commercial, consumer-oriented Christmas. From the opening scene of a Christmas show window being decorated, commerce frames the story. (A Macy's newspaper advertisement, spinning into focus, is also used to set the story's day and time.) An elderly gentleman, who is convinced that he is Kris Kringle, is out for a Thanksgiving stroll and happens upon preparations for the Macy's parade. Discovering the Macy's Santa Claus to be shamefully drunk, Kris Kringle protests to the parade's organizer, a Macy's executive named Doris Walker. Desperate to replace the inebriated Santa, Walker convinces Kris Kringle to fill in. With a long white beard and a jolly mien, Kris proves quite a success in the parade, and afterward Macy's hires him to be its store Santa Claus for the season.[119]

The toy-department manager, Mr. Shellhammer, is convinced that Kris Kringle is ideal for the job. "I just know with that man on the throne," he declares, "that my toy department will sell more toys than it ever has. He's a born salesman. I just feel it." Initiating Kris into his job, Shellhammer offers "a few tips on how to be a good Santa Claus" to Kris Kringle, who is quite sure he knows the role firsthand. "Here's a list of toys that we have to push," Shellhammer tells Kris. "You know, things that we're overstocked on. Now you'll find that a great many children will be undecided as to what they want for Christmas. When that happens you immediately suggest one of these items." This advice occasions Kris to lament such crass manipulation to one of Macy's janitors, a young man named Alfred. "Imagine making a child take something he doesn't want just because [Shellhammer] bought too many of the wrong toys. That's what I've been fighting against for years—the way they commercialize Christmas." Alfred, in full agreement with Kris, follows with the movie's strongest speech against commercialization: "Yea, there's a lot of bad isms floating around this world, but one of the worst is commercialism. Make a buck, make a buck. Even in Brooklyn it's the same: Don't care what Christmas stands for. Just make a buck, make a buck." Market and festival, entrepreneurial calculation and meaningful celebration, are pictured as utterly oppositional.

But the story is hardly a thoroughgoing critique of the commercial Christmas. Kris Kringle himself actually displays considerable faith in the modern Christmas as it is staged in America's great department stores. After the Macy's parade, he dutifully announces to the throngs: "You'll find toys of all kinds at Macy's." Indeed, his chief resistance to commercialism as Macy's Santa Claus consists in sending people to other stores, such as Gimbel's, when he knows that a better or more affordable toy or gift is available elsewhere. And ironically this novel practice of recommending other stores works to Macy's advantage. One woman announces to a surprised Mr. Shellhammer, "Well, listen, I want to congratulate you and Macy's on this wonderful new stunt you're pulling. Imagine sending people to other stores. . . . Imagine a big outfit like Macy's putting the spirit of Christmas ahead of the commercial. It's wonderful. Well, I'll tell you I never done much shopping here before. But I'll tell you one thing from now on I'm going to be a regular Macy's customer." The movie rejoices in such ironies. R. H. Macy himself pronounces Kris Kringle's actions to be a great new "merchandising policy."[120] "We'll be known as the helpful store, the friendly store, the store with a heart, the store that places public service ahead of profit," Macy proclaims, and then after a short pause adds, "and consequently we'll make more profits than ever before." Kris's unexpected advice is quickly turned into a strategic "game" of the marketplace—one that Gimbel's can play just as well as Macy's. The commercial Christmas is recognized as all-consuming: It turns resistance or countervailing sentiments to its own ends. The very values of giving, charity, reciprocity, and public service are made part of the commercial Christmas, and goodwill becomes an indispensable technique of merchandising, a stunt, a trick of the trade. The movie both exposes and exalts this capitalist magic and the paradoxes that this sorcery creates.

Ambivalence toward the modern Christmas extends beyond the character of Kris Kringle and his simultaneous blessing and condemnation of commercialism. Disenchantment also affects Doris Walker and her daughter, Susan, two of the other central characters in the movie. A manager for Macy's, one of whose chief responsibilities is the Thanksgiving parade, Doris Walker knows Christmas is about the bottom line—the hiring and firing of Santa Clauses, the orchestration of floats and balloons, the costs of bands and acrobats. The machinery of celebration is all too clear to her; Christmas has been utterly demystified for her through commercial calculation and hard-boiled realism. The parade she organizes has nothing to do with festivity; it is all about the successful inauguration of the holiday shopping season. She has tried to pass on this tough-mindedness to her young daughter, for whom there is to be "no Santa Claus, no fairy tales, no fantasies of any kind." The reenchantment of the holiday for Doris and Susan becomes Kris Kringle's mission. They are his "test case": To have them believe in Santa Claus is to show that the modern Christmas can be redeemed, that Christmas stories can still come to life, even in a world where "we're all so busy trying to beat the other fellow and making things go faster and look shinier and cost less." The movie hinges on the possibility of recovering myth, fantasy, faith, imagination, and sentimentality within a world of economic self-interest and enlightened rationality.

In this motif, the movie plays on a theme at the heart of the modern Christmas—the romantic longing for enchantment in the face of the disenchanting forces of the Enlightenment and a market economy. This nostalgia for "old traditions and holiday customs," terribly imperiled by "the cold and selfish spirit" of modern society, had been a familiar theme for nineteenth-century antiquarians and sentimentalists. Thomas Hervey, for example, in his popular *Book of Christmas* in 1837 pronounced the romantic credo in defense of "the old festivals" and "the community of enjoyment which they imply": "We love all commemorations. We love these anniversaries, for their own sakes." The romantic disdain for the "sneering, scoffing mood" of modernity—for its doubters and demythologizers, for its purveyors of suspicion and skepticism—became a cultural refrain at Christmas. The festival was seen as one remaining island of faith and fantasy in a flood of modern cynicism. *Miracle on Thirty-Fourth Street* thus makes the same affirmation of faith as the famous editorial response to little Virginia O'Hanlon's query in the *New York Sun* in 1897: "Yes, Virginia, there is a Santa Claus." Like the editorial, the movie was an avowal of "faith, fancy, poetry, love, [and] romance" in a world of vanishing wonder and mystery.[121]

By the end of the movie, Kris Kringle emerges victorious, and all that he stands for—"kindness and joy and love"—seems vindicated. This victory, though, is not won without a fight, and remains tenuous. Macy's staff psychologist is convinced that Kris is "insane," that he is suffering from a "fixed delusion" and should be institutionalized. Temporarily committed to a mental ward, Kris Kringle lashes out against the store psychologist and the modern values he represents. This nail-biting clinician is "dishonest, selfish, deceitful, vicious—and yet he's out there and I'm in here. He's called normal, and I'm not. But if that's normal, I don't want it." Kris's "lunacy hearing" thus becomes a referendum on imagination and creativity in a ruthlessly "realistic world," on fancy and "sentimental whim" in a world of managers hell-bent on "getting ahead." Constituting something of a Foucauldian drama, the movie pits modern forms of "truth" and "reason" against the marginalized domains of myth and faith. At Christmas, these subjugated discourses are, like Kris himself, allowed out of the asylum. But apparently it is only at Christmas that such languages and symbols break free and gain plausibility; even then, it is with a pragmatist's wink at the masquerade—adult credulity put on for the sake of children. Ostensibly the story makes believers out of everyone, but, underneath, this Santa Claus faith still seems make-believe.

Also by the end of the film, Doris Walker, the divorced careerist, has been brought around to a more traditional maternalism and sentimentalism. Kris Kringle's miracles act, in effect, to restore her to more-familiar gender codings—tenderness, sentimentality, and faithfulness as she advises her daughter that "faith is believing in things when common sense tells you not to." But hers remains a peculiarly modern devotion—one that points more to American patterns of prosperity than to traditional forms of religious belief or community. Indeed, her daughter's newfound faith in Santa Claus—"I believe . . . I believe . . .," Susan reiterates in a mantra of positive thinking—is finally rewarded with a new house on Long Island, complete with a backyard swing. (The house has gotten considerably larger and more plush in the 1994 remake.) For daughter (and mother), Kris Kringle proves his mysterious powers by making this home a reality. This is the ultimate Christmas present, the consummate act of middle-class consumption—a nice home in the suburbs, safely distant from the disenchanting scenes of the city. Faith will be rewarded with prosperity and security, and the American Christmas is the vehicle of that promise. The movie, having gone one way and then another, completes its circuit: It critiques the commercial Christmas, the smoke and mirrors of market calculation, the superficial shine and whirling speed of modernity, but it stays to celebrate the gospel of abundance and the enchantments of the consumer culture. Nostalgic for premodern simplicity, faith, and miracle, the movie pins its hope and trust on the postwar culture of the suburbs.

PUTTING CHRIST IN CHRISTMAS AND KEEPING HIM THERE: THE PIETY OF PROTEST

In 1992 several ministerial leaders, Protestant and Catholic, came together to issue a proclamation condemning the commercialization of Christmas. Included among the coalition's members were many of the luminaries of the American churches: Calvin Butts, Joan Brown Campbell, William Sloane Coffin, Theodore Hesburgh, and Joseph Lowery, among twenty or so other denominational and seminary leaders. Molded around concerns about community, family, spirituality, poverty, and the environment, the proclamation was especially biting in its attack on the commercial usurpation of religious authority at Christmas: "We have seen the spirit of Christmas reduced to a carnival of mass marketing. Consumption has taken on an almost religious quality; malls have become the new shrines of worship. Massive and alluring advertising crusades have waged war on the essential meaning of the spiritual life, fostering the belief that the marketplace can fulfill our highest aspirations." Though displaying fresh energy and perspicacity, the critique still had the ring of an old, well-rehearsed chorus. American Christians have long cast a wary and discouraged eye on Christmas "abuses," seeking in one way or another to purify, reform, sanctify, or decommercialize the festival. As was the case with New Year's observances, conflicts about how to solemnize Christmas, particularly how to sort out Christian and commercial enactments, have been a recurrent feature of American religious life.[122]

Throughout the nineteenth century, religious expressions of reproach toward the Christmas bazaar were always more than balanced by acceptance of Christmas abundance, and most church folks, like William Mactier or Clara Pardee, appeared quite at home in the holiday marketplace. The favorable reception of O'Neill's handkerchief church, like the warm embrace of Wanamaker's Christmas cathedrals a few decades later, suggested the harmonious convergence of Christian celebration and commercial spectacle. Often, indeed, the churches themselves contributed to the Christmas fair, sponsoring (and advertising) their own holiday bazaars of Christmas gifts and "FANCY ARTICLES" to raise money for charities, missions, or building funds. Likewise, publishers of religious periodicals happily added to the broadening expanse of Christmas promotions as they vigorously competed for holiday advertising revenues. "Christmas advertisers can not reach so many Christmas buyers in any other way so cheaply and easily as by advertising in these papers," the Religious Press Association advised in 1891. "Their every reader is interested in the celebration of Christmas."[123] Holiday advertisements, whether appearing in the *Sunday School Times* (one of Wanamaker's favored periodicals) or the *Christian Recorder* (a weekly of the African Methodist Episcopal Church), filled the December issues of religious publications in the late nineteenth century.

Christmas as it was celebrated in Victorian Sunday schools was anything but austere. With Santa Claus on hand, sometimes presiding from a festooned booth or captaining a treasure-laden ship, all the little scholars received presents—whether sweets, books, cards, or toys. (A notably strong synergy existed between the department-store Santa Claus and his Sunday school counterpart in the late nineteenth century.) Engravings depicting the Sunday school Christmas often pictured images of affluence and plenty, mirroring similar visions of Christmas abundance on holiday trade cards. Indeed, the Sunday schools were such an established consumer market at Christmas by the 1870s and 1880s that Macy's, Wanamaker's, and other stores made special advertising pitches to church-school leaders for their business, as did various supply houses and lithographers. "TOYS AND DOLLS FOR SABBATH SCHOOLS AND FAIRS," an Edward Ridley and Sons ad proclaimed in 1877. "SUPERINTENDENTS . . . WILL FIND OUR STOCK OF HOLIDAY GOODS COMPLETE."[124] Thus, in various ways, the churches were drawn into the new commercial Christmas, and their embrace of the consumer-oriented version of the feast was hardly unwitting or half-hearted: The churches often happily participated in the construction of the Christmas bazaar.

But the easy acceptance of Christmas was itself something new for most American Protestants in the late nineteenth century, and widening alienation from the holiday marketplace would be built on deep-seated Protestant suspicions about the festival. In the seventeenth and eighteenth centuries, Puritans and Presbyterians had given up on the holiday entirely, seeing suppression as the best path of reform. "Can you in your *Conscience* think, that our *Holy Saviour* is honoured, by *Mad Mirth*, by long *Eating*, by hard *Drinking*, by lewd *Gaming*, by rude *Revelling*; by a *Mass* fit for none but a *Saturn*, or a *Bacchus*, or the Night of a *Mahometan Ramadam*?" Cotton Mather had asked in a sermon in 1712, and for most of his meetinghouse auditors the question was safely rhetorical: Good New England Congregationalists had purged the holiday from their lives and could simply wag their heads at misguided Anglicans or

62. "Christmas Eve at Our Sunday School," from *Christmas Chimes and New Year Greeting*, Wanamaker store souvenir, 1879, 5.

irreligious revelers who kept up the celebration.[125] Similarly, when Philip Fithian, a Princeton-educated Presbyterian, served as a tutor on the Robert Carter plantation in Virginia in the early 1770s, he found himself surrounded at Christmas by holiday entertainments, foxhunts, pranks, dances, feasting, and noise. A few years later he was relieved to be back among his own people, where on Christmas "Not a Gun is Heard—Not a Shout—No company or Cabal assembled—To Day is like other Days every Way calm & temperate—People go about their daily business with the same Readiness, & apply themselves to it with the same Industry." This Puritan hope of prophetic cleansing long energized American Protestant critiques of Christmas.[126]

Pitted against the Puritan dream of holiday purgation was a churchly vision of consecration. Anglicans commended both the religious observance and the festive hospitality of Christmas as great blessings, looking to contain holiday conviviality within the structures of church life. At the same time, though, they shared the Puritans' dismay about the myriad ways that holiday lewdness, drunkenness, obscenity, and brawling dishonored Christ. In 1773 the *Virginia Gazette*, for example, reprinted an essay on Christmas from the *London Magazine* that concluded:

> Here is enough of Mirth, of Merriment, and of Sporting. Here is enough of every thing suitable to the Time and Occasion; of every Thing, except Religion. The most sacred Festival in our Kalendar, instead of being celebrated with that pious Joy, that Christian Cheerfulness, which were the great Purposes of its Institution, is converted into one continued Scene of Riot, Profligacy, and Debauchery. . . . We celebrate the Festivity of our Saviour, as if we were ministering the mad Orgies of Bacchus.

Puritans and Anglicans often displayed similar alarm about Christmas riot and excess, but whereas one group hoped to abolish the celebration altogether, the other sought to hallow the occasion and redeem the exultation, to perpetuate "an innocent and laudable festivity" by which people were made "more generous, more virtuous, and more religious." Despite fundamentally different views of the Christian calendar, these leading colonial traditions both bequeathed rich languages of holiday protest.[127]

The churchly vision of consecration picked up support from eighteenth-century Anglican evangelicals, who, in turn, helped broker this perspective to their American counterparts. As they did with New Year's, the early Methodists wanted to transform the popular festivities of Christmas into stirring evangelical observances through prayers, exhortations, testimonials, love feasts, and new hymns (such as Charles Wesley's "Come, Thou Long-Expected Jesus" and "Hark! the Herald Angels Sing"). The sentiments of George Whitefield were indicative of these hopes. In a sermon on "the true Way of keeping Christmas," Whitefield sharply contrasted the sinful and pious ways of observing that holy season. Those who ate and drank to excess, those who played cards and dice, those who neglected their worldly callings, those who indulged in luxury and extravagance, misspent the holiday, but these abuses did not mean that the devout should spurn Christmas. Instead, redeeming and reclaiming Christmas, turning it to evangelical ends, was Whitefield's call. And he was not beyond singling out his own devotional fervor at Christmas as an example of how Christians should redeem the season. In *Christmas Well Kept, and the Twelve Days Well Spent*, Whitefield used his journal to model a new Christmas of tireless evangelism, unflagging prayer, and unstinted worship—a pattern so commendable indeed that even a New England writer remarked, "Would to GOD that *Christmas*, if it must be observed, were kept something after *this Manner* thro' all *Christendom*!"[128]

Even while many American evangelicals kept up the Puritan attack on Christmas, others picked up some of the evangelical Anglican moderation of Whitefield and the Wesleys. As the itinerant preacher Freeborn Garrettson commented in his journal on Christmas Day in 1824, "We must avail ourselves of this festival," not slight it like those "in the Presbyterian way."[129] But making religious use of this celebration was always easier said than done. After preaching at a Christmas service in South Carolina in 1805, Francis Asbury sounded the old note of despair, moaning that "*Christmas day* is the worst in the whole year on which to preach Christ; at least to me." Another entry in his diary about a Christmas service some years earlier in Virginia gave a sense of why Asbury was so doleful: "I felt warm in speaking; but there was an offensive smell of rum among the people."[130] Throughout the colonial and antebellum periods, those like Asbury who tried to redeem Christmas faced sizable obstacles. As Elizabeth Powell noted in her Louisiana diary in 1856, "Blessed be God for ever having given us a Christmas to commemorate; although it has been celebrated in this place, to-day by feasting." Through much of the nineteenth century, the Christianization of Christmas was a quite fragile proposition, tentative and fragmentary. Every time a pastor tried to remind his congregants that Christmas was a solemn religious event that "should be observed in the heart as well as at the hearth, in the temple as well as at the table," he seemed to have to admit that the most visible observances of the season were "rioting and vain amusement"—shooting guns, callithumpian music, practical jokes, heavy drinking, and the like. The churches were invariably hard-pressed to communicate the devotional dimensions of Christmas; the raucous plebeian versions of the celebration always threatened to drown them out.[131]

Confessedly, those Protestants in the Puritan mold were partially to blame for the sorry state of Christmas devotion in the colonial and antebellum worlds. The tradition of holiday purgation, long shared in by Congregationalists, Presbyterians, Baptists, Quakers, and many Methodists, bequeathed a model of thorough desacralization that actually helped Christmas go its secular way in American culture. Time and again, these Protestants insisted that Christmas was just like any other day, that it was without "any peculiar sanctity." At best, Christmas was an object of "mistaken piety"; at worst, it was the occasion of superstition and corrupt tradition.[132] Given these presuppositions about the idolatry of the ancient church calendar, when low-church Protestants began their home-centered recovery of Christmas in the middle decades of the nineteenth century, they often welcomed it back explicitly as a "social holiday," not as a "religious observance." As one Sunday school publication, the *Baptist Teacher*, editorialized in 1875, "We believe in Christmas—not as a holy day but as a *holiday* and so we join with our juveniles with utmost heartiness of festal celebration. . . . Stripped as it ought to be, of all pretensions of religious sanctity and simply regarded as a social and domestic institution—an occasion of housewarming, and heart-warming and innocent festivity—we welcome its coming with a hearty 'All Hail.' "[133] A Holiness Methodist publication in the 1880s took a similar tack: It accepted Christmas as a day of family reunions and good works, but the feast, all the same, was without "the authority of God's word" and smacked of Roman Catholicism. Hence the journal's blunt conclusion: "We attach no holy significance to the day." It is not hard to see in this radical Protestant perspective a religious source for the very secularization of the holiday that would eventually be so widely decried. With the often jostling secularism of the Christmas bazaar, Protestant rigorists simply got what they had long wished for—Christmas as one more market day, a profane time of work and trade.[134]

But many low-church Protestants increasingly found this unhallowed version of Christmas wanting and longed to recover more than the domestic sociability of the holiday. The example of the Philadelphia businessman and Presbyterian trustee William Mactier is suggestive in this regard. Mactier and his family headed to their church on Christmas Day in 1859, which happened that year to fall on a Sunday: "We all went to Church to hear a sermon on the Nativity, as was natural to expect; but Dr. Macdonald preached on *Death* and *Resurrection*. The sermon was excellent, but as I thought inappropriate, and not in unison with the feelings and flow of thought of most of his hearers." What Mactier often did, and he was joined by a growing number of his Protestant contemporaries, was to attend an Episcopal church on Christmas and Easter, where the sermons and services were "appropriate." On Christmas 1861, he noted in his diary: "Attended the Episcopal Church and heard an appropriate discourse from Dr. Dod, the Rector." He found the same appropriateness a few years later in a Good Friday service in a Moravian church; Good Friday was another holy day that was anathema to his Presbyterian pastor. The pressures to adapt church services to these lay expectations became increasingly acute and were hard to ignore. In an article in 1857, even the New England–based *North American Review* advised outright imitation of "the Romanists and Episcopalians" in their religious observance of Christmas and lamented the residue of "Puritan zeal" that still impeded the holiday's full acceptance among "all Christian denominations." "There are abundant indications," the essayist concluded, "that, if the clergy would initiate the movement, the laity are prepared to make Christmas among us the universal religious holiday, which all considerations of piety, domestic affection, and traditional reverence unite to proclaim it."[135]

The churchly vision of consecration, long familiar to Episcopalians, Catholics, Lutherans, and Moravians, had achieved wide cultural ascendancy by the last decades of the nineteenth century. A small but revealing example of this tilt can be seen in a letter describing a Christmas celebration in one evangelical Sunday school in 1882. Having long been content with "the usual" entertainments—a Christmas tree and a bunch of little presents for the children—the Sunday school switched for the first time to a new Christmas emblem, "a rude imitation of the stable of the Nativity . . . with the Star of Bethlemen shining in through a window."[136] (The trouble that this Sunday school teacher had spelling Bethlehem underscored the novelty and unfamiliarity of these holiday symbols for many Protestants, even in the 1880s. This ignorance could easily be turned on evangelicals: *Ave Maria*, a Catholic devotional journal, enjoyed poking fun at a Protestant Sunday school teacher who "did not know that Christ was born, nor why christians keep Christmas as a holiday.")[137] At first more comfortable with the domestic sides of the holiday—the stockings for children, the visits from Santa Claus, the decoration of Christmas trees, and the homecoming of family dinners—a growing number of Protestants slowly reappropriated the religious emblems of the holiday. A list of Christmas things for the 1820s and 1830s in the United States could reasonably have made few religious allusions, but a half century or so later a good list would have needed to contain several Christian references—Nativity scenes and new Sunday school pageants among them. In 1877 the *New York Times* remarked that formerly Christmas observance had been "devoted chiefly to eating and drinking" and that, as for churchgoing, "only a few" had gone "to join in the songs of praise." Now church chimes, tolling the solemnity, had deposed the rough music of callithumpians; scriptures about "the lowly stable," the angel, the shepherds, and "the wise men's visit" had replaced "a ghost story or two" told around a blazing fire; and "responsive crowds," instead of noisily thronging the streets, flocked to special church services. This was, the paper thought, Christmas as it should be. For all those reform-minded folks who had long despaired about the Christmas carnival, Christianization seemed finally to be making some real progress.[138]

One of the surest signs of this heightened religious espousal was the unparalleled burst of new Christmas hymnody from the 1840s through the 1880s. The new hymns included "Once in Royal David's City" (1848), "It Came upon the Midnight Clear" (1849), "When Christmas Morn Is Dawning" (1856), "There Came a Little Child to Earth" (1856), "We Three Kings" (1857), "O Little Town of Bethlehem" (1868), "In the Bleak Midwinter" (1872), "There's a Song in the Air" (1874), "Love Came Down at Christmas" (1885), and "Away in a Manger" (1887). There were also new arrangements or English translations for "O Come All Ye Faithful" (1841), "Joy to the World" (1848), "O

Come, O Come, Emmanuel" (1854), "Good Christian Men, Rejoice," (1855), "Hark! the Herald Angels Sing" (1856), "Angels We Have Heard on High" (1862), and "Angels from the Realms of Glory" (1867).[139] These new hymns, all of which became an integral part of the holiday's repertory, reflected and helped further Christmas's modern consecration. As this upsurge in popular Christmas hymnody suggested, the holiday was increasingly experienced across wide sections of the culture as far more than a domestic party, a street free-for-all, a well-stocked bazaar, or a Puritan bugbear. The process of sacralization always remained incomplete, but by the end of the nineteenth century Christmas had come to stand out as a major religious event in American culture—a time to recount biblical stories of the Incarnation, sing religious hymns, stage Sunday school pageants, view Nativity scenes, decorate church interiors, hold special services, and contemplate God's mysterious work of redemption. This deepened sense of the feast's sacredness, when combined with traditional Protestant fears of holiday extravagance, would make a potent mix for a piety of protest aimed at the Christmas bazaar.

Early complaints about the impact of commerce on the holiday centered on how merchandising affected the rituals of gift giving, particularly how the marketplace had made Christmas presents a matter of fashion and ostentation. In 1849 the *Sunday School Advocate*, for example, detected wastefulness and superficiality in the abundance of holiday gift books and annuals. These books, with their "gaudy exterior" and "trickery of ornament," were "mere gew-gaws of fashion" and "gilded trash." To take delight in the Gothic bindings of books was a commentary on the self; Protestant simplicity, transparency, and interiority demanded an unadorned exterior. In this evangelical world, books, like true selves in which interior and exterior corresponded, could be judged by their covers. Genuine holiday gifts, this writer thought, should avoid mere display and should especially concentrate on books of devotion and moral instruction—in other words, books of "lasting good" that could be read again and again, not holiday annuals that were, by definition, made for the season and then easily forgotten. In short, the *Sunday School Advocate* appealed for Christmas books that encouraged traditional forms of devotional reading based on familiarity and repetition, not holiday annuals that celebrated modern forms of literary fluff founded on novelty and fashion.[140]

Soon the religious critique widened. In 1871 another evangelical publication, the *Ladies' Repository*, expressed a broadened concern with the growing fondness for lavish gifts of all sorts on various festive occasions. In particular, the writer lamented "the jingle of gilded trinkets" for Christmas and the "glittering inventory of bridal presents" for the "modern fashionable wedding." "The *commercial* aspect of gift-making" was turning these modern rituals into a frivolous show of social status and acquisitiveness, transforming joyful giving into "a sharp, sordid, bargaining spirit." To this essayist, presents for Christmas and weddings had come to be more about style, costliness, and display than about "spontaneous loving impulse," more about the duplicate articles of the modern mart than about the originals of painstaking handicraft. The author's fears concerning Christmas's fate ran high: The celebration was fast degenerating into "a hot-bed of stimulated gratification" for overly pampered children. Romantic anxieties about the impact of the market on gift giving, already familiar from the debates over the tokens of St. Valentine's Day, increasingly dogged Christmas as well.[141]

By the closing decades of the nineteenth century, these views on the commercial distortion of holiday gift giving found ever more frequent expression. The *New York Times*, for example, extolled the simplicity and sentiment of homemade Christmas gifts over the lavishness of "bought presents" in a caustic editorial in 1880. "Very few Americans have the moral courage to be economical or even sensible at this season of the year," the paper scolded in fine republican and Protestant tones. "It seems the fashion to be extravagant, almost reckless, in expenditure, and people of all classes vie with each other in the costliness of their presents until the rivalry in only too many cases becomes nothing more nor less than vulgar ostentation and coarse display of money-bags." Some, seeing this loosening of economic restraint and the ascendancy of a consumer ethic at Christmas, blamed not the shopping habits of the people, but "the dominance of the store-keepers' influence." According to the *American* in 1887, merchants were the ones who were chiefly responsible for "multiplying gifts," for "increasing their costliness," and for "exaggerating all the bad tendencies" of holiday gift exchange. The shopkeepers now "began the Christmas season with the beginning of the month. Week after week they [fill] their windows and spread their counters with the things which the customs of the season compel people to buy." "Let us get back to first principles," the journal exhorted. "What is Christmas for? Not to enrich the shop-keepers." Dislodging Christmas from the marketplace was seen as a requirement for preserving it as a time of worship, reunion, and "old fashioned sports."[142]

What the critics suspected was that, in an atmosphere of commercial artifice and promotion, Christmas gifts meant less and less; they were becoming little more than a "compliance with a social necessity," an empty and wearisome responsibility, a mechanical gesture. "We are really slaves of our Christmas shopping lists," one writer moaned in 1906. The vastly extended customs of Christmas gift giving were repeatedly pictured as a source of social anxiety and exhausting strain, and the Christmas rush was taken to be a prime indication of lost simplicity and modern complexity, the very emblem of a neurasthenic age. In the whirl of fashion, status, and social obligation, Christmas gifts themselves were seen as one more source of deceit and insincerity; they were too easily caught in a web of "small hypocrisies and calculated generosities." They became little more than "a game of grab and graft," a matter of "swapping and trading"—that is, they often seemed more agonistic than integrative, more like a calculated market exchange than a sentimental gift exchange. By the turn of the century, articles with titles like "Christmas Insincerities," "The Oppression of Gifts," "The Value of Limitations," "The Unchristian Christmas," and "Save Christmas!" were standard holiday fare, and Edward Bok, the influential editor of the *Ladies' Home Journal*, was making it an annual rite of his to rue the compulsions and complexities of Christmas gift giving. All along these critics etched their resistance to the holiday marketplace in hoary juxtapositions: surface versus substance, guise versus transparency, luxury versus simplicity, self-interest versus selflessness, artificiality versus genuineness.[143]

Another area of persistent concern for Christmas's critics was how the poor fared during the holiday. Christmas mutuality and charity had long been crucial holiday themes, and the popularity of Dickens's *Christmas Carol* (1843) had made Christmas generosity a Victorian convention: To remember the poor was an obligation of the season. This requirement of Christian benevolence was one of the most important sources for religious protest about the jarring displays of Christmas affluence. As in Dreiser's story, the contrast between the holiday observances of the wealthy and those of the poor was perpetually unsettling. Harriet Beecher Stowe in a Christmas story in 1853 suggested the basic contours of this devout remonstrance, this passion for social equity:

> "Whose birth does Christmas commemorate, Ella?"
>
> "Our Saviour's, certainly, aunt."
>
> "Yes," said her aunt. "And when and how was he born? in a stable! laid in a manger; thus born, that in all ages he might be known as the brother and friend of the poor. And surely it seems but appropriate to commemorate His birthday by an especial remembrance of the lowly, the poor, the outcast, and distressed; and if Christ should come back to our city on a Christmas day, where should we think it most appropriate to his character to find him? Would he be carrying splendid gifts to splendid dwellings, or would he be gliding about in the cheerless haunts of the desolate, the poor, the forsaken, and the sorrowful?"

This moral was one that the social-gospel movement would take to heart as it tried to turn the traditional commitment to Christmas charity into sustained economic justice for laborers, the poor, and the oppressed—that is, to move from a "spasm" of holiday goodwill to systemic reforms.[144]

The social-gospel critique of Christmas commercialism had something of the prophetic passion of Jesus' running the moneychangers out of the temple. In a children's story, first published in 1887, that required a certain precocity to appreciate, Washington Gladden had Santa Claus take to the pulpit to deliver a rebuke to those who were making Christmas "a pig's feast"—that is, a celebration in which the rich gave bright gifts that they obtained through wealth generated by the grinding exploitation of their workers. In Gladden's story, Santa flashes a stereopticon slide of an elegant Christmas gift—a necklace of gold and diamonds—that one rich man had bought for his wife, and the image elicits gasps of desire and delight from the congregation. But the prophet quickly warns that "things are not always what they seem." To afford this bejeweled chain for his wife, the man had fettered hundreds of women, "cramped" and "emaciated," to their work in the garment factory he owned. Gladden's tale was, at bottom, another Protestant story of unmasking, of seeing beneath glittering surfaces to hypocrisy, avarice, and exploitation—that is, seeing things as they really are.[145]

Other social gospelers, particularly the poet and journalist Edwin Markham, tried to expose the inequities and injustices that Christmas's intense seasonal market created. Markham was especially concerned with the callous mistreatment of children as laborers, who were pushed all the harder in the three months before Christmas to meet the demands of the holiday rush. Focusing specifically on the use of child labor in the confectionery industry, Markham noted how twelve-hour days regularly became fourteen-hour days during the Christmas season. The holiday grind was mind numbing and physically debilitating, "murderously monotonous" in its drudgery. "In the name of the young child," Markham commented in 1907, "we make Christmas an abomination to thousands of working children." The confectionery industry served Markham's prophetic purposes especially well. With Christmas candy evoking images of the simple holiday insouciance of children, Markham was able to pound home his sardonic message. "What irony of civilization is this," he said, "one band of children wasting their bodies and souls to make a little joy for the rest."[146]

Labor issues were the principal concern for social gospelers in their critique of the modern commercial Christmas. "Cannot the church save the day from degradation and the people from cruel overwork?" Walter Rauschenbusch asked about Christmas in 1911. "The solicitations of our commerce have corrupted it and turned it into a time of frantic buying and selling, which drives all workers at terrible pressure." These stresses were felt not only in factories and sweatshops, but also in retail establishments. Like the Tiffany's clerk who complained in his diary about his tiresome holiday toil, shopgirls and delivery boys were often overwhelmed by work at Christmas with little or no additional compensation in return. Progressive Era reformers threw themselves behind various crusades to remove "the Christmas curse" of long hours and frantic labor that plagued retail clerks. One movement, which began in New York City in the 1890s and coalesced as a national cause in the 1910s, was the Shop Early campaign. Designed to encourage consumers to do their Christmas shopping both earlier in the day to cut down on the evening hours of stores as well as earlier in the season to lessen the last-minute crush of Christmas crowds, the Shop Early campaign garnered extensive religious, political, and commercial backing. Moderately successful in shortening working hours for retail clerks, the Shop Early movement had another upshot as well. It provided a moral imperative for the extension of the holiday shopping season: "FOR THE SAKE OF HUMANITY, SHOP EARLY," was its battle cry. Beginning one's Christmas shopping around Thanksgiving or even earlier was cast as an act of civic responsibility and virtuous citizenship. Thus, in the putative pursuit of fairness for store employees, this reform movement ironically ended up providing a crucial buttress for the temporal expansion of Christmas shopping.[147]

A final area of concern for the critics was how the flourishing holiday marketplace threatened to eclipse the religious meanings of Christmas. The vision of fully hallowing Christmas, even as it had made considerable progress in the second half of the nineteenth century, always seemed frail, and the holiday bazaar received growing blame for the renewed peril of Christmas piety. For example, in 1896 a convocation of ministers was convened in New York City at the Gospel Tabernacle in order to look for ways to divert the "intemperate gayety and extravagant expenditure" of Christmas "into more spiritual and scriptural channels." For these pastors, the old difficulty of making "this holiday a holy day indeed" had taken on the new problem of how to rein in the lavishness of New York's Christmas bazaar. Some years later another pastor framed the new holiday predicament for Christians this way: Christmas had been captured by a modern paganism that was "commercial, self-seeking, anti-Christian in its very essence." In this new paganism, it was feared that the Christmas spirit had come to be indistinguishable from the capitalist spirit.[148]

For those critics who worried about the loss of Christmas's religious meanings, Santa Claus, in particular, came in for censure. Increasingly viewed more as a booster of festal indulgence than a benign gift giver, Santa Claus was thought to obscure, rather than complement, the scriptural stories about the Incarnation. One Lutheran commentator in 1883 labeled Santa Claus a species of American heathenism, and the transformation of the German Christ-Kindlein into the American Kris Kringle was seen as a sad case of secular debasement. Likewise in the first two decades of this century, the *Sunday School Times* made it a small crusade to minimize Santa Claus's presence in

63. "For the Sake of Humanity, Shop Early," *American City* 13 (November 1915): 406.

Protestant church schools and turn attention more squarely on the Nativity. Christmas was not "Santa Claus Day" or "Santamas," the paper insisted, and those Victorian Protestants who had made Kris Kringle the center of their Sunday school entertainments had gotten terribly off track. "Have we not, in a word, been chiefly honoring Santa Claus instead of Christ?" the paper asked in 1909. As one convinced reader of the *Sunday School Times* wrote from California, "The thoughtful Christians who have studied it have decided not to use the name 'Santa Claus' any more, but to teach the trusting little ones that it is through Jesus that we receive all the blessings of Christmas." Such concern about Santa Claus was not confined to Protestants. One Roman Catholic priest, James Cotter, wrote in 1917, "In America, Santa Claus is rapidly usurping the Babe's throne in the children's affections, making the holy name of sacrifice a term for greed." Though few Christians wanted to take the puritanical step of abolishing Santa Claus, many agreed that the saint had become "discouragingly mercenary," an icon of acquisition and consumer longing, distressingly at odds with the Christian meanings of the feast. There was simply little way of seeing him any longer, as James K. Paulding had in 1836, as "the poor man's saint," a self-sacrificing exemplar of Jesus' identification with the indigent.[149]

By the early decades of this century, the pervasive intertwining of Christmas and the commercial culture was a recurrent worry for American Christians, and that jolly denizen of the North Pole was only the tip of the iceberg.

Though Christians at times rejoiced that Christmas had been raised to the largest, most extensive festival in the culture, there was also a tone of dashed hope in religious appraisals of the holiday, a timbre that echoed the disillusionment that many of the faithful had come to feel regarding the failing efforts to make the nation avowedly Christian. In a Christmas editorial in 1912 the *Sunday School Times* crystallized that double feeling. Somehow the holiday had been both lifted up and hollowed out at the same time; even as it had been sacralized, Christmas had been secularized:

> On the surface, the Christmas spirit seems to pervade everything. Never before was there so much Christmas giving. Merchants have ransacked the earth to find articles to sell, and people have bought lavishly. But commercialism has come in and Christ has been crowded out. There was no room in the inn for the mother of Jesus when the great Birthday came. Is there much more room for Jesus this Christmas in the immense Christmas business which is making the merchants so happy? There is love in many hearts, and the giving in many homes is holy and beautiful. But out of the great bulk of the giving the soul has gone. The day has come to be to many families a burden instead of a delight. Never before was the day so widely or so expensively observed, but its deep and sacred meaning has been too greatly obscured.

Amid the shopping, the cards, the Toyland Santa Clauses, the packages, and the lights, the festivities of winter once again seemed to allow only marginal room for Christ. The holiday bazaar had become the central motif in the new refrain about what had gone wrong with Christmas in modern American culture.[150] In Christian piety the Christmas drama demands an unreceptive world, a crowded inn, and the marketplace increasingly served that purpose. Overburdened shoppers and calculating merchants had taken the place of soused bacchanalians and masked mummers in the familiar emplotment of the Christmas story as a tale of salvation overlooked and slighted.

Distress about "the commercialization of Christmas" had become a standard subject of religious protest by the 1930s and 1940s. The views of one pastor, expressed in a Christmas sermon in 1938, were typical of what had become a habitual chorus: "At Christmas time when spiritual values should be uppermost in the minds of people, the land is inundated by a tidal wave of commercial activity and materialistic self-seeking that quite obliterates the quiet, peaceful, spiritual meaning of the birth of Jesus Christ."[151] Such sentiments finally coalesced in 1949 into a quite visible movement that went under the still-familiar banner, "Put Christ Back into Christmas." First sparked by a poster and billboard campaign by the Milwaukee Archconfraternity of Christian Mothers, the movement received extensive media coverage and wide denominational backing over the next decade. For one city after another, stories were told of community-wide campaigns in which Christ had been restored to the center of Christmas. Protestant ministerial associations, Catholic lay organizations, civic councils, and educational groups all came together to put up Nativity scenes, to distribute posters and automobile stickers, to hold "Christ in Christmas" parades, and to plaster billboards with the campaign's slogan.[152]

Perhaps what was most striking about the new campaign, however, was not its protest of Christmas commercialism, but its consecration of it. The movement to "put Christ back into Christmas" ultimately underscored how deeply the modern Christmas was enmeshed in the commercial culture and how easily criticism of the consumer-oriented holiday was translated into a merchandising idiom. Among the Milwaukee confraternity's chief backers in 1949 had been two hundred of the city's merchants, and that pattern of religious and commercial cooperation played itself out from one town to another in the 1950s. An account of how Christ was restored to Christmas in Evanston, Illinois, in 1951 can stand for dozens of similar cases. Over the summer a coalition of local priests, ministers, lay people, educators, and civic leaders had come together to form the Christian Family Christmas Committee. Included among the lay people were some "professional advertising men, copywriters and art directors, who loaned their skills unstintingly," and it was in "the city's commercial life" that the campaign achieved its "most astounding success." Window show cards of the Nativity, drawn up and distributed by the committee, were prominently displayed in Evanston's shops, and merchants agreed to use the slogan "Put Christ Back into Christmas" in their advertising. Marshall Field's set up "a most artistic Nativity design" in one of its large windows, and other department stores in the town devised similarly towering displays of the Holy Family and the Three Wise Men. Banks, restaurants, hospitals, and public parks were also adorned with "Christmas cribs." In Evanston, as elsewhere, the campaign was a concerted attempt to reclaim the holiday's religious meanings within, rather than apart from, the modern consumer culture. In the end, the movement had much in common with Wanamaker's Christmas cathedrals; both consecrated the holiday marketplace; both treated Christmas as a Constantinian rite of American Christendom. "Put Christ Back into Christmas" wound up being a benediction for the Christmas bazaar.[153]

Keeping Christ in Christmas has obviously continued to exercise American Christians from one year to the next since the 1950s. Among the most salient examples of the continued critique of the modern Christmas has been the ecumenical group Alternatives, which was organized by a Protestant pastor, Milo Thornberry, in 1973 explicitly for the purpose of protesting "the commercialization of Christmas." Based in Ellenwood, Georgia, Alternatives now

64. "Keep Christ in Christmas," Knights of Columbus billboard, 1993.

publishes materials embracing American holidays and celebrations generally, but the focus of the group's concern remains Christmas. With support from several Catholic dioceses and mainline Protestant bodies, the association annually publishes a sophisticated critique of America's "Santa Claus theology" entitled *Whose Birthday Is It, Anyway?* for use in the churches. Distributing 150,000 to 200,000 of these booklets each year to congregations, Alternatives has for twenty years encouraged resistance to the "consumer Christmas."[154]

The aims of Alternatives resonate deeply with previous protests about the Christmas bazaar over the past century: namely, to keep gifts simple, heartfelt, and meaningful; to remember the poor in substantial ways and pursue paths toward economic justice; to make the season a sacred time of prayer, contemplation, and self-examination; and to resist the consumer gospel at Christmas that equates buying and spending with fulfillment and happiness. In prophetic witness, Alternatives has sought to lift up the Christian stories of Christ's advent over those of Santa Claus, who has become "a god of material wealth and consumption," obscuring and distorting the gospel. (In contrast to Jesus, who brings "good news to the poor," Santa rewards the rich and makes the holiday "a cruel hoax" for the penniless.)[155] Alternatives offers a piety of protest with something of the old Puritan dream of holiday cleansing and something of the venerable ecclesial vision of consecration—a Christmas both purged and redeemed. As has been the case for earlier critics, Alternatives has had a tough row to hoe. Powerful cultural myths insulate the modern Christmas from the thrashings of each Amos who comes along: Prophets are quickly turned into Scrooges and Grinches, cheapskates and skinflints, joyless precisians and hopeless idealists. But these stereotypes have hardly quieted those among the faithful who have recurrently dissented from the modern Christmas bazaar.

The American marketplace has served for more than a century and a half as a site of competition about the meanings of Christmas. The contest has revealed deep ambiguities in the culture—fundamental tensions between asceticism and indulgence, simplicity and affluence, piety and spectacle, religion and consumerism, Christ and culture. Often the tensions have seemed to dissolve, as in Clara Pardee's diary, Wanamaker's Christmas cathedrals, or the "Put Christ Back into Christmas" campaign. At other times the tensions have remained taut, as in the stinging commentaries of various critics from Washington Gladden to Milo Thornberry. For all the billions of dollars in sales that the modern Christmas generates, the holiday bazaar has remained a realm of contest, not fiat, a place of disaffection and estrangement as well as joy and excitement, a site of not a little ambivalence, paradox, and contradiction.

4
Easter Parade

RVING BERLIN'S popular musical of 1948, *Easter Parade*, starring Fred Astaire and Judy Garland, opens with a wonderful shopping scene. It is the day before Easter 1911. Astaire's character, Don Hewes, sings and dances his way along the streets of New York past a dry-goods store and through millinery, flower, and toy shops. "Me, oh, my," he sings, "there's a lot to buy. There is shopping I must do. Happy Easter to you." In the millinery store, saleswomen model elaborate Easter bonnets and mellifluously offer their wares: "Here's a hat that you must take home. Happy Easter. . . . This was made for the hat parade on the well-known avenue. This one's nice and it's worth the price. Happy Easter to you." Everywhere Hewes goes he buys things—a bonnet, a large pot of lilies, a toy bunny. By the time he leaves the florist he has purchased so many presents that he is followed by three attendants who help him carry all the packages. In the toy store, quite overtaken with the possibilities, he lets out a song that could easily pass for a toy catalogue: "A bunny for my honey, a dolly with a curl, an airplane, an electric train, and a teddy bear for my girl, a kitty for my pretty, a castle for my love—Gee, what do I see? Brother, if that's a drum, that's for me. I'm drum crazy. Yes, I'm drum crazy. Yes, I'm plum crazy for drums."[1] Don Hewes is plum crazy about gifts and goods; he is a consumer on a spree. And Easter is the occasion for it.

With a boyish exuberance, Don Hewes prepares for Easter by shopping. His efforts are aimed not at readying himself for church or sacrament, but at ensuring that his companion will make a fine appearance in New York's fashion parade. The opening chorus chirrups this theme: "In your Easter bonnet with all the frills upon it, you'll be the grandest lady in the Easter parade. I'll be all in clover, and when they look you over, I'll be the proudest fellow in the Easter parade." Fulfillment consists in seeing and being seen, in having his consort admired with envious gazes. When Hewes and his new dance partner, a humble showgirl who doubles as a barmaid, actually encounter the fashion promenade the next day, she is overawed. "I can't believe I'm really here," she gasps. "You know, I used to read about the Easter parade in New York, and then I'd look at the pictures of the women in their lovely clothes and dream that maybe someday I'd. . . ." Her voice trails off in wonder and dreamy aspiration. The only religious image in the film appears in the last scene, when the Easter parade has returned for another year. A Gothic church looms as a dim backdrop for the fancily dressed couples who stroll by in a streaming concourse of fashion and affluence.

The film is not primarily about Easter, of course, but about Astaire and

Garland and their marvelous dancing and singing. But the movie and Berlin's popular theme song are illuminating texts about the American Easter all the same. From at least the 1880s into the 1960s, this dress parade was one of the primary cultural expressions of Easter in the United States, one of the fundamental ways the occasion was identified and celebrated. The holiday blossomed in the late nineteenth century into a cultural rite of spring with elaborate floral decorations, new clothes, fancy millinery, chocolate bunnies, candy eggs, greeting cards, and other gifts. The movie, like the Easter parade itself, embodied an expansive public faith in American abundance: "Everything seems to come your way," the chorus lilts. "Happy Easter!"

In his recent novel, *Operation Shylock*, Philip Roth celebrates Irving Berlin's *Easter Parade* for its creative de-Christianization of the festival, for its promotion of a "schlockified Christianity" in which the bonnet overthrows the cross. But in many ways, Berlin was merely offering a catchy, hummable benediction for the fashionable modern festival that American Christians had been busily creating for themselves over the previous century. This consumer-oriented Easter actually had deep religious wellsprings, and the juxtapositions of Christian devotion and lavish display were as richly polychromatic as the holiday flowers and fashions themselves. An understanding of the growing significance attached to church decoration in the second half of the nineteenth century is of first importance in making sense of this modern Easter. These religious patterns of embellishment, in turn, fed commercial holiday displays and spectacles of Easter merchandising. Lushly adorned churches provided the backdrop for finely dressed congregants and for the efflorescence of the Easter parades in New York City and elsewhere. With the Easter parade also came a new surfeit of Easter goods—cards, confections, and novelties. This bewildering array of trinkets, warmly welcomed into home and Sunday school, sharply recast the holiday's iconography. All the while, this Easter fanfare elicited biting criticism from devotees of simplicity and plainness, from those who were alienated from the faith of comfortable materialism. This estrangement was etched in distinctly gendered terms. The complementary, yet contested, relationship between American Christianity and the modern consumer culture nowhere found clearer performance than in the Easter festival.[2]

"IN THE BEAUTY OF THE LILIES": THE ART OF CHURCH DECORATION AND THE ART OF WINDOW DISPLAY

The Gothic church that flickers in the last frames of *Easter Parade* stands in the background, perhaps a nostalgic image—distant, unobtrusive, evanescent. Yet to understand the development of the Easter parade as a cultural (and religious) event, this neo-Gothic edifice and others like it need to be brought into the foreground. Churches such as Trinity Episcopal Church, St. Patrick's Cathedral, and St. Thomas's Episcopal Church in New York City, with their rich Gothic ornament, are central, not peripheral, to this story. The elaborate decorations that these splendid urban churches created for ecclesiastical festivals such as Christmas and Easter are crucial for fathoming the emergence of a fashionable Easter in the second half of the nineteenth century. The newly cultivated art of church decoration, in turn, helped inspire inventive window trimmers and interior designers in their creation of holiday spectacles for merchandising purposes.

Easter, even more than Christmas, remained under a Puritan and evangelical cloud in the antebellum United States. Though various denominations preserved the holiday—most prominently Episcopalians, Roman Catholics, Lutherans, and Moravians—their celebrations were, until the middle of the century, local, parochial, and disparate. The festival only became a nearly ubiquitous cultural event in the decades after 1860 as low-church Protestant resistance or indifference gave way to approbation and as Episcopalian, Roman Catholic, and new-immigrant observances became ever more prominent. Middle-class Victorians, as fascinated as ever with the romantic recovery of fading holiday traditions and the cultivation of new home-centered festivities, discovered lush possibilities in this spring rite. "A few years ago and Easter as a holiday was scarcely thought of, except by the devout," the *New York Herald* reported on "Eastertide" in 1881. "Now all are eager to join in the celebration." Between about 1860 and 1890, Easter took distinctive religious and cultural shape as an American holy day and holiday.[3]

In an article on Easter published in 1863, *Harper's New Monthly Magazine* suggested the growing embrace of the feast in American culture. "It is one of the obvious marks of our American religion," the article related, "that we are noticing more habitually and affectionately the ancient days and seasons of the Christian Church." Easter, following Christmas's rising popularity, showed "unmistakable signs that it is fast gaining upon the religious affection and public regard of our people." "We have carefully noted the gradual increase of observance of the day," the journal continued, "and can remember when it was a somewhat memorable thing for a minister, not Catholic or Episcopal, to preach an Easter sermon." What the magazine found most revealing of "this new love for Easter," however, was the increasing use of elaborate floral decorations for the festival. "Easter flowers are making their way into churches of all persuasions," the magazine applauded. "One of our chief Presbyterian churches near by decked its communion-table and pulpit with flowers for the third time this Easter season." The writer praised Easter floral displays for their artistic taste and devotional symbolism—their "ministry of the beautiful." The splendor of Easter flowers embodied the new, compelling allure of the festival.[4]

In lauding Easter flowers, the *Harper's* piece was celebrating the expanding art of church decoration. As a liturgical movement, this art bloomed in England and the United States in the middle decades of the nineteenth century. An outgrowth of the ritualist or Catholic turn within Anglican and Episcopalian circles, the new forms of church decoration meshed with the Gothic revival in Victorian church architecture and ornament. English writers such as William A. Barrett and Ernest Geldart led the way in formalizing the rubrics of modern church decoration in a number of handbooks that helped foster and guide the burgeoning art on both sides of the Atlantic. These writers codified a new aesthetic for church adornment, nostalgically medieval and Gothic in its vision, but decidedly Victorian and modern in its elaboration. They cultivated what the historian T. J. Jackson Lears has called "the religion of beauty"—a devotional love of liturgical drama, material symbolism, polychromy, sumptuous music, and graceful ornament. They wanted to fill the churches, as one handbook attested, with "sermons in stones, in glass, in wood, in flowers, and fruits, and leaves."[5]

Much of this ritual adornment focused on the high holy days of Christmas and Easter. Festooning the interior of churches with evergreens, flowers, vines, mosses, berries, leaves, wreaths, illuminated texts, emblems, tracery, and other devices became a holiday tradition. "Few fashions," Edward L. Cutts commented in 1868 in the third edition of his handbook on church decoration, "have made such rapid progress within the last few years as the improved fashion of Decorating our Churches with evergreens and flowers for the great Church festivals." By 1882 another leading advocate of the "new fashion," Ernest Geldart, could remark that "it requires an effort of memory to recall the days when, save a few ill-set sprigs of holly at Christmas, none of these things were known."[6]

Christmas initially led the way in church decoration, but Easter soon came to rival, if not surpass, the winter feast for special adornment. Ernest R. Suffling commented on Easter's ascent in his manual *Church Festival Decorations*: "Decorating the church at Easter, which a generation ago was but feebly carried out, has now become a recognized and general institution, and at no season of the year is it more appropriate. The joy of our hearts at the Resurrection of our Saviour—the seal of the completion of His work on earth—must surely be even greater than on the festival of His birth. The festival, coming as it does in early spring, is best commemorated by the use of as many flowers as possible."[7] Weaving garlands around pillars, covering reading desks and fonts with fresh blooms, hanging wreaths from arches and rails, erecting floral

65. Ernest Geldart, ed., *The Art of Garnishing Churches at Christmas and Other Times: A Manual of Directions* (London: Cox Sons, Buckley, 1882), plate 3.

crosses on the altar or communion table, filling windowsills with bouquets, setting up vine-covered trellises, and creating pyramids of lilies—in short, putting flowers everywhere—became an Easter vogue of vast proportions. As the *Ladies' Floral Cabinet* observed in 1885, "the graceful drapery of flowers" had come to be an essential part of Easter worship, and this "growing taste" for floral decorations in the churches was, the magazine thought, "one of the most cheering signs of the times."[8]

One way to render specific the rising importance of floral decorations at Easter is through diaries. The journal of Henry Dana Ward, rector of St. Jude's Episcopal Church in New York City, survives for the years from 1850 to 1857, and it suggests the budding interest in Easter flowers. He mentioned no special floral displays for his Easter services from 1850 to 1854, but in 1855 he noted that "the recess behind the Table was furnished with three pots of flow-

66. Easter church decorations, *Ladies' Home Journal* 34 (April 1917): 3.

ers in full bloom and the Font with the same in partial bloom." Ward thought that the flowers, all "Egyptian lilies," were pretty and pleasing, adding to the solemnity of the service. Regarding these decorations, as well as new coverings for the communion table and the pulpit, he took comfort that "no one was offended by these small novelties." He also made clear that his forays into festal decoration were tame compared to those of some other Episcopal churches. Visiting an afternoon Easter service at Trinity in 1857, he found the ritualism and decorations excessive: "They make *too much* of a good thing—chant the Anthems to death—and make a show of flowers on the Font & the reading Desk."[9] Decades before "the concept of show invaded the domain of culture" in the form of showplaces, showrooms, and fashion shows, churches such as Trinity were cultivating a festive, luxuriant, and dramatic religious world through the increasingly ornate art of church decoration.[10] This sense of Easter decorations as a show or spectacle would become all the more evident in the decades after the Civil War.

The diary of a young man who worked as a clerk at Tiffany's in New York City in the early 1870s suggested the dramatic impression that Easter decorations made. For Easter 1873, he went to a morning service at Christ Church and an afternoon service at St. Stephen's, both of which he found "magnificent," if fearfully crowded. The two churches, "well trimmed with beautiful flowers," were stunning in their decorations. "At Christs Church," he said, "the burning star they had Christmas was over the alter besides the decorations of flowers. At St Stephens was arranged in the same manner—gas jets[.] Over the alter (as if it was there without anything to keep it there) was suspended a cross and above over it a crown. The effect was very good[,] the flaming of the gas making it so brilliant." The decorations clearly made a lasting and strong impression on this young man (here at Easter he still remembers the blazing star from the previous Christmas). The ornaments were almost magical in allure. (The cross and crown, suspended in air, are supported by hidden devices.) Indeed, he seemed far more overawed by the decorations that he saw in New York's Episcopal and Catholic churches than by anything he came across in New York's stores. For theatrical effect, the stores in the 1870s still had much to learn from the churches.[11]

The special floral decorations for Easter received particular attention in women's diaries. An active Baptist layperson in New York City, Sarah Anne Todd, commented in her diary on a visit to an Episcopal church for an Easter service in 1867: "Being Easter Sunday the Church was handsomely dressed with flowers." Likewise, in her diary the New Yorker Elizabeth Merchant often made note of the Easter display of flowers: "Our church was beautifully dressed with flowers," she wrote of Easter 1883; "The church was lovely with flowers," she recalled of Easter worship in 1886; "Flowers perfectly beautiful & Mr Brooks splendid," she eulogized on the occasion of two Easter services at Trinity Episcopal that she and her son enjoyed in 1887. Another New York woman, Mrs. George Richards, made similar notations about Easter in her diary, writing tellingly in 1888: "Easter Day, Communion Sunday. Flowers in church. Alice & I took the children to the Church to see the flowers." Decorations seen, as much as sermons heard or eucharistic elements received, stood out in the memories that these women recorded. For women especially, who often took particular responsibility for these floral displays, Easter in the churches was a time for flowers.[12]

The implications and consequences of the new fascination with Easter decorations were manifold. Certainly, and perhaps quintessentially, this art constituted an important new medium for religious expression. The decorations were devotional; their "double purpose" was to glorify God and edify Christians. At Trinity Episcopal in 1861, the *New York Sun* reported, the Easter floral decorations were "in fine taste": "Flowers suggestive of the fundamental doctrines of Christianity composed the ornaments, and were so grouped as to indicate the cardinal truths of religion. In the centre of the altar was a floral globe mounted by a cross, and expressive of the redemption of the world." Floral decorations, testifying to the promise of new life, became for Victorians one of the dominant ways of communicating the Christian message of resurrection. This floral piety was evident in the *New York Herald's* account of Easter services at St. Alban's Episcopal Church in 1868: "The blossom and bloom of life . . . hung in grand festoons upon altar and lectern; they peeped out from every nook and cranny available for the purpose; they typified the resurrection at every point." To make certain that the devotional significance of the decorations remained clear, the churches often prominently displayed illuminated scriptural texts, usually drawn in intricate Gothic lettering. Arches and altars, chancels and choirs, brimmed with monumental affirmations: "He is risen"; "I am the Resurrection and the Life"; "Now is Christ risen from the dead, the first-fruits of them that slept"; "O death, where is thy sting? O grave, where is thy victory?" Easter decorations were a form of popular piety that evoked the ancient coalescence of the rebirth of spring and the resurrection of Christ.[13]

In their devotional dimensions Easter decorations also suggested a sentimental and domestic version of Christian piety. Easter, *Harper's* said, was "winning our household feeling as well as our religious respect"; it served as a liturgical affirmation of the eternality of "family affections," as a celebration of "the great sentiment of home love." This domestic tenor was evident in the increasing overlap of church and home decorations: Lilies, floral crosses, and distinctive Easter bouquets, for example, ornamented Victorian altars and parlors alike. The decorative result was to join the church and the home in a shared, overarching design—"the House Beautiful."[14] Moreover, flowers suggested how Easter was becoming preeminently "the festival of sacred remembrance." Easter blooms, lilies especially, were presented in the churches as personal memorials for "departed kindred and friends"; they were hopeful, powerful tokens of the restored wholeness of familial circles. Indeed, the new love of Easter flowers was at one level the liturgical counterpart to Elizabeth Stuart Phelps's Victorian bestseller *The Gates Ajar*—a sentimental, consoling portrayal of heaven in terms of home, family, and friends. The new Easter helped reinforce the Victorian predilection for picturing heaven more as a place of human relationships and domestic reunions than as a God-centered realm of divine praise, light, and glory.[15]

The new passion for floral decoration clearly carried consequences that were not only devotional and domestic. For one thing, issues of competition and emulation crept into the Easter displays. The handbooks warned against the tendencies toward extravagance and rivalry: "Never try to beat the record," Ernest Geldart instructed. "Pray don't let it be your ambition that prompts you to 'beat' anything you have ever done, and above all, don't try to beat your neighbour's efforts." Admonitions notwithstanding, competition became an acknowledged undercurrent in holiday church decoration. Who would have the most beautiful and extensive floral displays? Who would have the most inspiring music, the most solemn, dramatic, and crowded services? As the *New York Herald* observed in 1881, "The Catholics and Episcopalians are, of course, the foremost in the observance of the season, but other denominations are not far behind, and all vie with each other to make their house the most attractive to the worshipper." In a culture increasingly fascinated with the religious and familial possibilities of Christmas and Easter, the dramatic, well-appointed services of Catholics and Episcopalians were alluring. "The congregations in most of the churches were large, especially in those of the Catholics and Episcopalians, where fine flowers and music were attractive," the *New York Sun* commented in a typical report in 1878.[16] In America's free-market religious culture, church decoration became another way of attracting parishioners and gaining attention. Members of less ritualist denominations—Presbyterians, Methodists, and even Baptists—learned to emulate Episcopalian and Catholic forms of holiday celebration in order to hold the allegiance of their people at these seasons of the year. Thorstein Veblen was wrong to view the "devout consumption" of the churches in the 1890s—their increasingly elaborate "ceremonial paraphernalia"—simply in terms of "status" and "conspicuous waste." (Such an interpretation was irredeemably monochromatic.) But he was right to see competition and emulation as component parts of Victorian church furnishing and decoration.[17]

Another unintended consequence of holiday church decoration was how it fostered modishness and exoticism. In 1867 the *New York Herald*, in commenting on the "elaborate floral decorations" for Easter at St. John the Baptist Episcopal Church, noted that the display included "one of the only three genuine palms known to exist in the United States." Similarly, an 1873 report on the Easter decorations in the Church of the Divine Paternity struck the same chord of rarity: "Surmounting the reredos was a magnificent cross made of lilies, on either side of which were two recumbent beds of roses. The altar was profusely covered with the rarest of exotics." Trinity Episcopal that same year was likewise said to have been "embowered in terraces of glorious exotics, pyramids of floral gorgeousness." Ernest Suffling, summarizing this trend toward floral exoticism—if not colonialist rampage—observed that where a few "indigenous evergreens" had formerly satisfied the church decorator, now "we ransack the whole world, for our grasses, flowers, and palms, our fruits and mosses." There was little that was traditional, antimodern, or medieval in searching out "rare evergreens," "choice tropicals," or "calla lilies of remarkable size and beauty, sent hermetically sealed from California." Style, taste, abundance, and novelty—the very values of the burgeoning consumer culture—became defining features of Easter decorations in the churches. The fashionable Easter given expression in the Easter parade and in turn-of-the-century department stores had its roots in the religious culture, which itself was becoming progressively more consumerist in its mode of celebration. At Easter, devout consumption fed its more worldly counterpart.[18]

A final, portentous consequence of the new art of church decoration was that it provided a model or repertory for holiday displays outside the churches in the marketplace. With Easter, even more than with Christmas, the commercial culture built its enterprise directly on the religious culture—on Christian patterns of decoration, display, and celebration. Church music, flowers, ornaments, banners, and other decorations all found their way into show windows and interior displays in late-nineteenth- and early-twentieth-century department stores. Easter decorations were clearly attractive for commercial appropriation; their associations with the church and liturgical solemnity, with women and the home, with fashion and affluence, were all useful connections for merchandising. With multiple layers of meaning, Easter emblems, popularized through church decoration, provided retailers with redolent symbols.

More broadly, the art of church decoration offered a useful aesthetic for the art of store decoration. The manuals for church decoration, flourishing by the 1860s and 1870s, provided a model for similar manuals on show-window design, the first of which appeared in 1889 and dozens of which followed. Church decorators, like their commercial counterparts after them, stressed the power of visual representation, the importance of harmonizing form and color, the careful planning of designs, and the expressive potential of lighting and glass. Church decorators also provided a principle of innovation, regularly experimenting with new decorative materials and warning against "sameness," "feeble repetition," and "distasteful monotony" in beautifying the sanctuary. This outlook intermeshed with the mounting desire of window trimmers and store decorators to bring seasonal variety and originality to their displays of goods. In such ways, the art of church decoration contributed to the formation of "the display aesthetic" that came to characterize the modern consumer culture.[19]

Irving Berlin's *Easter Parade* in itself suggests the migration of church decoration into the marketplace: Don Hewes passes the show window of a dry-goods store that is trimmed with Easter lilies, as is the interior of the millinery shop he patronizes. The transformation of church decorations into store embellishments was evident as early as the 1880s and 1890s. "Make a gala week of the week before Easter," the *Dry Goods Chronicle* exhorted in 1898. "Tog your store out until it shines with the Easter spirit. . . . Blossom with the Easter lily, give your store a dress in keeping with this Easter festival. . . . It may cost something to fit your store to look equal to the occasion, but it will be worth all it may cost." This kind of advice was regularly put into practice. "The store is in harmony with the occasion," Wanamaker's Easter catalogue boasted in 1893. "Easter Symbols are everywhere in the decorations. . . . Easter merchandise is all over the store."[20] By the turn of the century, such Easter displays had become standard trade preparations: Lavish store decorations were considered essential for imparting and evoking the Easter spirit and for attracting holiday shoppers.

Trimming a store for Easter meant a profusion of seasonal folk symbols such as rabbits, chicks, and eggs, often on a gargantuan scale (massive rabbits to go with the towering Santa Clauses of Christmas or the mammoth cakes of New Year's). As at Christmas, though, store decorations at Easter entailed a surplus of Christian iconography. The *American Advertiser* offered this description of a "delicate and pleasing" Easter window in a Chicago jewelry store in 1890:

> The window floor was covered with white jewelers' cotton in sheets, looking pure as snow. A cross of similar material and whiteness was slightly raised above the level of the window-floor, in the middle rear part of the window. On each side of the window was a calla lily blossom, the flower being cut short off below the bloom. Inside the lily, like a drop of purest dew, sparkled a diamond—just one on each lily. The cross was slightly twined with smilax, which also bordered the back of the window. A white rose was scattered here and there, and on the cross and on the white window floor were displayed a few gems and trinkets,—not enough to distract the attention or give the appearance of crowding. . . . Taken altogether the display was the perfection of good taste and artistic skill.

The cross and lilies, staples of church decoration, became mainstays of the window dresser's art—repeated centerpieces for the display of goods, whether millinery, greeting cards, or even groceries.[21] In this case, jewelry and other items were actually attached to the lilies and the cross, making the link between them direct and tangible.

Designs for show windows also played on the sentimental, domestic dimensions of Victorian Easter piety. One window trimmer bragged in 1896 of a crowd-stopping Easter display: Entitled "Gates Ajar," the window was trimmed from floor to ceiling "with spotless white silk handkerchiefs entwined with ferns and smilax from the millinery stock and plants from the hot-house." The focal point of the window was "a flight of five steps, at the head of which was a large double gate, partially opened, so as to show one large figure in white silk and pretty little cherubs (dolls with wings of gold and silver paper) as if in the act of flying." This show-window glimpse of silky

67. Easter decorations, Simpson-Crawford department store, New York City, 1904.

68. Easter show window of millinery, from [Charles A. Tracy, ed.], *The Art of Decorating Show Windows and Interiors*, 3d ed. (Chicago: Merchants Record, 1906), 314.

white seraphs and everlasting life dovetailed with the alluring domestic heaven depicted in Elizabeth Stuart Phelps's *Gates Ajar* and its sequels. In *The Feminization of American Culture*, Ann Douglas wryly comments that reading Phelps's novels about heaven with all their luminous detail about domestic furnishings and possessions "is somewhat like window-shopping outside the fanciest stores on Fifth Avenue." Window trimmers and store decorators had the same intuition. In their appropriation of Phelps's themes, they made explicit the otherwise implicit interconnections between this domestic piety and consumerist ideals.[22]

Store decorations for Easter were often more elaborate than such relatively modest show windows, and sometimes rivaled the churches in what one window trimmer called "cathedral effect[s]." This decorative intricacy was epitomized in the Easter adornment in Wanamaker's in Philadelphia. As was the case at Christmas, Wanamaker's Grand Court was transformed at Easter into a religious spectacle. Statues of angels, thousands of lilies and ferns, displays of ornate ecclesiastical vestments, religious banners and tapestries, and mot-

69. Easter display of tea, from Alfred G. Bauer, *The Art of Window Dressing for Grocers* (Chicago: Sprague, Warner, [1902]), 80.

70. Greeting-card show window for Easter, *Greeting Card* 5 (March 1933): 5.

71. Wanamaker's Grand Court, Easter 1931.

toes proclaiming "He is Risen!" and "Alleluia!" all found a place in Wanamaker's during the Easter season in the early decades of the twentieth century. The store's grandest Easter spectacle, however, was the repeated display, which had begun by the early 1930s, of two monumental canvases by the Hungarian artist Michael de Munkacsy—one painting (twenty feet eight inches by thirteen feet six inches) entitled *Christ before Pilate* and the other (twenty-three feet four inches by fourteen feet two inches) entitled *Christ on Calvary*. Painted in 1881 and 1884, respectively, these works had been widely exhibited and heralded in this country and had achieved international repute in their day as grand masterpieces. Purchased by John Wanamaker as favored treasures for his own impressive collection of art, the paintings eventually graced the Grand Court on a nearly annual basis during Lent and Easter. The exhibition of paintings with this level of acclaim was something that the churches could rarely match. Easter displays such as these brought into sharp relief the dynamic interplay of art, piety, and commerce in the American marketplace. Like Christmas in the Grand Court, Easter in Wanamaker's epito-

72. Wanamaker's Grand Court, Easter 1957.

mized the translation of the Gothic revival and the art of church decoration into a commercial idiom.[23]

Discerning the meaning and significance of the various Christian emblems that found their way into show windows and department stores is no easy task. What did religious symbols—such as the cross, lilies, church replicas, or the Agnus Dei—come to symbolize when placed within the context of Easter displays? In the ersatz, artful, and cunning world of the marketplace, the meanings of symbols were particularly unstable and slippery. Perhaps such religious emblems became quite literally so much window dressing—that is, artificial, distracting, and illusory fluff, little more than splashes of color and attractive packaging, a vapid and insincere mimicry of liturgical art. Certainly the employment of religious symbols as merchandising icons carried an undeniable artifice and doubleness, a sharp edge of deception. In their intramural discussions of display techniques, window trimmers were often quite candid about their purposes. L. Frank Baum, who started in the fantasy world of show windows before moving on to the *Wizard of Oz*, commented matter-of-factly on the place of the cross in Easter displays: "The cross is the principal emblem of Easter and is used in connection with many displays, being suitable for any line of merchandise. To be most effective it should be a floral cross." The essential object in window dressing was, after all, to sell goods, and religious symbols, like all display props, were used self-consciously to maximize this effect.[24] Creatively negotiating the borderland between commerce and Christianity was part of the window trimmer's calling, and these Easter icons were, at one level, simply another trick of the trade.

But these displays represented more than commercial artifice. The widespread infusion of religious symbols into the marketplace also suggested the deep hold of Christianity on the culture and indicated anew how "adaptable" American religion was to "popular commercial forms."[25] Far from eschewing Christian emblems, retailers seized the opportunity to consecrate their stores through holiday decorations. Often enough, churchgoing merchants employed these emblems straightforwardly to evoke and affirm the old-time piety; certainly Wanamaker understood his cathedral-like decorations and his in-store choir concerts in religious terms. The density of spiritual referents was, after all, what made these symbols so powerful; it is also what made them so useful. Still, the manipulation, misappropriation, or displacement of Christian symbols was rarely the issue for merchants or customers. In these displays Christian hopes and consumerist dreams regularly merged into a cohesive cultural whole. Rather than shunting aside the church, turn-of-the-century department stores (and the emergent mass culture that these institutions represented) accorded Christianity considerable cultural authority during the holidays.

In appropriating Christian symbols merchants were, at one level, achieving exactly what liberal Protestant pundits had been calling for: namely, the wholesale consecration of the marketplace. In a tract published in 1891, for example, social-gospeler George Herron exhorted "the Christian business men of America" to "make the marketplace as sacred as the church." "You can draw the world's trades and traffics within the onsweep of Christ's redemptive purpose." Wanamaker and other merchants like him were seen by many Protestants as the consummate consecrators of wealth and the market. In the "one undivided Kingdom of God," commerce and Christianity would harmoniously support one another, cohering in a millennium of fulfilled progressivism. The turn-of-the-century celebrations of Christmas and Easter in the department stores were the rites of that liberal cultural faith in abundance and amelioration. At the same time, they were a modern Protestant staging of the "festive marketplace" of the early modern world in which the church's time converged with the "brimming-over abundance" of the fair. Again, Christians like Wanamaker looked backward, even as they moved forward into the heart of modernity.[26]

The seemingly happy convergence of Christianity and consumption at Easter suggested in itself, however, a profound transformation in the meaning of Christian symbols. The stores clearly presented a new gospel of prosperity that was far removed from traditional Christian emphases on self-abnegation and divine sacrifice. "When I survey the wondrous cross on which the Prince of glory died," Isaac Watts had versified in the eighteenth century in lines his Victorian heirs still sang, "My richest gain I count but loss, and pour contempt on all my pride. . . . All the vain things that charm me most, I sacrifice them to his blood." Surveying the wondrous cross within a show window or a department store effectively shifted the foundations of this crucicentric piety from self-denial to self-fulfillment. The context in which these symbols appeared suggested a substantial revision of the faith—a new image of piety at peace with plenty and at home in the new "dream world" of mass consumption. This was no small subversion. Traditional Christian symbols of self-abnegation had come to legitimate luxury, elegance, and indulgence. The cross had become one of the charms of the merchandiser's art, its religious power absorbed into the new magic of modern commodities and advertising. It would not be long before the cross itself became a fashion accessory, a bit of costume jewelry for the modern styling of the self.[27]

PIETY, FASHION, AND A SPRING PROMENADE

The vogue for Easter flowers and church decoration intertwined with other Easter fashions—those in clothing and millinery. Of an Easter service at Christ Church, an Episcopalian congregation on Fifth Avenue, the *New York Herald* wrote in 1873: "More than one-half of the congregation were ladies, who displayed all the gorgeous and marvelous articles of dress which Dame Fashion has submitted to be the ruling idea of Spring, and the appearance of the body of the church thus vied in effect and magnificence with the pleasant and tasteful array of flowers which decorated the chancel." In a similar vein, a reporter compared "the costumes of the ladies" at St. Patrick's Cathedral for Easter 1871 with "a parterre of flowers." Since spring millinery fashions actually tended to include various flora and fauna, such comparisons were not mere similes. Fashions in flowers and dress, indeed, interpenetrated one another. In 1897, for example, violets were reported to be in greater demand than any other Easter flower "because the violet, in all its various shades, is the predominating color in dress." The development of the Easter parade along Fifth Avenue was in part connected with the popularity of visiting the different churches to see their elaborate floral decorations. "Many will go to church to-day to see the flowers," the *New York Times* observed in 1889, "and not a few are accustomed to join the parade on Fifth-avenue from church to church, just to look at the beautiful productions of nature." In many ways, the Victorian love of Easter flowers and ornate church decoration blossomed naturally into the famous promenade of Easter fashions.[28]

Having new clothes for Easter or dressing up in special ways for the festival was never simply about modern forms of fashion and display. The practice had deep roots, or at least resonances, in European religious traditions and folk customs at Easter. Sacred times—baptisms, weddings, funerals, fasts, and feasts—warranted special forms of dress, material markers of holiness and celebration. Uncommon or distinctive garb for Easter, like the Sunday best of the Sabbatarian or the special vestments of priests, had long communicated the solemnity of the occasion. The special raiment might be as simple as new gloves, ribbons, or stockings, or as stunning as a wholly white outfit. Conventions were localistic and diverse, but the overarching point was captured in an Irish adage: "For Christmas, food and drink; for Easter, new clothes." A frequently recited maxim from Poor Robin distilled such holiday expectations into a couplet:

> At Easter let your clothes be new,
> Or else be sure you will it rue.

This old English saying itself became part of the Victorian memory about Easter, a selective slice of Easter folklore that helped people situate their own interest in new attire for the holiday within the comforting framework of tradition. As the *New York Herald* noted in 1855, "There is an old proverb that if on Easter Sunday some part of your dress is not new you will have no good fortune that year."[29]

The parade of Easter fashions in New York City emerged as a distinct religious and cultural event in the 1870s and 1880s, and the Easter services of the churches were at the center of it. An account in 1873 in the *New York Herald* of "the throngs of people" going to and from church suggested the parade's incipient form:

> They were a gaily dressed crowd of worshippers, and the female portion of it seemed to have come out *en masse* in fresh apparel, and dazzled the eye with their exhibition of shade and color in the multitudinous and variegated hues of their garments. Fifth avenue, from Tenth street to the Central Park, from ten o'clock in the morning till late in the afternoon, was one long procession of men and women, whose attire and bearing betokened refinement, wealth and prosperity, and nearly all these were worshippers of some denomination or another, as the crowds that poured in and out of the various religious edifices along the line of the avenue amply testified.

By the end of the 1870s the "fashionable promenade" was more clearly set in the early afternoon, ensuing at the conclusion of the morning church services: "In the afternoon," the *Herald* reported in 1879, "Fifth avenue was a brilliant sight when the thronging congregations of the various churches poured out upon the sidewalks and leisurely journeyed homeward." *Le beau monde* flowed out of the churches into a vast concourse of style, affluence, and luxury. Contemporary fashion and Christian festival were confluent; the one enlarged the other.[30]

In the 1880s the afternoon promenade of Easter churchgoers became all the more "the great fashion show of the year." By 1890 the procession had achieved standing as a recognized marvel on New York's calendar of festivities and had taken on its enduring designation as "the Easter parade." As the *New York Times* reported in 1890, "It was the great Easter Sunday parade, which has become such an established institution in New-York that the curious flock to Fifth-avenue almost as numerously and enthusiastically as they do to see a circus parade." A spectacle of new spring fashions, prismatic colors, seasonal bouquets and corsages, elaborate and ever-changing millinery, New York's "great Easter parade" was an occasion for people "to see and be seen." By the mid-1890s, day-trippers from New Jersey and Long Island as well as other visitors flocked to the Fifth Avenue pageant to survey the fashions and to join in the promenade. Thus, having begun as a procession of fashionable and privileged churchgoers, the parade quickly became a jostling, crowded scene—"a kaleidoscope of humanity that changed incessantly and presented a new picture with every change."[31]

The emergence of the Easter parade clearly presented a choice opportunity for dry-goods and millinery establishments. Surprisingly, however, retailers were not overly quick to push the promotional connection between Easter and seasonal fashions. While Christmas was already garnering the advertising attention of New York's emergent dry-goods palaces in the 1840s and 1850s, Easter went unnoticed. Spring openings were a merchandising staple for New York firms by the mid–nineteenth century, yet no advertising efforts were fabricated to link spring bonnets or other spring fashions explicitly to Easter. In the 1850s and 1860s, newspaper advertisements for seasonal apparel remained the same before and after Easter. Through the mid-1870s, few, if any, attempts were made to create a specific market for the holiday, even though the connection between Easter and new spring styles was already apparent in New York's most fashionable churches. Only in the late 1870s did New York's merchants begin to exploit the growing religious link between Easter and fashion. According to Ralph M. Hower, Macy's first began to promote goods specifically for Easter in its newspaper advertising in 1878, and this coincides

73. Easter parade, New York City, ca. 1903.

with the early efforts of other retailers. For example, in the *New York Sun* in 1878 E. Ridley and Sons advertised "Trimmed Bonnets and Round Hats, Manufactured for Easter," and Lord and Taylor made a similar pitch. In the 1880s almost all the leading department stores would join in this kind of advertising, thus bringing spring fashions and Easter into an explicit and ever-deepening alliance.[32]

By the 1890s, the promotion of Easter within the dry-goods industry was in full swing. There was no bigger event in the trade's calendar. "Easter is preeminently the festival of the dry goods trade," the *Dry Goods Economist* concluded in 1894. "Much of the success of the year's business hangs upon the demand experienced during the weeks just preceding Easter." Retailers did all they could to stoke the desire for Easter fashions. "Everything is done during these days to influence the shopper to buy," the *Dry Goods Economist* observed of the Easter season in 1894. "Windows are trimmed with all the art at the dresser's command and with as much study as the Royal Academician gives to a magnificent painting." Merchants had clearly come to see their role in the Easter festival as more than one of simply responding to a demand for seasonal goods. Instead, their goal was to expand the market, to deepen and widen these holiday customs. "Women may be induced to think more and more of something special for Easter by telling insinuations judiciously put in your advertising," the *Dry Goods Chronicle* theorized in 1898. "Women may be induced to forego the satisfying of some actual need in order to gratify an Easter fancy, provided you prod their vanity with suggestive advertising and supplement it with a fetching store display." As was the case with so many other dimensions of the expanding consumer culture, women were condescendingly cast as the arch-consumers at Easter and received most of the attention in its promotion. If merchants had been slow to get on the Easter bandwagon in the 1860s and 1870s, they were among its loudest trumpeters and trombonists by the 1890s. Through their tireless promotions, they helped define Easter as "a time for 'dress parade' and 'full feather.'"[33]

A spectacle of faith and fashion, the Easter parade was assuredly a multivalent ritual, a multilayered cultural performance. For the devout the season's new clothes were part of a synthesis of piety and material culture: As the gray of winter and the darkness of Lent and Good Friday gave way to the rebirth of spring and the Resurrection, the sumptuous hues of Easter fashions reflected these transitions. New Yorker Elizabeth Orr suggested this dense interplay of themes in her diary entry about Easter in 1871:

> Easter Sunday came in bright and beautiful[,] has been one of the most beautiful Spring days I ever experienced. Every one seemed to be influenced by the weather, bright happy faces. Most every one out in their holiday clothes gotten up for the occasion. Dr Eddy gave us one of his good discourses on the reserection of Christ and his followers. Oh that I may be one of that number! "Am I his or Am I not" should be a question with us. I know and feel my sinfulness, and he came to save just such a sinner. I repent every day, and trust I am forgiven. Oh that happy day when we will have no more sin to repent of, but constantly [be] in the presence of our Lord and Master.

In Orr's recollections of the day's activities, the beautiful spring weather led naturally to promenading in holiday clothes, which connected seamlessly, in turn, with pious reflections on sin, repentance, and resurrection. Easter devotion was part of a rich mix of experiences in which impressions of clothes and sunshine and smiles flitted alongside the ringing words of the pastor's sermon.[34]

Elizabeth Merchant's diary entries on Easter displayed the same sort of tangled synthesis of seasonal rejoicing, new clothes, and resurrection. The Saturday before Easter in 1881 she noted: "Went to town looking for Easter cards

74. *(Left)* "New York Shop-Girls Buying Easter Bonnets on Division Street," *Harper's Weekly*, 5 April 1890, 256.
75. *(Right)* "The Maiden's Prayer," George W. Miles advertisement, trade card, ca. 1885.

& buying myself a dress . . . with linings &c. then went to Bible class & heard a lovely lecture from Dr. Hall on the resurrection." In another passage she waxed eloquent on the interconnections between the new life of Easter and the vernal revival: "Oh! Such a perfect day! trees budding birds singing—grass is green & sky so beautiful with its fleecy clouds. All the air full of sweet Spring sounds. I long to be out Enjoying every Moment at this season of so much beauty. There is an immense Robin red breast hopping and flying over the lawn! Oh God will the resurrection of our frail bodies be glorious like this waking of nature from the cold death of Winter?" Elizabeth Merchant readily combined the satisfactions of Easter shopping with the deeper mysteries of Christianity and nature. The same overlay of experiences was captured in Clara Pardee's clipped entry for Easter 1883: "A lovely Easter day—Out to church & walked up 5th Ave. Crowds of people—spring hats." Marjorie Reynolds was similarly terse in her notes about Easter in 1912: "Robed in new white corduroy. To the Brick [Church] with Oliver & a bunch of flowers. I don't know [what] I enjoyed more . . . a packed church . . . beautiful music & a good sermon . . . on the Av. afterwards w[ith] O[liver] & Mr. M[iddle] up to 59th St." The clear reconfiguring of Easter by the burgeoning consumer culture did not necessarily lessen the feast's religious power; instead it added to its sensuous richness and complexity. In these women's diaries, there was no necessary movement away from salvation to self-fulfillment, no hard-and-fast opposition between Christian soteriology and cosmopolitan display. For religious and cultural critics, it would prove all too easy to associate the feminized domains of church decoration and Easter fashion with vanity and immodesty. (One trade writer tellingly spoke of the "masculine contempt" for flowery forms of dress and millinery.) In these women's jottings, however, church and parade, fashion and festival, coalesced into an undivided whole.[35]

As Irving Berlin's movie suggests, all the spring promenaders and curious onlookers hardly maintained this synthesis of piety and materiality. As at any festival, a wide range of motivations and expectations animated those in attendance. Tens of thousands and eventually hundreds of thousands clogged New York's fashionable thoroughfares for the Easter parade, and people took their bearings from various sources, sometimes divergent, often overlapping. Some went forth from the churches on errands of benevolence, making their way to hospitals and orphanages with flowers to brighten up the holiday for others. Some were abroad mostly to court and flirt and ogle; almost all were seeking diversion and entertainment of one kind or another. Not a few came out to work the milling crowds: thieves and pickpockets with quick hands, street vendors and peddlers with various wares. At the same time, many members of Veblen's leisure class graced the avenue, showcasing their status, urbanity, and importance, perhaps most interested in the parade as a theater of social prestige. Also, many who were frankly indifferent to religion joined in the procession—those, as the *New York Herald* groused in 1890, who had heard "no Easter benediction" and whose holiday glow "came from a brandy cocktail with a dash of absinthe in it." In all, the parade presented a mélange of characters who moved to various rhythms.[36]

Certainly among the loudest drummers was fashion: Lovers of new spring apparel and millinery, devotees of the latest style and vogue, peopled Fifth Avenue. The Easter parade, as Irving Berlin's movie highlighted, was indeed a celebration of the consumer culture—its capitalistic abundance, its unfettered choices, its constantly changing styles. If there was ever a holiday spectacle that apotheosized the "American way of life," this was it. New York's dress parade was a tableau of American prosperity. Eventually it even came to be seen as a parable about the bounties of American enterprise that contrasted sharply with the failures of Soviet Communism. "Fifth Avenue on Easter Sunday," a *New York Times* columnist wrote in 1949, "would probably irritate

Stalin more than he is already exasperated with the United States. . . . It will take a long series of five-year plans before the Soviet woman can buy a dress, a hat or a pair of shoes for anything near the price a New York working girl paid for her Easter outfit."[37] In 1955 the *Saturday Evening Post* was even more blunt about the parade's cultural meaning: New York's springtime pageant stood as "a reflection of the American Dream—that a person is as good as the clothes, car and home he is able to buy." In this writer's reckoning, the church's celebration of Easter was "incidental" to this wider public affirmation of American prosperity. The Easter parade's peculiar trademark was, to be sure, a gospel of wealth and refinement. Christian celebration in modern American culture ebbed easily into a public faith in boundless abundance, changing fashions, and consumer choice.[38]

Still, the Easter parade remained a polysemous event, hardly reducible to a surface of fashion, respectability, and buttoned-up conventionality. Beneath its consumerist credo were carnivalesque tinges reminiscent of old Easter Monday traditions of mummery, which, as at New Year's, included outlandish costumes and boisterous conviviality. (How else but in terms of the fantastical and the improvisational could one explain the large hat worn by one woman in 1953 that contained both a replica of the Last Supper and a live bird in a cage?) In many ways, the Easter parade was an unstructured, boundless, liminal event: There was "no apparent beginning, ending, organization or purpose." People flowed in and out of it; it was something of a leisurely free-for-all where fashionable promenaders, idle spectators, and publicity mongers merged into a closely commingled throng. The Easter parade may have begun in the 1870s as a parade of refinement—a middle- and upper-class staging of gentility, a sort of ritual primer for immigrants and the working class on the accoutrements of respectability—but by the turn of the century it had more than a hint of the crowded, unpredictable energy of a street fair in which both Lenten and bourgeois strictures met the ancient solvent of Easter laughter. Certainly the residual form of the parade that survives today in New York City is more costumed frolic than genteel show.[39]

The creative, playful possibilities were also seen in the roles women assumed in this public drama. With their elaborate dresses and millinery, they took center stage. In a culture in which men and their civic associations had long dominated formal street parades, and in a culture in which rowdy male youths had long made carnivalesque festivity and violence their special domain, the Easter parade was decidedly different. In contrast to the home-centered celebrations that so often prevailed among middle-class Victorian women, and in contrast to the commonly minimal role of women as spectators on the edges of civic ceremony, the Easter parade was preeminently about women in public procession. Whereas most nineteenth-century parades re-

76. *(Left)* "The Eternal Question," *Spokesman-Review*, 9 April 1908, 1.
77. *(Right)* "Easter hats," Gage Brothers advertisement, 1906.

volved quite literally around the *man* in the street, the Easter procession turned this convention on its head. Its very fluidity, its unplanned and unchoreographed quality, and its close connection to the churches made possible the breaking of "the powerful gender taboo" that governed so much of American ceremonial life.[40]

The parading of women in Easter millinery also served as a subversion of Pauline (and evangelical Protestant) views about head-coverings as emblematic of female modesty and meekness. The new world of Easter millinery was about the assertion of the female self; about a world of mirrors and studied appearances ("You cannot have too many mirrors," one book on the art of millinery advised); about self-transformation through bewitching lines, fabrics, and colors; about the fashioning and refashioning of the self in a parade of protean styles. Millinery was a creative art, a woman-dominated enterprise in which customers and designers often joined in a whimsical play with ornamental materials—feathers, ribbons, flowers, silk, taffeta, and brocade. To be sure, Victorian women's fashions were often restrictive and oppressive, even contorting the female body, but this parade of Easter millinery appeared more subversive than tyrannical, a grand street theater of chameleon inconstancy and springlike possibility.[41]

Among the most far-reaching consequences of New York's dress parade is that it became a cultural model for spin-off observances around the country. Parallel events cropped up in other major cities, such as Philadelphia and Boston, and appeared in smaller towns as well. The cultural diffusion of New York's great Easter procession became especially evident in satellite resorts such as Coney Island, Asbury Park, and Atlantic City, where the new Barnums of commercialized leisure reproduced facsimiles for their own purposes. In these places the Easter parade was transformed into an excursion, a tourist attraction. The *New York Herald* reported that at Coney Island in 1925, the local chamber of commerce had organized, with the help of several manufacturers, "a fashion show and Easter parade." To augment the proceedings the promoters had hired fifty "show girls" to parade in bathing suits; the crowds were overwhelming. No less hucksterish were the proceedings at Atlantic City, where by the 1920s the Easter parade was attracting annual crowds of two hundred thousand and more. Like Coney Island, Atlantic City was an excursionist's wonderland, and the parade there presented a kaleidoscopic scene of lolling, laughing pleasure seekers—a boardwalk carnival of costuming and consumption. Easter, like other American holidays, became a vacation. Begun in an outflow of the churches, the Easter parade climaxed in an amusement for that ultimate consumer, the tourist.[42]

"A BEWILDERING ARRAY OF PLASTIC FORMS": EASTER KNICKKNACKS AND NOVELTIES

Complementing the profusion of Easter flowers and the parade of Easter fashions was a plenitude of new Easter gifts. Beginning in the late 1870s, the number of goods for Easter—cards, toys, plants, flowers, confectionery, and other novelties—mushroomed at an astonishing rate. The commercial production of endless varieties of Easter eggs was but one example of this proliferation. "There are," the *New York Herald* marveled in 1881, "paper eggs, wooden eggs, satin and silk eggs, plush eggs, tin eggs, silver eggs, gilt eggs, gold eggs, glass and china eggs and sugar eggs." Priced from ten cents to more than a hundred dollars and ranging in size from the Lilliputian to the Brobdingnagian, Easter eggs had rolled out of the field of folk custom into the American marketplace. So deep-rooted in European popular culture and so fecund in its symbolic associations, the egg at Easter was the perfect emblem

78. Easter parade, Atlantic City, 1905.

to commercialize. "Time was when Easter was only Easter—and eggs were only eggs," the *Herald* concluded. "But now Easter is a great and general holiday—a sort of second Christmas,—and Easter eggs are alike articles of value and works of art." In a word, Easter eggs had become commodities. As went eggs, so went the holiday: Easter was transformed in the last decades of the nineteenth century into "a fashionable festival" of " 'knicknacks,' oddities and presents."[43]

The rapid proliferation of Easter goods in the 1880s and 1890s was striking, if not stunning. "It is within a period of two years," the *New York Times* marveled in 1882, "that the custom of making presents on Easter has come to be a well-observed fashion." Before this, the *Times* reported, few holiday tokens were exchanged, and those that were tended to consist of simple homemade items such as dyed hard-boiled eggs. In her regional study of Easter in Lancaster County, Pennsylvania, the historian Elizabeth Clarke Kieffer also found the late 1870s and early 1880s to be the crucial years of transition. Through the mid-1870s Lancaster newspapers paid only brief attention to Easter, and even these limited notices were more often critical of the holiday's "superstitious" customs than supportive of the feast's liturgical enactment. When one newspaper in 1880 finally "caught the holiday spirit" with a front-page article on local celebrations, it focused on the growing welter of Easter whatnots and souvenirs:

> Never in all our history has there been so marked an observance of Easter as during the present season. The confectionery windows are filled with eggs of every description, many of them of rich and costly design, as well as the mythical rabbits that laid the eggs, and the nests to lay them in. Bookstores have large assortments of Easter cards, carrying with them instruction as well as beauty, and on market this morning the florists . . . quickly sold their entire stock, people buying them with the greatest avidity for home and church decorations.

In the late 1870s and early 1880s seasonal goods, gifts, and displays increasingly demarcated the holiday's observance: Easter seemed to be as much about novel merchandise as about church services or folk rituals. "Easter," the *New York Times* summarized in 1882, "has come to be a day on which the exchanging of presents has become as common and fashionable as on Christmas."[44]

If the Victorian Easter never quite made it to the level of a second Christmas, it certainly came to mirror the winter feast. Diaries from the late nineteenth century suggest the growing importance of Easter as an occasion for cards and gifts. In the 1860s and 1870s Elizabeth Merchant took no notice of the holiday as a gift-giving occasion, but in the 1880s she regularly recorded giving and receiving small tokens of friendship, especially Easter cards. For the holiday in 1883 she reported that "Miss Anna sent me lovely books last eve. & Mrs Lathrop card & cake." In 1890 she noted typically that she had received "lovely Easter cards & sent some few." Similarly, Mrs. George Richards received flowers, three plants, and a baby picture for "Easter presents" in 1885 and a book and a bouquet of flowers in 1887. In 1890 Clara Pardee reported that her son Harold "had lots of pretty Easter gifts"; in 1893 she noted that "the children had a lovely Easter & lots of gifts"; and in other years she similarly registered her children's happiness with Easter and the season's treats. In doting on her delighted children, Pardee suggested the holiday's new familial, home-centered quality. The prevalence of Easter presents for children—candy, eggs, and toys—paralleled Santa Claus's coddling of the little ones. At the same time, the new rituals, especially the exchange of cards among women, extended beyond children and family to include an intimate circle of friends. The redefinition of Easter in terms of cards and gifts necessarily meant refocusing the holiday on personal relationships and private associations, on the bonds within families and among friends, more than on the larger attachments of church and community.[45]

All the new Easter goods and gifts—whether candy rabbits, toy chickens, silk-fringed cards, bonbon boxes, or gilt eggs—may seem like trifles, but their impact on the holiday was anything but trifling. They helped create a more secular and nationalized iconography for the holiday. Liberally borrowing from various folk traditions as well as freely devising new emblems, merchants patched together disparate symbols and customs on their way to fashioning the holiday's modern material forms. Take the Easter hare or rabbit, for example. Connected especially to German folk beliefs, the rabbit made its passage from being an ethnic tradition and local legend into a well-nigh pervasive artifact in large part through the commercial culture. Katharine Hillard, writing in the *Atlantic Monthly* in 1890, commented that "of late years" the Easter rabbit had come to vie with the Easter egg for "supremacy in the confectioners' shops." "The hare-myth," she observed, had "come over to America . . . in the shape of the confectioners' Easter hares." The *New York Times* offered additional description of the emblem's commercial dissemination in 1896: "Easter is the season for rabbits, or 'hares,' as they figure in Easter literature. They fill the shop windows in all forms of bonbon boxes and in all styles of dress. They are in the toy shops, looking very natural, made of white cotton flannel." The confectioner's mold, the greeting card, and the toy shop gave shape, standardization, and scope to the holiday's symbols: Rabbits became popular, nearly ubiquitous emblems of the festival in turn-of-the-century America through this symbiosis of folklore and commerce.[46]

This synergy was important. Increasingly the cultural bridges that con-

79. Easter novelties, F. C. Cassel advertisement, *Confectioners' Journal* 25 (February 1899): 52.

nected people to folk legends and symbols were not agrarian celebrations or venerable storytellers, but merchants, manufacturers, and their wares. The new Easter goods were based on facsimile, mechanization, and mass production; they took the place of the traditional links that had joined Easter, nature, and folk culture. Satin, glass, or wooden eggs competed with real eggs; toy rabbits substituted for wild ones; artificial flowers surpassed actual blooms for Easter millinery; taxidermic or marshmallow chicks rivaled their flesh-and-blood counterparts; commercial dyes for Easter eggs replaced natural dyes that had been made at home from such things as onion skins, spinach leaves, or walnut hulls (the Paas Dye Company in Newark, New Jersey, opened in 1879 and made a specialty of manufacturing and packaging commercial dyes for Easter eggs);[47] and soon enough thin green strips of plastic or cellophane for Easter baskets even supplanted the grass of the mythic hare's nest. At every turn mass-produced imitations displaced the "genuine" article. Modern manufacturing redefined the holiday in terms of commercial facsimile. In a report in *Scientific American* in 1906 entitled "How Easter Eggs Are Made by the Thousand," the writer underlined this trend: "A remarkable development of modern manufacturing activity is found in the numerous industries, some of astonishing magnitude, which have sprung from popular customs." Leading examples were Easter eggs, Easter candy, and Easter toys. (In the last category, the writer specified "the plaster rabbit, beloved of the youth of the land" and "the ocher-colored chick, with its wobbly wire legs." Wire and plaster—again, these were the things of the factory, not nature.)[48] A holiday, long tied in folk belief and ritual to nature, became saturated with standardized, ersatz manufactured goods. The market stretched its way into the realm of popular custom and into the world of nature and offered convenient surrogates for both.

The new Easter goods and gifts further suffused the holiday with the values of the consumer culture. Novelty, fashion, and variety were the reigning principles, whether the product was candy, cards, eggs, or toys. Every year, for example, Louis Prang would have a new line of Easter cards ready, and always, so the advertising insisted, the choices were lavish, the styles exquisite, and the art unsurpassed. Prang's announcement in his annual catalogue of Easter goods in 1891 was typical in its emphases: His "new line" would be found to outclass in "refined taste, chaste and delicate designs[,] and appropriate selections" any the firm had ever offered. The accent was always on "variety, beauty and richness of design," on "elaborate, elegant and desirable styles." His cards for 1893, he assured, were done in "the most fashionable shades." Beyond cards, Prang's Easter novelties ran the gamut of fancy bonbon boxes, special Easter books and booklets, sachets, and glove cases; "new designs" were emphasized for almost every item. Confectionery and other industries displayed the same values. Soon, for instance, it was not enough to have an ordinary rabbit; instead, the confectioner's hare itself became a creature of fashion and oddity. It played a drum or was put in harness like a horse or was dressed up in the latest styles. By the 1930s, in a series of hybridized fusions, chocolate bunnies drove cars, played the accordion, or golfed; they themselves, in other words, had become model consumers. Such goods are suggestive of the nested quality of modern shopping—one commodity points to another commodity, which points to another, and so on. The consumerist ideals of novelty and modishness permeated the simplest of the holiday's symbols.[49]

Easter souvenirs and novelties were important as well because they helped codify and promote a distinctly secular iconography for the holiday. Easter trade cards are good examples of the merchant's part in circulating and publicizing a broadly seasonal, secular imagery. Like those disbursed at Christmas, trade cards at Easter were distributed to customers as holiday souvenirs and advertisements. They featured some greeting card–like image on the front and anything from merely the name of the store to a detailed list of available products on the back. Surviving collections of trade cards suggest that these Easter souvenirs, like their Christmas counterparts, highlighted nonreligious symbols: Eggs, rabbits, cherubs, chicks, baskets, butterflies, pansies, daisies, and sweetly innocent young children predominated. Also, their messages of holiday greeting tended to avoid specific religious convictions: "Easter Souvenir, Compliments Worcester Skating Rink"; "Wishing You Every Easter Blessing: Bonbons, Chocolats, H. Maillard New-York"; "An Easter Greeting, 1891, Compliments of S. S. Long & Brother." The seasonal symbols of Easter trade cards in their folksy imagery and in their avoidance of religious specificity offered generic public forms of holiday representation.[50]

The new iconography of Easter gifts and goods was never exclusively secular; as with their show windows, merchants remained happy to employ religious emblems. Like Easter flowers and fashions, Christian symbols and seasonal emblems often complemented one another. This was quite evident with Easter greeting cards, which blossomed as a holiday vogue in the early 1880s. While of wide variety and ever-changing design, Easter greeting cards were nonetheless governed by certain conventions and prevailing fashions. No image was more pervasive than flowers. In keeping with church decoration and with card designs for other holidays, floral motifs dominated Prang's early Easter cards. These floral designs easily combined with religious messages and short quotations of Scripture. "Thanks be to GOD, which giveth us the victory through our LORD JESUS CHRIST," read one of Prang's silk-fringed Easter cards from 1881. Above the biblical inscription was a spray of light-blue pansies. Floral crosses, lilies, and scriptural mottoes, all familiar from church decoration, became equally commonplace on Easter greeting cards of the 1880s and 1890s.[51]

Religious, folk, and seasonal symbols often existed side by side on Easter cards in a hodgepodge of images and a potpourri of sentiments. Prang's announcement about Easter cards for 1885 suggested the emergent mélange

80. "An Easter Greeting," S. S. Long and Brother advertisement, trade card, 1891.

81. "Easter Souvenir," Worcester Skating Rink advertisement, trade card, ca. 1885.

82. "Thanks Be to God," Louis Prang Easter card, 1881.

of holiday symbolism: "All the new Easter Cards strike the note of joy, and they are, if possible, even more artistic than those of past seasons. Delicate spring flowers, singing birds, children, and the emblematic egg play their part in turn, and it is hard to say which are the most happily appropriate." Christian iconography was regularly thrown into the mix of symbols, one more set of images to be toyed with in this play of holiday fantasies. On a Prang card from 1888, for example, a poem beginning "Jesus Lives" is imprinted on the image of a large egg nestled in a bouquet of spring flowers. On another card, a basket of eggs sits in a clump of spring grasses and violets; the message reads "HE IS RISEN." On still another, a Prang card from 1882, a young girl in a spring hat and dress exchanges glances with a bird; the printed sentiment connects this image with popular Easter piety: "Bird and brook and child rejoice / In the Easter gladness, / In the Life that follows Death: / Joy that follows sadness." Snippets of religious sentiment were mixed with cheerful images of spring to put forth a delicate, softly lighted Easter piety.[52]

More-engrossing religious images also appeared on greeting cards, however. Sometimes, for example, the resurrected Lord was imagined as a cherub, reborn in the heavenly innocence of childhood, a blurring of Easter piety into the sentimentalism of Christmas devotion. Angelic images of young girls were often presented as embodying the resurrected Christ in what amounted to an apotheosis of the feminine. Jesus himself often became an androgynous figure in these popular depictions; with flowing hair and delicate features, the risen Christ was invariably surrounded by flowers, cultural markings that decidedly "feminized" the Savior. Since these cards, like those for other holidays, circulated mostly among female friends and relatives, these renderings of the divine were doubly important, embodying a domestic, woman-centered spirituality. Like the sentimental and feminized devotion of popular Victorian fiction, these Easter images may have presented an unsystematic and diffuse spirituality, sunny and reassuring, but sadly insubstantial and unsophisticated (as critics such as Ann Douglas might well view them). Yet as a countervailing Protestant piety in which faith and materiality easily commingled and in which the smallest of trinkets affirmed the eternal, these Easter cards were important in much the same way holiday flowers and fashions were. They formed part of a female world of piety and ritual, one in which the Savior himself was often remade in the ideal image of middle-class Victorian women and their children—pure, innocent, and tender. In their mundaneness, in their quotidian conventionality, Easter cards effectively reimagined popular Christian piety, simply disregarding the terrifying, melancholiac dimensions of the Calvinist past as well as the medieval fascination with the pain and suffering of the crucified, bleeding Savior.

83. “Bird and Brook,” Louis Prang Easter card, 1882.

84. "He Is Not Here," Marcus Ward Easter card, 1884.

85. "Christ the Lord Is Risen To-day," Bufford Easter card, ca. 1880.

86. "The Lord Is Risen Indeed," Bufford Easter card, ca. 1880.

87. Prang's Easter Cards, poster advertisement, ca. 1885.

88. Prang's Easter Cards, poster advertisement, ca. 1885.

The churches did not simply stand on the sidelines as merchants went about shaping a new iconography for Easter, but instead participated in the proliferation of new Easter souvenirs and knickknacks. Having provided the impetus for ornate floral displays and fashionable attire, the churches also had a role in this aspect of the holiday's commercialization. This was especially evident in Protestant Sunday schools, where children often received from their teachers small holiday mementos such as cards, candy, flowers, eggs, booklets, or souvenir pins. The trade catalogues of the David C. Cook Company, a large Protestant publisher in Chicago, were suggestive of these trends. In its annual guide for 1886, "EASTER SUNDAY SCHOOL SPECIALTIES," the firm boasted that Sunday schools "all over the land are beginning to take advantage of the Easter season, not only for suitable decorations and exercises, but also in the use of inexpensive, appropriate school gifts." Small Easter gifts, tokens of reward and appreciation, were claimed to result in "heightened interest and increased attendance" for the church school; they were touted, in short, as a promotional gimmick. Offering special Easter entertainments, programs, tickets, decorations, and cards in 1886, Cook continued to augment his holiday materials as the years went by. For such companies as Cook's, the Sunday schools proved a good holiday market. At the major festivals of Christmas and Easter and at some smaller in-house celebrations such as Children's Day, late-Victorian Sunday schools became small-scale "consumption communities" in which a wide variety of holiday souvenirs and trinkets circulated.[53]

Cook's company especially offered Easter cards as appropriate Sunday school gifts, and these tokens were among the most common mementos given to pupils. While Cook's cards focused on religious images and sentiments, the Sunday schools did not confine themselves to specifically Christian emblems. Two examples in the Smithsonian's collections suggest this. One, signed on the back "M[ethodist] E[piscopal] Sunday School Your Teacher S. A. Snow 1881," carries a picture of a nest with eggs surrounded by flowers and the simple motto, "Wishing you every easter blessing." The other, from a Lutheran Sunday school in Lebanon, Pennsylvania, from 1884, was emblazoned with a large egg and a small child chasing a butterfly.[54] Many Victorian Protestants (though surely not Lutherans) had long been disconnected from Easter and the rest of the church year. Without a traditional liturgical framework in which to place Easter, they patched together their Easter observances from various sources, picking up liturgical pieces here and there, responding to popular desires for both spiritual uplift and entertainment, and creating Easter programs for children in the Sunday schools that were consonant with the commercial valences of the wider culture. Again, modern American renderings of Easter drew on (and concocted) a mix of symbols and traditions, and

89. "Wishing You Every Easter Blessing," Methodist Sunday school souvenir, 1881.

90. "Easter Greeting," Lutheran Sunday school souvenir, 1884.

these Sunday school trinkets were little fragments in this pasticcio, little bits for Protestant bricolage.

In the 1880s and 1890s the material forms of the modern Easter—chocolate rabbits, mass-produced eggs, greeting cards, baskets, toy chicks, and the like—settled snugly into place as fixtures of the holiday. In surveying how Easter was celebrated in Philadelphia stores in 1897, an article in the *Confectioners' Journal*, entitled "Easter Among the Confectioners," wondered at the dazzling, disorienting profusion of Easter novelties: "Most of the retail stores presented a very bewildering display of goods and, as a rule, they were neatly placed in the windows, making a pleasing effect to the eye. . . . Occasionally one encountered a store so heavily laden with fancy notions as to set spectators to wondering where they all came from, whose deft hands moulded them, or how the human imagination could supply material for such a bewildering array of plastic forms without losing sight of Easter altogether." Although the journal went on to assure its readers that all these fancy notions remained "wonderfully apropos of the Easter season," the question lingered. Was Easter as a religious feast lost sight of amid this "bewildering array of plastic forms," this mishmash of fancy goods, this seeming babble of kitsch?[55] It was a question that would perplex not a few critics.

RAINING ON THE EASTER PARADE: PROTEST, SUBVERSION, AND DISQUIET

All the display and fashion of the modern American Easter bewildered various people and inspired recurrent cultural criticism. Distressed commentators presented a wide range of intellectual perspectives from social-gospel principles about economic justice to bedrock Puritan and republican convictions about simplicity and plainness. Above all, critics saw this as a cultural contest over the very meaning of Easter. Could the age-old Christian message of redemptive sacrifice and resurrection at the heart of Holy Week shine through the modern fanfare of style, novelty, and affluence? It was a struggle in ritual, liturgy, and performance to define what the values of the nation were and what Christianity demanded of its adherents. Seen from the perspective of the long history of the church, the struggle embodied perennial strains between Christ and culture, God and mammon. Viewed from the narrower span of American religious history, the conflict evoked familiar tensions between Puritan theocentrism and Yankee anthropocentrism, between otherworldly hopes of redemption and consumer dreams of material abundance, and between republican notions of male virtue and the corresponding fears of effeminacy and foppery.

Critics worried regularly about Easter extravagance. This "vaunting of personal possessions" in a parade of fashions abraded deep-seated cultural values of simplicity, frugality, and self-denial. Although waning in the face of the expanding consumer culture, these principles continued to hold considerable allegiance, and concerns about Easter fashions brought these cultural tensions into sharp relief, perhaps particularly so since as a religious event Easter was expected to undergird, not subvert, the traditional values of austerity, thrift, and moderation. Challenges to Easter extravagance took various forms. One Nazarene minister in Illinois in 1930, for example, gained notice with a bit of evangelical showmanship: He protested the predilection for turning Easter into "a fashion show" and a time of luxury by leading worship "attired in overalls." Likewise a Methodist minister in New Jersey in 1956 made the same point by wearing old clothes to conduct his Easter service. The worldliness of the Easter parade, the swaggering of "supreme ego, self-interest, [and] self-conceit," the searing contrast between Jesus' suffering and humiliation on the road to Calvary and the modern "fanfaronade of women in silks and furs" jarred a writer for the *Christian Century* in 1932. Two decades later another contributor to the same weekly wondered at the Fifth Avenue procession in which all seemed to cry "Look at me!" To its critics, the Easter parade was a giant spectacle of vain self-assertion.[56]

Commentary on the American Easter sometimes cut deep to fundamental issues of social and economic justice. Like the Christmas rush, Easter preparations put huge burdens on workers to meet the surging demand for holiday goods and to satisfy the throng of holiday shoppers. Edwin Markham, poetaster of the social gospel whose "Man with the Hoe" (1899) launched him to fame as a crusader against dehumanizing labor, spotlighted the crushing hardships of the holiday seasons in a series of blistering, reform-minded essays on child labor. Fired in part by his understanding of Jesus as a socialistic and progressivist visionary, Markham laid into "this generation of the colossal factory and the multitudinous store and the teeming tenement-house," all of which darkened even the joys of Christmas and Easter. "To thousands of those who depend on . . . the fashion-plate for light and leading," he blasted, "Easter means only a time of changing styles—a date on which to display new spring gowns and bonnets—a sort of national millinery opening. But to the workers in the shadow, . . . it means only a blind rush and tug of work that makes this solemn festival a time of dread and weariness. They might truly say in tears, 'They have taken away my Lord, and I know not where they have laid him.'"[57]

Markham aimed his sharpest attacks at sweatshops where children labored late into the night at piecework wages over artificial flowers for millinery to satisfy "the season's rush." He estimated that three-quarters of those making this product in New York City, the center of the industry, were children under the age of fourteen. "There is no other Easter preparation," he concluded, "where children are so cruelly overworked as in the making of artificial flowers." These "vampire blossoms" robbed children of education, health, and play:

> I lately visited a factory where a group of girls were making artificial roses. They were working ten hours a day, some of them getting only a dollar and a half a week. . . . Swiftly, rhythmically, the ever-flying fingers darted through the motions, keeping time to the unheard but clamorous metronome of need. Many of the girls had inflamed eyes. . . . The faces were dulled, the gaze was listless. Here was another illustration of the tragedy in our civilization—the work that deadens the worker.

The sweatshop exploitation of women and children, raised to feverish levels during the holiday rush, was to Markham "the tragedy behind the flaunting festoons of our Easter Vanity Fair." Even Markham, however, had a hard time seeing the international, colonialist scope of the trade, the children of the Philippines or China plaiting materials for the American market. Such labor was often treated as part of the exoticism or "romance of millinery." "It is a pleasure . . . to know," one trade writer concluded, "how the peoples in the far corners of the earth toil for the adornment of our heads."[58]

Still, Markham raked the muck on Easter fashions with unusual breadth as well as directness. Writing with a second-person bluntness that indicated again the gendered nature of this contest, Markham blasted: "Perhaps, last Easter, you, my lady, wore one of those pretty things of lace and chiffon trimmed with shining beads and made at midnight by your starved-down sister." Like Washington Gladden, Walter Rauschenbusch, and other social reformers, Markham pressed the middle class to see their complicity in the suffering of the urban poor, to recognize that their choices as consumers were deeply interwoven with issues of economic justice, and to understand that their festive indulgence and intensified consumption at Christmas and Easter turned the screws on workers in city sweatshops and tenements. But since, in the gendering of consumption, women were seen as the chief devotees of fashion and novelty, these attacks were always directed far more at women than at men. In raining on the Easter parade, critics inevitably aimed their sharpest barbs at the supposed vanity and folly of women. Where Protestant women such as Elizabeth Merchant and Clara Pardee had worked out a synthesis of piety and materiality, male critics such as Markham were often sharply alienated from this world of millinery, flowers, and dress.[59]

Issues of social justice were also raised within the Easter parade itself as New York's colossal spectacle became the occasion for turning grievance into ritual. Protesters exploited the carnivalesque, fantastical potentialities within the procession to create a platform for various causes. During the Great Depression, groups of the unemployed, for example, paraded in "battered top hats, lumberjack coats, frayed trousers and broken shoes." If their social commentary was not clear enough, some carried placards or banners: "ONE FIFTH AVENUE GOWN EQUALS A YEAR OF RELIEF." The inversion of the fashionableness and capitalistic excesses of New York's Easter procession was often used as a tool for labor and socialist protests. The Fifth Avenue extravaganza invited other kinds of pickets as well. In 1966, for instance, a group of about fifty antiwar demonstrators saw in the parade the possibilities of subversion. "While you march down the avenue in your new clothes, the clothing is being burned off the backs of men, women and children in Vietnam," their flyers and signs declared. The Easter parade as an embodiment of American complacency and abundance called forth protesters and critics who used it as an occasion to question the values that underpinned this rite of spring. The meanings of the festival were thus never univocal, but contested and challenged, always subject to inversion and antithesis. The very modishness and ostentation of the Easter parade provided the wedge for critics to open up issues of economic fairness and social justice—the lever by which to turn the whole ritual upside down.[60]

The chief protests against the modern rendering of Easter centered on the tensions between commercialism and Christianity, between secular goods and religious meanings. The Presbyterian pastor Zed H. Copp put the conflict in its starkest terms at a Philadelphia ministers' gathering in 1932: Through "commercialization of the Holy Week," he said, the Easter bunny, colored eggs, and confectionery treats are substituted for "the cross of Christ and the open tomb of the resurrection." He saw in these substitutes, as in the symbolic preeminence of Santa Claus at Christmas, "a combined insidious attack on . . . the traditions of the church and on Christianity itself"—ersatz replacements that tended "to paganize our children and blind their spiritual sight." Cast in these terms, the contest conjured up venerable conflicts: What was Christian, what was pagan in the celebration? How sharp a line should be drawn between church practices and folk customs? How much allowance should be made for popular amusements and seasonal mirth? The worries about commercial distractions were in many ways the latest round in a centuries-long contest to lift up the religious meanings of the holiday against various semiotic competitors. It was, in short, another attempt "to make Easter a thoroughly *Christian festival*" rather than a hybridized, springtime romp.[61]

Sampling two instances of the religious critique of commercialization—one from the 1930s and the other from the 1950s—shows both the content and contours of this perspective. A Methodist church in White Plains, New York, in 1935 garnered attention in both the *New York Times* and the *Literary Digest* for a report assailing the modern "commercial" Easter as a "travesty." The church argued that the material forms "cultivated" by "commercial interests," from new clothes to greeting cards to candy rabbits, diverted people from their devotion to the resurrected Christ. The report, supported unanimously by the congregation, decried the social obligations and merchandising exploitation that had grown up around these customs. "In particular we have been led to feel that we simply must have new Spring clothes for Easter Sunday," which, the report said, add "nothing to the atmosphere of reverence" in the church's worship. In stirring tones the church's minister, the Reverend C. Lloyd Lee, endorsed the report, which had been initiated by a layman and New York businessman, Harold V. Atwell. "We have lost Christmas through the commercial interest," Lee exhorted, "and I don't want to lose Easter. We crucified the given Christ on His birthday. Shall we now bury the living Lord beneath the rabbits, the eggs, satins, finery and thoughtlessness? We say no. We want to celebrate Easter in religion from now on." The critique was double-edged: first, commercial manipulation created burdensome social pressures that undermined free and unfeigned participation in the festival, and second, the market elevated customs, symbols, and gifts that competed with or displaced the religious emblems and meanings of Easter.[62]

The church's report did not go unchallenged. The local chamber of commerce was quick to denounce the position of the White Plains Methodists as "ridiculous." The church was quite out of line: Buying new clothes *was* an unassailable necessity of the season, and, what is more, the chamber of commerce insisted, "the Easter bunny is second only to Santa Claus in the traditions of the people." The *New York Times* weighed in with an editorial against the church's view of commercialism, arguing that the church had "swallowed whole the favorite doctrine of the 'sales-pressure' school of thinkers": "This holds that people virtually never buy anything because they need it or want it or like it, or because people have always bought it. Not at all! The American people buys things which it does not need and does not want and would never have thought of buying if it were not wheedled and mentally coerced and propagandized and advertised into buying by people who make a profit thereby. It is the doctrine of high-pressure salesmanship as explaining the whole economic life of a people." The *Times* thought that this view would have "some small measure of truth" in a few cases, such as with "what the florists have done to spread Mother's Day, and what the necktie interests have done for Father's Day." But commercial coaxing seemed hardly the explanation for the widespread delight in Easter finery, for the satisfaction taken in new spring fashions. The church's report and this editorial rejoinder revealed the tensile polarities that tug at all interpretations of modern commerce and advertising, cultural production and consumption: manipulation versus freedom, seduction versus desire, market orchestration versus consumer improvisation. Easter may seem an odd location for these suspicions and debates, but to find such concerns here, as elsewhere, underlines the pervasiveness of the market system.[63]

The second case of contested commercialism is an episode involving New York's Easter parade in 1952. Television coverage of the Fifth Avenue fashion parade brought out growing numbers of publicity seekers—models, celebrities, and promoters of various products—and in 1952 the collision between "the decorum of worshippers" and the growing "carnival of commercialism" reached a crisis point. With St. Patrick's Cathedral as their backdrop, professionals were employed to model different hats and designer clothes; one woman "in black tights, advertising a hair lotion, pirouetted on a platform" that was set up as a stage to catch the attention of the crowd and the television crews; celebrities came by to promote their current films or shows; the actress Vivian Blaine modeled five hundred thousand dollars worth of pearls for the Imperial Pearl Company; and criers carried pennants and placards and wore outlandish costumes to advertise various businesses, such as a local amusement park. Television, it was said, had turned the Easter parade into an "electronic Coney Island." Such televised antics were seen by many as "carrying commercialism beyond bearable limits," and this controversy set into motion moderately successful efforts at reform that extended over the next decade.[64]

A sense of scandal or even abomination characterized the critiques of this Easter carnival of 1952. Within a week of the event, the Protestant Council of the City of New York had issued "a public protest against this unseemly demonstration," saying that "Christian people of all churches, and indeed all decent-minded citizens" had been "shocked and scandalized": "When models are displayed in tights in front of our churches, and use the steps of a cathedral as a theatrical dressing-room; when Fifth Avenue is turned into a stage for the crassest commercialism of the hucksters of radio and television, the whole affair takes on the aspect of a Mardi Gras and this on a day of the deepest religious significance." Predictably ill at ease with the transgressive, the Protestant Council sought to purify New York's Easter celebration and to contain its bursting hybridity. Indeed, in a bid to restore the essential boundaries between the sacred and profane, a bill was even introduced in the City Council that would have prohibited "'any commercial, business, advertising or broadcasting activity' on a public street within 500 feet of a place of worship."[65]

While this bill languished in the City Council, other measures were successfully carried out. The following year the police were enlisted to restore the parade's dignity, guarding the churches and their immediate environs from publicity seekers and in some cases forcibly excluding any recalcitrant exhibitionists from the procession on Fifth Avenue. Ministers and civic leaders also sought and received assurances from ABC, CBS, and NBC not to repeat the "disgraceful commercialism" of the previous year; all three networks announced appropriate restraints on their coverage. Commentary in 1953 was in wide agreement on the success of these reforms and on the restored dignity of the occasion. In accounts of the parade in 1960 police bans on "advertising and commercialism" were still being emphasized, and 1952 was hailed as the turning point in the "decommercialization of the Easter Parade." Though these efforts to control the Barnumesque (and carnivalesque) undercurrents of the parade gradually weakened and ultimately failed, they suggest the lengths to which the churches and civic government were willing to go in their joint campaign for a reverent, appropriately bounded Easter. This 1950s campaign to save Easter was the coincident counterpart of efforts to "put Christ back into Christmas." Both causes hoped to restore and maintain Christianity as part of America's civic creed, and both saw these Christian feasts as the ritual anchors of that public faith.[66]

The same sorts of worries about commercialization are still regularly heard today in religious circles. Admittedly Easter fashions are rarely the concern now; the millinery industry has gone into eclipse over the last three decades, and spring openings for clothes have come, as they did before the 1880s, to predominate over the Easter trade. But the overarching concern about secular goods displacing religious referents is still very much alive. Charles Colson displayed a familiar disquiet when he editorialized in *Christianity Today* in 1986 that commercially promoted symbols such as the Easter bunny may be "cute" and "entertaining," but they are also "deadly." They divert "our attention from the centrality of the Resurrection." In a pluralistic society that tries to reduce religious and cultural differences to "the lowest common denominator," Colson wrote, "holy days such as Christ's birth and resurrection survive only if adorned with commercial trinkets." Similarly, the ecumenical Christian group Alternatives, long committed to resisting the commercialization of Christmas, also continues to make the case against "the annual Easter clothes, card, flower and candy blitz." In one of their stories a church-school teacher asks a group of preschoolers one Easter morning, "What happened on the third day?" And the reply comes back, "The Easter bunny brought eggs." In another of the group's images, suggestive of the lingering Protestant fear of festive hybridity, an apotheosized rabbit emerges from the tomb offering a sign of blessing. Critics have long bemoaned the secular, popular, and commercial aspects of Easter, entering into an ongoing cultural contest to define the meanings of the holiday—Resurrection Day, rite of spring, shopping event, or somehow all of these at the same time.[67]

91. Easter satire by Tom Peterson, from *To Celebrate: Reshaping Holidays and Rites of Passage* (Ellenwood, Ga.: Alternatives, 1987), 102.

Finally, it is important to underline again that this cultural contest over the meaning of Easter was (and is) not simply one of polarities: anxious critics versus unabashed celebrants; clear-eyed prophets versus profit-seeking merchants; ascetics versus sybarites. When people faced such tensions in their own celebrations of Easter, they resolved them variously or simply lived with them. For example, the Reverend Morgan Dix, rector at Trinity Episcopal Church in New York, a parish as fond as any of elaborate floral decorations and the display of Easter finery, found himself wondering in 1880 if festal ornamentation had become too extravagant. Was the church turning into "a hot-house"? One writer in 1883 considered Easter floral adornments in the churches attractive and appropriate, but still questioned whether the churches had, "even without intention, become but poor imitations of the theatre in their efforts at exhibition." The writer praised "simple" floral decorations but rejected costly ones that displayed a "foolish pride and a selfish ambition to out-do all others." Others suggested that Easter flowers should be distributed after church to the poor; still others recommended forgoing them and giving the money to charity. Unresolved tensions, ambiguities, and contradictions were evident also in Edwin Markham's career. At one time a critic of the "multitude of baubles" and "unmeaning trinkets" of the commercialized Easter—the "flimsy cards," the "glass eggs," the "paste chickens," the "plaster rabbits"—Markham turned around and happily sold some of his verses for sentiments on greeting cards. Not even the sharpest critics were exempt from the tensions they highlighted.[68]

Some experienced these polarities and sought self-consciously to harmonize them. Reflecting on the Easter parade in 1905, a writer in *Harper's*, for example, recognized the tensions that many felt between mere "outward adornment" and the religious meaning of the festival. "I have known," he reported, "women to say that they avoided springing new frocks on an admiring world on Easter Sunday because they did not wish to intrude so trivial a thing as millinery upon a religious festival of such deep significance." But it "seems to me," he said, "that if one gets the right point of view, all the outward tokens of Easter are harmonious with the inner spiritual meanings of it." The flowers and clothes had sacramental importance; they were "outward manifestations" of Easter's religious solemnity and significance. One minister, writing in 1910, summarized both the tensions and their potential resolution: "One dislikes the element of fashionable frivolity which has come to mark some people's keeping of the Easter feast; but, apart from that, as the city shops and streets break out into fragrant and beautiful bloom, one realizes the close kinship between heavenly and spiritual things and things material and earthly." This was always the core religious concern—how to mediate piety and materiality, flesh and spirit, faith and riches, otherworldly salvation and cosmopolitan display, the inward and the outward, surface and substance, in a world of proliferating goods.[69]

In a recent reminiscence about Easter Sundays while he was growing up in a small town in Virginia, Samuel Pickering, Jr., evokes these complex, tensile mediations with a fine eye for local color. His memories serve as an apt summary of the complexities—rather than the simplicities of a Thorstein Veblen or a Philip Roth—of what was going on in these modern forms of Easter piety and display. "Easter was even more joyous than Christmas," he recalls. "Men stuck greenery onto their lapels and the women bloomed in bright bonnets. Some ordered hats not simply from Richmond but from Baltimore and Philadelphia. On Easter Sunday the congregation could not keep still as each new hat caused much neck craning and comment." He remembers, in particular, Miss Ida, a reserved woman known for her elaborate Easter bonnets, which she embellished herself with innumerable artificial flowers ordered from New York until "her head resembled a summer garden in full bloom." When it looked one Easter as if Miss Ida was not going to make her usual appearance, the church's celebration sagged: "Miss Ida's absence had taken something bright from our lives, and as we sat down after singing ['Hail Thee, Festival Day'], Easter seemed sadly ordinary." But then Miss Ida appeared, with a still-grander hat, the centerpiece of which was "a wonderful sunflower." "Our hearts leaped up," Pickering recollects, "and at the end of the service people in Richmond must have heard us singing 'Christ The Lord Is Risen Today.'" His memories are rich ones: On a cold reading, they testify to the diffusion of the Easter parade and the reach of the Easter market—the implication of the imaginative Miss Ida in New York's urban economic structures. But the point of the story is a warmhearted affirmation of the piety within holiday dress, and this needs to be recognized without erasing exploitation or ignoring the immigrant labor that makes possible Ida's inventiveness. Pickering recalls an unexpected grace. Miss Ida's Easter bonnets did not so much overshadow the cross as reveal a joyous community of faith; they were densely material celebrations of bodily resurrection and promised rebirth. It was these sorts of mediations, not always successful and more prominent among women than men, that energized these modern forms of Easter observance.[70]

Easter, more than Christmas, disclosed the role of the churches in the rise of consumer-oriented celebrations. The enlarging scope of "devout consumption" was seen in the elaborate displays of Easter flowers and other church decorations. The conflux of consumption and Christianity was nowhere more evident than in the streaming parade of Easter fashions as the stylish poured into and out of the churches. New holiday gifts and souvenirs, such as Easter cards, had found a substantial market in the Sunday schools. Even as most Christians embraced and helped facilitate this new Easter, others demonstrated considerable wariness about where this alliance between Christian celebration and the consumer culture was headed. They foresaw the dim outlines of Irving Berlin's *Easter Parade* or Philip Roth's "schlockified Christianity" in which the holiday became a synonym for shopping, abundance, and the American way of life, a ritual display of plenty. Still, the critics rarely fathomed the complexity of the drama that so disturbed them, the hybridized commingling of faith and fashion, renewal and laughter, piety and improvisation that paraded before them. With Easter, as often as not, the stores had followed the lead of the churches; with Mother's Day, merchants would quickly take charge, and its Protestant founder would soon be left to wonder what she had wrought.

5
Mother's Day Bouquet

IN THE 1910s and 1920s, American merchants found a new holiday to promote, "the most sentimental of all days," Mother's Day. Commercial florists took the lead in advertising the holiday, helping invent the celebration. Other trades soon joined the parade. Predictably, the greeting-card industry displayed particular foresight and enterprise. An early etiquette book published by the National Association of Greeting Card Manufacturers in 1926 proclaimed that "every mother should receive a card with just the right sentiment." And many mothers did; indeed, by recent estimate, 150 million cards are sent annually at Mother's Day, making it the fourth-largest card-buying occasion in the United States behind Christmas, St. Valentine's Day, and Easter. Telephone calls to Mom, restaurant dinners for her, bouquets, candy, and department-store gifts, among other possibilities, all complement the custom of giving cards and all entail their own special promotions. One early card manufacturer, Ernest Dudley Chase, commented in 1926 that he found the sudden growth of "the Mother's Day card business" to be "phenomenal." Yet the boom in Mother's Day business was not half so remarkable as the sudden advent of the holiday itself. Twenty years earlier it had not existed; by the late 1920s it was one of the more prominent holidays in the American calendar and one of the most promising commercial events.[1]

The rise of Mother's Day as an American holiday is inextricably bound up with the story of Anna Jarvis and her well-meaning efforts to establish the event as a fixture in the American calendar. Her campaign took shape in the matrices of her own religious upbringing in West Virginia and in the larger world of evangelical Protestantism. The churches, long accustomed to staging special days in the Sunday schools, played a crucial part in the invention of this new maternal festival. But the holiday was immediately a celebration with multiple "homes," and one of them was the marketplace. From the outset the industry that took primary responsibility and credit for selling the holiday was commercial floriculture (a word of nineteenth-century coinage that seems peculiarly suited for academic currency in the late twentieth century). The history of the floral industry and its extensive patronage of the new holiday provides a crisp picture of the mechanics of commercialization in the early twentieth century, the increasingly systematic ways by which an industry went about building a market for its product around celebration and ritual.

In what, by then, had nearly the status of cultural refrain, critique followed commercialization. Anna Jarvis was the loudest and most querulous in attacking those who turned her holy day into a market day, but her bitterness was symptomatic of wider feelings of unease over the directions in which modern celebrations were headed. But expressions of alienation were soon overmatched by varied attempts at emulation: Mother's Day quickly came to function as a model for the spin-off of other market-rich observances. In this regard, Father's Day was the preeminent example, and it, too, readily combined folksy church roots with modern entrepreneurialism. Its Spokane-based "founder," Sonora Dodd, was always at ease with business leaders and trade groups, and the holiday quickly came under the formal sponsorship of merchants, especially the Associated Men's Wear Retailers, a trade bureau in New York City that set up a national committee in the 1930s to promote the event. But satire and suspicion always fenced in Father's Day; for many, it seemed like old-fashioned humbug, the calendrical equivalent to a Barnumesque mermaid propped up each year on the third Sunday in June. From Mother's Day and Father's Day, it was only a short step to such proposals as Sweetest Day, Grandparents' Day, Professional Secretaries' Day, Child Health Care Day, Bosses' Day, or even National Clean Up Your Desk Day—that is, to the construing of the calendar as a pliant testing ground for one industrial, benevolent, or mindless promotion after another.

ANNA JARVIS AND THE CHURCHES: SOURCES OF A NEW CELEBRATION

Anna Jarvis, the leader of what she herself liked to refer to as the "Mother's Day Movement," was nothing if not diligent and determined in the pursuit of her cause. A Methodist layperson, Jarvis spent a good part of her time in the first four decades of this century promoting the new holiday, especially in the churches and Sunday schools, but also in just about any other forum in which she could find a hearing. Jarvis envisioned Mother's Day, in her words, as "a holy day," even in a truly grandiloquent moment as "a divine gift," a Sabbath celebration of maternal love and sacrifice, "not as a holiday" at the disposal of various "trade vandals" and "trade pirates." Sometimes prophetic, sometimes captious, sometimes despondent, often enough all three, Jarvis regularly bewailed "the mire of commercialism" into which her solemn and sentimental occasion progressively sank. In her life and work, recalcitrance and disillusionment commingled. Mother's Day embodied the mounting tensions in American culture between festival and marketplace, between Christian celebration and complacent consumption, and Jarvis herself would experience those strains with peculiar intensity.[2]

Born in 1864, a few miles outside Grafton, West Virginia, Jarvis grew up and came to adulthood in this small, rural community. Both of her grandfathers had been preachers in the area, and her father, Granville, was a local

92. Anna Jarvis, ca. 1895.

merchant, moderately successful in various lines of trade. Though a Baptist in upbringing, the father left little impression on his daughter as being a man of piety; a member of a Masonic order, he may well have taken most of his social and religious bearings from that fraternity. A heavy drinker in later years with a sharp temper, he often seemed distant and withdrawn from the family. The daughter, not surprisingly, oriented most of her world around her mother for whom she was named. The religious, benevolent, and educational enterprises of the mother were the daughter's inheritance. After taking courses for two years at Augusta Female Seminary in Staunton, Virginia, in the early 1880s, Jarvis, then nineteen, returned to Grafton to work as a teacher in a public school. She also took on the roles of church organist and Sunday school teacher in one of Grafton's Methodist churches, where her mother had been actively involved for years.

In 1891 Jarvis began to look beyond the confines of Grafton and hoped to follow the example of her two brothers, one of whom had moved to Baltimore and the other to Philadelphia, in striking out on her own. She looked first to Chattanooga—a place, bragged her uncle who lived there, "more than 10 times the size of Grafton," where "there is always room for the 'survival of the fittest.'" Pleased that his niece was finally cutting the apron strings, the uncle unkindly wrote that in leaving home she would "really commence a new life,—one worth living." The uncle likewise admonished his sister not to agonize over her separation from her daughter. "So, please dry up," he counseled her, "and send your child off on her *triumphal march* with gladness, not in sorrow, and tears." Single (she would never marry) and fired with what her uncle called "laudable ambition," the younger Jarvis left small-town West Virginia and her mother for the big city.[3]

Chattanooga proved but a brief way station. Jarvis moved the next year to Philadelphia, drawn there by her entrepreneurial brother Claude and the even grander possibilities conjured up by that city. There Jarvis worked first as a stenographer for Edison Electric Light Company and then as a writer for Fidelity Mutual, an insurance company. Though sometimes she grew "so tired of the city" that she pined for the West Virginia countryside and for reunion with family and friends, she never moved back home. She wound up spending the rest of her life in Philadelphia. This long separation from home and mother would provide an integral theme for her later Mother's Day movement. Writing home to Mother or going back home to visit would form a cornerstone of Jarvis's cause. The longing for home ties, for rootedness and remembrance, would help sustain her own efforts and would give her holiday emotional resonance with all those other sons and daughters of this period who had made similar breaks. Not coincidentally, it would also provide one of the basic advertising themes for the floral industry; commercialization would be built on the very vulnerability and social importance of these familial ties.[4]

Living in Philadelphia, Jarvis had to content herself with reconnecting with home through letters. In particular, she carried on a warm and frequent correspondence with her mother ("I have not heard from you this week," her mother wrote worriedly in one letter, "and feel so much afraid you are sick"). A tender and devoted companionship glowed in their letters. "I think I love you more and more each day," her mother wrote in 1898; "no name ever sounds so sweet as yours to me." Not long after her father died in December 1902, Anna wrote her mother: "You are more to us now than ever, and we all want to take care of you so we can have you with us a long time, for you are such a dear, good mother." It is no wonder that the daughter would always stress the importance of writing letters home to Mother as the appropriate commemoration of Mother's Day and that no mere postcard, telegram, or even telephone call would suffice. Letter writing was the medium that sustained her intimate relationship with her mother for nearly a decade and a half of often painful separation. "Write Home" would thus be among her most favored and insistent slogans in her Mother's Day work.[5]

Soon after their father's death, Anna and her brother convinced their mother to move to Philadelphia. When they were reunited in late 1903, the daughter became the main comforter for her mother in her last year and a half of life, especially in her final illness. After her mother's death in early May 1905, Anna remembered her life warmly in recollections penned for friends and relatives. What she recalled about her mother, what she committed to paper, suggests her paragon for motherhood. The sketch reveals the sorts of values and strengths that she admired in her mother and that, in turn, she hoped to preserve and commemorate.[6]

Jarvis remembered her mother especially for her evangelical piety and practice. She noted her mother's spiritual lineage with pride: Her mother was the daughter and granddaughter of Methodist ministers, and that side of her family liked to boast of ties back to the founding years of the Wesleyan movement. The daughter saw her mother's strong denominational identity as a source of independence in her marriage: Though she had wed a Baptist, her husband "never disestablished my mother from the church of her father." (This basis for autonomy nicely parallels Hillary Rodham Clinton's resolute Methodism in her marriage to a Baptist.) To the daughter, her mother's life was true to these evangelical roots, and Jarvis carefully recollected her mother's involvement in the church—her decades-long work in the Sunday school, her leadership in local church societies on issues of education and benevolence, her patterns of daily prayer, her favorite Bible verses, and her annual fasts on Good Friday (a piece of the traditional church year that had survived among some Methodists). The daughter also remembered her mother's graces at meals and made particular note of how it was her mother, not her father, who took responsibility for this familial devotion around the table. Such small acts of worship were the substance of the popular Protestant piety in which Jarvis was reared; one sees in these seemingly trivial little bits of devotion the tangible, unfeigned habits of evangelical faith. When Jarvis swung her mind to the task of memorializing her mother in ritual, she would turn naturally to the churches, the Sunday schools, and their forms of worship.[7]

What stood out most in the daughter's memories of religious ardor was her mother's abiding affection for certain cherished hymns such as "Nearer, My God, to Thee" and "Jesus, Lover of My Soul." These songs were still warm with the fervor of the camp meeting; revivals remained a regular feature of popular

Protestantism in this era, and a notably large one had stirred up the Methodists in Grafton in 1898.[8] A half century earlier at another revival, Anna's mother had experienced conversion at the age of twelve, and the daughter recalled how her mother considered one "old Methodist hymn" in particular—"O, How Happy Are They Who Their Savior Obey"—to be her "conversion hymn." She sang it over and over again at the time ("I could not get it out of my heart," she told her daughter), and it stayed with her throughout her life. She kept the song marked with a blue ribbon in her hymnal and annotated it with the phrase "Sing this at the Last."[9]

These hymns are translucent windows into the piety that the daughter admired in the mother, a spirituality of otherworldliness and fortitude, of hope and holiness in the face of heartrending affliction. Her mother's life had been filled with nearly endless grieving. Seven of the eleven children whom her mother bore died in early childhood, and these deaths tragically haunted her to the end of her life. In at least two cases she experienced grim premonitions of a child's death. In one dream, for example, she was forced to carry a young daughter in an Abrahamic journey to "the top of a high mountain. I had to pass through a field of stuble, and being in my bare feet and burdened by the weight of my child whom I was carrying to protect her little feet from the roughness of the ground, I climbed the hill in the greatest agony, and can now see the tracks of blood I left behind as the stuble pierced my aching feet." Though waking in a cold sweat before she reached the top of the mountain, she saw in the dream a sign of her daughter's imminent death, that all her protectiveness, pain, bleeding, and sacrifice would not spare her child the dark providence that awaited her. On her own deathbed, in a vision of both profound sorrow and consolation, she had a dream in which she saw Jesus "right across the street" with "a whole lot of little children." "They were such nice little children," she told her daughter, "and I saw them all so plainly."[10]

The hymns offered the counterpoint to the pain and desolation that the daughter saw piercing her mother's life. They harbor a piety both plaintive and hopeful. Strength and resilience come in glimpses of "Beulah land, sweet Beulah land" (the hymn, "Beulah Land," was another that Anna remembered her mother singing repeatedly). Amid storm and tempest, Jesus offers refuge; the Lord is a source of "sweet comfort and peace." Even as the believer looks to a distant, shining shore, the "stony griefs" of this world are not denied in these hymns, but faced with mournful directness. Nearness to God comes through prayer and song, through crosses and self-denial, and fulfillment is found in the transcendent, in treasures "laid up above," not riches accumulated here below; contentment is looked for in heavenly mansions, not earthly estates. The self in its brokenness and pain is made whole through conversion and sanctification, through spiritual experience rather than material reward.[11] Intoned in "that old time way," these revival hymns reverberated throughout the mother's life—at home, in solitude, in prayer, at worship, in death—incantations of sorrow and triumph.[12]

"What a beautiful emblem of christianity her life was," a friend wrote about Anna's mother, and this is certainly the picture that the daughter painted in her recollections. She also equally emphasized another dimension of her mother's life—namely, her commitment to home and family. These domestic responsibilities were, the daughter said, her mother's "every-day religion": caring for her children, nursing them in illness, looking after her husband, and attending to him in his old age. (He was ten years her senior.) As dedicated as her mother may have been to this familial trust, Jarvis did not recall these maternal obligations without regret. It saddened her that her mother's hopes to have a college education had been thwarted by "home responsibilities" and that her mother's "own pleasure and ambitions" had been "restrained by the ties of motherhood."[13] The irony that Mother's Day would hallow the very institutions that held her mother back seems never to have sunk in with the daughter, nor, apparently, did the incongruity that her nearly total dedication to this cause was made possible because she herself was free of the maternal and domestic obligations that she celebrated. Perhaps Mother's Day was, in part, a monument to the strains that she experienced between her "laudable ambition" and the omnipresent cultural idealization of motherhood, which she saw exemplified in her mother and which she had forgone. Perhaps the holiday was a ritual of penitence and absolution for the daughter, who found herself torn between new aspirations and old abnegations.

Jarvis's memorial for her mother began with personal remembrance. She carefully preserved letters praising her mother's life and spirit and sent copies of a cherished picture of her, along with a favorite prayer, to those who sent condolences. The transition from private to public memorial began in 1907 in the Methodist Sunday school back in Grafton where her mother had served all those years. Working to have a memorial table and a memorial picture of her mother placed in the Sunday school, Jarvis also helped arrange a special service at the church in May 1907 in memory of her mother's work there.[14] After this Sunday school observance, her vision widened to honoring her mother on a much grander scale—by honoring all mothers with their own special day on the second Sunday in May.

What prompted Jarvis to shift from conventional forms of remembrance and memorial to this far larger, even grandiose, scheme is hard to divine. Her love and admiration for her mother clearly remained paramount, but inspiration for this specific kind of observance may have come from a variety of sources. Having been a church organist and a Sunday school teacher, she was well versed in the red-letter days of American Protestantism and was deeply familiar with the round of special days in the Sunday school. The festive programs for Christmas and Easter stood out as the big events, but these were woven into a rich calendar of plays, pageants, and special observances. Children's Day, held on the second Sunday in June, had been a fixture in the Sunday schools of Victorian Protestants since the 1870s and 1880s, and any number of other special occasions—Temperance Sunday, Roll Call Day, Decision Day, Missionary Day, and the like—dotted the year. The invention of Mother's Day was certainly continuous with this evangelical Protestant world.[15]

Children's Day and other like-minded religious observances were clear precursors: In Jarvis's eyes, Mother's Day, like Children's Day, was foremost a celebration of the Christian home and family, and Protestant modes of celebration—hymns, prayers, Scripture readings, homilies, recitations, and pageants of Sunday school children—shaped the liturgies that she promulgated. But Mother's Day was not only a family day; it was also a "memorial day." Most obviously, it memorialized Jarvis's own mother, but by extension it was intended to recall all departed mothers. In the calendar, Mother's Day would stand in close proximity to Memorial Day, which hallowed the sacrifices of sons for their country. The new holiday would balance these filial sacrifices with the sacrifices of motherhood. To Jarvis (and others), it seemed peculiarly fitting for Mother's Day to become "part of our Memorial Month, when we honor our holy dead." Women had taken the lead in orchestrating and perpetuating services of remembrance and bereavement in the aftermath of the Civil War, and Decoration Days, in their various local and sectional incarnations, were solemn times of memory, consolation, and floral tributes. Hence Jarvis's newly minted ritual would draw power and legitimacy from another woman-led, flower-strewn, memory-laden, sacrifice-redeeming, flag-honoring holiday of Victorian vintage, Memorial Day.[16]

Mother's Day may also have had other ritual sources besides Children's Day and Memorial Day. It is possible that Jarvis had heard of the calls of Julia Ward Howe for Mothers' Peace Day celebrations, which Howe had promoted since the 1870s as events in early June in which mothers of the world were to commit themselves to the cause of world peace. As late as 1893, Howe was still suggesting a Mother's Day dedicated to peace, wondering forlornly (and naively) whether women might remake the Fourth of July into such an occasion.[17] For maternal celebrations of peace, Jarvis may also have looked closer to home for inspiration. Among her mother's good works in and around Grafton had been efforts to organize special rituals of reconciliation after the Civil War, Mothers' Friendship celebrations, which were designed to bring together neighbors who had split over the conflict in this border region.[18] Or perhaps Jarvis looked farther afield—to the Old World custom of Mothering Sunday, a mid-Lent celebration focused on returning home and paying homage to one's mother. But she never mentioned Howe or Mothering Sunday, and never intimated any connection between her special day and other special days in the Sunday schools. And while she liked to see her movement as an extension of her mother's labors on behalf of "home, church, and community," she nonetheless was always quite insistent that "Mother's Day celebrations . . . were founded by me." She was not one to spread the credit around; this was her idea and her day, and she would always jealously protect it.[19]

Whatever sources or precursors there may have been and whatever organizations ended up being instrumental in the holiday's promotion, Jarvis certainly deserves the lion's share of the credit for the invention of Mother's Day. From 1908 on, her organizational energy, especially her letter-writing campaign on behalf of the event, was phenomenal. Assembling what she called the Mother's Day International Association—a committee that she directed in its task of promoting the new holiday—Jarvis, under the aegis of this association, tirelessly got in contact with politicians, newspaper editors, and church leaders. Though she encountered her share of skeptics, she met with considerable success, even in the early years of observance. On the second Sunday in May 1908, the first official Mother's Day services were held in various cities and towns around the country, with Jarvis herself helping orchestrate services in Philadelphia and Grafton.[20] By 1910, the Young Men's Christian Association, the World Sunday School Association, and several other religious and benevolent groups had lent their support. Jarvis's own church, the Methodist Episcopal Church, formally embraced the holiday at its General Conference in 1912. Protestant luminaries, such as William Jennings Bryan, J. Wilbur Chapman, and Russell Conwell, quickly chimed in on her side. Jarvis also won Mother's Day endorsements from a string of mayors, governors, and congressional leaders; this political backing found fruition in Woodrow Wilson's presidential proclamation giving national recognition to the holiday in 1914. As one Congregationalist paper at the time wrote effusively about the rising prominence of Mother's Day in the American calendar, "Not Christmas, nor Easter, nor Children's Day has stirred such depth of sentiment."[21]

In some ways the meteoric rise of Mother's Day was a tribute to Jarvis's ingenuity and persistence. But the holiday's rapid ascent was clearly attributable to more than the doings of one pious and dedicated woman. Its success also had deep religious, social, and political sources: the long-standing republican and evangelical idealizations of motherhood; the privatizing, domestic course of nineteenth-century religion; the conservative fears of feminism and female suffrage; the misgivings about urban migration and the consequent erosion of filial attachments; and the civic and patriotic associations of the occasion, which would be especially accentuated after the American entry into World War I. (By political proclamation, Mother's Day was a "flag day," and these civil-religious tones were everywhere apparent in the holiday's enactment.)[22] Mother's Day, to be sure, struck a resonant chord across wide segments of the culture, and this full-throated resonance is what would make the holiday such sweet music to the florists and other merchants. The new holiday had a web of private meanings for Anna Jarvis, a web of religious sentiments and familial memories, but in its public unfolding, Mother's Day added all kinds of strands.

For the churches, the holiday seemed a godsend. In the 1910s and 1920s (and often enough thereafter) Mother's Day served as a kind of solace for many American Christians, Protestants and Catholics alike, who feared that the "new womanhood" was threatening the very institutions of motherhood, domesticity, and the family. Mother's Day offered the assurance, as a writer in the *Homiletic Review* put it in 1917, that "women are still at their old tasks."[23] For Protestants, the holiday underscored the traditional themes of motherly influences in matters of evangelism and salvation, themes grown familiar from a century of maternal associations and female missionary societies. For Catholics, the holiday offered another occasion to recall that sacred model of self-denying motherhood, the Virgin Mary, and to emphasize anew sacramental obligations within the parish.[24] Even within Protestant ranks the holiday inspired extensive reconsideration of Mary's role in the divine order of things. A plethora of sermon ideas on this topic (and even a number of illustrations of the Virgin and child) found growing space in the May issues of Protestant periodicals like the *Homiletic Review*. W. Lloyd Warner, struck by the importance of Mother's Day in the church year in the 1950s, observed in his classic study of Yankee City (Newburyport, Massachusetts) how the Protestant congregations had "welcomed back" the Virgin Mary through their Mother's Day liturgies.[25] Overall, the churches' celebrations of the holiday painted, as they often still do, a traditional picture of self-sacrificing domesticity and sentimental piety. The very ceremonies that emerged in the churches for honoring mothers on this day—for example, lauding the oldest and most-recent mothers present or the mother with the most children with her—were ways of ritually enclosing or bounding all women into motherhood and domesticity.

But in fairness to Jarvis and to all those daughters who rushed to affirm Mother's Day, a small prophetic glint shone amid the old saws on motherhood and home. One of Jarvis's favorite devices that she used in defense of Mother's Day was a playful litany that she recited on the patriarchy of the American calendar: "Washington's Birthday is for the 'Father of our Country'; Memorial Day for our 'Heroic Fathers'; 4th of July for 'Patriot Fathers'; Labor Day for Laboring Fathers; Thanksgiving Day for 'Pilgrim Father[s]'; and even New Year's Day is for 'Old Father Time.'"[26] Of course, Mother's Day hardly constituted an inclusion of all women; indeed, not even Jarvis herself, since she remained unmarried and childless, found inclusion within its rubrics. Nonetheless, Mother's Day potentially carried with it a larger vision of rectification. Jarvis, and some after her, saw in Mother's Day a ritual of correction and inclusion, a recognition of all mothers alongside the nation's fathers. The florists, too, would be among those who would appropriate this logic as a selling point for the day.[27]

All along, Mother's Day was hardly confined to hidebound formulations. As it moved quickly out of Jarvis's and the churches' control, the holiday became a cultural rite open to diverse or competing enactments—that is, a cultural "text" susceptible to variant, contested, and improvised readings. Here and there, for example, social-gospel perspectives on poverty, birth control, or the exploitation of working women found space in the holiday.[28] Mother's Day thus came to act, in part at least, as a temporal location for cultural debates about women, justice, and equality; indeed, the observance eventually provided a ritual occasion for various groups to raise pressing social issues. As part of the Poor People's Campaign in 1968, for instance, Coretta Scott King led a Mother's Day march in support of poor mothers and their children. Under the banner of "Mother Power," she exhorted "black women, white women, brown women and red women—all the women of this nation" to take up this "campaign of conscience." In the 1970s the National Organization for Women employed Mother's Day to stage rallies for the Equal Rights Amendment, to promote broadened access to child care, and to hold their own "Give-Equality-for-Mother's-Day" banquets. Likewise, in the 1980s the Women's Party for Survival, founded by Helen Caldicott, reappropriated Julia Ward Howe's idea of Mothers' Peace Day celebrations and used the holiday as an occasion for antinuclear demonstrations.[29]

Even as the holiday opened up into competing and conflictual enactments, prevailing interpretations—about women as guardians of the Christian home, about modern celebrations as domestic affairs, or about mothers as fountainheads of democratic government in bringing up sons to be virtuous citizens—remained little diminished. All along, too, commercial renderings of the festival stood out as among the most formative and pervasive "readings" or "performances" of the celebration. Gift advertisements, store displays, trade journals, and show windows were crucial purveyors of the observance, and flowers, above all, became the quintessential material expression of the holiday. Regularly in the popular media its "nation-wide commemoration" was attributed not to Anna Jarvis or the churches at all, but instead to "the notoriety fostered by florists."[30] How was it that one industry managed to play such a large role in the holiday's prosperity?

COMMERCIAL FLORICULTURE AND THE MORAL ECONOMY OF FLOWERS: THE MARKETING OF MOTHER'S DAY

The success of Mother's Day hinged in good measure on its commercial potential and promotion. Without the systematic, sustained campaign of commercial florists (and eventually other industries as well), Mother's Day would certainly have been a smaller observance and might well have remained a parochial event; it might even have gradually withered away like other Protestant days of the early twentieth century such as Children's Day or Temperance Sunday. If not simply, as many in the industry liked to think, a "florist-made" holiday, Mother's Day was deeply enmeshed with commerce and consumption. Already in 1913 the *Florists' Review*, with characteristic exaggeration and bluster, congratulated the industry for its part in making the holiday a national observance: "For the success of the 'day,' we are to credit ourselves, us, we, the members of the trade who know a good thing when they see it and who are sufficiently progressive to push it along—Mothers' day is ours; we made it; we made it practically unaided and alone."[31]

The growth of commercial floriculture in the United States over the course of the nineteenth century mirrored in microcosm the expansion of the consumer culture. In the first half of the century, books on floriculture often commented on the "instructive lessons, tending to moral and social virtue," that could be learned from cultivating flowers. The focus of flower books was obviously on practical matters—when and how to plant, how to construct greenhouses or hotbeds, how to lay out a garden, or how much to water—but a whole complex of virtues and values was also connected with floriculture. For example, Roland Green's *Treatise on the Cultivation of Ornamental Flowers* (1828) offered, along with detailed botanical lists and horticultural rules of thumb, this advice: "As every valuable plant must be defended, and every noxious weed removed; so every moral virtue must be protected, and every corrupt passion and propensity subdued." Similarly, Thomas Bridgeman's *Florist's Guide* (1835) contained a didactic chapter entitled "The Matrimonial Garden" that urged readers, among other things, to root out "AVARICE, like some choking weed." In flower books one often found homiletic reflections on God and nature as well as on mundane virtues such as industry, frugality, domesticity, and orderliness. In this typological world, one could, through cultivating flowers, refurrow some of the basic lines of the moral universe.[32]

Commercial floriculture introduced new dimensions into the moral economy of flowers. In his pathbreaking work for the development of the industry, *Practical Floriculture* (1869), Peter Henderson provided the first handbook for the trade. Previous flower books had been written for amateur home gardeners; Henderson's work, published fifteen years before the organization of the Society of American Florists, pioneered in the field of what he tellingly called "flower manufacturing" and included such chapters as "The Profits of Floriculture" and "How to Become a Florist." His book also anticipated the rise of an impressive panoply of trade journals for the floral industry over the next three decades: *American Florist* led the way from Chicago in 1885; the *Florists' Exchange* followed from New York in 1888; and *Florists' Review* commenced in Chicago in 1897.[33] In concentrating on the business of flower production and merchandising, Henderson, like the various trade writers who followed him, modified many of the values given expression in the earlier volumes on ornamental floriculture.

Where flower gardens had stood as moral lessons about order and self-discipline, Henderson rejoiced in the extravagant use of cut flowers. He held up to would-be florists the prospect of great sums of money to be made through the indulgence and encouragement of the profuse display of flowers. His new heroines were "rich and fashionable belles"; he made particular mention of one who sallied forth to promenade with a bouquet in each hand and with six others strung from her arms "as trophies." By 1887, when the fourth edition of his book appeared, Henderson was able to tell of a wedding in which six hundred dollars was spent on one "floral canopy" and in which the overall bill for flowers totaled five thousand dollars.[34] Peter Henderson's view of flowers was far removed from that of Roland Green or Thomas Bridgeman. Commercial floriculture brought the values of the consumer culture to the floral world: Flowers could be produced in lavish amounts and in luxuriant variety at any time of the year and could be made into stunning arrangements with ever-changing colors and shapes to please "that erratic jade, Dame Fashion."[35] In turn, they could and should be consumed lavishly. Cut flowers, in their superfluity and quick exhaustibility, were apt symbols of the burgeoning consumer culture.

Yet commercial florists, in their efforts to promote the consumption of their product, built upon, as much as transformed, the traditional meanings of flowers. For Victorians, flowers harbored a complex language; they were, in an anthropological trope, good for thinking. Redolent of sentiment, flowers were seen as a wonderful vehicle for the conveyance of diverse feelings; different flowers could embody highly complex emotions—sorrow, remembrance, hope, faith, longing, and love (the last, in varying degrees of purity and passion). Besides their sentimental meanings, flowers could also evoke an array of social significations. Associated especially with women and the home, flowers were symbols of femininity and domestic happiness (hence they proved a "natural" choice for Mother's Day, even as they would fall flat as a gift idea for Father's Day). Symbolic associations with religion were also prominent as the extensive floral decorations for Christmas and Easter amply testified. Thus when people purchased flowers as gifts, decorations, or memorials, they were tapping into a lush symbolic medium, rich in possibilities for giving expression to a range of sentiments, emotions, and relationships. As Emerson observed in his essay on gifts, "Flowers and fruits are always fit presents; flowers because they are a proud assertion that a ray of beauty overvalues all the utilities of the world. . . . [D]elicate flowers look like the frolic and interference of love and beauty."[36]

The industry thus played upon and reinforced the already rich cultural meanings of floral tributes, commercializing the Victorian language of flowers with great effectiveness. In some cases, retailers actually gave out complimentary booklets or souvenirs with titles like "Whispers from Flowerdom" or "The Boudoir Language of Flowers" that made explicit the commercial interest in appropriating this popular medium of expression and that spelled out for uninitiated consumers the specific meanings of various flowers. This commercialization of the Victorian language of flowers would be encapsulated in the highly successful national advertising slogan of the Society of American Florists, "Say It with Flowers." Introduced as part of the society's first national publicity campaign in 1918, the jingle achieved the talismanic status for which every pitchman yearns. It became part of the vernacular; it was echoed in song, comedy, and other popular media and was imitated by fellow retailers in different lines of trade.[37]

To make purchasing cut flowers a regular part of people's lives, commercial floriculture soon discovered what several other industries were discovering at the same time: namely, the commercial value of celebration and ritual. Almost as much as the greeting-card industry had, commercial floriculture built its success on special occasions, holidays, and life passages. In Peter Henderson's volume in 1869 this had only been inchoate—for example, in his directions for various wreath designs for funerals. Despite the growing fashion of church decoration, he made no explicit linkage of Easter with lilies or other flowers, and, so far as Christmas and New Year's were concerned, he merely made the

93. "Say It with Flowers," *Saturday Evening Post*, 4 May 1918, 52.

simple suggestion that poinsettias would make excellent adornments, since they were "in full perfection at the holidays." Thirty years later, in another commercial florists' manual, Easter and lilies were synonymous, and poinsettias were simply dubbed "the Christmas flower." By the turn of the century, Easter, Christmas, New Year's, and Memorial Day had clearly emerged as red-letter days for the industry. In another thirty years the cycle of commercial floriculture had widened further to include St. Valentine's Day, Thanksgiving, and Mother's Day; promotions playing on themes from other holidays, such as Washington's Birthday, Lincoln's Birthday, St. Patrick's Day, Halloween, and Armistice Day, were also employed. In 1914 the *American Florist*, the charter journal for the industry, summed up the trade's view of holidays in bold terms: "There are a number of these days in the year, but not too many certainly for the florist. Anything that operates to give him more of these holidays does just so much to put more money into his pocket and makes the new home or the new automobile that much more certain."[38]

The immediate inspiration for this bold remark from the *American Florist* was Mother's Day. As part of the first observance of the holiday, Jarvis had urged people to wear white carnations in honor of their mothers, a simple floral badge chosen because the carnation had been among her mother's favorite flowers. This seemingly innocent suggestion created in itself an unprecedented demand for white carnations for the second Sunday in May, sending prices up and actually causing annual shortages in some places. It also provided the opening wedge for the industry, which quickly attempted to expand the flowers associated with the day beyond the white carnation. In 1910 the *Florists' Review* was already urging that churches, homes, Sunday schools, and cemeteries be decorated with flowers for the holiday. The trade was soon promoting the notion that flowers should also be given to one's mother as a gift, and by 1912 the industry was offering various Mother's Day bouquets. Throughout the 1910s the florists were the primary merchants promoting Mother's Day as they forged a solid link between the day and their product. Competition mounted in the early 1920s from confectioners, department stores, stationers, and jewelers, but the commercial florists, helped by Jarvis's initial suggestion, had clearly gotten a jump on the others. As the *American Florist* happily reported in 1919, "All the other holidays of the year have features that are taken advantage of by various lines of business, but the second Sunday in May is purely a floral holiday, which can and should be made of great advantage to the entire trade."[39]

The florists' sizable share of the Mother's Day market in 1919 was built on a decade of work during which the trade amply displayed its acumen at commercializing the calendar. Trade journals, not surprisingly, played a leading role from the start. The *Florists' Review*, the *American Florist*, *Horticulture*, and the *Florists' Exchange* all noted the day in its first year of observance in 1908. The *Florists' Review* took the lead, publishing an excited letter from Chapin Brothers of Lincoln, Nebraska, in its issue of 14 May 1908. "Again Nebraska is ahead," the letter announced of Lincoln's observance of Mother's Day. "It's a sentiment that appeals to every man and boy, and people bought flowers that never bought before. . . . We hope to make it a holiday for the United

States. Crowd it and push it; it has Decoration day beat [by] a mile, and comes when flowers are cheap and plenty. Get a swing on your pen, but give Lincoln, Neb., the credit. We grow big men and big ideas here." If slightly more restrained in its diction, the *American Florist* was similarly sanguine and hortatory: "Let us one and all, keep the anniversary before us and make it with each recurring season the greatest floral event of the year."[40] Once alerted to Mother's Day in 1908, the trade journals never lost their enthusiasm. Year after year, these publications mapped out elaborate campaigns for the industry's promotion of the holiday.

As the letter from Chapin Brothers suggests, one of the primary tasks the trade journals performed was exhorting the florists themselves to push the new holiday. Clearinghouses for horticultural advice and new marketing ideas, the publications were also platforms for cheerleading. "Let every one boost Mothers' Day—talk it up, make a fuss about it, believe in it, get enthusiastic over it," the *American Florist* advised. "The sentiment is here; it is only waiting to be awakened. Get together, boys, and arouse it." Such zeal was constantly enjoined. The Lord helps those who help themselves; that was the leading tenet in this gospel of business initiative. "Are you a real, live wire, wide-awake florist?" the *Southern Florist* queried. "If so, how are you preparing to augment your sales on Mother's Day? Have you advertised it, talked it, preached it, sung it, and then followed the same route over again?" With such rhetoric the trade journals sought to establish the most important precondition for the success of the holiday within the industry: The florists themselves had to be sold on the newly invented occasion before they could sell it to others. Without the proper enthusiasm and dedication on the part of those in the industry, articles in the journals warned, Mother's Day might be only a passing fad or might be channeled in directions of little or no benefit to the trade. (Such scenarios were, indeed, quite conceivable.) Thus admonished about the possibilities of failure and rallied by visions of creating a great floral occasion, the trade primed itself to devote considerable time and money to making the holiday an American institution.[41]

The exhortations in the trade papers encouraged boosting Mother's Day "in every possible way," and this meant, in a word, advertising. The florists' unbounded faith in advertising echoed the wider business orthodoxy of the period: "Advertising of the right kind," the *American Florist* asserted in 1913, "will create the demand." Or, as the *Southern Florist* put the matter a few years later, "You can make [Mother's Day business] as big as you want it to be. ADVERTISE!" With this conviction, the trade plied every angle in promoting the day. The *Florists' Review* made only a partial list when it summarily reviewed advertising venues for the holiday's "exploitation": "window decorations,

94. Mother's Day advertisement, *Florists' Review*, 25 April 1918, 8.

newspaper display advertising—cooperative and individual—handbills, articles in newspapers and periodicals, reminder cards in delivered packages and stickers on them."[42] Banners on the sides of delivery trucks or on streetcars, show cards, circulars, direct mailings to customers, and posters or other displays around town were also common parts of Mother's Day advertising.

All along, two staples of florist advertising were the twin arts of poetry and window decoration. Dripping with sentiment, poetic verses—or what the *Florists' Review* more accurately called "poetic propaganda"—were seen as particularly suited to Mother's Day. "Only the poet can do justice to this subject," the *Florists' Exchange* concluded. Such promotional poems, composed for reprinting in newspaper advertisements or on placards, usually included floral slogans, especially the ubiquitous refrain, "Say It with Flowers." Closely allied to poetry for "the artistic florist" were the pictures of filial obligation and maternal devotion painted in show windows. For florists, as for other merchants, window decoration was a portentous medium, and Mother's Day offered the trade a new eye-catching opportunity—one played on regularly with scenes of Mother surrounded by flowers. "Every window . . . is a story, a tale with a plot to it," the *Florists' Review* observed, and in its windows of late April and early May the trade told stories of mothers made happy by sons and daughters who remembered to send flowers, tales of familial relationships renewed and affirmed through floral gifts.[43]

In 1917 the industry began to expand its horizons to include advertisements for Mother's Day flowers in national magazines; the first, under the sponsorship of the Chicago Florists' Club, appeared in *Literary Digest* in May 1917, and the next year the Society of American Florists committed the industry to a broadened national campaign. The florists were also quick to push Mother's Day through the latest advertising media, including, at least as early as 1914, slides of Mother's Day advertisements for showing in moving-picture theaters.[44] Indicative, too, of this technological edge in the holiday's promotion was the prominence given the services of the Florists' Telegraph Delivery Association (FTD). Organized in 1910, well timed to the rise of Mother's Day, FTD encouraged sons and daughters far from home to have flowers wired to Mother across the miles.[45] By the 1920s the trade was already issuing Mother's Day publicity over the radio, and in the 1950s the first national television commercial for the industry was an FTD advertisement for Mother's Day.[46] Repetition was acknowledged as a key to any successful advertising campaign, especially in the introduction of a new product. The same was true, the florist industry was convinced, in the introduction of a new holiday, as the trade conveyed its Mother's Day message each year through any and all means it had at its disposal.[47]

The trade's promotion of Mother's Day did not end with the pursuit of the expected advertising channels, but embraced a broad view of publicity. In April 1910 the *Florists' Review* issued this general reminder: "Well, what have you started to help along Mothers' day? Seen the mayor about issuing a proclamation? Called the ministers' attention? Spoken to the local newspapers? . . . We can't expect ready-made flower days—we've got to do something to work

95. Mother's Day show window, *Florists' Review*, 3 May 1923, 28.

them up." The first item, getting a mayoral proclamation, was regularly hailed as a trade goal. Already in 1908, the excited letter from Chapin Brothers had noted that the mayor of Lincoln had issued a Mother's Day proclamation, and it suggested that florists take the lead in obtaining such proclamations in the future. Retailers thus joined Jarvis in pushing Mother's Day as a civic event, and, given their numbers and their geographic diffusion, they rightly saw themselves as far better positioned than Jarvis's Philadelphia-based association to procure the holiday's widespread political promulgation.[48]

Political proclamations were only part of a larger strategy. The churches were also to be urged to hold "special services." If most churches hardly required encouragement from local merchants, the florists were nonetheless called on to preach to the converted—to get the word out to ministers and congregants who, it was felt, would no doubt be supportive. And the testimonies flowed into the trade journals that the florists out in the field were doing the job. Typical was the report from Kenosha, Wisconsin, in 1911: "I went to our mayor and he issued a proclamation. . . . I also went to nearly every pastor in town." The *American Florist* suggested how the trade saw the use of the churches in its publicity work: "In some communities, flowers have been furnished by the trade, so that each Sunday school scholar is given one to wear; this being another form of advertising and trying to make the custom universal." In such cases, the churches, like the mayors who issued proclamations at the trade's urging, were made part of a publicity campaign—an advertisement—for the florists.[49]

Along with ministers and mayors, newspaper editors were on the list of people to visit in order to obtain broad publicity for Mother's Day. Recipients of a good part of the florists' advertising expenditures, the newspapers were, as a rule, predisposed to cooperate with their clients. In Spokane, Washington, for example, the local florists jointly ran a number of newspaper advertisements for Mother's Day in 1915 "in return for which the newspapers gave a full column of reading matter telling the origin of Mother's Day and developing public sentiment in a proper manner." Happily, it was reported, this campaign "made Mother's Day business" in Spokane "as large as [the business] the day before Christmas." This use of the newspapers was a commonplace recommendation in the trade journals: The goal was to ensure that articles "telling the history and purpose of Mother's Day" annually appeared in the papers. "It is a matter of education," the *American Florist* commented of Mother's Day in 1919, "that brings about a custom that will in time become universal." Recurrent articles about Mother's Day in the newspapers helped provide that education.[50]

To make what was, after all, a very short history newsworthy required a satisfying story of origins, and Anna Jarvis and her mother provided that. Ascribing the holiday to the self-sacrificing dedication of one woman who was inspired out of love and grief for her noble and even more self-sacrificing mother, the trade saw in Jarvis and her story "more publicity for Mother's Day than money can buy." Daughter and mother were thus seen as assets for advertising, even as promotional icons; their pictures appeared time and again in trade publications and, often at the trade's urging, in newspapers and other popular media. At some level, mother and daughter came to serve as a facade for the florists and other merchants: Jarvis's sincerity and commitment became window dressing for the trade, a surface of devoted selflessness that helped veil commercial self-interest. This guise soon nettled Jarvis, and after 1920 she spent much of her time trying to expose what she saw as the trade's humbug.[51]

Despite Jarvis's pique, merchants had discerned an important lesson in publicizing the story of her and her mother: When it came to inventing holidays, women were vital sponsors. With such Mother's Day spin-offs as Father's Day, Grandparents' Day, Secretaries' Day, and Bosses' Day, merchants looked in each case to a woman as the "founder." These stories of origin, spread through press releases and trade publications, were helpful for suggesting that these holidays were somehow authentic, genuinely sentimental, and appropriately populist. Similarly, when it came to building up Armistice Day in the wake of World War I, one trade writer in the *Florists' Exchange* offered this blanket advice: "Someone, preferably a woman of determination and pluck, must be the one to enthuse our legislators and the public." The trade quickly lifted up Mrs. Simeon Shaw, the wife of a Methodist minister and a mother of nine from Canyon City, Texas, for her proposal to honor the world's soldiers with floral tributes. It was her touching idea, the trade said, to turn Armistice Day into an "International Flower Day." Like its various successors, Jarvis's story served inescapably promotional ends, and that feature remains one of the principal implications of its annual retelling. In this context, even the scholarly narration of Jarvis's tale becomes promotional, all too easily made a part of the holiday's cultural (and commercial) legitimation.[52]

Even more than the "history" surrounding Jarvis and her mother, the holiday's "sentiment" was recognized as the key to both its popularity and its promotion. Theirs, the florists knew, was a business "founded on sentiment," and they were well aware of the part they needed to play in helping deepen the sentimental power of the holiday. Editors at the trade journals, quite caught up in the event's sentimental possibilities, waxed as eloquent and theological about Mother's Day as any minister. "It is a celebration based upon, redolent of, radiant with the highest, most sacred and most tender sentiments," the *Florists' Exchange* rhapsodized. In an article entitled "Mother's Day—A Second Eastertide," the same journal grew even more reverent: "Is there not, after all, as much of the spirit of resurrection in Mother's Day as in Easter? Is there any thought more holy, more imperishable, more immortal than that of motherhood? Shall we be any less thankful for the blessing of an earthly mother than for that of a Heavenly Father?" How better to give expression to such lofty sentiments and reverent feelings than through "the mystical, beautiful language of flowers"? Flowers were, indeed, powerful emblems of holiness and worship in the culture—time and again, they blessed times of sorrow and loss, love and celebration, sacrifice and hope, rebirth and resurrection. Florists were thus to see their windows and stores, as the *Florists' Exchange* put it, as "an altar of God's love and grace." The real calling of the trade finally was an almost religious, sacramental, or ministerial enterprise, that is, to mythologize and dignify holiday rituals, Mother's Day most immediately.[53]

The trade knew that there were delicate boundaries between sentiment and business, that it had to cultivate the emotive potential of Mother's Day without calling attention to the commercial interests of the industry. For example, the Toledo Florists' Club, reporting on its Mother's Day advertising in 1916, noted that "the publicity was designed to keep the commercial phase in the background and to give prominence in a dignified manner, to the beautiful sentiment of the day." The advertisements for Mother's Day were to tug at the heart with studied evocations of home, childhood, separation, love, frailty, and memory. The florists, keenly aware that they could "kill the day" with ill-conceived or tactless marketing, carefully appropriated and emphasized in their advertising the revered values of motherhood, home, family, and faith. Such sentiments and images helped disguise, or at least mute, the commercial designs of the trade. The *American Florist* offered this laconic bit of advertising advice for the holiday in 1916: "The commercial aspect is at all times to be kept concealed." And it was sentiment, above all, that concealed. It was precisely the profound depth of sentiment that Mother's Day evoked that made the commercial uses of the holiday possible. Without all the varied associations of motherhood, florist advertising would have meant little and profited less. It was indeed the sentiment that counted.[54]

The extensive involvement of the floral industry in founding and shaping Mother's Day as a national observance illustrates how far the process of commercialization had moved by the 1910s and 1920s. The full panoply of commercial forces was marshaled on a national scale with thorough systematization, familiarity, and sophistication. More than that, Mother's Day suggested a new stage in the commercial management of the calendar: The florist industry did not simply capitalize on existing holidays, like St. Valentine's Day or Easter; the trade actually helped invent a new celebration, molding the occasion to its economic advantage and creating a solid link between its product and the new ritual event. The success that the florists experienced with Mother's Day intensified interest in generating new festivals for commercial ends. In this, Mother's Day helped set a pattern that became characteristic of the American calendar and American public life: the proliferation of invented occasions under the auspices of various trades.

PIRATES, PROFITEERS, AND TRESPASSERS: NEGOTIATING THE BOUNDS OF CHURCH, HOME AND MARKETPLACE

The welling up of sentiment never concealed commercialism completely, especially not from Anna Jarvis, for whom the use of such high sentiments for commercial calculation or obfuscation was nothing short of an abomination. To Jarvis, the mystification of Mother's Day gifts and goods was continually mystifying. Her crusade became peculiarly one of unmasking the florists and other profit seekers. With prophetic ire and caviling irascibility she attacked the "charlatans, bandits, pirates, racketeers, kidnappers and other termites [who] would undermine with their greed one of the finest, noblest, truest Movements and celebrations known." Embittered at every turn by "greedy tradesmen," she repeatedly lashed out at those who "have feasted on our

Cause" and who seemed willing to "take the coppers off a dead mother's eyes." Hers became a quest to preserve the putative purity of Mother's Day, to keep "any money taint" from profaning it—in short, to maintain boundaries of consecration around home, church, and motherhood.[55]

That commerce and consumption should so disturb Jarvis was not self-evident. Initially she had happily cooperated with merchants; John Wanamaker, for example, had been among her earliest backers in Philadelphia, making his store available for Jarvis's Mother's Day programs, championing the occasion for the Sunday schools, and creating holiday souvenirs for the event. (Again, Wanamaker's mix of motives was evident; his commercial boosterism combined sincerely with religious sentimentality, and Jarvis apparently never questioned his intentions or his integrity.) Jarvis was greatly indebted to her brother Claude, a successful Philadelphia businessman, for financial backing of her cause, and she drew as well on the resources of other moguls in the area such as H. J. Heinz.[56] She also took pride in her own business life with Fidelity Mutual, where her literary responsibilities apparently included work in advertising, though she soon resigned from this position to devote herself full-time to the work of her Mother's Day International Association.[57] Early on she even sought favor with her soon-to-be arch-nemesis, the florist industry, seeing in commercial floriculture an ally in the promotion of her floral emblem, the white carnation. She happily spoke to florist clubs about her cause, accepted sizable donations from them, and even printed up her own Mother's Day placards for display in store windows. Hardly alienated from modern forms of commerce, promotion, and publicity, Jarvis initially seemed at home in that world, an energetic and entrepreneurial woman with a new holiday to sell.[58]

But harmony and cooperation soon gave way to anger and alienation. As it became clear that the florists were molding her "holy day" to their own ends, Jarvis became increasingly indignant and resentful. Charges of "commercialism" strained her relationship with the trade, and in 1920 tensions finally snapped, producing utter estrangement. Jarvis, ever defensive about Mother's Day, formally denounced the industry with scathing and widely publicized attacks on its "profiteering." Hoping, she said, "to settle the floral question for all time," she proposed substituting celluloid buttons for white carnations as the holiday's official badge and urged people to stop buying flowers or any other gifts for the occasion. "Flowers are not used," she pronounced wishfully in 1921, "and Mother's Day has not any connection with florists or other tradesmen."[59] For its part, the trade was quick to retaliate: It cut off any official support it had given her, ceased to credit her with any special authority over the day, and became harshly dismissive and even contemptuous toward her.[60]

In this last-ditch battle to root commerce out of Mother's Day, Jarvis clearly lost. In 1922 the *Florists' Review* happily reported that Jarvis's campaign against the industry had been "completely squelched," noting in sinister tones that trade associations around the country had, in several cases, pulled strings to keep her attacks out of the press. Many in the industry even saw a silver lining in the whole brouhaha: Jarvis's repeated "vaporings" against commercialization actually resulted in increased publicity for Mother's Day. Controversy, too, was good advertising—and even better, it was free.[61]

Jarvis's forlorn critique of commercialization was multilayered. At the shallowest level, her denunciations seemed no more than the cranky harangues of someone who was unwilling to accept the fact that the holiday was no longer her own special province, that power over the holiday's celebration had become culturally diffuse, and that she no longer exercised singular control or authority over it. In some sense, her concerns then were not so much with the corrosive, hollowing, or profaning effects of commercialism, but instead with the power that businesspeople were claiming over the holiday's enactment at her expense. "It is not for strangers to meddle with," she said in a phrase suggestive of her deep personal identification with this work. She wanted everyone interested in Mother's Day to come through her and her Philadelphia committee, and anyone who did not—whether merchants, ministers, or politicians—was subject to withering rebuke. Thus she often characterized others who took up the cause and offered their own versions of Mother's Day activities as "grafters," "infringers," "trespassers," "usurpers," or "dead beats." Her disdain extended to those interested in turning the holiday to benevolent purposes, particularly fund-raisers for philanthropies. Such "charity charlatans" were to her almost as accursed as the florists and other "hard-boiled trade operators."[62] At bottom, Jarvis wanted to maintain for herself the power to determine how the holiday was celebrated, and she was unwilling to let that power slip away without prolonged protest.

The critique was also about who would get credit for Mother's Day. If she could not have power, she at least wanted recognition and flattery. She detested the florists for claiming the holiday as their own creation, just as she disdained anyone else who came forward with claims of having had the idea before her (of whom there were many). She went to great lengths, for example, to discredit the Fraternal Order of Eagles for maintaining that the organization had staged the first Mother's Day in February 1904. Likewise she regarded the notions of broadening out Mother's Day into Parents' Day and spinning off a Father's Day as commercial scams aimed at undermining the "sacred basic standards" that only her international association maintained pristinely. As late as 1941, seven years before her death at the age of eighty-four, she was still complaining about "fake M[other's] D[ay] founders, historians, etc.," all of whom seemed hell-bent on depriving her of her place in the sun.[63]

But Jarvis's protest was founded on more than selfish motives. Substantively she was concerned with issues of sincerity, simplicity, home, and religion; all of these she wanted to protect or safeguard from the "money taint." Matters of sincerity and genuineness absorbed her, and much of her alienation centered on the way commercially produced trinkets, gifts, and cards were surrogates for real expressions of affection and closeness. To Jarvis, letters and visits were better ways to bolster and affirm one's relationship with Mother than such mass-produced gifts of the marketplace. For example, greeting cards, she said, were "a poor excuse for the letter you are too lazy to write." "Any mother would rather have a line of the worst scribble from her son or daughter, than any fancy greeting card."[64] To Jarvis, such commodities were inadequate for the task of self-expression; rather than being vehicles of intimacy, they were unauthentic and even self-serving. Sons, she said, all too often give a box of candy to their mothers, only to "eat most of it themselves." Contained within her crotchety, often trifling castigations of "trade vandals" for their "Mother's Day rake off" was a concern for artless feeling and unaffected gifts—the offering of self, instead of things.[65] Hers, she said, was an "altruistic, sincere work," and she wanted it filled with heartfelt expressions of love, free from "the commercial grip of buying and giving" and free from the "ulterior motives" of money-getters, retailers, and promoters.[66] As one pastor, who shared Jarvis's concerns, prayed in a litany for the holiday, "*Good Lord, deliver us* [f]rom the unreality of superficial sentiment, from commercial exploitation, and from all lip service to motherhood."[67] For Jarvis and other critics, these were essential tensions or juxtapositions: The "camouflage" and "deception" of merchants darkened the transparent "sacrifice" and "sincerity" of Mother's Day. The dialectics of pretense and purity, disguise and integrity, permeated (and energized) the rhetoric of protest. In the marketplace the good, the beautiful, and the true seemed all too easily subsumed by artifice and manipulation.[68]

A second substantive concern was that of simplicity in celebration. On this point, Jarvis showed little penchant for consistency. She herself hardly cultivated the old evangelical ethic of plainness and austerity. As much as anyone, she was a lover of Victorian elegance and finery; she filled her Philadelphia home with charming bric-a-brac and bibelots, and the house was appointed with a marble foyer, stained glass, and fine mahogany fireplaces.[69] Yet she remained fearful of extravagance and, like both the critics and the apostles of Easter fashions, drew the line at excessive consumption in circuitous and unpredictable ways. On this score, choosing to found a festival was in itself a perilous decision, especially for a Protestant: It was a cultural form particularly susceptible to indulgence and immoderation. Jarvis clearly did not want to provide another ritual occasion for dissipation. Mother's Day was to be a sober and solemn commemoration, centered on church and home, faithful to the memory of her own mother's sacrifice and avowed temperance. Not surprisingly, then, she saw merchants as subverting this simplicity of celebration and encouraging exorbitance instead. She expressed her position time and again after 1920: "We are opposed to the great waste of money for flowers for funerals, holidays, Mother's Day and similar occasions. We do not wish Mother's Day to have any longer any responsibility for such waste."[70] To Jarvis, the commercial florists' celebration of consumption, display, and indulgence—the floral canopies, the pyramids of exotics, the lush bouquets, the intricate wreaths—cut against the older ethic of frugality and self-restraint. Though simplicity appeared to be merely a residual concern for Jarvis (perhaps in this regard the otherworldly, self-denying piety of her mother was more her measure than her own habits), this collision of the consumer culture with deep-seated fears of luxury and prodigality certainly helps explain her profound alienation from commercialism.

At its deepest level, Jarvis's protest was based on her perception that commerce obscured, subverted, or profaned two of her central missions—her hope to emphasize the moral uplift of the home and her desire to stress the abiding rituals of evangelical Protestantism. Her mother's domesticity and devotion were clearly the models for both objectives, and songs such as "Nearer, My God, to Thee," "Jesus, Lover of My Soul," and "Home, Sweet Home" evoked for Jarvis the correct liturgical moods.[71] Merchants, though happy enough to see such dimensions of the holiday flourish, obviously had other venues in mind besides home and church for the holiday's enactment. They wanted to add shops, stores, and restaurants as primary staging grounds for the holiday and hoped that commercial gift giving would become an essential and obligatory part of the celebration.

This conflict of visions between Jarvis and the merchants was embedded in a wider clash of cultural values, centered on religion and gender. At the core of the contest were deep-seated cultural oppositions—the home-centered, religious world of women versus the commercial, self-aggrandizing world of men. Joining Jarvis in her critique, a writer in the *Christian Advocate*, Laura Athearn, worried that Mother's Day was becoming nothing but "the tool of commercial interests," that the onslaught of "expensive gifts" and "falsely sentimental advertising" was obscuring the religious benefits of this festival of the Christian home. "Commercial influences must be abolished in any celebration of Mother's Day," she warned, "if spiritual values are to be conserved." The dichotomies could hardly have been clearer: The "spiritual values" of home, motherhood, and Christianity were set against the "commercial interests" of marketplace, advertising, and profit making. The profane world of commerce was seen as threatening the boundaries that encircled the sacred time of home and church; Jarvis, after all, had instituted this familial "holy day" on a Sunday precisely to underscore its hallowedness, its separateness from workaday time or merchant's time. All along the celebration drew energy from anxieties about the loosening of filial attachments, the all-absorbing demands of enterprise, the seductive lure of the cities, and the neglect of home ties. Ideally Mother's Day would act as a buffer against the threatening, harried, money-grubbing world of trade, but the ritual could hardly accomplish this if it were itself consumed by commerce. Jarvis's disaffection (and that of others) was thus drawn in a chiaroscuro of church versus marketplace, home versus trade, women versus men.[72]

These poles, with all their complex interrelationships and tensions, animated the cultural contest over the holiday. Chagrin about the commercialization of Mother's Day was redoubled precisely because of the perceived violation of such cultural boundaries or categories. To Jarvis and other religious critics (of whom there were sundry), the "invasion" of market exchanges into the domains of home, church, and motherhood was transgressive. This sense of commercial contamination was suggested in the proposal of one Methodist minister in Mount Vernon, New York, in 1921. He proposed replacing commercially produced flowers with a simple, handpicked dandelion as an emblem for the holiday. This modest proposal, which was given surprisingly wide play, embodied a religious desire to purify the holiday by removing the blot of lucre and profit—that is, to keep the interests of the market out of a church-centered celebration focused on the supposed selflessness of motherhood.[73] To the florists, such religious recommendations, whatever their anthropological or cultural provenance, were absurd. For example, when a number of clergymen in 1920 publicly sided with Jarvis in her campaign against commercialism, the *Florists' Exchange* dismissed their "hue and cry" in no uncertain terms. Figuring that "usually this class of minister has no business experience," the paper concluded that "a business man hearing this idealistic talk, and realizing full well that it is not practicable, pays no further attention to it." In other words, when ministers would not give their blessing to such commercial activities, businesspeople need not worry: Pragmatic economic actions were unaccountable to such impractical, "effeminate" religious ideals. In these small moments of conflict the simple, seemingly banal rituals of Mother's Day brought the contested cultural boundaries between church and marketplace into sharp relief.[74]

Once again, though, the contest between commerce and Christianity should not be seen as one of uncomplicated polarities: meetinghouse versus countinghouse, home versus mart, church versus business. Just as Jarvis had appropriated show cards and other advertising techniques for promoting her own version of the holiday, the churches regularly turned to commercial venues for their own festive materials and publicity. Quick to demonstrate that they shared the commercial acumen of their compatriots in business, church leaders often employed special advertising for Mother's Day services in hopes of packing the house as at Christmas and Easter. The churches were skilled in using special days for promotional, bureaucratic, and benevolent ends. The Methodist Episcopal Church, for example, had officially instituted Children's Day at its General Conference of 1872 not so much out of any exalted sentiment, but as a fund-raising event for its Board of Education. Likewise in the African Methodist Episcopal Church the event was designed to solicit donations for its national Sunday School Union and its Church Extension campaign. The churches sprinkled their calendars with special observances that served as occasions for collections for various causes—missions, temperance, education, and the like.[75] The popular Protestant calendar was (and is) a web of "stewardship" Sundays of one kind or another. The liturgiologist James F. White has even gone so far as to liken this round of "promotions" in the churches to "the yearly cycle of the department store."[76] Certainly the churches were familiar with the promotional possibilities of holidays and were not averse to cultivating them in ways that would have been familiar to their compatriots in the marketplace. As the *Florists' Review* advised, the trade should get the newspapers "to interview the ministers about what special services the churches will have" for Mother's Day (and other holidays). "There isn't anything needs advertising more than a church does and they all will jump at the chance."[77] In America's voluntaristic milieu the churches, like merchants, were immersed in the free market; the idioms of competition and promotion were widely shared across the culture.

Also, as at Christmas and Easter, denominational publishing houses offered for sale various Mother's Day materials. These included special Sunday school souvenirs, postcards, bookmarks, bulletins, and celluloid buttons for the occasion.[78] With this, as with other holidays, such religious kitsch was a familiar part of church celebrations. The little items related to Sunday school festivities often found their way into scrapbooks or onto bedsteads (or later onto refrigerator doors). It was the material components of ritual that frequently stood out in people's memories. When, for example, Kate Bartine was interviewed in 1947 at the age of eighty-one about her participation in one of the first Children's Day services seventy-five years earlier, what she remembered was "the lovely white dress" and the "store flowers" that she had gotten for the occasion.[79] New clothes and pretty bouquets—the very materials of celebration—for most were the stuff of pleasant memory, not maddened protest. As at other holidays, people remembered Mother's Day (and family and church and home) through flowers, cards, and other palpable emblems.

That the relationship between commerce and Christian celebration was not simply conflictual, but creative and interactive, can be seen in the place that red and white flowers assumed in the folk liturgies for Mother's Day. Jarvis hoped initially to introduce white carnations into Sunday schools and church services as a universal emblem for the holiday; in her repeated explication, this would stand as a symbol for maternal purity, faithfulness, and love. In part because of shortages of white carnations and in part to widen the variety of flowers associated with the day, florists increasingly promoted wearing red flowers in honor of living mothers and white flowers in memory of deceased mothers. Commercial jingles tirelessly promoted this revision of Jarvis's single-minded emphasis on white carnations:

> White flowers for Mother's memory.
> Bright flowers for Mothers living.[80]

This florists' distinction quickly worked its way into popular observances in the churches, and the semiotics of red and white flowers for Mother's Day are ones still familiar to many low-church Protestants. That this little piece of folk practice should come from the "fakelore" or "folklure" of commercial floriculture underlines the influence of the marketplace on the churches. But this simple, small gesture of honor and remembrance was no less popular for having been appropriated and adapted from a commercial idiom.

For all the points of overlap and interaction, the relationship of the churches with the commercial culture remained awkward and ambiguous. The simmering conflicts over Mother's Day, which reached a boil in Jarvis's protests, suggested another variation on the theme of displacement: The expanding consumer culture threatened to transform many of the core values of traditional Protestant piety, here embodied in the devotional world of Jarvis's mother. The cultural redefinition of womanhood in terms of consumption continued to accelerate in these decades, and Mother's Day became in many ways an ironic embodiment of these mounting cultural changes. Envisioned by Jarvis and her religious allies as an enshrinement of evangelical verities about church and home, the holiday became in its wider cultural expression a consumer fête and commercial bonanza. In the 1910s a shibboleth for the occasion had been the hymn "Blest Be the Tie that Binds";[81] in the 1990s its hallmark could be summed up in one company's slogan, "Celebrate Mother's Day with a Shopping Spree."[82] The holiday, indeed, is now worth close to $9 billion in retail sales, and its ongoing religious connections seem culturally faint by comparison to its robust presence in the marketplace.[83]

THE INVENTION OF FATHER'S DAY: THE HUMBUG OF MODERN RITUAL

> What do you buy for a man who has everything, you hear the women remark amongst themselves, no matter how lacking their men. You simply didn't buy a man a present because it was beautiful. Beauty, flowers, candlesticks, a china cup, a silver server, the perfect fragrance women owned or needed. As though fathers or husbands could provide but not desire things.
>
> *Susan Bergman, "Presents" (1992)*[84]

The success of Mother's Day was an inspiration. It set merchants, church folks, crackpots, and comedians to dreaming about the invention of any number of other holidays. In the outpouring of sometimes serious, sometimes snide proposals (Parents' Day, Friendship Day, Baby Week, Sister Day, Mother-in-Law Day, and the like), Father's Day emerged as the most obvious and extensive spin-off from this new maternal celebration. Once the country had a Mother's Day, a Father's Day seemed all but inevitable. So much a natural consequence of Mother's Day, the idea for Father's Day can hardly be seen as the original brainstorm of any one group or individual. The idea was quickly floated in various circles—in local churches, in letters to the editor, in service clubs, and among merchants and trade organizations. But the impetus for Father's Day eventually crystallized around two sources: first, a young woman named Sonora Dodd who, beginning in 1910, worked through Protestant churches and local groups in Spokane, Washington, to push for a new holiday, and second, the National Council for the Promotion of Father's Day, a trade bureau organized in 1938 by the Associated Men's Wear Retailers in New York City. (The latter aimed to systematize and nationalize the disparate Father's Day promotions that various industries, including its parent group, had already undertaken.) Though both Dodd and the retailers' council were, each in its own way, quite serious about the significance of this new holiday for Dad, they were always hard-pressed to get others to consider it with due solemnity. For many, it seemed like a bit of trickery, a joke, a send-up for Will Rogers or Groucho Marx. Despite the long-term success of the Father's Day Council in getting the occasion established on the calendar (Richard Nixon finally signed off on it as a national observance in 1972), cynicism has always feasted on the holiday. Perhaps no other event brought out quite so clearly the ironies of ritual and celebration in a modern consumer culture.

The "founder" of Father's Day, Sonora Smart Dodd, was born in 1882 in a little town in Arkansas that had been named after P. T. Barnum's singing sensation, Jenny Lind, a fitting dash of humbug for a woman whose own story became inextricably entwined with the ballyhoo of promoters. As a child, Dodd moved west with her family, settling in eastern Washington, where in 1898 her mother died, leaving her father, William Jackson Smart, a farmer and Civil War veteran, to raise six children on his own. Already in 1909 Mother's Day had come to Spokane, and Dodd, by then a young wife with an infant son, listened to her pastor's ringing tributes to Mother with some sense of imbalance. It was her widowed father, after all, who had held her family together, and surely the nation's fathers deserved similar praise and honor. "I liked everything you said about motherhood," she told her pastor at Central Methodist Episcopal Church after his Mother's Day sermon, "but don't you think father should have a special day, too?"[85] The remark soon proved more than an incidental, at-the-church-door observation on a minister's sermon. In June 1910, with backing from local officers in the Young Men's Christian Association, she turned her suggestion into a petition to the Spokane Ministerial Association urging a parallel observance for fathers.

Dodd's petition was a classic blend of popular Protestant liturgics, sentimentalism, moral reform, and republican civics:

> The beautiful custom of Mothers' Day suggests the question, Why not a Fathers' Day? This question is further emphasized by the celebration in our Sunday schools of Children's Day.
> A Fathers' Day would call attention to such constructive teachings from the pulpit as [it] would naturally point out:
>
> The father's place in the home.
> The training of children.
> The safeguarding of the marriage tie.
> The protection of womanhood and childhood.
>
> The meaning of this, whether in light of religion or of patriotism, is so apparent as to need no argument in behalf of such a day.[86]

The petition closed by suggesting the third Sunday in June, the week after Children's Day, as the appropriate time for the observance and by urging the wearing of roses as the suitable counterpart to the carnations of Mother's Day. In that vast Protestant world of home protection, Father's Day was one more little salvo. (Not coincidentally, Dodd was also a champion of the local work of the Women's Christian Temperance Union.)[87] The utility of the event, as Dodd had predicted, proved self-evident to Spokane's ministerial association. The group endorsed her petition, and several of the pastors in town set about planning worship services around the theme of fatherhood.

Larger cultural debates about gender immediately framed the enactment of Father's Day in the Protestant churches of Spokane. The holiday's observance was quickly set within long-running religious contests over the relative feminization and masculinization of American Christianity. As initially envisioned by Dodd, Father's Day sounded distinctly "feminized," with core concerns about Father's role within the home and the protection of womanhood. (In Dodd's view, what was particularly notable about her father was how well he had assumed the domestic responsibilities of raising six "motherless" children. Her own father's virtues were thus presented in notably "maternal" ways; in some sense, then, her father was admirable because he had become a surrogate "mother.") In this context, the images of fatherhood were often tender, gentle, sensitive, and companionate: "True fatherhood," one Spokane woman versified, presented "a friendly bulwark, safe and kind," not "a great peak, forbidding, cold, remote." The church rituals that were developed for the event often simply mirrored the sentimental, flower-filled liturgies of Mother's Day. For example, one Spokane church in 1916 honored "the oldest father, the father with the largest number of children and the father with the youngest child" each with a bouquet, symbolically (and perhaps a little subversively) encircling the men of the church within the world of pious domesticity.[88]

But these tender familial appeals were hardly the only ones that Spokane's religious enactments of Father's Day conveyed. The YMCA as well as various local ministers often had more virile, muscular images of faith and fatherhood in mind in their understanding of the celebration's intent. Like the interdenominational Men and Religion Forward movement of 1911–12, which went under the banner, "More Men for Religion, More Religion for Men," boosters of Father's Day quickly seized the occasion as an opportunity to affirm the robust masculinity of Christianity. Indicative of this was the title of the sermon preached by the Presbyterian pastor Conrad Bluhm in the first year of the holiday's observance: "The Knighthood that Never Retreats." To Bluhm, Father's Day was, like the strapping and valiant men whom he idealized, "rugged, husky, [and] stalwart"; the event, forceful and warriorlike, was "the heavy artillery by which God Almighty will storm the citadel of sin." Even more than that, the celebration was a welcome reminder of the patriarchal potency of the faith: "It was Fathers' Day when Abraham left Ur of Chaldees. It was Fathers' Day when Noah built the ark. It was Fathers' Day when Christ chose the

Twelve. . . . The New Testament is strictly masculine. The antecedents and pioneers of Christian faith were men. The Bible is a man's book and its lessons are his life-task." Bluhm even did some counting in his concordance to underline his point: "The word Father is found in the Bible 1650 times; Mother but 311 times. It is a Fathers' book." Elizabeth Cady Stanton might have written such meditations as bits of satire, but Bluhm was perfectly serious; his was the "manly" oratory of a Billy Sunday or a John Roach Straton.[89]

While Dodd's familial, home-protection rhetoric was easily translated into the muscular Christianity of the YMCA, the Men and Religion Forward Movement, and the Laymen's Missionary Movement, there obviously remained much common ground among Spokane's Protestant ministers and those churchwomen who supported the new holiday. Sermonic messages to fathers about their obligation to concern themselves with the spiritual welfare of their families and the dangers of evading these responsibilities were suggestive of these allied purposes. Other Father's Day messages—for example, those on the importance of fathers setting appropriate civic models for their children—were simply the coin of the realm. At bottom, Father's Day offered another opportunity to explore the modern perils of the Christian home and to call for renewal of "the family altar, the family table, the family pew, [and] the family carriage."[90]

Some of the same machinery that was being mobilized on behalf of Mother's Day was soon marshaled for Father's Day. As Jarvis had done for her holiday, Dodd formed a committee to spread and perpetuate the new celebration. She and her coworkers sought political endorsements for the event, answered inquiries about it from around the country, talked it up in service clubs, and helped stage local celebrations at churches, public parks, and fairgrounds. This was clearly far from a one-woman show in Spokane; various women spoke about the celebration in different congregations in the early years of the holiday's observance, and already in 1911 the YWCA had joined the YMCA in sponsoring local services. But despite these concerted activities, Father's Day was hardly a crowning success, even in Spokane. By 1919 there was little trace of the celebration in the *Spokesman-Review*, and it largely dropped out of view as a local event in the 1920s, only occasionally meriting a special sermon or program. By then, Dodd herself was on to other things; independent and resourceful, she went to study at the Art Institute of Chicago, reimagined herself as a poet and painter, worked for awhile in Hollywood in fashion design, and apparently concerned herself very little with Father's Day. For a time, the holiday looked as if it might prove about as enduring as crepe-paper streamers, perhaps simply remembered as a piece of local color from the Spokane of the 1910s.[91]

96. Spokane Father's Day Association (Sonora Dodd seated third from left), from Grace Willhoite Hitchcock, comp., *Father's Day Silver Anniversary, 1935* (Spokane: Lighthouse Publishing, 1935), unpaginated.

Yet, however tenuous its place even in Spokane's local calendar, the holiday did not die. Dodd herself was back in town permanently by the early 1930s and started working again on behalf of the celebration, especially helping orchestrate a twenty-fifth anniversary observance in 1935. Receiving growing credit from newspapers and trade organizations as the "founder" of Father's Day, she even started appearing on radio programs in which she was honored for her inventiveness.[92] Also, as Father's Day gained wider national exposure in the media and through merchandising, civic-minded Spokanians became more interested in claiming the holiday as their own creation. In the mid-1930s the event became a notable one again in the *Spokesman-Review*; the local Father's Day committee increased its activity; and pastors contrived special sermons in numbers (and themes) comparable to the early 1910s: "Jesus Portrays the Ideal Father," "Fatherly Fathers," "Some Masculine Factors Needed in Life and Religion," "The Heart of a Father," "Honor Thy Father," "The Responsibility of Fatherhood," and "The Father Who Thought Grandad Was Mistaken," among other similarly polished gems of the preacher's art.[93]

Notwithstanding the respect that some of the faithful in Spokane accorded the new rite, advocates of Father's Day had a major public-relations problem from the outset. To be sure, Dodd's idea had attracted some favorable attention around the country: William Jennings Bryan lauded it in 1910 as a fine idea; Woodrow Wilson signaled his approval telegraphically during a Spokane Father's Day program in 1916; several mayors and governors had issued the requisite proclamations; and some churches, Sunday schools, and interdenominational organizations had embraced the idea. For all that, it was still quite evident that Father's Day was regularly garnering attention for the wrong reason: Namely, many people found it laughable. Something of this problem can be seen in the fate of two proposals at the Presbyterian General Assembly in 1911. One urged the observance of Mother's Day in Presbyterian churches throughout the country, and the other supported the establishment of a Father's Day. The first resolution was easily approved, but when a pastor from Oklahoma followed up with the proposal for Father's Day, it was simply "greeted with laughter."[94] Even the *Spokesman-Review* admitted in 1927 that "ever since its inception Father's day has attracted the attention of the wags more than the sages and orators." As one booster lamented, the advance of Father's Day had been severely hampered by the fact that "no one took the day seriously"; indeed, those who seemed most prone to notice the event, he moaned, were editorial humorists who derived "a great deal of pleasure" from making fun of " 'Poor Father' and his special day." Dodd often said that one of her motivations in inaugurating the holiday had been to rectify the glib, mocking portrayals of Dad as an irresponsible loafer in such popular songs of the era as "Everybody Works But Father." In practice, however, her new rite invited a fresh gush of sarcasm.[95]

What was it that the wags found so funny about Father's Day? It was partly the absurd possibilities entailed in imagining the proliferation of observances to cover all relationships—siblings, cousins, grandparents, and in-laws. For example, one letter writer to the *New York Times* in 1914, having heard of the suggestion for a Father's Day, simply satirized the notion with a proposed calendar that included Maiden Aunty's Day and Household Pet Day.[96] While Mother's Day had inspired some spoofs like this, for Father's Day this became a recurrent gag. Similarly, when the dandelion was suggested as a Mother's Day flower, it was aimed at cleansing the observance of floral profiteering; when the same suggestion was made in connection with Father's Day, it was simply a joke. The dandelion was said to be the best flower to commemorate Father because "the more it is trampled on, the more it grows." Even supposedly serious recommendations for Father's Day activities often flirted with the comical: "A fine surprise for father on Father's day," the *Spokesman-Review* suggested, "would be for the whole family to reach the breakfast room ahead of him and, remaining standing until he entered, greet him with: 'Hail to the chief!' " As the *New York Times* observed in 1938, supporters of Father's Day invariably had to undertake their promotions "in the teeth of quipsters and a lack of paternal enthusiasm."[97]

This perceived lack of fatherly excitement was a crucial part of the fun for cynics and satirists. Father's Day was comical in part because fathers seemed so out of place or uncomfortable in this holiday world of sentimental gifts and domestic flattery. The "little remembrances" of flowers, cards, and novelties became funny when showered on Father; they opened up a line of humor that played on the gendered incongruities of holiday gift giving. As one editorial writer on the holiday put the matter in 1925, fathers have "no talent for the fribbles and frabbles and furbelows with which Mother signalizes well-being." Similarly, one greeting-card manufacturer confessed in 1926 to a real Father's Day predicament: "Mannish-looking cards are hard to design," he concluded, "in any scheme that will be beautiful." Even when the gifts were recognizably "mannish"—ties, tobacco, and shirts—fathers did not seem to fare much better. Indeed, by the 1920s, the prevalence of unbecoming Father's Day ties was already a matter for snide cynicism. One writer in 1929 mocked "this infernal practice of giving father a mess of neckties as a token of affection. Red, blue, orange, purple—all the colors of the rainbow, and a few added for luck." Then he added in typically gendered tones, "My appeal to the women-folk is this: Lay off the neckties for Father's Day." Like the men in Susan Bergman's story "Presents," fathers appeared poor candidates for easy inclusion in the sentimental, feminized domain of domestic gift giving: "You simply didn't buy a man a present because it was beautiful." In commenting on the lackluster success of Father's Day in comparison to Mother's Day, one New York florist put his finger on the problem in 1928: "It has been nothing like Mother's Day. . . . I figure it out that fathers haven't the same sentimental appeal that mothers have. You know how it is yourself."[98]

This awkwardness of engaging fathers in the sentimental beauties of domestic gift giving was a recurrent source of playful humor. Indeed, in the editorial cartoons on the holiday in the *Spokesman-Review*, Father's Day exchanges appeared as a kind of practical joke; Dad was bewildered by the attention or even somehow duped by these tokens of affection (some of which were clearly purchased more with the giver than the receiver in mind). Also, and this was a source of particular satire, Dad was seen as the one who, in the end, would have to pay for all these gadgets and trinkets. The bills for Father's Day gifts were viewed as circling back to him, so that he was made to pay, quite literally, for his own undoing:

> The Old Man wept, and his teardrops swept
> Like rain on the Summer hills.
> 'Twas Father's Day and his hair turned gray,
> For he knew he must pay the bills.[99]

But certainly this type of joke was not only at Father's expense: It underlined how holiday gifts often took their meaning from inequality or financial dependence, how women and children often remained subject to the largess of men,

Today is father's day

Tomorrow will be the day after

97. "Today Is Father's Day," *Spokesman-Review*, 18 June 1911, 1.

Father's day.

98. "Father's Day," *Spokesman-Review*, 20 June 1915, 1.

and how middle-class fathers and husbands did not need or require such "gifts." They could simply purchase what they wanted—the right ties, cigars, liquors, or golf clubs—on their own without having to rely on the generosity of family and friends.[100] Father's Day humor certainly underlined these familial hierarchies. At the same time, however, such drollery suggested how the rite could be turned into a practical joke through gag gifts that gently mocked these very discrepancies. Admittedly, compared to the Rabelaisian satires of Mardi Gras, these little mockeries were pallidly tame, but in a middle-class consumer culture, joke gifts—whether bizarre ties or derisive cards—have long been a notable source of burlesque and play.

Perhaps the most important fount of Father's Day sardonicism was the holiday's commercial humbug. Anna Jarvis predictably sneered about the ballyhoo surrounding Father's Day, seeing the whole observance as a poorly disguised plot of "some necktie, tobacco, whiskey and lottery promoters." With "millions of dollars back of its promotion," it was, Jarvis knew in her bones, "an absolute failure as to sentiment or uplift." If Jarvis's acid resentment mirrored her usual disposition, her skepticism about the holiday's commercialism was nonetheless widely shared. To the *Christian Advocate* in 1951, Father's Day appeared to be "little more than the afterthought of manufacturers of neckties and fishing tackle." Likewise, one father interviewed by the *New York Times* in 1928 pronounced his blanket disdain: "I think it's a lot of hooey." Opinions reported in the same newspaper the year before were not much warmer: "Some one is trying to work those 'Lindy' ties off on us"; "I think it's a lot of bunk." The snide perception that the holiday was an inane hoax and that merchants were responsible for putting it over on people found ample expression. Father's Day, more than any other celebration up to that time, demonstrated the corrosive cynicism that had come to hedge in modern rituals in a world of advertising and promotion.[101]

There was, however, a flip side to these Father's Day suspicions: namely, Americans had often indulged a peculiar fondness for Barnumesque humbug and hokum. As Neil Harris has suggested, Barnum's art of deception, his commercial sleight of hand, and his theatrics of trickery were widely admired and appreciated for their very outlandishness and gall. And certainly there was much about Father's Day that possessed those brazen qualities. To some, the holiday's deep embeddedness in commercial and promotional matrices was pleasantly amusing. As a writer for the *Spokesman-Review* observed in 1927, "What Mother's day is to the florists and confectioners, Father's day . . . is to the necktie trust. The cravat industry has placarded the country with appeals to the nation's offspring to give their fathers neckties. The point is that it might have been worse. The claim might have been staked out by the crayon enlargement people." Observers often found it funny how people bought up gaudy ties or bad cigars or pasteboard greetings for Dad. (It was funny, too, how fathers had to feign appreciation for these things and actually wear, smoke, or display them.) That such holiday merchandise could be moved was part of the wonder of American enterprise and salesmanship. The holiday was both engaged and resisted through such droll, ironic commentaries.[102]

Advertisers themselves recognized this wider cultural tendency to see Father's Day gifts as humbug, and one solution was to incorporate this into holiday promotions and to try to turn it to commercial advantage. For example, one Spokane advertiser of menswear pictured a father saddled with the "absurd" gifts of "a mandarin robe, a turkish water-pipe and Indian clubs." The cautionary advice: Do not be taken in by others (or, in this case, quite literally the "other"); what Father really needs and wants are true-blue Arrow shirts. Similarly, another advertisement presented a father lamenting the "screaming green and yellow seat covers for the car," the bad cigars, and the "red leather volume of Love Lyrics" that he had received the preceding Father's Day. The subtext was that Emry's House of Quality, with its fine ties and silk socks, was a refuge from the wiles and tawdry wares of other merchants. In the sometimes carnivalesque air of the American marketplace, the very absurdity and humbug of Father's Day gifts could be used to sell the celebration. Such wry twists of merchandising logic had an almost Adornoesque quality to them: "The triumph of advertising in the culture industry is that consumers feel compelled to buy and use its products even though they see through them." Father's Day promotions were regularly umasked and mocked, even by merchants themselves, but it nonetheless got progressively harder for consumers simply to leave the event unheeded and unobserved. Still, the supposed folly of Father's Day was received playfully; its odd presents, products, and promotions were often turned into a species of modern holiday entertainment.[103]

The influence of merchants in making Father's Day proved even more apparent than in the propagation of Mother's Day. In Spokane, Dodd sought out merchants for their support from the first, and that backing was readily obtained. She asked local merchants to put up display cards publicizing the observance and urged them to construct show windows featuring Father's Day gifts. As a graduate of a local business school and an astute self-promoter, she was altogether comfortable in the world of advertising, fashion design, window display, and trade promotions (indeed, in 1914 the Spokane Advertising Club made her a life member for her work on behalf of Father's Day).[104] Not surprisingly, then, Father's Day in Spokane was produced as much in stores and through advertisements as it was through churches and the YMCA. In the first years of observance, promotional sidebars in department-store advertisements hailed the new event and described the homage due Father for his love

99. "Emry's, the House of Quality," *Spokesman-Review*, 16 June 1938, 2.

and fortitude. Similarly, a Father's Day show window at Spokane's Graham and Co. in 1910 borrowed heavily from the display conventions of other civic holidays; it featured George Washington as "the Father of His Country," a silk American flag, and the placard "Remember Father," all of which combined to highlight a number of holiday gift items. To these sentimental and patriotic portrayals were shortly added more-straightforward advertising slogans such as "Give Dad a Tie," "He Needs Hosiery," or "Father's Day Tie Special."[105]

The holiday soon garnered commercial sponsorship well beyond Spokane—patronage that was diffuse and polycentric. In Chicago, for example, a businessman and Lions Club president, Harry C. Meek, was an active booster for the holiday in the 1910s and 1920s and for a time even asserted that he had originated the event (which may well have been a true enough claim for the Chicago area).[106] Tobacconists, florists, stationers, and men's clothiers were all involved in various local and national promotions by 1930, and each trade worked the standard channels of publicity. In 1921 the *Florists' Exchange* noted in familiar fashion that Father's Day presented "an excellent opportunity for additional business if rightly developed. . . . Now is the time for every retailer to start a little campaign for Father's Day." By 1925, the National Board of Tobacco Salesmen was sending out eighty-five thousand display cards to local retailers to announce the holiday's approach, and the number of Father's Day show cards for cigars and tobacco was in the hundreds of thousands a few years later. Similarly, *Men's Wear: The Retailer's Style and Merchandising Authority*, pushing a host of promotions, was regularly buoyed up by the new event, "a bang-up success." Amid these diffuse campaigns, the Associated Men's Wear Retailers of New York City took an increasing lead, hoping to give existing Father's Day advertising national direction and coordination.[107]

In the early- to mid-1930s the Associated Men's Wear Retailers were sponsoring the usual promotions: store cutouts, posters, placards, window-trimming contests, newspaper advertising, and radio publicity. The group had its own Father's Day Committee, which had come up with the forthright slogan, "Give Dad Something to Wear," and it was already working on getting the holiday "decreed" a state and national observance. At its heart, the group had sugarplum visions of turning the celebration into "a second Christmas," at least so far as "the sale of men's wear gifts" was concerned. (Once again, Christmas inspired ardor: The notion of somehow creating a second one lit up the imagination of retailers, whether at Easter or Father's Day. By the mid-1980s, the Father's Day Council was convinced that the group had achieved its dream: "Father's Day has transcended a day of celebration into a 'season' of three weeks, has become a 'Second Christmas' for all of the men's gift-oriented industries.") Always keeping the pulse on national promotions, the group esti-

Give Dad a Tie

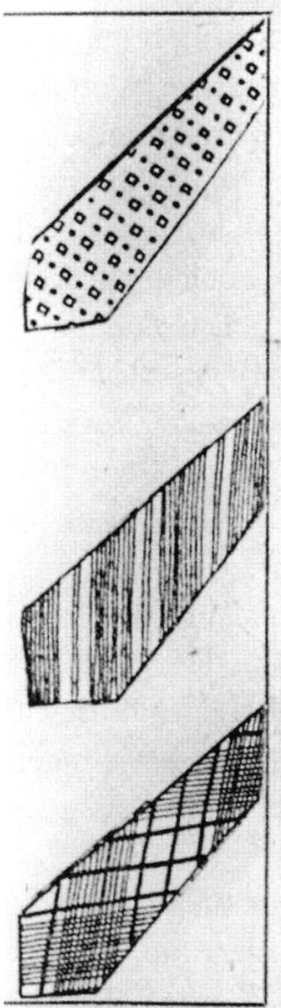

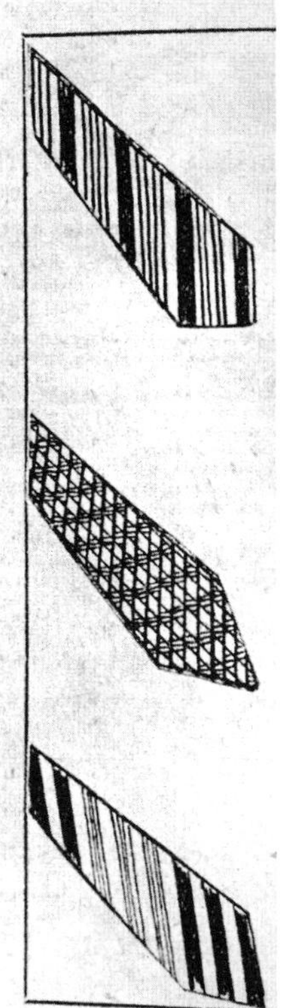

Next Sunday is Father's Day—instituted by a Spokane woman, and now nationally observed. It gives sons and daughters an opportunity to express their affection for their Dads with a remembrance—say, a tie—

A Large Variety at $1.50

Made from serviceable domestic silks in small, conservative figured designs and stripes, in almost every color.

Then we have hand tailored ties with a wool lining that will please Dad because they tie well, look well and wear well. Of course, there's a great variety of patterns and colors in these; the silks are imported—**$1.50 to $7.50.**

Other Things Dad Would Like

Fruit-of-the-Loom Shirts **$2 and $2.50**
Manhattan Shirts **$2.50 and up**
Golf Sweaters and Hose
Golf Clubs and Balls
Imported French Handkerchiefs

THE CRESCENT

RIVERSIDE & WALL STORE FOR MEN RIVERSIDE & WALL

100. "Give Dad a Tie," *Spokesman-Review*, 14 June 1929, 12.

mated in 1937 that more than a million dollars was spent for Father's Day advertising in magazines and newspapers. But the group also recognized that observance of the holiday was still "spotty"; according to one survey, only one in six fathers in 1937 had been duly honored "with socks, ties, suspenders, pipes, and other gifts." With Father's Day, as with other holidays, market surveys were increasingly used to monitor ritual observances, and this new surfeit of corporate statistics represented a quintessential rationalization and quantification of modern forms of gift giving.[108]

With clear recognition of the work yet to be done, the Associated Men's Wear Retailers expanded their Father's Day Committee in 1938 into a larger group with a bigger reach, the National Council for the Promotion of Father's Day. This reformulated Father's Day Council linked arms with a number of other trade groups, including the National Retail Dry Goods Association, the National Association of Retail Clothiers and Furnishers, and the National Association of Tobacco Distributors, in an attempt to manage the holiday as a "merchandising event" in a more systematic way. This was a council with powerful connections, a who's who of New York merchants, not a monopolizing culture industry, but certainly an aspirant, influential bunch. Among its members were advertising and publicity directors from Macy's, the May Company, Bloomingdale's, and Arnold, Constable, and Company; a New York advertising executive, Alvin Austin, was put in charge of the council, and William Weintraub, publisher of *Esquire*, was named its chair. The aim of the group was to boost sales through increasing the demand for gifts, and to do this it needed to get Father's Day accepted, as one council member said, as "a real day, . . . firmly established in the minds of every one." In other words, the group wanted to authenticate the celebration, to give it cultural legitimacy. It wanted to reverse the widespread perception of the holiday as mere commercial artifice or humbug, confessedly a problematic task for a council made up of merchants, advertisers, and public-relations executives.[109]

The Father's Day Council kept up the strategies of promotion put together over the previous decade by the Associated Men's Wear Retailers and regularly issued exuberant accounts of increasing sales. But in its quest to make Father's Day "real," the council knew that far more was required than advertising. (In this regard, Macy's offered special assistance in 1941 with a popular, widely covered "Father's Day Sports Parade," which constituted that department store's own peculiar brand of "genuine" celebration.) For its part, the council kept working on the political angle, and though federal recognition remained slow in coming, more and more governors obliged the group with family-extolling, father-lauding proclamations. Over the next decade the council also tried to refashion itself into a civic-minded group devoted to the holiday's "non-commercial, public-service phases." In 1949, the executive director, Alvin Austin, gamely announced that what was most important about Father's Day was its "sentimental and spiritual character." The group's slogan was appropriately retailored: "Remember Father, Molder of Our Children's Future—For a Safe World Tomorrow Teach Democracy Today." Ironically, in trying to move away from the ballyhoo of earlier promotions, the group seemed only to up the ante on humbug. "Give Dad Something to Wear" had at least been utterly transparent; now the council put a far more complex face on its motivations: sentiment, spirituality, democracy, freedom, community benefit, and family cohesion. Nonprofit public service notwithstanding, after the 1949 campaign the council delighted in the estimated $106 million in holiday sales volume. This proud emphasis on profits could not be laid aside because it remained crucial to legitimating the council to its various trade backers. As Austin explained in 1949, "Some think that like Christmas, Father's Day is here to stay and needs no organized effort. That is a fatal mistake. If the central bureau and organization promotion were discontinued, Father's Day would die a miserable death." From the 1940s on, the Father's Day Council thus positioned itself in this dual, tensile way: a public-minded champion of a "spontaneous" community event and a catalytic promoter of a highly orchestrated retailing campaign.[110]

For Dodd, there was nothing incongruous or contradictory about the dual mission of the Father's Day Council. Alvin Austin enlisted her in the council's work from the beginning, and she always sang its praises for carrying on her project and regularly gave it credit for the actual establishment of the holiday nationally. But Dodd's role remained far more than one of sidelines cheerleader; even from Spokane, she was an indispensable player for the council. Austin himself told and retold her story, and the group still includes her "grass-roots," "out-West" tale in its annual press releases, attempting to reproduce the holiday through representations of it as a populist, prairie-inspired phenomenon—an "authentic" homespun heritage far removed from Madison Avenue. Dodd herself continued to thrive on commercial promotion; in this, she was the very antithesis of Jarvis. Indeed, after the 1910s she talked little about the churches, the YMCA, or the YWCA; she saw her best, most enduring allies in the business community. They offered warm tributes and traveling money; as she said, the nation's merchants had always been "very kind to me." While she declined to become the spokesperson for any one line of Father's Day goods (the invitations were sundry), she happily endorsed the various "Gifts-for-Father" campaigns of the Father's Day Council. All along she simply loved gift giving and considered fathers richly deserving of this familial reciprocity (and her sentimental love for presents, resonant with deeper romantic views of the relational power of gifts, should be read as quite serious and sincere). When asked directly about the "commercialism" of Father's Day in 1972, six years before her death at the age of ninety-six, she responded, "Oh, I like it, I love it. I love seeing fathers get gifts. Besides all the cards, advertising and special promotions have done one major thing—focused attention on observance of the day." Even from a convalescent home three years later, she was hortatory: "Father's Day is best celebrated by showering the fathers with gifts on his special day." By then, the Father's Day Council estimated the holiday to be worth more than $1 billion in retail sales.[111]

Dodd and Father's Day had moved along a distinctly secular trajectory. "Hundreds of new ties, socks, pipes, cigars and golf clubs went into service yesterday," the *New York Times* noted in 1936. "It was Father's Day." The holiday presented an unblinking enshrinement of things, of gifts both sincere and playful, heartfelt and humorous; as a rite, it had come to be identified almost exclusively by this profusion of holiday presents and by the wonders of humbug. It was increasingly equated, too, with the indulgence of Dad, a Sunday holiday of "utmost freedom" for him. He could stay in bed, receive familial tributes, untroubled by the usual harassments, one of which was being nagged about church attendance. Put in the wishes of one Father's Day greeting card of the 1920s: "May you sleep as long as you want in the morning. May you have the newspaper when you want it and as long as you want it. . . . Here's hoping no one asks you to drive the car or go to church." In images of holiday consumption, paternal leisure, and domestic ease, the public celebrations of churches and community groups faded into the dim shadows. To the extent that Father's Day ever overcame the wags and cynics, it did so through the private, gift-centered observances of home and family and through evocative images of fatherly indulgence and consumption.[112]

After the advent of Mother's Day and Father's Day, commercial designs for the calendar grew only bolder. In 1916 the National Confectioners' Association came up with the bright idea of Candy Day, slated it for the second Saturday in October, and valiantly promoted it as a day to give little presents of sweets to one another. In 1919 Joyce C. Hall floated the idea of Friendship Day for the first Sunday in August, a date chosen as a slow period between other holidays, and the Greeting Card Association buoyed up the occasion with the usual raft of promotions. (In the peculiarly innovative logic of American business, the association claimed that the proposed fête warranted "widespread acceptance" because, "like all worthwhile special days," it was "unsupported by tradition.") In 1926 leaders within the doll industry launched the Better Play for Childhood League, which sought to commandeer the Sunday school occasion of Children's Day as a promotional event for toy retailers, an appropriation that Marshall Field's and other department stores had already

101. Friendship Day advertisement, *Greeting Card* 2 (August 1930): 2.

been experimenting with since the 1890s. Delaying the retailing version of Children's Day to the Saturday after the churches' celebration (in an increasingly crowded calendar, this made it the day before Father's Day), the doll industry provided a new slogan for the occasion: "Give Toys for Children's Day." In 1933 and again in 1939, the National Retail Dry Goods Association felt emboldened enough to try to move the celebration of Thanksgiving back a week in order to lengthen the Christmas shopping season. Franklin Roosevelt refused in 1933, but obliged in 1939, proclaiming the holiday for 23 November, instead of the last Thursday of the month, 30 November that year. Though the move proved highly controversial (some denounced it as a desecration), the retailers' association predicted an extra 10 percent in holiday sales and more than a billion-dollar stimulus for the nation's economy. "Franksgiving," as some political satirists dubbed it, was among the better indices of the ever-expanding claims of the market on American holiday celebrations.[113]

Thus did the invention of Mother's Day and Father's Day herald a steady stream of specially designated days, weeks, months, or even years. From Child Health Care Day to Professional Secretaries' Week, from National Pretzel Month to the Year of the Bible, the American calendar became a web of promotions. In a cultural jumble of publicity stunts, the new events often seemed to be self-mocking commentaries on the whole notion of national observances (what is it exactly that is *national* about National Hosiery Week?). Indeed, the very process of gaining congressional and presidential recognition for such commemorations has developed into a ludicrous governmental burden: 35 percent of all bills passed in the 99th Congress involved the creation of "a commemorative time period," and reformers have vainly tried to call a halt to such trivial activities. Perhaps the all-consuming rhythms of modern enterprise were best encapsulated in the retailing novelty of giveaway calendars, which had come into vogue at the turn of the century and on which businesses printed advertisements about their goods and services. The new calendars were praised as "a living advertisement 365 days in the year."[114] In the twentieth century, commercialization took in the whole calendar. Time was consumed.

EPILOGUE

April Fools? Trade, Trickery, and Modern Celebration

In 1898, the holiday chronicler William Walsh noted how American confectioners and owners of toy shops had taken to selling "April Fool candy" for All Fools' Day. Mostly "for juvenile use," the candy was "made of gun-cotton plentifully spiced with Cayenne pepper, coated with sugar, and appetizingly colored." For a day devoted to pranks and practical jokes, the deceptive confection seemed an appropriate commodity, just the thing with which to fool someone. In the eighteenth and nineteenth centuries, 1 April was notorious as a day of "hoax," "imposture," and "unreality," a little carnival of humbug and folly. "The great object is to catch some person off his guard," Robert Chambers explained in 1863, "to pass off upon him, as a simple fact, something barely possible, and which has no truth in it; to impose upon him, so as to induce him to go into positions of absurdity." "For successful April fooling," he added, "it is necessary to have some considerable degree of coolness and face; also some tact whereby to know in what direction the victim is most ready to be imposed upon by his own tendencies of belief." As an emblem for a commercial culture of Barnumesque hoaxes and ballyhoo, the holiday was ideal: Turned ever so slightly, Chambers's advice on April fooling could have served as counsel for peddlers, advertisers, and mountebanks. It is no wonder that Melville both set and published his grand masquerade, *The Confidence-Man* (1857), a tale of a guise-shifting swindler on a steamboat full of dupes and skeptics, on All Fools' Day.[1]

An occasion rife with artifice and subterfuge, April Fools' Day furnishes an appropriate trope for modern celebrations as tricks of trade. Over the course of the nineteenth and twentieth centuries, suspicion and disbelief increasingly shadowed modern rituals: What, critics asked, were "cunning" stationers and booksellers putting over on people with all those fancy billets-doux for St. Valentine's Day? What were Christmas and Easter but occasions for merchants to sell things, to entice the credulous and to enrich themselves? What were Mother's Day and Father's Day but the most blatant humbug, the respective fantasies of florists and menswear retailers? In a commercial culture, more and more people expressed a loss of confidence in holiday rituals; more and more critics indulged the snide cynicism that modern celebrations were ruses or pseudo-events, something trumped up to take people in, counterfeit spectacles. In the marketplace, ritual seemed to become as artificial as window dressing, something like a hoax or an imposture, something like All Fools' Day. As was the case with the sugar-coated, cayenne-laced candy of the confectioners, modern celebrations seemed a deception. "No trust" was the creed of the confidence man, and over the rituals of the modern mart lurked specters of suspicion and illusion, unreality and disbelief.[2] When celebrants feel that they have to be on guard against the artfulness of merchants, impetuosity and enchantment easily fade from the festivities. All too typical was the holiday dismissal of one undergraduate when asked by a writer for the alumni/alumnae magazine how she was going to celebrate St. Valentine's Day: "I think it's Hallmark's excuse to make money."[3] In the marketplace of guise and self-interest, rituals forfeit believability; they often seem about as trustworthy as patent medicines, about as real as Santa's beard. Engaging rituals on such terms becomes an exercise in irony, at best a tongue-in-cheek celebration of camp, at worst a sneer at triviality. What the *Weekly Florist* said of Memorial Day in 1925 seemed to be the case with many rites of modernity: "It is becoming another banal holiday with no real purpose behind it."[4] The journal's advice pointed more to the problem than to the solution: Revive the celebration through tactful advertising.

But who was being fooled by all this "face" and tact? Resistance to merchant-concocted, consumer-oriented holidays was considerable. Industry trade journals were littered with failed ideas for new feasts—abortive schemes that testified to the real limits of commercial stratagems. Florists envisioned, however briefly, making great floral events out of such occasions as All Saints' and All Souls' Days, Teachers' Day, St. George's Day, Baby Week, McKinley Day, and Poppy Day—all to little or no avail.[5] Likewise, Joyce Hall's notion of Friendship Day went over like a lead balloon; as one greeting-card manufacturer confessed, there was "little real enthusiasm for this new day," despite the usual holiday promotions. One retailer actually chided those among his colleagues who thought they could put over on the public any special occasion that they dreamed up or got wind of. His case in point was a proposal for a new international flower day, Hero's Day, to be held in connection with Armistice Day. The gullible among his associates, he rightly warned, were in for "a sad, sad awakening"; he said of himself, "I will not permit myself to be fooled into the belief that we can . . . put this over." There were a lot of confidence games in American culture, and merchants were always playing them on each other as much as on their customers. For occasions such as Hero's Day, Baby Week, or McKinley Day, most florists themselves seemed unconvinced, and "the great American public" could easily ignore or even scoff at such ill-conceived devices.[6]

That holiday consumers were nobody's fool was apparent in Candy Day, that 1910s brainchild of the National Confectioners' Association (NCA). Mobilizing the familiar forces—newspaper and magazine advertising, window displays, posters, and many other "special publicity stunts"—the NCA sought through Candy Day "to make the nation Candy-Conscious" or, put more directly, "to increase the daily consumption of candy." The trade was already well versed in the promotion of red-letter days (evident in the industry's success with St. Valentine's Day, Easter, and even April Fools' Day), and the NCA saw Candy Day as potentially an even better commercial proposition, since other industries would not be able to "step in and realize upon the holiday sales the confectioners had created." Candy Day, pretty much by definition, would be for the candy industry. But something went gravely wrong. The trade journal *Candy Factory* crystallized the problem in 1923 in an article entitled "Can Candy Day Be Put Over?": "What is the reaction of the public to a day merely to increase the sales of merchandise?" it asked. "Are they enthusiastic over a holiday that has for its avowed purpose the sale of candy? The answer, we are inclined to think, is that they are not." Even efforts in Candy Day advertising to evoke the "finer sentiments" and "tender feelings" of familial love and to suggest the need to show that love "in a material way" by buying boxes of candy as gifts seemed to miss the mark. Candy Day appeared "a bit too commercial a proposition to go over in many territories." One trade writer located the nub of the problem: So many of these occasions were being promoted by different industries that such observances were "becoming more or less of a joke." (It was this same view of ritual as "joke" and "bunk" that had long eaten away at Father's Day.) Trade expectations for Candy Day foundered on the reality of consumer indifference and even ridicule. Few Americans charged off on the fool's errand that the confectioners had devised.[7]

Yet the NCA was hardly disabused of its own humbug. Attempting to soften the event's commercial edge by renaming it Sweetest Day, the trade redoubled the holiday's promotion. (It is still an industry event.) If falling well short of industry dreams to accomplish for confectionery what the florists had achieved with Mother's Day, Candy Day was not an out-and-out failure either. It provided a new advertising theme, attracted some notice, and reportedly increased sales in several cities—"this in the face of the fact," one trade journal marveled, "that there was no particular reason for Candy Day other than that those who were in the candy business wanted to sell more candy." (The amused, hoaxing tone was unmistakable.) Far from being disillusioned by holiday promotions, the industry continued to expand them. If Sweetest Day had not fulfilled expectations, other holidays—such as Mother's Day, Halloween, and Thanksgiving—remained terribly promising. Christmas and Easter demonstrated these possibilities: What had been done with them "can be done with other Holidays." Candy Day only underlined the industry's taken-for-granted conviction that celebrations were indispensable for trade. It also suggested, though, that most folks saw through such commercial trickery and even had fun making light of its clumsy overtness. (There was, after all, little tact or "face" in these promotions.) Perhaps, most of all, events like Sweetest Day pointed to (and furthered) the widening perception of modern holidays as weightless commercial shams.[8]

Resistance to the commercial rhythms and rites of modernity was evident as well in the dashed hopes of various businesspeople and industrialists who wanted to stabilize the date of Easter. This movable feast, which could fall on any date between 22 March and 25 April, flew in the face of the full rationalization of time and the calendar; the "absolute regularity" of time, epitomized in the adoption of Standard Time and in the clockwork discipline of factories, was a cornerstone of modern industry and commerce. As George Eastman, who was absorbed with issues of calendrical reform and whose Kodak cameras left their own distinct imprint on American holidays, explained in 1927, "the 'wandering' Easter" caused difficulties for various "commercial lines of business," in particular the apparel and tourist industries. Early Easters, especially when spring weather had yet to take hold, "often cut down the volume of Easter retail trading" as well as the amount of holiday travel. For managers, advertisers, planners, and economic analysts, the wobbling Easter was an irritant; the feast's movement introduced an annoying, needless variable into the tracking of market data and skewed seasonal, month-to-month comparisons. Eastman's solution, endorsed by various merchants and industrialists (and some church leaders), was to fix Easter in mid-April. Despite commercial inconvenience and entrepreneurial concern, Easter continued to meander on a course set for it in the fourth century.[9]

The "wandering" Easter is an emblem: Religious rhythms have often proved perdurable in their unfolding encounter with commercial constructions of time. The saints' days of modern America are hardly confined to holiday sales for St. Valentine's Day or Washington's Birthday, but flourish in local shrines for Catholic saints or in Afro-Baptist services in honor of Martin Luther King, Jr. The preparatory seasons of Advent and Lent have never been wholly absorbed into Thanksgiving Day parades or pre-Easter specials. Nor has Epiphany, the feast of the Three Kings, been lost amid after-Christmas clearances; thriving community celebrations from New York City to Miami to Santa Fe bespeak the persistence of street festivities alongside the sales events of malls. The church's time, as seen in its great feasts of Christmas and Easter, has proven a crucial auxiliary of merchant's time in American culture, but the former did not simply sanctify the latter; the two versions of time have also continued to move in competing as much as complementary directions. Faith in timeworn rituals has often balanced the cagey suspicions and distrust people feel for merchandising devices. Still, as Melville well knew, the skepticism that commercial artifice invites is not easily contained: It readily slides into the metaphysical.

The persistence of distinctive religious rhythms suggests the larger tension in modern American holidays between the sacred and the secular. It would be easy to see this story—the marketplace's colonization of ritual—as a tale of woeful secularization: St. Valentine changing from the church's miracle worker into the stationer's matchmaker; New Year's resolutions moving from the pious to the self-actualizing; Christmas shifting from a time of topsy-turvy commotion and Christian remonstrance to an occasion of rationalized commercial magic; Easter turning into a millinery show and a stronghold of kitsch; Mother's Day and Father's Day progressing from Protestant-inspired liturgical events into major retailing campaigns. But those sorts of secular trajectories, while real, disguise an equally important story—that the sacred and the secular have been ceaselessly combined and recombined, that these categories have regularly dissolved in lived experience. The holidays have resided in the borderlands, in the commingling of religion and marketplace, in the hybridity of faith, family, shopping, and presents: for example, the easy flow between Christmas gifts and the divine gift, Santa Claus masks and Sunday school pageants, floral displays and the Resurrection, or show-window crosses and affirmations of faith. In this story the sacred and secular have often reversed themselves, the marketplace becoming a realm of religious enchantment and the churches a site of material abundance and promotional gimmicks. What one sees finally in these modern holiday rituals is this: how secular much of the sacred is and how sacred much of the secular is.

The confused intermingling of sacred and secular points to another area of contestation, that of localism versus nationalization. The modern market represented a kind of ritual imperialism, extending the same sorts of goods and ceremonies from one place to another, nationalizing the emblems of holiday observance from greeting cards to Santa's department-store throne, from chocolate Easter bunnies to Christmas tree lights. The consumer culture—more than folk tradition, local custom, or religious community—increasingly provided the common forms and materials for American celebrations. Commerce even had a globalizing impact on ritual as American holidays were exported—Christmas shopping in Korea, Mother's Day flowers in Germany, Santa Claus in England. As has been the case for cars, soft drinks, fast food, and theme parks, a world market has emerged over the twentieth century for the commodities of American celebration. No corporation better epitomizes this multinational trend than Hallmark. A truly "international business empire," the company now reaches "consumers in over one hundred countries around the world."[10]

Japan offers a prime example of this internationalization of American-brand, consumerist versions of celebration: Christmas, Halloween, St. Valentine's Day, and even St. Patrick's Day all have distinct commercial renderings. As one Tokyo merchant explained, "In Japan, these events have no religious meaning at all. We just take the form and use it to sell." In a fine piece of humbug, Kentucky Fried Chicken of Japan has run campaigns promoting takeout buckets of chicken as the traditional food for the Christmas holidays, actually quintupling sales for the period from 23 to 25 December. For the Japanese version of St. Valentine's Day, in which women give gifts to men, chocolate sales were worth $495 million in 1992. But international markets have hardly created a mass holiday culture, homogeneous and undifferentiated. The Japanese versions of consumerist celebrations represent original contrivance as much as standardization. White Day on 14 March, balancing the gifts of St. Valentine's Day with presents from men to women, is itself a homegrown retailing holiday. Similarly, Halloween has been sponsored by the Japan Biscuit Association as a day for eating biscuits, promoting ceremonies that are improvisations on American rituals, not imitations, though the whole idea has fallen about as flat in Japan as Candy Day did in the United States. With holidays and the consumer culture, there is a tensile story to tell of persistent variegation and ceaseless commercial replication, popular obstinacy and market expansion. As James Clifford has written in another context, "Modern ethnographic histories are perhaps condemned to oscillate between two metanarratives: one of homogenization, the other of emergence; one of loss, the other of invention. In most specific conjunctures both narratives are relevant, each undermining the other's claim to tell 'the whole story,' each denying to the other a privileged, Hegelian vision." As the critic Stephen Greenblatt found in his encounter with a videocassette recorder in Bali, the export of American commodities and rituals simultaneously diminishes the autonomy of local cultures and generates new forms of hybridity, syncretism, and difference.[11]

Another consistent point of tension in modern holiday observance has centered on issues of gender. In the nineteenth and early twentieth centuries, middle-class women were drawn into an alliance with the consumer culture in the creation of refined, home-centered, shopping-laden holiday rituals. This feminization of festivity provided a temperate alternative to the carnivalesque world of rough music and the largely male repertory of parades, mumming, noisemaking, carousing, and street violence. It also meant that the new holiday rituals—centering on home, family, food, stores, gifts, and cards—were the peculiar obligation of women to orchestrate. This nineteenth-century configuration of holiday observance has come under increasing strain in the late twentieth century as more and more middle-class women have entered the work force and have found the familial, relational demands of the "traditional" forms harder to sustain. As trend-watchers in the greeting-card industry are well aware, the new forms of women's work hold the potential to transform old forms of women's work, including gift-giving customs, all the way down to such traditions as Christmas cards or Mother's Day cards. It is conceivable that these contemporary shifts may ultimately lessen the commercialization of the holidays—the less time for shopping and gift giving, the smaller the claims of the marketplace. But it also holds the potential for further market penetration of family celebrations in the form of caterers and decorators in which holiday meals and embellishments themselves become "subcontracted."[12] These shifting time pressures for women have also been a boon for mail-order houses; even as the original wish book, the Sears Roebuck catalogue, has passed from the scene, others arise to take its place and aim to "simplify" holiday shopping.

Among the most important arenas of tension regarding consumer-oriented celebrations has been the realm of conservation and ecology. From Arbor Day to Earth Day, rituals have been dreamed up to counter the pursuit of novelty and the headlong depletion of resources that have so often characterized the modern culture of consumption. First celebrated in Nebraska in April 1872, Arbor Day led the way as an experiment in conservationist ritual, staged in response to mounting anxieties about rapid deforestation. Embraced by the National Education Association in 1884, the holiday found its institutional abode in the public schools and in the innumerable tree-planting ceremonies of schoolchildren. In some cases, though, grander civic celebrations emerged: In Cincinnati in 1882, fifty thousand people came out for a huge Arbor Day procession, and whole groves of saplings were planted in one fell swoop.[13] As in the wider conservation movement, much about Arbor Day was utilitarian in aim—making certain that there would always be enough trees to satisfy fuel, building, and industry needs from one generation to another. But the event was also informed by emergent preservationist ideals, ones that saw in the new festival of tree planting a ritualized reversal of "our wicked wastefulness and contempt" toward nature. By 1888 the holiday was officially observed in thirty states and territories, and by the turn of the century, it had become something of a national event. Soon added to Arbor Day were other preservationist events, including Bird Days, given encouragement as public-school events by the Audubon Societies from the 1890s into the 1910s. For the National Association of Audubon Societies the real nemesis was the millinery industry (by 1900, two hundred million birds were being killed annually to supply plumage for the trade), and Bird Days were one little way of questioning the feathery parade of American millinery fashions. Turn-of-the-century bird protectionists sought to convince Americans that consumer choices (here the widespread use of feather ornaments) carried serious ecological consequences in an "age of extermination."[14]

Ecological ritual came into its own with the first Earth Day on 22 April 1970. The substance of this festival of the earth was hortatory (teach-ins and speeches); the carnivalesque masking and costumes were macabre (gas and face masks); the rituals of revulsion were sardonic (burying or bashing gas-guzzling cars and "dump-ins" at city halls). Borrowing wider strategies of social protest and demonstration for the environmental movement, the new holiday echoed, enlarged, and in some sense displaced Arbor Day (22 April had been the day set for Arbor Day in Nebraska). Earth Day gave new energy and exposure to that great new ritual of environmentalism—recycling. It gave new scope as well to rituals of anticonsumption (for example, the spurning of plastics and nonreturnable bottles), rituals that could be endlessly extended and replicated (the rejection of aerosol cans, certain detergents, styrofoam cups, disposable diapers, and so forth). With its annual reenactment and with especially large celebrations on the tenth anniversary in 1980 and the twentieth in 1990, Earth Day has come to stand as a ritualized embodiment of the environmental movement and its resistance to consumerism. That Earth Day has its own cards and T-shirts and even its own fast-food advertising almost goes without saying (even Arbor Day was picked up by some turn-of-the-century department stores—free seedlings to go with the sale prices). Ritualized protests against consumption and commercialism have regularly been caught in the very web of what they decry. The dominant discourse of consumption has all along displayed a striking capacity to absorb the counterdiscourses of anticonsumerism, simplicity, and preservation.[15]

The African American festival Kwanzaa is increasingly exhibiting this same predicament of resistance and co-optation. A week-long celebration stretching from the day after Christmas to New Year's, Kwanzaa is relatively new, having been invented in 1966 by the sociologist Maulana Karenga in a gesture of constructive anthropology, or what might be called applied Durkheim. Founded as a countercultural celebration of racial solidarity and self-determination, the festival was intended, the young Al Sharpton explained to a group of Harlem schoolchildren in 1971, as a "way of de-whitizing" the festivities of winter. To Karenga himself, Kwanzaa was set up in direct opposition to "the high-priced hustle and bustle of Christmas buying and selling"; it was an explicit alternative to the "European cultural accretions of Santa Claus, reindeer, mistletoe, frantic shopping, [and] alienated gift-giving." Yet as observance of the festival has spread more widely in the African American community, it has taken on increasingly consumerist forms. At a Kwanzaa Holiday Expo at the Jacob Javits Convention Center in New York City in 1993, three hundred exhibitors were on hand with everything from "Kwanzaa cards and wrapping paper" to "teddy bears in African garb." Such corporate giants as Anheuser-Busch, Hallmark, J. C. Penney, and Pepsi-Cola sent representatives. Hearing of the trade extravaganza, Karenga remarked, in angry tones that Anna Jarvis would have appreciated: "This is a capitalistic society where they rent wombs and sell bodies. One can expect they will try to commodicize. The challenge of the African people is to avoid the problems of commercialization that they've learned from other holidays like Christmas." African American entrepreneurs at the trade show were more sanguine: "Black people need not be embarrassed about making money," one woman noted. "That is what pays the rent and that is what makes America tick." The issues in the debate are old, but with Kwanzaa, as with Christmas, they are proving no less contested for that grizzled familiarity.[16]

Certainly many have felt about commercial ingenuity much as this African American businessperson does: It is what makes America tick, and the holidays are none the worse for this entrepreneurial merchandising. As the *American Florist* argued in sweeping terms in 1914, "The American people are a money-making people, and it does not detract from the sacredness of an occasion for them to make money out of it. It takes none of the sacredness away from Christmas because department stores and florist stores and other business places gain money thereby. It does not lessen the sanctity of the Resurrection for the florist to make money from the flowers he disposes of at Easter." The author was willing to go still further: The holidays were actually enhanced through commercial aggrandizement, through the rich and varied goods of the marketplace. American celebrations were, indeed, "made possible only through the fact that money is made from them." Sponsorship by merchants was crucial to the very enactment of modern rites, and most Americans, this trade writer testified, were quite content with commercial versions of festival. After all, money-making people knew what the marketplace was like, knew what it was like to scramble for "all the many good things that money can buy"—homes, cars, college educations.[17]

As self-consoling (and self-serving) as such trade defenses might be, they contain an important grain of truth. Resisting the machinations of merchants was not particularly important to most people most of the time. Whatever humbug, exploitation, or imposture resided in modern celebrations (and there was plenty), alienation was only one leitmotif in a larger chorus of affirmation. People found play, fun, trickery, romance, and charivari in the little exchanges of valentine greetings; they found joy in the "social carnival" of New Year's visits and gifts; they looked to the fanfare of the Christmas marketplace for excitement, color, possibility, and sometimes even faith; they wore bright Easter costumes and sometimes constructed outlandish Easter bonnets in a parade that combined something of the mummer's imagination with more-pedestrian fashions.[18] With Children's Day and Mother's Day, sentiments were no less serious for being maudlin, and, even with Father's Day, gifts were certainly as much sincere gestures of reciprocity and affection as tokens of droll cynicism (and even presents of the latter sort invited clever gags, not simply snide skepticism about the humbug of merchants and the sentimental failings of fathers).

Confidence in modern ritual turns in unlikely ways: "A Mall Halloween: Trick-or-Treating for a Distrustful Time" read a recent *New York Times* headline. Parents head to shopping centers with masked children to celebrate where they can trust the treats of merchants to be what they seem. Likewise, adult revelers are encouraged to turn to Hallmark's Boo Bazaar for costumes and accessories, for "fun and fantasy in their Halloween look." Accessorizing the American Halloween, with "ghoul jewels" such as dangling-bat earrings or with "wacky caps" and vinyl masks, is now a $400 million enterprise—a flowering of holiday novelty lines that were first cultivated at the turn of the century. (As the celebration has grown into a major seasonal festival, the holiday has even gained its own industry publication, fittingly entitled *Selling Halloween*.) "Celebrants are enjoying more freedom and individuality in creating a particular Halloween look," one marketing strategist recently averred. "They want to be different with a look that is entirely their own."[19] It sounds like the old promises of a valentine writer: the unleashing of individuality and imagination through the luxuriant, festive choices of the marketplace. Again, though, it is an assurance fraught with contradiction, if not poignancy; it seems barely believable, this confident pledge, this bourgeois hope, that Mall-oween can provide both sanctuary and freedom, both safety and fantasy, both predictability and possibility, both transparency and masquerade, both control and carnival. Perhaps the contemporary Halloween, as it migrates off the streets and into the malls, is a symbol of the very paradoxes at the heart of modern American celebrations—carnivalesque trickery turned into a commodity, another capitalist containment of the license of popular ritual, another transformation of folk ceremony into camp parody. But, as with the candy of All Fools' Day, farce, play, and ingenuity remain.

ACKNOWLEDGMENTS

Forgive me my denomination and my town.

John Updike, A Month of Sundays (1975)

The usual acknowledgments—of good friends and generous foundations—follow below. But some other forms of acknowledgment also seem warranted. Acknowledgment implies, after all, not only appreciation, but also admission. The ingenuous avowal of historical detachment—the empiricist's pretense "to be objective, to be no one in particular," in poet Vicki Hearne's fine phrase—is a costly pose. Historians, like ethnographers, are learning to be more forthright about their own positionings. My hope in these (dis)closing pages is to be self-referential without being self-absorbed, reflexive without being solipsistic.[1]

Let me admit, then, that the bourgeois holidays that I have described are my holidays; they are the ones I grew up with: Christmas stockings and crèches, valentines at school, Easter baskets filled with candy and recycled kitsch (the egg-shaped containers of L'eggs hosiery turned into silvery holiday packages), unpleasant encounters with department-store Santa Clauses, Easter lilies and sunrise services, Halloween costumes and masks from Woolworth's, Mother's Day cards not only for Mom, but also for grandmothers and great-grandmothers. (Of the last, my mother has reminded me with occasional installments of holiday cards found preserved among my grandmothers' belongings. It is telling from the standpoint of highbrow—and male—disaffection that I cannot remember the last time I bothered with such tokens.) And while I am at it, let me confess, too, that I am a liberal Protestant born of a largely Methodist background. These middle-class Protestant circumstances have inevitably shaped the very things I have found interesting to pursue and accentuate. My own holiday memories of home, church, and marketplace have stalked my research: They have flitted through my mind like the quavering frames of the silent home movies through which I can still replay one celebration or another—birthday parties, Christmas mornings, or even a whole montage of Pet-and-Bike Parades (a quintessential suburban procession if there ever was one).

Perhaps some will think that those bourgeois environs explain why I have a less than critical voice about these modern forms of celebration, why I am not so suspicious of the cultural producers nor so snide about the ardent consumers as I should be (so judged from suitably Marxist, Veblenian, or Adornoesque perspectives). After all, one of my grandfathers was a traveling salesman in Nebraska (and later in southern California), peddling tires from one place to another with considerable adeptness and verve: how critical was I likely to be of the go-getters and self-promoters I have studied? Indeed, Joyce Hall and my grandfather probably traveled the same routes fifty miles west of Omaha. Perhaps others, however, will think that my liberal Protestant identification explains why themes of alienation, resistance, and jeremiad loom so large (or, conversely, why they do not loom large enough—one more liberal captive of modern culture). Strike the *perhapses*. But there are interpretive gains as well as limitations in my affinities with this middle-class Protestant world, and these gains are in the realm of understanding and forbearance.

Included in one of the Christmas cards that one of my grandmothers sent me over the years was a little story about her favorite Christmas growing up on the outskirts of Dallas, South Dakota, in the 1910s. Her parents took her and her brothers to town for one "last peek at the toys" in the store windows. She had already wished for "a small iron stove and a doll," but on seeing a "fascinating mesh Christmas stocking" filled with "tiny gifts," each individually wrapped and each constituting a "miniature wonder," her desires instantly changed. Somehow that "beautiful stuffed stocking" appeared the next morning under the tree, and my grandmother "spent hours opening and examining each and every item it contained." (Her imagination seemed far better served by the fantastic mysteries of that stocking than by the rather restrained domestic hope for a stove and a doll.) My grandmother's final line: "Santa had heard my prayer." Here again, close to home, is that distinctive mix of religion, celebration, and consumption that runs through so much of what I have studied. It may not make for classical theology, but it is a prominent piety in American life, a dreaming of fulfillment, a prayer of possibility. My gentleness with these American renderings of faith and festival, my appreciation for the wonders of holiday gifts and for the marvels of the marketplace, take rise from such little "miracles" or "graces" of popular experience—in my grandmother's story and in my own memories. Such stories need to be contextualized and historicized, but I cannot tell them with contempt. I have viewed them with an eye for the humble magic of things, for the miniature wonders of modern ritual, for the tiny freedoms of fancy in a marketplace of enchantment and humbug.

A second familial example underlines the value of this interpretive stance. Aunt Ida wrote to my great-grandmother Minnie about another Christmas in South Dakota, this one in 1947. It is a letter of grotesque detail—how cousin Clarence lost his arm in a gory accident—but it is also a letter about "our big day Christmas whitch is so famous throughout the Nation." "I got *your* Card—

with 50 other Cards—and many thanks, *it* was sure a pretty one," she informed her sister. "I got quite a few presents," and there followed a sprawling list of gifts that displayed a web of both kinship and friendship. "Blanch & Geo[rge] sent me a big towel and wash cloth with hand crochet around the edges, & Jessie & Geo[rge] sent a towel. Gladys a box of toilet soap. Loretta a box of stationary & one of those Ball point pens." And on went her enumeration of gifts and relations for a page and a half, the things inseparably joined to the people who gave them, little objects that might serve in day-to-day life as sparks of memory of amiability and connection. Then Aunt Ida switched to describing the feasting, a salmagundi of festive fare, enjoyed by a large gathering of family and friends—"children and grand children and great grand children." "We sure had lots of good things for dinner. We had 9 chickens and two of them weren't even carved. . . . [W]e had Mince, Apple, & Pumpkin pie, three cakes, Pea Salid, potato Salid, Vegetable salid prepared with Jelo & two fruit salids, two fruit dishes of Cran Berries, Corn & sweet potatoes baked & sugared real fancy." And that account, too, went on for a page and half, moving right on down to the "Coffee & Baked Beans" and "oh yes, tooth picks and Candy & Nuts." Again, there is more of Rabelais's banquet for all the world, more utopian abundance, preserved in modern forms of celebration than is usually acknowledged. As the Russian literary critic Mikhail Bakhtin surmised, such plenitude had increasingly been turned inward toward the family, but saying that as a kind of withering reproof of bourgeois ritual is hardly enough.[2] For Aunt Ida at the holidays, life itself seemed to be "sugared real fancy," and that sweetness needs to be savored.

It is to the voices of common folks like Aunt Ida that interpreters of the consumer culture, holidays, domesticity, religion, and ritual need to attend. I have tried to listen to these voices, from Mary Root to William Mactier to Clara Pardee, to attend to the quotidian and the ordinary without assuming an interpretive model of decline, control, banality, or manipulation. I pursued in my first book, *Holy Fairs*, one version of this paradigm—the bourgeois reform of popular religion, which indeed helps make sense of the early modern world and the diminution of certain types of festivity. But, as a form of narrative closure, it all too easily mires middle-class folks and their rites in a one-dimensional netherworld. Repressed, neurasthenic, and even hysterical, the bourgeois are left holding the dim candles of the carnivalesque, terrified by a shadow circus of released inhibitions and enclosed in a cluttered interior of kitsch with a host of tepid domestic rituals to perform.[3] I have tried to accord the same respect to these feminized, commodified, middle-class forms of piety and celebration as is so readily accorded the topsy-turvy world of carnival. In this regard, the relevant interpretive traditions for engagement come from experience-near forms of ethnographic analysis or from the domain of cultural studies with its crumbling hierarchies and its pursuit of the popular and the everyday, not from the elite aestheticism that runs through so much cultural criticism from Thorstein Veblen to the Frankfurt School to Ann Douglas. Modern holidays, in their very commodification, remain Jello-thick with meaning. Like Janice Radway in her efforts to take romance novels and their readers seriously, interpreters need to puzzle out the popularity of greeting-card sentimentalists like Edgar A. Guest. That Joyce Hall made a good deal of money with Guest's verses is one thing; that my great-grandmother Minnie bothered to save a small cache of "My Favorite Poems" and that Guest's tear-jerking lines on "Crops and a Child" and "Going Home for Christmas" were among them is something else again.[4]

This social location within a middle-class Protestant world has hardly led me to a monologic narrative of praise and celebration. I dare say there is still plenty of alienation and contestation to go around, arising out of cultural negotiations internal to bourgeois, Protestant mentalities as well as out of countless cultural alternatives that have recurrently challenged those ways of seeing and acting. Critical distance persists, inherent in the suspicions and complexities entailed in the wide-ranging cultural debates over modern forms of celebration and commerce. The power of the market, the politics of capitalist innovation, and the dialectics of cultural production and consumption abide. So, too, do the pangs of religious estrangement—the abrasions of spirit that the trivialization of faith entails, the varied disenchantments that a modern commercial culture generates. "For this your mother sweated in the cold," Edna St. Vincent Millay wrote in "To Jesus on His Birthday," "For this you bled upon the bitter tree: / A yard of tinsel ribbon bought and sold; / A paper wreath; a day at home for me."[5] Edna St. Vincent Millay, *Collected Sonnets* (New York: Harper and Row, 1988), 68. Cognizant of my own ambivalences, I have dealt with these tensions not by erasure or effacement, not by some interpretive sleight of hand that pretends to have cleared everything up. I have tried instead to preserve ambivalence and multivocality, to construct a complex and open-ended narrative of shifting perspectives that invites others to join in and redirect the story. There is no closure or finality in such a narrative, only circling dialogue, a playful conversation that Aunt Ida and my great-grandmother, who always wanted me to be a preacher, would have appreciated. Actually the word they preferred was not conversation, but *visiting*, a good expression, rich with a sense of place, of lived experience, of talking and eating and laughing, of shared lives, of leisurely yet ephemeral connections.

Looking back over these acknowledgments, I am struck by how quickly I stopped talking about myself and started writing about female relatives—grandmothers and great aunts, now dead—how readily I sought refuge in documents, how fond I remain of historical distance, how problematic scholarly self-disclosure is. I am also struck by how quickly I turned back to the abstract processes of interpretation and away from the practical possibilities of celebration. But, as Nietzsche asked, "What good is all the art of our works of art, if we lose that higher art, the art of festivals?" It is a vital question to keep posing, here on the edges of postmodernity, especially as academic folks look rather wanly to playful prose, to carnivalized texts, for the conviviality of festival and the commensalism of celebration. As the masks, fantasies, and subversions of carnival are turned into wordplay, it is all the more important to consider more deeply the festive repertories of home, community, religion, street, and marketplace, to continue the romantic—even quixotic—enterprise of redeeming holiday liturgies amid and against (and now beyond) modernity.[6]

That nineteenth-century man of letters Robert Chambers, who spent many of his days and years collecting curiosities about popular calendrical customs, feared as death approached that it had been all the work on his two compendious volumes on the holidays that had killed him. For helping me to escape such an unfortunate demise in my own seemingly interminable tracking of the holidays, I give credit to all those who have offered their support, assistance, insight, and commentary along the way.

The Theological and Graduate Schools at Drew University are a most agreeable place for scholarly pursuits, for writing and teaching. I have experienced four different Theological School deans in my first six years at Drew, but each one—Thomas Ogletree, James Ault, Robin Lovin, and Janet Fishburn—mustered institutional support for my research and writing. I have also received considerable encouragement from Drew colleagues and students for which I am appreciative. I am indebted, in particular, to graduate students Daryl Elliott, Kristina Lacelle-Peterson, Pamela Klassen, and Paula Much for their research assistance. Pamela, in particular, took time away from her own work on the Mennonites to help me with mine on merchants.

In addition to support from Drew, I have received indispensable backing from the National Endowment for the Humanities in the form of a Fellowship for University Teachers. The Center of Theological Inquiry in Princeton, New Jersey, provided me with a most hospitable place for scholarly residence during my leave in 1991–92. Thanks are owed the Louisville Institute for the Study of American Protestantism for providing a stipend for summer research in 1993. The book was finished at the Shelby Cullom Davis Center for Historical Studies at Princeton University in the fall of 1994. Such support has been invaluable. Similarly indispensable has been the commentary of various scholars on different incarnations of this research, whether as conference papers, journal articles, or actual chapters: my thanks to Virginia Burrus, Jon Butler, Matthew Dennis, Richard Wightman Fox, Edwin Gaustad, R. Marie Griffith, Catherine Hutchins, Jackson Lears, Edward Linenthal, Roland Marchand, Alexis McCrossen, Colleen McDannell, and David Thelen. A number of archivists and curators went out of their way to help me, particularly John Fleckner and Ann Kuebler at the Smithsonian, Kimberly Rich and Sharman Robertson at the Hallmark Historical Collection, Georgia Barnhill at the American Antiquarian Society, and Maja Keech at the Library of Congress. Private collections of books, objects, and ephemera are often an untapped resource for historians, and I thank two collectors in particular—Betsy Beinecke Shirley and Jack Golden—for allowing me to use their materials. The generous counsel and good humor of Ann Wald and Sara Mullen at Princeton University Press have made the process of bringing this book into print doubly rewarding.

I have had the luxury of thinking through the issues of this project in various publications over the last several years, and I am grateful for permission to reprint these essays in revised and expanded form in this book. These works include: "The Easter Parade: Piety, Fashion, and Display," *Religion and American Culture* 4 (Summer 1994): 135–64; "Time, Celebration, and the Christian Year in Eighteenth-Century Evangelicalism," in *Evangelicalism: Comparative Studies in Popular Protestantism in North America, the British Isles, and Beyond, 1700–1990*, ed. Mark A. Noll, David W. Bebbington, and George A. Rawlyk (New York: Oxford University Press, 1994), 90–109; "The Fashioning of a Modern Holiday, St. Valentine's Day, 1840–1870," *Winterthur Portfolio: A Journal of American Material Culture* 28 (Winter 1993): 209–45; "Christianity in the Marketplace: Christmas and the Consumer Culture," *Cross Currents* 42 (Fall 1992): 342–56; and "The Commercialization of the Calendar: American Holidays and the Culture of Consumption, 1870–1930," *Journal of American History* 78 (December 1991): 887–916.

I owe a special debt of gratitude to John Merrill—friend, scholar, photographer, horticulturist, and at one time the shadowy butler for the Master of Forbes College—for a lengthy discussion during a leisurely walk that helped me decide to write this book and not another that I had been contemplating. Also, as before, Edwin Gaustad, Albert Raboteau, and John Wilson have offered unflagging support along the way.

As at holidays, so at other times, my parents have always been there for me, and this book is small reciprocation, another of those incommensurate academic gifts.

NOTES TO INTRODUCTION

1. Jacques Le Goff, *Time, Work, and Culture in the Middle Ages*, trans. Arthur Goldhammer (Chicago: University of Chicago Press, 1980), 29–42; Thorstein Veblen, *The Theory of the Leisure Class: An Economic Study of Institutions* (New York: Random House, 1934), 119.

2. Daniel J. Boorstin, *The Americans: The Democratic Experience* (New York: Random House, 1973), 157–64. For statistics on the Christmas market, see William Severini Kowinski, *The Malling of America: An Inside Look at the Great Consumer Paradise* (New York: William Morrow, 1985), 78; Steve Weiner, "Marshall Field Does Christmas in a Big Way with a Big Eye on Profits," *Wall Street Journal*, 29 November 1984, 1; and Blayne Cutler, "Here Comes Santa Claus (Again)," *American Demographics* 11 (December 1989): 32. For the notion of a "temporal map," see Eviatar Zerubavel, *The Seven Day Circle: The History and Meaning of the Week* (Chicago: University of Chicago Press, 1985), 2.

3. These observations are borne out by the perusal of the holiday advertisements in any metropolitan newspaper. For these specific examples and citations, see *Newark Star-Ledger*, 13 February 1990, 3; ibid., 2 July 1991, 12; *New York Times*, 9 June 1991, sect. OH, 3; and ibid., 13 June 1991, A7. The "Mall-oween" example is from a WCBS news report for 29 October 1991; on this transformation, see also the epilogue.

4. For the cartoon, see *New York Times*, 2 June 1991, sect. 4, 4. On the now somewhat outmoded notions of "fakelore" and "folklure," see Tom E. Sullenberger, "Ajax Meets the Jolly Green Giant: Some Observations on the Use of Folklore and Myth in American Mass Marketing," *Journal of American Folklore* 87 (1974): 53–65, and Richard M. Dorson, *American Folklore and the Historian* (Chicago: University of Chicago Press, 1971), 3–14. For taking the productions or creations of "mass culture" seriously as composite forms of folklore and popular culture, see Lawrence W. Levine, "The Folklore of Industrial Society: Popular Culture and Its Audiences," *American Historical Review* 97 (1992): 1369–99. For an example of such a Halloween parade, see Garrison Keillor, "Halloween Capital of the World," *New York Times*, 31 October 1991, A27.

5. "Celebrate Christmas, Not Commercialism," November 1992, Campaign to Take Commercialism out of Christmas, Center for the Study of Commercialism, Washington, D.C. (copy in author's possession).

6. Josef Pieper, *In Tune with the World: A Theory of Festivity*, trans. Richard Winston and Clara Winston (New York: Harcourt, Brace, and World, 1963), 45; Jo Robinson and Jean Coppock Staeheli, *Unplug the Christmas Machine: A Complete Guide to Putting Love and Joy Back into the Season* (New York: William Morrow, 1991), 15. See also Robert Lee, *Religion and Leisure in America* (New York: Abingdon, 1964), and Richard A. Horsley, *The Liberation of Christmas: The Infancy Narratives in Social Context* (New York: Crossroad, 1989).

7. For a recent critique of Christmas-Chanukah distortions, see Lawrence A. Hoffman, "Being a Jew at Christmas Time," *Cross Currents* 42 (1992): 357–63. On the

history of how the American Chanukah was remade into a "commodified" domestic festival, see Jenna Weissman Joselit, "'Merry Chanuka': The Changing Holiday Practices of American Jews, 1880–1950," in *The Uses of Tradition: Jewish Continuity in the Modern Era*, ed. Jack Wertheimer (New York: Jewish Theological Seminary of America, 1992), 303–25, and Andrew R. Heinze, *Adapting to Abundance: Jewish Immigrants, Mass Consumption, and the Search for American Identity* (New York: Columbia University Press, 1990), 71–79.

8. See, for example, Alessandro Falassi, ed., *Time out of Time: Essays on the Festival* (Albuquerque: University of New Mexico Press, 1987), 4–5; Harvey Cox, *The Feast of Fools: A Theological Essay on Festivity and Fantasy* (Cambridge, Mass.: Harvard University Press, 1969), 22–23; and Peter Burke, *Popular Culture in Early Modern Europe* (New York: Harper and Row, 1978), 178.

9. Ralph Waldo Emerson, *The Collected Works of Ralph Waldo Emerson*, vol. 3, *Essays: Second Series* (Cambridge, Mass.: Harvard University Press, 1983), 94.

10. See especially David Cheal, *The Gift Economy* (London: Routledge, 1988); Grant McCracken, *Culture and Consumption: New Approaches to the Symbolic Character of Consumer Goods and Activities* (Bloomington: Indiana University Press, 1988); Mihaly Csikszentmihalyi and Eugene Rochberg-Halton, *The Meaning of Things: Domestic Symbols and the Self* (Cambridge: Cambridge University Press, 1981); and Arjun Appadurai, ed., *The Social Life of Things: Commodities in Cultural Perspective* (Cambridge: Cambridge University Press, 1986).

11. The notion of "regulated improvisations" is borrowed from Pierre Bourdieu's discussion of his mediating construct of *habitus* in *The Logic of Practice*, trans. Richard Nice (Stanford: Stanford University Press, 1990), 57. On cultural invention and reception, see Levine, "Folklore of Industrial Society," 1398.

12. Louisa May Alcott, "A March Christmas," in *"May Your Days Be Merry and Bright" and Other Christmas Stories by Women*, ed. Susan Koppelman (Detroit: Wayne State University Press, 1988), 32. On the gendering of mass culture as female, see Andreas Huyssen, *After the Great Divide: Modernism, Mass Culture, Postmodernism* (Bloomington: Indiana University Press, 1986), 44–62. For the privileging of public ritual over domestic ritual, see, for example, Mary P. Ryan, *Women in Public: Between Banners and Ballots, 1825–1880* (Baltimore: Johns Hopkins University Press, 1990), 19–57. There are several notable exceptions in the scholarly literature that take domestic holiday rituals seriously on their own terms. See, for example, Nada Gray, *Holidays: Victorian Women Celebrate in Pennsylvania* (University Park: Pennsylvania State University Press, 1983).

13. See the discussion of dialogism and heteroglossia in Gary Saul Morson and Caryl Emerson, *Mikhail Bakhtin: Creation of a Prosaics* (Stanford: Stanford University Press, 1990), 49–58, 139–45.

14. Henry Bourne, *Antiquitates Vulgares; or, The Antiquities of the Common People* (1725; reprint, New York: Arno Press, 1977), x.

15. Harry Spencer Stuff, *The Book of Holidays: What—When—Where—Why* (Los Angeles: Times-Mirror, 1926), 12–13, 36, 43, 64; Edward M. Deems, comp., *Holy-Days and Holidays: A Treasury of Historical Material, Sermons in Full and in Brief, Suggestive Thoughts, and Poetry, Relating to Holy Days and Holidays* (New York: Funk and Wagnalls, 1902), v.

16. See David Cressy, *Bonfires and Bells: National Memory and the Protestant Calendar in Elizabethan and Stuart England* (Berkeley and Los Angeles: University of California Press, 1989); Richard P. Gildrie, "The Ceremonial Puritan: Days of Humiliation and

Thanksgiving," *New England Historical and Genealogical Register* 136 (1982): 3–16; Winton U. Solberg, *Redeem the Time: The Puritan Sabbath in Early America* (Cambridge, Mass.: Harvard University Press, 1977), 1–58, 167–96, 298–302; James P. Walsh, "Holy Time and Sacred Space in Puritan New England," *American Quarterly* 32 (1980): 79–95; Eugene Genovese, *Roll, Jordan, Roll: The World the Slaves Made* (New York: Random House, 1972), 573–84; William H. Wiggins, Jr., *O Freedom! Afro-American Emancipation Celebrations* (Knoxville: University of Tennessee Press, 1987); Susan G. Davis, "'Making Night Hideous': Christmas Revelry and Public Order in Nineteenth-Century Philadelphia," *American Quarterly* 34 (1982): 185–99; Roy Rosenzweig, *Eight Hours for What We Will: Workers and Leisure in an Industrial City, 1870–1920* (Cambridge: Cambridge University Press, 1983), 65–90, 153–68; Sean Wilentz, "Artisan Republican Festivals," in *Working-Class America*, ed. Michael Frisch and Daniel Walkowitz (Urbana: University of Illinois Press, 1983), 37–77; Samuel Kinser, *Carnival, American Style: Mardi Gras at New Orleans and Mobile* (Chicago: University of Chicago Press, 1990); Robert Anthony Orsi, *The Madonna of 115th Street: Faith and Community in Italian Harlem, 1880–1950* (New Haven: Yale University Press, 1985); Michael Kazin and Steven J. Ross, "America's Labor Day: The Dilemmas of a Worker's Celebration," *Journal of American History* 78 (1992): 1294–1323; Catherine Albanese, "Requiem for Memorial Day: Dissent in the Redeemer Nation," *American Quarterly* 26 (1974): 386–98; Conrad Cherry, "Two American Sacred Ceremonies: Their Implications for the Study of Religion in America," *American Quarterly* 21 (1969): 739–54; Timothy J. Meagher, "'Why Should We Care for a Little Trouble or a Walk through the Mud': St. Patrick's and Columbus Day Parades in Worcester, Massachusetts, 1845–1915," *New England Quarterly* 58 (1985): 5–26; and John F. Wilson, *Public Religion in American Culture* (Philadelphia: Temple University Press, 1979), 67–93.

17. See Boorstin, *Americans*, 157–64; James H. Barnett, *The American Christmas: A Study in National Culture* (New York: Macmillan, 1954), 33–36, 55–58, 79–101; William B. Waits, *The Modern Christmas in America: A Cultural History of Gift Giving* (New York: New York University Press, 1993); Heinze, *Adapting to Abundance*, 68–85; J. A. R. Pimlott, *The Englishman's Christmas: A Social History* (London: Harvester Press, 1978), 120–33; Tommy R. Thompson, "Sales, Santa, and Good Fellows: Celebrating Christmas in Omaha," *Nebraska History* 68 (1987): 127–41; and Russell W. Belk, "A Child's Christmas in America: Santa Claus as Deity, Consumption as Religion," *Journal of American Culture* 10 (1987): 87–100. Though focused on Christmas, Boorstin's eight pages range the farthest in looking at the transformation of American holidays into "festivals of consumption." Barnett's book on Christmas remains among the best places to start for consideration of that holiday, but, because Barnett is primarily a sociologist of the contemporary culture, his historical material is thin. His treatment of the commercial dimensions of Christmas is confined almost wholly to the 1920s and later; see especially 79–80. Heinze's book is excellent on the commercial transformation of the Jewish holiday cycle in American culture.

18. On the interpretive tensions between this metanarrative of homogenization and the reverse construct of emergence and invention, see James Clifford, *The Predicament of Culture: Twentieth-Century Ethnography, Literature, and Art* (Cambridge, Mass.: Harvard University Press, 1988), 16–17. On the wider dispersion of the carnivalesque, see Peter Stallybrass and Allon White, *The Politics and Poetics of Transgression* (Ithaca: Cornell University Press, 1986), 171–90. Stallybrass and White see this dispersion especially in terms of art and literature, while presenting the bourgeois repression of carni-

valesque pleasures as pathological, precipitating neurosis and hysteria. Though it allows that in the bourgeoisie "a tiny spark of the carnival flame" survived, the work of Mikhail Bakhtin has been crucial in setting the pattern for juxtaposing folk carnival humor with middle-class seriousness, for telling a story of carnival's disintegration and decline through the repressiveness of bourgeois family life. The story needs to be retold without this easy, predictable plot. See Mikhail Bakhtin, *Rabelais and His World*, trans. Hélène Iswolsky (Cambridge, Mass.: M.I.T. Press, 1968), 18–19, 33, 37, 53, 106, 276.

19. See, for example, Micaela Di Leonardo, "The Female World of Cards and Holidays: Women, Families, and the Work of Kinship," *Signs: Journal of Women in Culture and Society* 12 (1987): 440–53.

20. "Sermonettes," *Millinery Trade Review* 11 (March 1886): 148; Reinhold Niebuhr, *Pious and Secular America* (New York: Scribner's Sons, 1958), 1–13. R. Laurence Moore's *Selling God* appeared too late for me to address it in depth here. His volume is also concerned with the hybridity of religion and marketplace in American culture, and I consider it an important counterpart to my research. He tends, however, to minimize the complex forms of alienation from commercialization, spectacle, and commodification; he concentrates on the strategies of producers rather than on the responses of consumers—on selling, rather than the dialectic of buying and selling; he also has little to say about ritual and celebration. For his minimal comments on Christmas, see R. Laurence Moore, *Selling God: American Religion in the Marketplace of Culture* (New York: Oxford University Press, 1994), 205–6. For another important recent contribution to this discussion of the complementarity of Christianity and the commercial culture, see William Leach, *Land of Desire: Merchants, Power, and the Rise of a New American Culture* (New York: Pantheon, 1993), 173–224.

21. Gillo Dorfles, *Kitsch: The World of Bad Taste* (New York: Universe Books, 1969), 129–30; Fredric Jameson, *Postmodernism; or, The Cultural Logic of Late Capitalism* (Durham: Duke University Press, 1991), 2. Clement Greenberg wrote the classic modernist statement on the subject in "Avant-Garde and Kitsch" for the *Partisan Review* in 1939; it is reprinted in Dorfles's volume (116–26). On the demystification of these cultural hierarchies, see Lawrence W. Levine, *Highbrow/Lowbrow: The Emergence of Cultural Hierarchy in America* (Cambridge, Mass.: Harvard University Press, 1988), especially 243–56. As a Marxist critic, Jameson sees the aesthetic populism of postmodernism—its openness to fashion and kitsch, to Las Vegas and the strip mall—as replicating the logic of consumer capitalism. See Fredric Jameson, "Postmodernism and Consumer Society," in *The Anti-Aesthetic: Essays on Postmodern Culture*, ed. Hal Foster (Port Townsend, Wash.: Bay Press, 1983), 111–25.

22. Kazimierz Siemienowicz, *The Great Art of Artillery of Casimir Simienowicz*, trans. George Shelvocke (London: J. Tonson, 1729), i.

NOTES TO CHAPTER ONE

1. *Dry Goods Chronicle*, 10 February 1900, 7; ibid., 28 April 1900, 20; *Dry Goods Economist*, 9 November 1895, 63.

2. John Bunyan, *The Pilgrim's Progress*, ed. Louis L. Martz (New York: Rinehart, 1949), 91–92.

3. Le Goff, *Time, Work, and Culture*, 29–42.

4. Quoted in James T. Dennison, Jr., *The Market Day of the Soul: The Puritan Doctrine of the Sabbath in England, 1532–1700* (Lanham, Md.: University Press of America, 1983), 2.

5. See Edith Cooperrider Rodgers, *Discussion of Holidays in the Later Middle Ages* (New York: Columbia University Press, 1940; reprint, New York: AMS Press, 1967), 28–62 (page citations are to the reprint edition), and Edward Vansittart Neale, *Feasts and Fasts: An Essay on the Rise, Progress, and Present State of the Laws Relating to Sundays and Other Holidays* (London: John Murray, 1845), 86–137, 175–204.

6. Quoted in Rodgers, *Discussion*, 65; see also 78–79, and Kenneth L. Park, *The English Sabbath: A Study of Doctrine and Discipline from the Reformation to the Civil War* (Cambridge: Cambridge University Press, 1988), 9–16.

7. Alessandro Falassi, "Festival: Definition and Morphology," in Falassi, *Time out of Time*, 1–2. A good account of the seamless combination of holy days and market days can be found in Robert J. Smith's ethnography of a Peruvian Catholic fiesta, *The Art of the Festival*, University of Kansas Publications in Anthropology, no. 6 (Lawrence, Kans.: n.p., 1975), 124–30. For evidence of just how venerable or classical these convergences were, see Joan M. Frayn, *Markets and Fairs in Roman Italy: Their Social and Economic Importance from the Second Century B.C. to the Third Century A.D.* (Oxford: Clarendon Press, 1993), 9, 133–44. For an especially keen analysis of the hybridity of the early modern fair, see Stallybrass and White, *Politics and Poetics of Transgression*, 27–79. Stallybrass and White see the "separation of the festive and the commercial" and the fear of "the fair's inmixing of work and pleasure" as peculiarly distinctive of capitalist rationality and bourgeois discipline (30).

8. See, for example, David Jaffee, "Peddlers of Progress and the Transformation of the Rural North, 1760–1860," *Journal of American History* 78 (1991): 511–35; T. H. Breen, "An Empire of Goods: The Anglicization of Colonial America, 1690–1776," *Journal of British Studies* 25 (1986): 467–99; and Peter Benes, ed., *Annual Proceedings of the Dublin Seminar for New England Folklife*, vol. 9, *Itinerancy in New England and New York* (Boston: Boston University, 1986). I have also been helped by the chapter on peddlers in Jackson Lears's *Fables of Abundance*, which he graciously shared with me in manuscript.

9. Allen Wiley, quoted in Charles A. Johnson, *The Frontier Camp Meeting: Religion's Harvest Time* (Dallas: Southern Methodist University Press, 1955), 224–25. See also 214–25, 227–28.

10. I have drawn this example from legal ordinances of 1804 and 1811, which appear as appendices in Bradford Verter, "Pinkster and Power: Slavery, Festival, and Rebellion in Post-Revolutionary Albany" (seminar paper, Princeton University, Department of Religion, 1992). See also Shane White, "'It Was a Proud Day': African Americans, Festivals, and Parades in the North, 1741–1834," *Journal of American History* 81 (1994): 19–22; Shane White, "Pinkster in Albany, 1803: A Contemporary Description," *New York History* 10 (1989): 191–99; and A. J. Williams-Myers, "Pinkster Carnival: Africanisms in the Hudson River Valley," *Afro-Americans in New York Life and History* 9 (1985): 10, 15.

11. Bakhtin, *Rabelais and His World*, 92; Kinser, *Carnival, American Style*.

12. Archibald A. Hill, "The Pushcart Peddlers of New York," *Independent*, 18 October 1906, 919. For examples of holiday peddlers in the festivities of nineteenth-century Philadelphia, see Susan G. Davis, *Parades and Power: Street Theatre in Nineteenth-Cen-*

tury Philadelphia (Philadelphia: Temple University Press, 1986; reprint, Berkeley and Los Angeles: University of California Press, 1988), 30, 32, 40–42, 62 (page citations are to the reprint edition).

13. Quoted in Rodgers, *Discussion*, 110.

14. John Northbrooke, *A Treatise against Dicing, Dancing, Plays, and Interludes, with Other Pastimes* ([1577]; reprint, London: Shakespeare Society, 1843), 44.

15. See Cressy, *Bonfires and Bells*, 190–206; Horton Davies, *The Worship of the American Puritans, 1629–1730* (New York: Peter Lang, 1990), 51–75; David D. Hall, *Worlds of Wonder, Days of Judgment: Popular Religious Belief in Early New England* (New York: Alfred A. Knopf, 1989), 166–212, 216, 219–20; William DeLoss Love, Jr., *The Fast and Thanksgiving Days of New England* (Boston: Houghton Mifflin, 1895); Gildrie, "Ceremonial Puritan"; Charles E. Hambrick-Stowe, *The Practice of Piety: Puritan Devotional Disciplines in Seventeenth-Century New England* (Chapel Hill: University of North Carolina Press, 1982), 96–103, 133–35; Christopher Hill, *Society and Puritanism in Pre-Revolutionary England* (London: Secker and Warburg, 1964), 145–218; Solberg, *Redeem the Time*; and Walsh, "Holy Time and Sacred Space."

16. See Walter Tittle, comp., *Colonial Holidays, Being a Collection of Contemporary Accounts of Holiday Celebrations in Colonial Times* (New York: Doubleday, Page, 1910), 35–37.

17. On this point, see especially Walsh, "Holy Time and Sacred Space."

18. Thomas Shepard, *Theses Sabbaticae; or, The Doctrine of the Sabbath*, in *The Works of Thomas Shepard* (Boston: Doctrinal Tract and Book Society, 1853), 3:259.

19. Puritans also experimented with this numerical calendar system. See Cressy, *Bonfires and Bells*, 198–99.

20. See Philip Schaff, ed., *The Creeds of Christendom* (New York: Harper and Brothers, 1878), 3:796; Samuel G. Barton, "The Quaker Calendar," *Proceedings of the American Philosophical Society* 93 (1949): 32–39; Richard Bauman, "The Place of Festival in the Worldview of the Seventeenth-Century Quakers," in Falassi, *Time out of Time*, 93–98; and David Hackett Fischer, *Albion's Seed: Four British Folkways in America* (New York: Oxford University Press, 1989), 8–11, 158–66, 368–73, 560–66, 743–47.

21. William S. Perry, ed., *Historical Collections Relating to the American Colonial Church* (Hartford: Church Press, 1870–78), 1:213.

22. David Cressy's conclusion on the fate of the English calendar in the seventeenth-century colonies pushes the point too far, but it is suggestive of the prevailing current: "The sweep of the Christian year narrowed to a succession of Sundays." See Cressy, *Bonfires and Bells*, 193.

23. Montesquieu, *The Spirit of Laws*, ed. David Wallace Carrithers (Berkeley and Los Angeles: University of California Press, 1977), 54, 335. For a detailed *Mémoire pour la suppression des fêtes*, see Joachim Faiguet de Villeneuve, *L'Ami des Pauvres, ou L'économe Politique, Ouvrage, dans lequel on Propose des Moyens pour Enricher & pour Perfectionner l'Espèce Humaine; Avec deux Mémoires Intéressans sur les Maîtrises & sur les Fêtes* (Paris: Chez Moreau, 1766).

24. [John Pollexfen], *Discourse of Trade, Coyn, and Paper Credit: And of Ways and Means to Gain, and Retain Riches* (London: Brabazon Aylmer, 1697), 49. For several examples of this type of calculation, see Edgar S. Furniss, *The Position of the Laborer in a System of Nationalism: A Study in the Labor Theories of the Later English Mercantilists* (Boston: Houghton Mifflin, 1920), 44–45.

25. Leonard W. Labaree, ed., *The Papers of Benjamin Franklin* (New Haven: Yale University Press, 1961), 4:86–87. See, for example, E. P. Thompson, "Time, Work-Discipline, and Industrial Capitalism," *Past and Present*, no. 38 (1967): 56–97; Gerard T. Moran, "Conceptions of Time in Early Modern France: An Approach to the History of Collective Mentalities," *Sixteenth Century Journal* 12 (1981): 3–19; and Michael O'Malley, *Keeping Watch: A History of American Time* (New York: Viking Penguin, 1990).

26. *A Letter from a Blacksmith to the Ministers and Elders of the Church of Scotland in which the Manner of Public Worship in that Church is Considered; Its Inconveniences and Defects Pointed Out; and Methods for Removing of Them Humbly Proposed* (New Haven: Oliver Steele, 1814), 26–28. See also Leigh Eric Schmidt, *Holy Fairs: Scottish Communions and American Revivals in the Early Modern Period* (Princeton: Princeton University Press, 1989), 179–83, 192–205.

27. "Camp-Meetings, and Agricultural Fairs," *Wesleyan Repository* 2 (August 1822): 140, 142. See also Terry D. Bilhartz, *Urban Religion and the Second Great Awakening: Church and Society in Early National Baltimore* (Rutherford, N.J.: Fairleigh Dickinson University Press, 1986), 87.

28. Charles Dickens, *A Christmas Carol in Prose. Being a Ghost Story of Christmas* (Boston: Ticknor and Fields, 1869), 12, 14, 19, 85–86, 104. On the *Carol* and its various incarnations, see Paul Davis, *The Lives and Times of Ebenezer Scrooge* (New Haven: Yale University Press, 1990).

29. On the response to Dickens on his American tour, see, for example, Barnett, *American Christmas*, 15–17, and Philip Collins, ed., *Charles Dickens: The Public Readings* (Oxford: Clarendon Press, 1975).

30. C. W. Moore, journal, 1842–71, 1:6–7, 185, 2: unpaginated (25 December 1846), Rare Books and Manuscripts, New York Public Library. Moore's journal is incomplete. For the years after 1853, there is simply not enough material to judge whether holidays became more important to him as a merchant, citizen, or Protestant.

31. For Whitney's dictum, see Ruth Webb Lee, *A History of Valentines* (New York: Studio Publications, 1952), 71. For Wanamaker's exhortation, see John Wanamaker, Store Editorial Letter, 10 February 1921, box 108, Wanamaker Collection, Historical Society of Pennsylvania, Philadelphia.

32. See Douglas A. Reid, "The Decline of St. Monday, 1766–1876," *Past and Present*, no. 71 (1976): 76–101; Bob Bushaway, *By Rite: Custom, Ceremony, and Community in England, 1700–1880* (London: Junction Books, 1982), 265–72; Rosenzweig, *Eight Hours for What We Will*, 65–90, 153–68; and Karen Sue Hybertsen, "'The Return of Chaos': The Uses and Interpretations of Halloween in the United States from the Victorian Era to the Present" (Ph.D. diss., Drew University, 1993), 29–99.

33. For an analysis of the debate on the King holiday, see William J. Starosta, "A National Holiday for Dr. King? Qualitative Content Analysis of Arguments Carried in the *Washington Post* and *New York Times*," *Journal of Black Studies* 18 (1988): 358–78.

34. See Pimlott, *Englishman's Christmas*, 77.

35. "Holidays," *North American Review* 84 (1857): 345–48, 357–60.

36. Ibid., 347.

37. Colin Campbell, *The Romantic Ethic and the Spirit of Modern Consumerism* (Oxford: Basil Blackwell, 1987).

38. "Holidays," 335; Sarah A. Myers, "New-Year's Day," *Ladies' Repository* 26 (Janu-

ary 1866): 32–33. On aristocratic refinement and democratic emulation, see especially Richard L. Bushman, *The Refinement of America: Persons, Houses, Cities* (New York: Alfred A. Knopf, 1992).

39. Breen, "Empire of Goods"; T. H. Breen, "'Baubles of Britain': The American and Consumer Revolutions of the Eighteenth Century," *Past and Present*, no. 119 (1988): 73–104; T. H. Breen, "Narrative of Commercial Life: Consumption, Ideology, and Community on the Eve of the American Revolution," *William and Mary Quarterly* 50 (1993): 471–501; Neil McKendrick, John Brewer, and J. H. Plumb, *The Birth of a Consumer Society: The Commercialization of Eighteenth-Century England* (Bloomington: Indiana University Press, 1982). Dating the beginnings of the modern consumer culture has been an issue of considerable debate: Answers range from at least the Renaissance to the late-nineteenth-century United States. Pinning down "origins" is finally less important than tracing the varied unfolding of this transformation in different periods and places. For one recent review of the issue of beginnings, see the first chapter in McCracken, *Culture and Consumption*. For the emergence of the consumer culture in the United States, the focus of the literature has long been on the years 1880 to 1930. See, for example, Simon J. Bronner, ed., *Consuming Visions: Accumulation and Display of Goods in America, 1880–1920* (New York: Norton, 1989), and T. J. Jackson Lears, "From Salvation to Self-Realization: Advertising and the Therapeutic Roots of the Consumer Culture, 1880–1930," in *The Culture of Consumption: Critical Essays in American History, 1880–1980*, ed. Richard Wightman Fox and T. J. Jackson Lears (New York: Pantheon Books, 1983), 3–38. Much recent work has pushed this discussion back in time to the larger British "empire of goods" in the second half of the eighteenth century, and the chapters that follow on St. Valentine's Day and Christmas, particularly the exploration of New Year's rites in the latter chapter, also push these "commercialization" issues back into the colonial and antebellum periods. For two helpful historiographical appraisals of current work on the culture of consumption, see Jean-Christophe Agnew, "Coming Up for Air: Consumer Culture in Historical Perspective," in *Consumption and the World of Goods*, ed. John Brewer and Roy Porter (London: Routledge, 1993), 19–39, and Ann Smart Martin, "Makers, Buyers, and Users: Consumerism as a Material Culture Framework," *Winterthur Portfolio: A Journal of American Material Culture* 28 (1993): 141–57.

40. "Holidays," 348–49.

41. Ibid.

42. On the themes of national versus local calendrical traditions, see especially Bushaway, *By Rite*, and Gavin Weightman and Steve Humphries, *Christmas Past* (London: Sidgwick and Jackson, 1987), 12–14, 21. Bushaway emphasizes the multiplicity of forces that fed national traditions over local ones in England: the work of folklorists and antiquarians, which tended to take local customs and depict them as national ones, the erosion of traditional parish and community structures, the decline of crafts and with them their distinctive holiday customs, the waning legal authority of local customs as popular rights, and the rising power of the Victorian middle class. He does not analyze the intertwined roles of commerce, consumption, and religion in this process and their intersection with middle-class Victorian versions of the holidays, which I would argue are the crucial variables in the American context.

43. See Diana Karter Appelbaum, *The Glorious Fourth: An American Holiday, an American History* (New York: Facts on File, 1989), 43; Len Travers, "Hurrah for the

Fourth: Patriotism, Politics, and Independence Day in Federalist Boston, 1783–1818," *Essex Institute Historical Collections* 125 (1989): 136–37; Cressy, *Bonfires and Bells*, 88–89; Alan St. H. Brock, *A History of Fireworks* (London: George G. Harrap, 1949); and James Cutbush, *A System of Pyrotechny, Comprehending the Theory and Practice, with the Application of Chemistry; Designed for Exhibition and for War* (Philadelphia: Clara F. Cutbush, 1825).

44. Masten and Wells, *Descriptive Catalogue and Price-List* (Boston: n.p., 1887), 2, 35–56; Masten and Wells, *Price-List: Fire-Works, Campaign Goods, Decorations, Etc.* (Boston: n.p., 1885), 16; Rochester Fireworks Co., *Programmes of Exhibition Assortments of Fireworks: Suitable for Lawn Displays, Summer Resorts, and Family Use* (Rochester: n.p., n.d.), 2, 4; E. Bennett and Co., *Manufacturers' Agents for the Excelsior Fireworks* (New York: n.p., 1876); Reuben Wood's Sons, *Pyrotechnics for Fourth [of] July, for Memorial Day, Washington's Birthday, Parades, Resort Openings, Conventions* (n.p., [1887]); *Advertising World*, 15 May 1899, 8. The statistic on the size of the industry is from Appelbaum, *Glorious Fourth*, 125. Outstanding collections of firework trade catalogues are available at the Hagley Museum and Library and the Winterthur Library, both in Wilmington, Delaware, and also in the Warshaw Collection of Business Americana at the National Museum of American History, Smithsonian Institution, Washington, D.C.

45. *Dry Goods Economist*, 12 June 1897, 53.

46. V. L. Price, "Make the Holidays Pay," *Candy Factory* 4 (April 1924): 18–19.

NOTES TO CHAPTER TWO

1. "Editors' Table," *Godey's Magazine and Lady's Book* 22 (February 1841): 95; "A New Fashion for Valentines," ibid., 38 (February 1849): frontispiece, 73–74; Harry Sunderland, "Kate's Valentine," ibid., 40 (February 1850): 119–21.

2. Joseph R. Chandler, "St. Valentine's Day," *Graham's American Monthly Magazine of Literature and Art* 34 (February 1849): 110–12; Sunderland, "Kate's Valentine," 119.

3. Collectors of valentines and other ephemera have produced most of the secondary work on the holiday's history in the United States. See Lee, *History of Valentines*; Frank Staff, *The Valentine and Its Origins* (New York: Frederick A. Praeger, 1969), and George Buday, *The History of the Christmas Card* (London: Spring Books, 1954), 45–52. The Ephemera Society of America recently devoted its annual proceedings to the topic of valentines; see *Ephemera Journal* 3 (1990). These works, though short on interpretation, remain useful surveys. For helpful observations on the expansion of valentine customs in English Canada from the 1840s to the 1860s, see Peter Ward, *Courtship, Love, and Marriage in Nineteenth-Century English Canada* (Montreal: McGill-Queen's University Press, 1990), 92, 96–100.

4. For this background on the cult of St. Valentine, I rely especially on the fine work of Jack B. Oruch, "St. Valentine, Chaucer, and Spring in February," *Speculum* 56 (1981): 534–65, and Henry Ansgar Kelly, *Chaucer and the Cult of St. Valentine* (Leiden: E. J. Brill, 1986). Though it is largely superseded by the above works, also helpful is the chapter on St. Valentine in Alfred L. Kellogg, *Chaucer, Langland, Arthur: Essays in Middle English Literature* (New Brunswick: Rutgers University Press, 1972), 108–45.

5. Oruch, "St. Valentine," 548.

6. On devotion to the saints and hagiography, see, for example, Peter Brown, *The*

Cult of the Saints: Its Rise and Function in Latin Christianity (Chicago: University of Chicago Press, 1981), and Thomas J. Heffernan, *Sacred Biography: Saints and Their Biographers in the Middle Ages* (New York: Oxford University Press, 1988).

7. See Kelly, *Chaucer*, 59–61, and Oruch, "St. Valentine," 538–42. For a perceptive nineteenth-century critique of this popular linkage of St. Valentine's Day to the Lupercalia, see John W. Hales, "St. Valentine's Day," *Antiquary* 5 (February 1882): 45. The invented histories of the eighteenth and nineteenth centuries continue to be repeated uncritically. See, for example, Jack Santino, *All Around the Year: Holidays and Celebrations in American Life* (Urbana: University of Illinois Press, 1994), 60, 67–71.

8. F. N. Robinson, ed., *The Complete Works of Geoffrey Chaucer* (New York: Houghton Mifflin, 1933), 366.

9. Kellogg, *Chaucer, Langland, Arthur*, 124. On Lydgate, see Kelly, *Chaucer*, 145, and Oruch, "St. Valentine," 559–60. The potential overlap of images of saintly love and sexual passion continued. Compare the devotional images in Max Bucherer, *Spitzenbilder, Papierschnitte, Porträtsilhouetten* (Munich: Einhorn Verlag, 1920), 15, 30, 37, 51, with the valentine images in William J. Petersen, "Postcard Holiday Greetings," *Palimpsest* 48 (1967): 569–84.

10. Ben Jonson, *A Tale of a Tub*, in *The Complete Plays of Ben Jonson*, ed. G. A. Wilkes (Oxford: Clarendon Press, 1981), 1:21–22.

11. Charles Wheatly, *A Rational Illustration of the Book of Common Prayer of the Church of England* (London: C. Hitch and L. Hawes, 1759), 54.

12. "Festivals and Holidays," *Chambers's Edinburgh Journal* 11 (January–June 1849): 221.

13. Bourne, *Antiquitates Vulgares*, 174.

14. Evidence on these traditions is helpfully collected in A. R. Wright and T. E. Lones, eds., *British Calendar Customs: England* (London: Folk-Lore Society, 1936–40), 1:103; 2:106–10, 151–54, 158, 199, 242–43; 3:41, 92, 100–101, 104, 111–13, 199, 227–28, 290–91.

15. Mrs. M. Macleod Banks, ed., *British Calendar Customs: Scotland* (London: Folk-Lore Society, 1937–41), 2:170.

16. See ibid., 2:170–72; Wright and Lones, *British Calendar Customs*, 2:146–54; and John Brand and Henry Ellis, *Observations on the Popular Antiquities of Great Britain* (London: Henry Bohn, 1849), 1:60–62.

17. Reprinted in Frank E. Bliss, comp., *In Praise of Bishop Valentine* (London: Chiswick Press, 1893), 147–49.

18. Bourne, *Antiquitates Vulgares*, 177.

19. The Herrick and Donne poems are reprinted in Bliss, *In Praise of Bishop Valentine*, 48, 58. For the courtly and monarchical uses of festivity, see Leah S. Marcus, *The Politics of Mirth: Jonson, Herrick, Milton, Marvell, and the Defense of Old Holiday Pastimes* (Chicago: University of Chicago Press, 1986).

20. Rosalind H. Williams, *Dream Worlds: Mass Consumption in Late Nineteenth-Century France* (Berkeley and Los Angeles: University of California Press, 1982), 8–9, 19–57, with quotations on 9, 19, 29, and 57.

21. Robert C. Latham and William Matthews, eds., *The Diary of Samuel Pepys* (Berkeley and Los Angeles: University of California Press, 1970–83), 8:184, 9:88–89. See also 2:38–40, 4:68, 7:70, 9:449.

22. See Wright and Lones, *British Calendar Customs*, 1:88, 2:150, and Staff, *Valentine*, 79, 81.

23. On the overlay of calendars in early modern England, see Cressy, *Bonfires and Bells*.

24. *The Butterfly's Birth Day, St. Valentine's Day, and Madam Whale's Ball: Poems, to Instruct and Amuse the Rising Generation* (Burlington, N.J.: D. Allinson, 1811), 9–11.

25. "Varieties," *United States Literary Gazette*, 15 December 1825, 237; "Valentine's Day," *Parley's Magazine* 4 (February 1836): 43; "St. Valentine's Day," *Ariel*, 5 March 1831, 180.

26. Samuel Woodworth, "Appendix: American Festivals, Games, and Amusements," in Horatio Smith, *Festivals, Games, and Amusements* (New York: Harper and Brothers, 1832), 334–35; "St. Valentine and Valentines," *Harper's Weekly*, 13 February 1858, 104.

27. *Philadelphia Public Ledger*, 14 February 1845, 2.

28. I have concentrated my research on Boston, Worcester, Philadelphia, and New York, all early centers of the valentine trade. But the fashion was hardly confined to the Northeast; it was increasingly national and even international in scope. The vogue, for example, had stretched into rural English Canada by the 1850s and 1860s. See Ward, *Courtship, Love, and Marriage*, 97–98.

29. See "Varieties," 237; William Hone, *The Every-Day Book; or, Everlasting Calendar of Popular Amusements* (1827; reprint, Detroit: Gale, 1967), 1:215; *Philadelphia Public Ledger*, 12 February 1848, 2; and W. H. Cremer, Jr., *St. Valentine's Day and Valentines: A Few Words on the Subject* (London: n.p., [1871]), 15.

30. *Boston Daily Evening Transcript*, 13 February 1843, 2; *Philadelphia Public Ledger*, 12 February 1848, 2. For useful, though incomplete, listings of American firms producing valentines or valentine writers, see Staff, *Valentine*, 136–37, and Lee, *History of Valentines*, 233–34. They miss R. Magee in Philadelphia, for example, who went into "the Valentine business" in 1841 and who in 1854 claimed to have two hundred employees devoted "entirely to this line of business," i.e., manufacturing and merchandising valentines. See *Philadelphia Public Ledger*, 13 February 1854, 2.

31. See E. M. Gilman to his sister (unnamed), 28 February 1842, box J4.15, Hallmark Historical Collection, Kansas City, Mo.; *Boston Daily Evening Transcript*, 18 February 1843, 2; *Niles' National Register*, 9 March 1844, 32; *Strong's Annual Valentine Advertiser* (New York: T. W. Strong, 1847), 2, American Antiquarian Society, Worcester; and *Massachusetts Spy*, 24 February 1847, 3.

32. *Philadelphia Public Ledger*, 15 February 1848, 2.

33. See the *Oxford English Dictionary*, s.v. "valentine," and Hales, "St. Valentine's Day," 49.

34. James Howe, "Verses to a Young Lady," 14 February 1788, box H4.11, Hallmark Historical Collection. For examples of combining poetic epigrams or mottoes with the traditional valentine lottery, see Latham and Matthews, *Diary of Samuel Pepys*, 8:65–66, and *Valantins, Questions D'Amour, et Autres Pieces Galantes* (Paris: Claude Barbin, 1669), unpaginated "Au Lecteur." This French text declares in its preface that "the game of drawing valentines was invented long ago; but it has been played with poetry only a little while" (author's translation). Pepys indicates, too, that drawing poetic mottoes was a new "fashion" in 1667.

35. Handmade cutwork valentine, undated, box "Oversize," Hallmark Historical Collection. For other examples of valentine tokens and puzzle purses made in response to drawn lots, see Lee, *History of Valentines*, 15–19, 28. For an example of the exchange of valentine love verses in late-eighteenth-century England, see [William Heard], *Valentine's Day, a Musical Drama, in Two Acts, as It Is Performed at the Theatre Royal in Drury-Lane* (London: T. Lowdnes, 1776), 9, 28.

36. See handmade valentines, boxes H3.12, H4.11, Hallmark Historical Collection, and valentines, box 2, American Antiquarian Society. See also boxes H4.2 and J4.15, Hallmark Historical Collection, and valentines, box 26, series 2, Norcross Greeting Card Collection, National Museum of American History, Smithsonian Institution, Washington, D.C. Ruth Lee and Frank Staff give a mistaken impression of the extent of handmade valentines in the United States before the 1840s. Lee especially portrays any and all handmade love tokens as valentines, many of which had nothing to do with St. Valentine's Day (for example, a heart-shaped German betrothal pledge dated 1753). Labeling these varied love tokens *valentines* is anachronistic.

37. Hickory Broom, "St. Valentine's Day," *Godey's Magazine and Lady's Book* 44 (February 1852): 149–51.

38. *The Complete Valentine Writer; or, The Young Men and Maidens Best Assistant* (London: T. Sabine, [1783]), frontispiece, A2, 56. Ruth Lee gives no source in claiming that valentine writers were known in England and North America as early as 1723. Sabine's is the earliest that I have seen. (A copy is available in the Hallmark Historical Collection.) The earliest example listed in the British Library's catalogue is from 1805. See Lee, *History of Valentines*, 14. Her claim, without additional substantiation, has been repeated in various places. Lee's date was probably a typographical error. Most likely she had in mind a valentine writer from 1823, not 1723, published by W. Borradaile in New York.

39. For a bibliographic checklist of 153 valentine writers, see Harry B. Weiss, "English and American Valentine Writers," *Bulletin of the New York Public Library* 43 (February 1939): 71–86.

40. See Peter Quizumall, *The New Quizzical Valentine Writer, Being an Excellent Collection of All the Humourous, Droll, and Merry Valentines, Ever Published* (New York: W. Borradaile, 1823); *The New Quizzical Valentine Writer, Being an Excellent Collection of All the Humourous, Droll, and Merry Valentines, Ever Published* (New York: S. King, 1828). This direct borrowing from British valentine writers is also evident in *Ladies and Gentlemen's Fashionable Valentine Writer* (New York: W. Mather, n.d.).

41. For one of these broadsheets, see *Cupid's Chit Chat* (New York: T. W. Strong, 1852) in valentines, box 1, American Antiquarian Society.

42. *The Sentimental Valentine Writer, for Both Sexes* (Philadelphia: Turner and Fisher, 1845), 3, 16.

43. See *St. Valentine's Budget, Being a Choice Miscellany of Elegant Poetical Pieces, Gay and Sentimental, Suitable for Valentines of Compliment, Friendship and Love* (New York: T. W. Strong, n.d.), 20–21, 23–24. This copy is at the American Antiquarian Society.

44. *Saint Valentine's Budget* in *Strong's Universal Valentine Writer* (New York: T. W. Strong, n.d.), 39, 57. This is a compilation of seven of Strong's discrete valentine writers into one "universal" valentine writer. This particular copy is in valentine writers, box 41, series 2, Norcross Greeting Card Collection. For a similarly marked-up chap-

book, see in the same box *A Collection of New and Original Valentines, Serious and Satirical, Sublime and Ridiculous, on All the Ordinary Names, Professions, Trades, Etc.* (London: Ward and Lock, [1857]), 48, 57.

45. *The Ladies' and Gentlemen's New and Original Valentine Writer* (Nashua, N.H.: J. M. Fletcher, n.d.), iii–iv; *Gems of Love; A Manual for the Valentine Writer* (New York: T. W. Strong, [1849]), unpaginated preface; *True-Love Knots for True Lovers; or, Cupid's Galaxy* (New York: T. W. Strong, 1850), iv; *Collection of New and Original Valentines*, 14–15.

46. Valentines, boxes H3.12 and H4.11, Hallmark Historical Collection.

47. See especially Campbell, *Romantic Ethic*, and Karen Lystra, *Searching the Heart: Women, Men, and Romantic Love in Nineteenth-Century America* (New York: Oxford University Press, 1989).

48. In her study of nineteenth-century courtship, Karen Lystra remarks that "Victorian lovers demanded self-expression of each other" and that "self-revelation became the primary symbol of intimacy, closeness, and sometimes even truth in nineteenth-century middle-class American culture." The successful commodification of sentiment, represented in the valentine writers and in valentines themselves, ran counter to the "free-form subjectivity" that Lystra finds in Victorian love letters. The emphasis within romantic love on sincere self-disclosure, however, does suggest why the publishers of valentine writers went to such lengths to stress flexibility and freedom. See Lystra, *Searching the Heart*, 33, 37.

49. Ann Douglas, *The Feminization of American Culture* (New York: Alfred A. Knopf, 1977), 255. In a parallel vein, see Arlie Russell Hochschild, *The Managed Heart: Commercialization of Human Feeling* (Berkeley and Los Angeles: University of California Press, 1983).

50. For the statistics on the growth of the industry, see David M. Potter, *People of Plenty: Economic Abundance and the American Character* (Chicago: University of Chicago Press, 1954), 168–69, 178–79. The literature on the history of advertising and display is abundant. I have been especially influenced by T. J. Jackson Lears, "Some Versions of Fantasy: Toward a Cultural History of American Advertising, 1880–1930," *Prospects* 9 (1984): 349–405; William Leach, "Strategists of Display and the Production of Desire," in Bronner, *Consuming Visions*, 99–132; Neil Harris, "The Drama of Consumer Desire," in *Yankee Enterprise: The Rise of the American System of Manufactures*, ed. Otto Mayr and Robert C. Post (Washington, D.C.: Smithsonian Institution Press, 1981), 189–216; Daniel Pope, *The Making of Modern Advertising* (New York: Basic Books, 1983); and Roland Marchand, *Advertising the American Dream: Making Way for Modernity, 1920–1940* (Berkeley and Los Angeles: University of California Press, 1985). The use of fantasy, festivity, romance, and the carnivalesque in the marketing of valentines pushes back by a half century the typical chronology for the emergence of such merchandising techniques in the United States.

51. *New-York Tribune*, 12 February 1847, 3; *Philadelphia Public Ledger*, 12 February 1848, 2.

52. *Philadelphia Public Ledger*, 13 February 1850, 2; *New-York Tribune*, 13 February 1846, 3; *Philadelphia Public Ledger*, 13 February 1847, 2; ibid., 14 February 1850, 2; ibid., 13 February 1846, 2. Zieber's St. Valentine may have inspired similar uses of Santa Claus, but some Philadelphia merchants were already trying in the 1840s to

establish themselves as Kris Kringle's headquarters. On merchandising experiments with Santa Claus, see the next chapter.

53. Campbell, *Romantic Ethic*, 227.

54. *Philadelphia Public Ledger*, 13 February 1850, 2; Leach, "Strategists," 131.

55. Turner and Fisher advertisement, *Fisher's Comic Almanac* (Boston: James Fisher, 1849), unpaginated. See also the Turner and Fisher advertisement in valentines, box 1, American Antiquarian Society. On the peddling of love charms and recipes for love, see Keith Thomas, *Religion and the Decline of Magic: Studies in Popular Beliefs in Sixteenth- and Seventeenth-Century England* (London: Weidenfeld and Nicolson, 1971; reprint, New York: Viking Penguin, 1973), 277–78 (page citations are to the reprint edition), and Albert J. Raboteau, *Slave Religion: The "Invisible Institution" in the Antebellum South* (New York: Oxford University Press, 1978), 279–80. On advertising and magic, see Raymond Williams, *Problems in Materialism and Culture* (London: Verso, 1980), 170–95; Lears, "Some Versions of Fantasy," 355, 397–98; and T. J. Jackson Lears, "Beyond Veblen: Rethinking Consumer Culture in America," in Bronner, *Consuming Visions*, 77–80.

56. For Strong's promotional journalism on the holiday, see "St. Valentine's Anniversary," *Yankee Notions* 1 (February 1852): 37–39, and "The History of a Valentine: A Very Short Story in Rhyme," ibid., 6 (February 1856): 38–39. For a brief sketch of Strong's career, see Harry T. Peters, *America on Stone: The Other Printmakers to the American People* (New York: Doubleday, Doran, 1931), 377–78.

57. See Strong's advertisements in *Yankee Notions* 6 (January 1856): 32; ibid., 7 (January 1858): 32; ibid., 7 (February 1858): 64; and ibid., 2 (February 1853): 64.

58. *Strong's Annual Valentine Advertiser*, 2–3; Strong advertisement, *Yankee Notions* 1 (February 1852): 39.

59. *Strong's Annual Valentine Advertiser*, 2.

60. Situating Esther Howland within this listing of firms should serve as a corrective to the fable that she somehow invented the American valentine and dominated the American market. Hers was certainly a leading enterprise, but stories about her role in introducing valentines are indicative of the ongoing commercial desire to point to a woman as the sponsor or originator of new holiday customs. Stories about Howland help "feminize" valentines and "engender" the impression that "feminine" sentimentality lies at their foundation, and thus lessen the "taint" of commercial (and male) self-interest. See the discussion of the commercial embrace of women as holiday founders in the Mother's Day chapter. For instances of the canard about Howland, see Staff, *Valentine*, 94; "Victorian Valentines," *Victorian Accents* 1 (Spring 1989): 65; and Dianne Watkins, "Esther Howland and the American Valentine," *Antique Review* 18 (February 1992): 33–35.

61. *Boston Daily Evening Transcript*, 13 February 1845, 2; *New-York Tribune*, 14 February 1848, 2; Michael Schudson, *Advertising, the Uneasy Persuasion: Its Dubious Impact on American Society* (New York: Basic Books, 1986), xxi.

62. Broom, "St. Valentine's Day," 149; "Editor's Easy Talk," *Graham's Illustrated Monthly* 50 (February 1857): 161–62; *Philadelphia Public Ledger*, 18 February 1850, 2. The hand-scrawled phrases "St. Valentine's Week" and "St. Valentine's Month" also show up on a number of manuscript valentines from the late 1840s. See valentines, box H3.12, Hallmark Historical Collection. For another indication of how these valentine exchanges spread well beyond the fourteenth, see Calista Billings, diary, 14–20 February 1849, Schlesinger Library Manuscripts, Radcliffe College, Harvard University.

63. *Philadelphia Public Ledger*, 18 February 1850, 2; *Ladies' and Gentlemen's New and Original Valentine Writer*, v.

64. *Ladies' and Gentlemen's New and Original Valentine Writer*, iv; *Philadelphia Public Ledger*, 14 February 1856, 2.

65. *Fisher and Brother's Catalogue* (Philadelphia: Fisher and Brother, n.d.), 30, in box "Card Catalogues and Art Magazines," Hallmark Historical Collection. On the changing gender patterns among store customers, see, for example, Elizabeth A. Perkins, "The Consumer Frontier: Household Consumption in Early Kentucky," *Journal of American History* 78 (1991): 495–96, and William R. Leach, "Transformations in a Culture of Consumption: Women and Department Stores, 1890–1925," *Journal of American History* 71 (1984): 319–42.

66. Sunderland, "Kate's Valentine," 119–21.

67. For an indication of the variety of valentines, see *Strong's Annual Valentine Advertiser*, 3–6; *New York Herald*, 14 February 1855, 1; and *Boston Daily Evening Transcript*, 9 February 1847, 2. For California and exploding valentines specifically, see, respectively, *New-York Tribune*, 12 February 1849, 3, and *Philadelphia Public Ledger*, 13 February 1845, 2.

68. *Boston Daily Evening Transcript*, 17 February 1845, 2; ibid., 10 February 1851, 2; *Strong's Annual Valentine Advertiser*, 5–6; *Boston Daily Evening Transcript*, 12 February 1847, 2.

69. "St. Valentine and Valentines," 105.

70. There are eighteenth-century French examples linking St. Valentine's Day to charivaris in which adulterers were mocked and to bonfires in which effigies of unfaithful valentines were burned, but I have come across nothing like this for St. Valentine's Day in Britain or the United States. See P. Saintyves, "Valentines et valentins: Les rondes d'amour et Cendrillon," *Revue de l'histoire des religions* 81 (1920): 162–63, 165. The literature on European charivaris is extensive. See, for example, Natalie Zemon Davis, *Society and Culture in Early Modern France* (Stanford: Stanford University Press, 1975), 97–123, 302–3. For their North American counterpart, see especially Bryan D. Palmer, "Discordant Music: Charivaris and Whitecapping in Nineteenth-Century North America," *Labour/Le travailleur* 3 (1978): 5–62.

71. *Philadelphia Public Ledger*, 15 February 1848, 2; Elton's advertisement in *Elton's Comic All-My-Nack for 1843* (New York: Elton, 1843), unpaginated; T. W. Strong advertisement in *Yankee Notions* 2 (February 1853): 64; "New Fashion," 73.

72. Both the Hallmark Historical Collection and the Norcross Greeting Card Collection have extensive holdings of comic valentines. Among the best specialized collections of caricature valentines from the mid–nineteenth century, however, is that of the Library Company of Philadelphia. It has about 650 comic valentines from ca. 1845–70, organized alphabetically by title or verse.

73. Valentines, box 21B, series 2, Norcross Greeting Card Collection.

74. "Scolding Wife," valentines, Library Company of Philadelphia; *New-York Tribune*, 14 February 1856, 1.

75. "You Ugly, Cross and Wrinkled Shrew," valentines, Library Company of Philadelphia.

76. "Corkscrew Tongue," ibid.

77. "Among the Women Who in History," ibid.

78. Emerson, *Essays: Second Series*, 94.

79. C. M. Kirkland, *A Book for the Home Circle* (New York: Scribner, 1853), 90–91.

80. "St. Valentine and Valentines," 105.

81. E. H. Hudson, "St. Valentine's Day," *Argosy* 25 (February 1878): 114; Richard Le Gallienne, *Good Bishop Valentine: A Prose Fancy* (New York: Village Press, 1913), 10; *New-York Tribune*, 14 February 1848, 2; *Christian Recorder*, 20 February 1869, 22; *New York Herald*, 14 February 1855, 1. See also *New York Times*, 15 February 1860, 4. While the genre of comic greetings never went out of style completely, by the 1880s and 1890s many of its coarser edges had been smoothed down. Louis Prang, the leading American publisher of holiday greetings in the late nineteenth century, played a large part in this shift: He always emphasized the high taste and quality of his products and eschewed the popular, transgressive edge of his predecessors. On Prang, see Luna Frances Lambert, "The Seasonal Trade: Gift Cards and Chromolithography in America, 1874–1910" (Ph.D. diss., George Washington University, 1980); Katharine Morrison McClinton, *The Chromolithographs of Louis Prang* (New York: Potter, 1973); and Peter C. Marzio, *The Democratic Art: Pictures for a Nineteenth-Century America, Chromolithography, 1840–1900* (Boston: Godine, 1979).

82. *The Letters of Emily Dickinson*, ed. Thomas H. Johnson (Cambridge, Mass.: Harvard University Press, Belknap Press, 1958), 1:63. Despite the "frowning brow" of Lyon and the other teachers, Dickinson reported that the young women had sneaked about 150 valentines into the post. The next year she said the missives were so plentiful that they had "flown around like, snowflakes." See 1:63, 76.

83. Richard Le Gallienne, introduction to Bliss, *In Praise of Bishop Valentine*, 2–3; Le Gallienne, *Good Bishop Valentine*, 4–5; *Boston Daily Evening Transcript*, 13 February 1845, 2. Perhaps the coup de grace to St. Valentine's religious significance came in 1969, when he was dropped from Rome's liturgical calendar. Saints Cyril and Methodius alone are lifted up for commemoration on 14 February. See Kelly, *Chaucer*, 47 n. 6.

84. *Boston Daily Evening Transcript*, 13 February 1845, 2; *New-York Tribune*, 14 February 1852, 5; Karen Halttunen, *Confidence Men and Painted Women: A Study of Middle-Class Culture in America, 1830–1870* (New Haven: Yale University Press, 1982), xvi. On the crucial issues of artifice and authenticity, see also Miles Orvell, *The Real Thing: Imitation and Authenticity in American Culture, 1880–1940* (Chapel Hill: University of North Carolina Press, 1989).

85. *Philadelphia Public Ledger*, 15 February 1848, 2.

86. "New Fashion," 73; "Cupid's Manufactory," *All the Year Round*, 20 February 1864, 36–40. On the perception in the 1880s and 1890s that Christmas gifts were being "contaminated" through mass production, see Waits, *Modern Christmas in America*, 18–21.

87. *New-York Tribune*, 15 February 1847, 3; "St. Valentine," *Harbinger*, 27 February 1847, 179; Helen Philbrook Patten, *The Year's Festivals* (Boston: Page, 1903), 68, 76, 90–92; *New-York Tribune*, 13 February 1843, 2.

88. Charles Lamb, "Valentine's Day: A Homily for the Fourteenth of February," from *Essays of Elia*, reprinted in *The Republic of Letters: Republication of Standard Literature* 3 (1835): 88.

89. William Mactier, diary, 1847–73, 14 February 1847, Rare Books and Manuscripts, Princeton University, Firestone Library, Princeton, N.J.; Sophia Root to (un-

named) sister, 21 February 1861, box J4.14, Hallmark Historical Collection. The actual valentine and envelope are preserved with the letter.

90. "St. Valentine and Valentines," 105; *Philadelphia Public Ledger*, 13 February 1847, 2. See, for example, Victorian Albums, L1.1, .7, .16, .19, .20, .34, Hallmark Historical Collection. See also the valentine scrapbook in box 7, series 2, Norcross Greeting Card Collection, and *Dick's Original Album Verses and Acrostics* (New York: Dick and Fitzgerald, 1879), 114–33. Most of the albums in the Hallmark Historical Collection come from the decades 1870 to 1900, though a few move back into the period from 1840 to 1870. Obviously all the valentines now in modern collections were saved in one way or another. It is clear that a substantial number in current holdings have been removed from albums; this is evident from glue and paper marks on the reverse side of many of them.

91. For elaborations of this association of women, cards, gift giving, and domesticity in subsequent celebrations, see Ryan, *Women in Public*, 37–51; Gray, *Holidays*; Waits, *Modern Christmas*, 80–86; and Di Leonardo, "Female World of Cards and Holidays."

92. Lamb, "Valentine's Day," 89.

93. Mary Moore, "Saint Valentine's Day," *Godey's Lady's Book and Magazine* 62 (February 1861): 119; valentines, box 28, series 2, Norcross Greeting Card Collection; T. W. Strong handbill, "Valentines! Leap Year Valentines!" 1848, greeting cards, Bella C. Landauer Collection of Business and Advertising Art, New-York Historical Society; *New-York Daily Tribune*, 14 February 1856, 1; ibid., 14 February 1852, 5.

94. *Richmond Dispatch*, 13 February 1854, 2; *Philadelphia Public Ledger*, 13 February 1856, 2.

95. *Letters of Emily Dickinson*, 1:63, 76.

96. For these pen names and the valentine to Ella, see valentines, boxes H3.12, H2.3, Hallmark Historical Collection.

97. *Strong's Annual Valentine Advertiser*, 2.

98. Gilman to sister, 28 February 1842.

99. Clifford Geertz, *The Interpretation of Cultures* (New York: Basic Books, 1973), 5–7, 412–53.

100. On this dimension of valentines and for visual examples of this "animated" quality, see Buday, *History*, 163–85.

101. Billings, diary, 17 February 1849, 20 February 1849. On the increasing legitimation of "polite hypocrisy" and masking in the middle-class culture of the 1850s, see Halttunen, *Confidence Men*, 153–90, quotation on 166.

102. *Philadelphia Public Ledger*, 13 February 1850, 2; *Boston Daily Evening Transcript*, 11 February 1853, 3; *Philadelphia Public Ledger*, 13 February 1850, 2.

103. "St. Valentine," *Confectioners' Journal* 18 (February 1892): 63; "Valentine's Day," ibid., 65.

104. "St. Valentine's Day," *Confectioners' Journal* 20 (February 1894): 70; "Make Candy Your Valentine," ibid., 49 (February 1923): 103.

105. "Sweets to the Sweet: The Confectioners Prepare for St. Valentine's Day," *Confectioners' Journal* 21 (February 1895): 61; Boorstin, *Americans*, 434–47.

106. George E. Milner, "How the Greeting Card Retailer Can Help Himself," *Greeting Card* 1 (May 1929): 5–6; "Building a Great Industry," ibid., (July 1929): 2; "Look for These Sales Helps," ibid., (September 1929): 14–15. The press release on "Trends" is

from the Greeting Card Association, Washington, D.C. On the development of the greeting-card industry, especially Louis Prang's company, see Lambert, "Seasonal Trade."

107. Joyce C. Hall (with Curtiss Anderson), *When You Care Enough* (Kansas City: Hallmark Cards, 1979), 4–17, 25. On Hall, see also Ellen Stern, *The Very Best from Hallmark: Greeting Cards through the Years* (New York: Harry N. Abrams, 1988), and *A Centennial Tribute to the Memory of Joyce C. Hall* (Kansas City: Hallmark Cards, [1991]).

108. Hall, *When You Care Enough*, 14, 26, 31–33, 38–39, 45, 54–55, 75, 92. For the current statistics, see William M. Stern, "Loyal to a Fault," *Forbes*, 14 March 1994, 58–59. In the latter part of Hall's memoirs, the insouciant images of the fluid marketplace of his youth fade into nostalgic local color before the seemingly inevitable progress of corporate empire—fine-tuned market surveys, improved display fixtures that set the industry standard, attentive advertising agencies, sparkling distribution centers, increasingly diversified product lines, computerized manufacturing plants, and sapient awareness of market segmentation, as well as keen commercial sponsorship of the arts.

109. *My Hallmark Date Book* (n.p.: Hall Brothers, 1948), in "Stationery Scrapbooks," Bella C. Landauer Collection; Hall, *When You Care Enough*, 94.

110. "1992 Valentine's Day Card Facts," news release, Hallmark Cards, Inc., December 1991; *Newark Star-Ledger*, 13 February 1990, sect. 1, 3; Judith Waldrop, "Romantic Gestures," *American Demographics* 14 (February 1992): 4.

111. See Breen, "Baubles of Britain," and Breen, "Empire of Goods."

112. *Boston Daily Evening Transcript*, 13 February 1845, 2; Chandler, "St. Valentine's Day," 110.

113. See Davis, "Making Night Hideous," 195–98; Ryan, *Women in Public*, 37–39, 50–51; and Hybertsen, "Return of Chaos," 95–100, 132–39.

114. Quoted in Elizabeth Hough Sechrist, *Red Letter Days: A Book of Holiday Customs* (Philadelphia: Macrae-Smith, 1940), 52–53.

NOTES TO CHAPTER THREE

1. The essay was reprinted a century later as a small volume of its own. See Leigh Hunt, *The Inexhaustibility of the Subject of Christmas: A Holiday Dissertation* (New York: William Bradford, 1937), 7–10.

2. *Philadelphia Public Ledger*, 25 December 1855, 2. A good example of this cultural and ethnic diversity in the American Christmas can be garnered from Elizabeth Silverthorne's regional study, *Christmas in Texas* (College Station: Texas A & M University Press, 1990). If a bit long on recipes and short on analysis, Silverthorne's book helpfully suggests the kaleidoscopic dimensions of Christmas in the United States.

3. Hunt's list does include the phrase "about cards?" but this should not be taken to mean Christmas cards, which would be anachronistic. He probably refers to calling cards for visits on New Year's Day; the phrase appears in proximity to New Year's in the list. Also, some of these items—such as reindeer and stockings—had begun to make their appearance in the United States before 1837 (most famously in Clement Moore's "Night before Christmas"), but they were not mentioned in Hunt's list. For reflections on Hunt's list in the English context, see Pimlott, *Englishman's Christmas*, 183.

4. There are a number of helpful secondary works that examine the nineteenth-

century transformation of Christmas. See Barnett, *American Christmas*; J. M. Golby and A. W. Purdue, *The Making of the Modern Christmas* (Athens: University of Georgia Press, 1986); Pimlott, *Englishman's Christmas*, 77–96; and Weightman and Humphries, *Christmas Past*. Of these books, only Barnett's volume focuses on the American Christmas; the others are concerned primarily with England, though they remain helpful texts for the middle-class transmutation of Christmas. Waits, *Modern Christmas in America*, concentrates on Christmas advertisements in mass periodicals in the period from 1900 to 1940; it is of limited help for the nineteenth century. Also suggestive on the middle-class domestication and annexation of Christmas are Stephen Nissenbaum, "The Month before 'The Night before Christmas,'" in *Humanists at Work: Disciplinary Perspectives and Personal Reflections* (Chicago: Office of Publications, University of Illinois at Chicago, 1989), 43–78, and Bushaway, *By Rite*, 264–74. For a recent historical and literary anthology, see Philip Reed Rulon, ed., *Keeping Christmas: The Celebration of an American Holiday* (Hamden, Conn.: Archon Books, 1990). For a recent collection of anthropological essays that puts contemporary Christmas observances in global perspective, see Daniel Miller, ed., *Unwrapping Christmas* (Oxford: Clarendon Press, 1993).

5. *The Virginia Almanack for the Year of Our Lord 1765* (Williamsburg: Joseph Royle, 1765), December page. For a full documentary account of such sources, see Mary R. M. Goodwin, ed., "Christmas in Colonial Virginia," 1955, Early American History Research Reports, no. 13, Colonial Williamsburg Foundation.

6. *The Virginia Almanack for the Year of Our Lord 1766* (Williamsburg: Joseph Royle, 1766), December page; *The Virginia Almanack for the Year of Our Lord 1767* (Williamsburg: Joseph Royle, 1767), December page.

7. *New-York Journal*, 2 January 1771, 239.

8. This account of New Year's festivities in New York in the 1820s was written by Gabriel Furman about 1830; the manuscript was edited and published as Gabriel Furman, "Winter Amusements in New York in the Early Nineteenth Century," *New-York Historical Society Quarterly* 23 (1939): 3–18, with quotations on 16–17. For secondary work on these carnivalesque festivities, see especially Davis, "Making Night Hideous," 185–99, and Davis, *Parades and Power*. See also Alfred L. Shoemaker, *Christmas in Pennsylvania: A Folk-Cultural Study* (Kutztown: Pennsylvania Folklore Society, 1959), and Genovese, *Roll, Jordan, Roll*, 573–84. For an example of maskers forcing their way into private homes, see H. E. Scudder, *Recollections of Samuel Breck with Passages from his Note-Books (1771–1862)* (Philadelphia: Porter and Coates, 1877), 35–36.

9. Furman, "Winter Amusements," 16–17.

10. Ryan, *Women in Public*, 29–30; "New Year's Day in New-York," *Hesperian* 2 (January 1839): 223–24; *New York Evening Post*, 2 January 1830, 2. See also "The Holidays," *Brother Jonathan*, 8 January 1842, 44, and "New-Year's Calls," *Broadway Journal*, 4 January 1845, 13–14. On calling cards for New Year's visits, see Buday, *History*, 16, 28–29, 43, 105. On the themes of domestication and the decline of wassailing on Christmas Eve, see Nissenbaum, "Month before 'The Night before Christmas,'" 43–78.

11. Bourne, *Antiquitates Vulgares*, 142–50; Buday, *History*, 16–19.

12. On this and other New Year's gifts, see William Sandys, *Christmastide: Its History, Festivities, and Carols* (London: Smith, [1854]), 37–42, 59–60, 99–101, 110–11, quotations on 91 and 101. See also A. F. Pollard, "New Year's Day and Leap Year in English History," *English Historical Review* 55 (1940): 182–84.

13. Excerpt from the *Monthly Miscellany* for December 1692, quoted in John Brand and W. Carew Hazlitt, comps., *Popular Antiquities of Great Britain* (London: John Russell Smith, 1870), 1:9.

14. Bourne, *Antiquitates Vulgares*, 142–45. See also Brand and Hazlitt, *Popular Antiquities*, 6–12, and Wright and Lones, *British Calendar Customs*, 2:24–28.

15. For such proverbial uses, see *South Carolina Gazette*, 28 December 1747–6 January 1748, 1; *Connecticut Courant*, 2 January 1792, 1; "Sermon LIX. A New Year's Gift," 1 January 1760, in Samuel Davies, *Sermons* (Philadelphia: Presbyterian Board of Publication, 1864), 3:52–72; Alexander Proudfit, *An Address to the Rising Generation as a New Year's Gift, for January 1, 1804* (Salem, N.Y.: Henry Dodd, 1804); and John Dunlap, *Short Addresses to Children, Youth, and Those Advanced to Old Age, as a New Year's Gift for January, First, 1805* (Cambridge, N.Y.: Tennery and Stock, [1805]).

16. *New York Evening Post*, 1 January 1803, 2. On these customs, see also Buday, *History*, 20–21, 25–26.

17. *The News-boy's Christmas and New-Year's Verses Humbly Address'd to the Gentlemen and Ladies to whom He Carries the Boston Evening-Post* (Boston: T. and J. Fleet, 1764), unpaginated broadside. For one more carrier address among hundreds, see *The New-Year's Verses of the Printer's Lad who Carries about the Pennsylvania Journal to the Customers Thereof, January 1, 1746* (Philadelphia: n.p., 1746). The anthropologist Annette Weiner puts the hierarchic dimensions of gift exchange in neatly concise form: "What motivates reciprocity is its reverse—the desire to keep something back from the pressures of give and take." See Annette B. Weiner, *Inalienable Possessions: The Paradox of Keeping-While-Giving* (Berkeley and Los Angeles: University of California Press, 1992), 43.

18. *New-York Journal; or, General Advertiser*, 27 December 1770, 235; 2 January 1771, 240. On late-eighteenth-century patterns of consumption and marketing, see especially McKendrick, Brewer, and Plumb, *Birth of a Consumer Society*.

19. *Philadelphia Public Ledger*, 21 December 1839, 3; *New York Evening Post*, 30 December 1816, 3; ibid., 31 December 1816, 3. For the promotion of the elegance and gentility of New Year's gifts, see also *Albany Argus*, 27 December 1814, 3.

20. "New Year's Day in France," *Godey's Magazine and Lady's Book* 42 (January 1851): frontispiece; Francis J. Grund, "Christmas and New Year's in France and Germany," ibid., 36 (January 1848): 7–8; "New Year's Gifts," ibid., 50 (January 1855): 90; "New Year's Day in France," *Album and Ladies' Weekly Gazette*, 19 July 1826, 3.

21. *Virginia Gazette*, 22–29 December 1738, 4. This kind of holiday advertisement remained quite rare in colonial newspapers. For example, microfilm runs of the *Virginia Gazette* for 1736 to 1751, the *South Carolina Gazette* for 1732 to 1763, and the *New York Evening Post* for 1744 to 1752 have been checked, and this process turned up no additional holiday advertisements.

22. For instances of advertisements for religious gifts for New Year's, see *Commercial Advertiser* (New York), 23 December 1820, 3; *New York Evening Post*, 23 December 1813, 3; ibid., 27 December 1813, 3; ibid., 31 December 1816, 3; and ibid., 22 December 1830, 1. For early examples of religious books as New Year's gifts, see Richard Standfast, *A New-Year's-Gift for Fainting Souls; or, A Little Handful of Cordial Comforts*, 7th ed. (Boston: S. Kneeland and T. Green, 1733); Aaron Kinne, *A New-Year's Gift, Presented Especially to the Young People in the First Society of Groton* (New London: T. Green, 1788); and *A New Year's Gift, Written a Few Years Ago by a Young Woman in*

England, and Presented to Her Nieces and Nephews, and Now Re-published (Concord, N.H.: Hough and Russell, 1792).

23. *Pennsylvania Journal and Weekly Advertiser*, 3 January 1784, 1. See also ibid., 31 December 1783, 3; ibid., 7 January 1784, 1; and ibid., 10 January 1784, 1. For an even earlier example of English children's books, such as *Nurse Truelove's Christmas Box and New Year's Gift*, advertised as holiday gifts on the American side of the Atlantic, see *New-York Journal, or General Advertiser*, 18 December 1766, 1, and ibid., 24 December 1766, 4. For an American edition of this volume of genteel advice, see *Nurse Truelove's New-Year's Gift; or, The Book of Books for Children* (Worcester, Mass.: Isaiah Thomas, 1786). For an early holiday broadside for children, see *A New Year's Gift for Children, Delightful and Entertaining Stories for Little Masters and Misses* (Boston: Fowle, [1754]).

24. For toys, see, for example, *Albany Argus*, 29 December 1818, 3, and ibid., 1 January 1819, 3.

25. For advertisements or articles featuring books and annuals, see, for example, *Harrisburg Chronicle*, 29 December 1831, 2; ibid., 5 January 1832, 2; *New York Evening Post*, 24 December 1833, 3; ibid., 23 December 1842, 1; ibid., 30 December 1842, 2; and *Philadelphia Public Ledger*, 23 December 1842, 1. For secondary literature on the gift books, see Ralph Thompson, *American Literary Annuals and Gift Books, 1825–1865* (New York: H. W. Wilson, 1936); Edwin Wolf II, *From Gothic Windows to Peacocks: American Embossed Leather Bindings, 1825–1855* (Philadelphia: Library Company, 1990); and Bushman, *Refinement of America*, 283–84.

26. See, for example, *New York Evening Post*, 4 January 1819, 3; ibid., 27 December 1819, 3; ibid., 23 December 1824, 3; and *Philadelphia Public Ledger*, 24 December 1839, 3. On festive and commercial uses of "gigantism," see Roger D. Abrahams, "The Language of Festivals: Celebrating the Economy," in *Celebration: Studies in Festivity and Ritual*, ed. Victor Turner (Washington, D.C.: Smithsonian Institution Press, 1982), 165–66, 171.

27. Mrs. William W. Todd, diary, 1 January 1846, manuscripts, New-York Historical Society; Frances Quick, diary, 31 December 1854, Schlesinger Library, Radcliffe College, Harvard University; Kinne, *New-Year's Gift*, 7; *A New Year's Gift: Pious Resolutions, Earnestly Recommended for the Consideration of All Who Believe Themselves Friendly to Christianity* (New York: n.p., 1809), unpaginated broadside. For other examples of these devout resolutions "to do something for Christ" in the coming year, see Mary Harris Lester, diary, 1 January 1848, manuscripts, New-York Historical Society, and "New-Year," *Sunday School Advocate*, 5 January 1847, 52. For the transition to more-secular resolutions, see, for example, "Good Resolutions," *Chambers's Journal*, 20 December 1879, 801–2; "New Year's Resolutions," *Independent*, 3 January 1907, 48–50; and Luther H. Gulick, "Health Resolutions—Good and Bad," *World's Work* 15 (January 1908): 9797–9800.

28. For the Puritan critique, see Samuel Mather, *A Testimony from the Scripture* (Cambridge: n.p., [1672]), 58, and Increase Mather, *A Testimony against Several Prophane and Superstitious Customs, Now Practised by Some in New-England, the Evil Whereof Is Evinced from the Holy Scriptures, and from the Writings both of Ancient and Modern Divines* (London: n.p., 1687), 37–38. For an Anglican counterpoint and summary of the debate, see Thomas Warmstry, *The Vindication of the Solemnity of the Nativity of Christ; Showing the Grounds upon which the Observation of that and Other Festivals Is Justified in the Church* (n.p., 1648), 22–25. For the concerns of a republican about New

Year's luxuries, see *New York Evening Post*, 3 January 1837, 2. For the devout resolution, see *A New Year's Gift: Pious Resolutions*, unpaginated broadside.

29. John Wesley, "A Plain Account of the People Called Methodists (1749)," in *The Works of John Wesley: The Methodist Societies: History, Nature, and Design*, ed. Rupert E. Davies (Nashville: Abingdon Press, 1989), 9:264. Of the new forms of Methodist worship, the watch night has been the least studied. It is arguably, however, the innovation of the widest and most lasting influence.

30. *Hymns for the Watch-Night* (London: Conference-Office, 1803), 11–12. For an excellent account of a watch-night service that captures its central religious themes, see Miriam Fletcher, *The Methodist; or, Incidents and Characters from Life in the Baltimore Conference* (New York: Derby and Jackson, 1859), 1:75–84.

31. *Hymns for the Watch-Night*, 2.

32. Frederick E. Maser and Howard T. Maag, eds., *The Journal of Joseph Pilmore, Methodist Itinerant* (Philadelphia: Message Publishing, 1969), 70. See also the revealing account of conflicts centered on a watch-night service in New York in 1777 in Samuel A. Seaman, *Annals of New York Methodism, Being a History of the Methodist Episcopal Church in the City of New York* (New York: Hunt and Eaton, 1892), 75–76. For later cases of conflict between watch-night participants and street rowdies, see *Philadelphia Public Ledger*, 3 January 1853, 2, and ibid., 2 January 1854, 2.

33. These two different types of opponents are portrayed with bold strokes in the ninth hymn in *Hymns for the Watch-Night*, 9–11.

34. George Whitefield, "A Penitent Heart, the Best New Year's Gift," in *Works* (London: Edward and Charles Dilly, 1771–72), 6:A2; *Philadelphia Public Ledger*, 28 December 1842, 2; "New Year's Visitations," *Earnest Christian and Golden Rule* 3 (January 1862): 36. I am indebted to Douglas R. Cullum for alerting me to the continued debates about New Year's among Free Methodists.

35. See, for example, *Philadelphia Public Ledger*, 18 December 1845, 4.

36. See *The Children's Friend, Number III: A New-Year's Present, to the Little Ones from Five to Twelve, Part III* (New York: William B. Gilley, 1821).

37. *Philadelphia Public Ledger*, 1 January 1841, 2. See also ibid., 2 January 1845, 2. On this reform and shrinkage of the holiday season, see especially Pimlott, *Englishman's Christmas*, 77–83.

38. *Philadelphia Public Ledger*, 25 December 1844, 2. For the Christmas tree, see W. H. Furness, "The Christmas Tree and Luther," *Sartain's Union Magazine* 5 (December 1849): 370–74; E. A. Starr, "The Christmas Tree," ibid., 376; Charles J. Peterson, "Christmas and Its Customs," *Peterson's Magazine* 34 (December 1858): 387–89; and "The Christmas Tree," *Godey's Magazine and Lady's Book* 41 (December 1850): frontispiece.

39. Woodworth, "Appendix," 341. For a similar account of the "grand spectacle" of toy and confectionery shops on Christmas Eve in Philadelphia, see *Philadelphia Public Ledger*, 25 December 1840, 2.

40. *New York Evening Post*, 29 December 1827, 2.

41. Ibid., 22 December 1827, 2. For earlier examples of somewhat more modest holiday exhibitions by the museums, see ibid., 21 December 1801, 2; ibid., 27 December 1813, 3; and *Poulson's American Daily Advertiser*, 1 January 1807, 3. For a later example, including Barnum's museum amusements, see *Philadelphia Public Ledger*, 19

December 1850, 3. On early-nineteenth-century museums and the American Museum particularly, see Neil Harris, *Humbug: The Art of P. T. Barnum* (Boston: Little, Brown, 1973), 33–57.

42. *New York Evening Post*, 24 December 1830, 2; ibid., 30 December 1824, 4; *Philadelphia Public Ledger*, 24 December 1839, 3. On *The Tempest* see Stephen Greenblatt, *Marvelous Possessions: The Wonder of the New World* (Chicago: University of Chicago Press, 1991), 121–22.

43. *Philadelphia Public Ledger*, 24 December 1844, 3.

44. *New York Evening Post*, 21 December 1839, 2; *Philadelphia Public Ledger*, 24 December 1845, 2.

45. *New York Evening Post*, 21 December 1860, 1; ibid., 22 December 1860, 1; *New York Times*, 21 December 1865, 8; ibid., 19 December 1869, 4; ibid., 21 December 1878, 4; ibid., 22 December 1881, 4.

46. For the most comprehensive treatment, see Charles W. Jones, *Saint Nicholas of Myra, Bari, and Manhattan: Biography of a Legend* (Chicago: University of Chicago Press, 1978).

47. Jones, *Saint Nicholas*, 340–42; Charles W. Jones, "Knickerbocker Santa Claus," *New-York Historical Society Quarterly* 38 (1954): 370–71.

48. See Jones, *Saint Nicholas*, 355.

49. [James K. Paulding], *The Book of St. Nicholas* (New York: Harper and Brothers, 1836), 216–17. It turns out later in the story, though, that St. Nick is quite a carouser himself.

50. See the Santa Claus poem in *New York Evening Post*, 26 December 1820, 1.

51. *Philadelphia Public Ledger*, 21 December 1842, 2.

52. *New York Evening Post*, 28 December 1815, 2.

53. For these quotations and diverse images, see Jones, *Saint Nicholas*, 351–53; Betsy B. Shirley, "Visions of Santa Claus," in *A Child's Garden of Dreams* (Chadds Ford, Pa.: Brandywine River Museum, 1989), 61–68; and Clarence P. Hornung, ed., *An Old-Fashioned Christmas in Illustration and Decoration* (New York: Dover, 1970).

54. Ernest Godfrey Hoffsten, *A Department Store Santa Claus* (Chicago: Denison, 1918), 7–8; *New York Times*, 28 November 1970, 23.

55. Clement C. Moore, *A Visit from St. Nicholas* (New York: Henry M. Onderdonk, 1848), unpaginated; *New York Evening Post*, 22 December 1830, 3. For an analysis of Santa Claus's link to the consumer culture, see Belk, "Child's Christmas in America." Belk locates Santa Claus's transformation into a god of consumption in the late nineteenth century.

56. Parkinson's claims appeared in an 1840 article written by Joseph R. Chandler, "The First Kriss-Kringle," which was then excerpted in James W. Parkinson, *American Dishes at the Centennial* (Philadelphia: King and Baird, 1874), 18.

57. *Philadelphia Public Ledger*, 21 December 1839, 3; *New York Evening Post*, 22 December 1830, 3.

58. *Philadelphia Public Ledger*, 25 December 1846, 2; ibid., 24 December 1845, 1.

59. Handbill, Graphic Arts Collection, Library Company of Philadelphia, no. 8004.f.8. Based on when Jones was in business by himself at this address on Chestnut Street (rather than with Parkinson) and based on when he used similar phrasing in his newspaper advertising, the handbill can be dated to about 1846. See *Philadelphia Public*

Ledger, 19 December 1846, 3; ibid., 23 December 1846, 1; and ibid., 21 December 1848, 3. On Ingham's sketch of St. Nicholas, see "St. Nicholas, on His New-Year's Eve Excursion, (as Ingham Saw Him,) in the Act of Descending a Chimney," *New-York Mirror*, 2 January 1841, 1. The engraving was also reprinted as a Christmas Eve excursion in *The Great Pictorial Annual Brother Jonathan* for 1845. See Hornung, *Old-Fashioned Christmas*, 29. On the shift to the theatrics of commodity exchange, see Leach, "Strategists," 106–7.

60. See Thomas Nast St. Hill, ed., *Thomas Nast's Christmas Drawings* (New York: Dover, 1978), and Jones, *Saint Nicholas*, 353–55. Nast is regularly credited with almost single-handedly creating the modern forms of Santa Claus imagery. Obviously his illustrations were important, but one needs to look at the other media—from cards to show windows to children's stories—that had a hand in making the modern Santa Claus.

61. David C. Cook Publishing Company was founded in 1875, but the earliest holiday trade catalogue for the company that I have come across is from 1886. See "David C. Cook's Holiday Annual 1886: Sunday School Supplies and Christmas Sunday School Specialties," Religion, box 2, Warshaw Collection of Business Americana. For more on Cook's holiday supplies, see the Easter chapter below. For another instance of Christmas supplies for the Sunday schools, including Santa Claus–emblazoned candy boxes and Santa Claus disguises, see "Holiday Catalogue of Bibles, Sunday School, and Church Supplies," American Baptist Publication Society, 1904, Warshaw Collection of Business Americana, churches, box 3.

62. See, for example, Harry Harman, *Window and Store Decorating for the Christmas Holidays* (Louisville: n.p., [1890]), and Harry Harman, *Harry Harman's Christmas Pamphlet for Window Displays and Store Decorating* (Louisville: n.p., 1891).

63. See Gray, *Holidays*, 21–26, 33–34, 45.

64. On the innovative importance of trade-card advertising, see Robert Jay, *The Trade Card in Nineteenth-Century America* (Columbia: University of Missouri Press, 1987), 1–3, 61. Jay only briefly mentions holiday trade cards (see 93, 95).

65. J. Lichtenstein and Sons (New York), "Greetings from Santa Claus," 1888, scrapbooks, dry-goods stores, Bella C. Landauer Collection.

66. *Dry Goods Reporter*, 7 December 1901, 19.

67. "The Mystic Spirit of Christmas," *Playthings* 7 (August 1909): 51–52. See also Antonia Fraser, *A History of Toys* (London: Weidenfeld and Nicolson, [1966]), 211, and James L. Fri, "The Business of Christmas Toys," *Current History* 47 (December 1937): 53–56. For one grand Toyland, see Sidney J. Rockwell's description of Macy's "Christmas Toy Department De Luxe" for 1911 in "The Christmas Campaign, III," *Playthings* 9 (November 1911): 29–36. For other reflections on the use of Santa Claus in the department store, see *Dry Goods Economist*, 7 December 1895, 57; ibid., 1 November 1902, 13; and ibid., 7 December 1907, 25.

68. For suggestive comments in the secondary literature on the commercial appropriation of street parades, see Davis, *Parades and Power*, 128–29, 170–73, and Leach, *Land of Desire*, 331–38. For Gimbel's parade, see Robert Strauss, "Sixty Years of History Is Parading By," *Philadelphia Daily News*, 19 November 1979, 33, and *Philadelphia Public Ledger*, 30 November 1928, 6. For Macy's and Hudson's, see Robert Hendrickson, *The Grand Emporiums: The Illustrated History of America's Great Department Stores* (New York: Stein and Day, 1978), 300–301. For earlier examples of this kind of department-

store use of the streets, see L. Frank Baum, *The Art of Decorating Dry Goods Windows and Interiors* (Chicago: Show Window Publishing, 1900), and *Dry Goods Economist*, 7 December 1907, 25. For another nineteenth-century example, see Ryan, *Women in Public*, 47.

69. See Barnett, *American Christmas*, 34, and Michael Vitz, "Educating Santa: Where They Learn the Golden Rules of the Red Suit," *Philadelphia Inquirer Magazine*, 20 December 1992, 18–24.

70. Robert L. May, *Rudolph the Red-Nosed Reindeer* (n.p.: Montgomery Ward and Co., 1939). In its original form, this complimentary store souvenir is quite rare. I have seen a copy at the Huntington Library in San Marino, Calif. For analysis of the story's themes, especially its ugly-duckling motif, see Barnett, *American Christmas*, 108–14. On the notion of folklore as "folklure" or "fakelore," see Priscilla Denby, "Folklore in the Mass Media," *Folklore Forum* 4 (1971): 113–21; Sullenberger, "Ajax Meets the Jolly Green Giant"; and Dorson, *American Folklore and the Historian*, 3–14.

71. *Advertising World*, 15 November 1899, 1.

72. For holiday trade catalogues, see Lawrence B. Romaine, *A Guide to American Trade Catalogs, 1744–1900* (New York: R. R. Bowker, 1960), 123, 125, 371–72. See also Gimbel Brothers (Philadelphia), *The Gimbel Holiday Book*, 1903, Hagley Museum and Library, Wilmington, Del., and John Wanamaker (Philadelphia), *Wanamaker's Gift Suggestions for the Puzzled Shopper, Christmas 1922*, Hagley Museum and Library, Wilmington, Del.

73. *Dry Goods Economist*, 1 November 1902, 13; Louis G. Quackenbush, "Capturing Christmas Trade," *Advertising World*, 15 November 1904, 1–2.

74. "Getting Christmas Business," *Merchants Record and Show Window* 22 (November 1908): 35; *Philadelphia Public Ledger*, 23 December 1856, 1.

75. Elizabeth Powell, diary, 25–31 December 1856, Bancroft Library, University of California, Berkeley, Calif.

76. Ibid., 25 December 1868, 25 December 1873.

77. Mactier, diary, 24 December 1847; Caroline Dunstan, diary, 23–25 December 1856, 21–25 December 1860, Rare Books and Manuscripts, New York Public Library.

78. Elizabeth W. Merchant, diary, 19 December 1864, 23 December 1864, 12 December 1872, Rare Books and Manuscripts, New York Public Library.

79. Clara Pardee, diary, 15 December 1885, 12–25 December 1893, manuscripts, New-York Historical Society.

80. Ibid., 13 December 1887, 21 December 1893, 11 December 1890, 8 December 1894, 18 December 1895, 11 April 1909, 25 December 1895.

81. Mactier, diary, 24 December 1858; Helen Lansing Grinnell, diary, 24 December 1864, Rare Books and Manuscripts, New York Public Library.

82. Dunstan, diary, 25 December 1857.

83. Merchant, diary, 25 December 1867, 25 December 1885, 25 December 1888.

84. The scholarly literature on the sociology and anthropology of gift exchange is extensive. For studies that especially address holiday gifts in the context of familial relationships, see Theodore Caplow, "Rule Enforcement without Visible Means: Christmas Gift Giving in Middletown," *American Journal of Sociology* 89 (1984): 1306–22; Theodore Caplow, "Christmas Gifts and Kin Networks," *American Sociological Review* 47 (1982): 383–92; and Cheal, *Gift Economy*.

85. Grinnell, diary, 26 December 1860. On the centrality of the Christmas tree in

the refashioned Victorian version of the festival, see Golby and Purdue, *Making of the Modern Christmas*, 61; on the luxuriant ornamentation of the tree, see Gray, *Holidays*, 4–5, 12, 17, 22–53.

86. Pardee, diary, 25 December 1899, 22 December 1938. Her children's Christmas lists are folded up in the back of the volume for 1899.

87. Mactier, diary, 24 December 1847, 21 December 1848.

88. Marguerite Delaware Du Bois, diary, 18 December 1907, 21 December 1907, Rare Books and Manuscripts, New York Public Library.

89. Pardee, diary, 16 December 1885, 6 December 1904, 21 December 1904, 22 December 1906, 21 December 1938. For an analysis of the prevalence of Christmas dissatisfaction based on contemporary observation and a historical survey of periodical literature, especially the *Ladies' Home Journal*, see Susan Camille Samuelson, "Festive Malaise and Festive Participation: A Case Study of Christmas Celebrations in America" (Ph.D. diss., University of Pennsylvania, 1983).

90. Anonymous, diary, 1872–73, 6 December 1873, 10 December 1873, 19 December 1873, manuscripts, New-York Historical Society.

91. Mrs. William W. Todd, diary, 25 December 1858.

92. Elizabeth Schuneman Orr, diary, 24–25 December 1871, 24–25 December 1872, Rare Books and Manuscripts, New York Public Library.

93. Merchant, diary, 21 December 1870, 26 December 1870.

94. Marjorie R. Reynolds, diary, 25 December 1910, manuscripts, New-York Historical Society.

95. Florence Colby Peck, diary, 25 December 1898, Rare Books and Manuscripts, New York Public Library.

96. Grace Eulalie Matthews Ashmore, diary, 25 December 1899, 25 December 1900, 25 December 1901, Rare Books and Manuscripts, New York Public Library; Christopher Lasch, *The Culture of Narcissism* (New York: Norton, 1978), 72; Claude Lévi-Strauss, *The Elementary Structures of Kinship*, trans. James H. Bell, John R. von Sturmer, and Rodney Needham (Boston: Beacon Press, 1969), 56.

97. Ashmore, diary, 25 December 1898, 25 December 1899, 25 December 1900, 25 December 1901.

98. Mary Knowlton, diary, 25 December 1905, Baker Library Manuscripts, Harvard University. Knowlton's diary is in the same volume with the diary of James Whiton, a Boston dry-goods merchant, manuscript no. 761, which covers the years 1843 to 1857.

99. Nellie Wetherbee, diary, 25 December 1860, Bancroft Library, University of California, Berkeley, Calif.

100. "Editor's Easy Chair," *Harper's New Monthly Magazine* 36 (February 1868): 396.

101. On the dance of the secular and the sacred in the commercial culture—"the play between spiritual longing and commodity fetishism"—see Jean-Christophe Agnew, "Times Square: Secularization and Sacralization," in *Inventing Times Square: Commerce and Culture at the Crossroads of the World*, ed. William R. Taylor (New York: Russell Sage, 1991), 2–13, quotation on 11. See also Moore, *Selling God*.

102. *New-York Tribune*, 5 December 1874, 5; "Christmas Scenes: The Doll Window at R. H. Macy & Co.'s," *Frank Leslie's Illustrated Newspaper*, 1 January 1876, 269, 271; *Dry Goods Chronicle*, 7 December 1895, 27. For the evolution of Macy's Christmas promotions, see Ralph M. Hower, *History of Macy's of New York, 1858–1919: Chapters in*

the Evolution of the Department Store (Cambridge, Mass.: Harvard University Press, 1943), 118–19, 169, 275. For various Christmas events in the department stores from the 1890s to the 1960s, see also "Christmas Promotions," case 3, Resseguie Collection, Baker Library, Harvard University.

103. *New York Herald*, 18 November 1894, 1.

104. *Printers' Ink*, 21 December 1898, 34. For other examples of such windows, see George J. Cowan, *Window Backgrounds: A Collection of Drawings and Descriptions of Store Window Backgrounds* (Chicago: Dry Goods Reporter, 1912), 56–59; Baum, *Art of Decorating*, 180; and *Dry Goods Economist*, 1 April 1905, 111.

105. John Wanamaker to an unnamed friend, 27 December 1881, Letterbook, Wanamaker Collection. For a brief overview of Wanamaker's career, see Hendrickson, *Grand Emporiums*, 75–79. For a far more expansive treatment, see Leach, *Land of Desire*, especially xv–xvi, 32–52, 194–215. For samples of Wanamaker's early Christmas promotions and souvenirs, see *Christmas Chimes and New Year Greeting* (1879), box 68, F-15, Wanamaker Collection; "Holiday Life at Wanamaker's" (1891), box 37A, F-11, Wanamaker Collection; and Wanamaker souvenir, "Christmas Eve—Hanging Up the Stockings," ca. 1879, no. 1975.F.7, Graphic Arts Collection, Library Company of Philadelphia.

106. For examples of the carol books, see box 25F, Wanamaker Collection. The Wanamaker message is from an undated carol book, simply called *Christmas Carols*, from ca. 1940. For the elaborate musical world created in Wanamaker's and other department stores, see Linda L. Tyler, "'Commerce and Poetry Hand in Hand': Music in American Department Stores, 1880–1930," *Journal of the American Musicological Society* 45 (1992): 75–120.

107. For store guides and photographs of these Christmas cathedrals, see boxes 11B, F-10, F-18; 12C, F-10; 12D, F-2; 12F, F-13, F-16; 20B, F-14; 24A, F-8; 25E, F-8, F-14; 65, F-9, Wanamaker Collection.

108. Sarah E. Quickel to Wanamaker's, 11 December 1950, box 7A, F-2, Wanamaker Collection; Charles James Hellier to Wanamaker's, 4 December 1950, box 7A, F-2, Wanamaker Collection. Letters of thanks like these apparently survive only for the Christmas celebrations of 1949 and 1950. The formulaic letter of acknowledgment from the company, offered in response to customers' letters, suggests that the store regularly received such notes from patrons. A store publication from 1925 noted: "Many of our friends have written us letters telling of the deep impression made upon them by this glowing presentation of the story and the song of Christmas." See "Splendors of Christmas Symbolism" (1925), box 5, F-9. Unfortunately none of these earlier letters has shown up in the Wanamaker Collection, which is still in the preliminary stages of full cataloguing, and so I have had to rely on the exchanges from 1949 and 1950. The collection contains more than a hundred boxes, plus allied materials such as the photograph albums of store decorator Howard L. Kratz.

109. This gesture was noted in "The Grand Court at Christmas" (1927), box 25E, F-8, Wanamaker Collection.

110. Mary M. Frank to Wanamaker's, 8 December 1950, box 7A, F-2, Wanamaker Collection; Howard L. Kratz to Rodman Wanamaker, 31 August 1926, Kratz Christmas Album, 1926, Wanamaker Collection.

111. Lewis M. Stevens to the editor of the *Evening Bulletin*, December 1949, box 7A, F-4, Wanamaker Collection.

112. Sister M. Franceline to Wanamaker's, 7 December 1950, box 7A, F-2, Wanamaker Collection. On Rich's celebration, see "The Stores Say It with Lights," *Business Week*, 14 December 1957, 118–22. On the Christmas windows of Miller and Rhoads, see Hendrickson, *Grand Emporiums*, 136.

113. See "John Wanamaker's Christmas Show History," box 43D, F-13, Wanamaker Collection.

114. Quotations from Mayor Dennis Lynch in Wayne R. Swanson, *The Christ Child Goes to Court* (Philadelphia: Temple University Press, 1990), 34.

115. Theodore Dreiser, *The Color of a Great City* (New York: Fertig, 1987), 275–83.

116. O. Henry, "The Gift of the Magi," in *The Complete Works of O. Henry* (New York: Doubleday, 1953), 7–11.

117. Ibid.

118. W. R. Rodgers, "White Christmas," in *A Little Treasury of Modern Poetry*, ed. Oscar Williams (New York: Scribner's, 1970), 492–93.

119. I base my interpretation on the original movie version (1947) of this story. The story was also published in book form after the movie's release with some small changes and additions. See Valentine Davies, *Miracle on Thirty-Fourth Street* (New York: Harcourt, Brace, 1947). All quotations are from the original movie version.

120. The presence of R. H. Macy's character in the film is anachronistic. He had died in 1877, and the store had long since passed out of the family's hands.

121. Thomas K. Hervey, *The Book of Christmas* (1837; reprint, London: Warne, 1888), 20–21; "The Devil at Christmas-Tide," *Outlook*, 18 December 1909, 846. The *New York Sun* editorial has been widely reprinted. I quote it from Martin Ebon, *St. Nicholas: Life and Legend* (New York: Harper and Row, 1975), 105–8.

122. "Celebrate Christmas, Not Commercialism." For one news report on the open letter, see *New York Times*, 29 November 1992, 29.

123. *Printers' Ink*, 2 December 1891, 679. For several examples of church fairs and bazaars, among innumerable instances, see *Philadelphia Public Ledger*, 24 December 1840, 2; ibid., 21 December 1842, 2; and ibid., 23 December 1844, 1.

124. For promotions aimed at the Sunday school market, see, for example, *Sunday School Times*, 15 December 1877, 2; *Commercial Advertiser* (New York), 15 December 1871, 3; Wanamaker, "Christmas Chimes," 5; J. and P. B. Myers (New York), "Catalogue of Sunday School Supplies for Christmas 1896," Winterthur Library, Winterthur, Del.; and Art Lithographic Publishing Co. (New York), "Christmas and New Year Cards," 1891, in box "Card Catalogues and Art Magazines," Hallmark Historical Collection.

125. Cotton Mather, *Grace Defended: A Censure on the Ungodliness by which the Glorious Grace of God, Is Too Commonly Abused* (Boston: B. Green, 1712), 19–20.

126. Robert G. Albion and Leonidas Dodson, eds., *Philip Vickers Fithian: Journal, 1775–1776* (Princeton: Princeton University Press, 1934), 149. For the earlier holiday festivities that surrounded Fithian, see Hunter D. Farish, ed., *Journal and Letters of Philip Vickers Fithian, 1773–1774* (Williamsburg: Colonial Williamsburg, 1943), 43–46, 49–55, 59–70.

127. *Virginia Gazette*, 30 December 1773, 1. See also ibid., 14–21 December 1739, 1.

128. George Whitefield, "The Observation of the Birth of Christ, the Duty of all Christians; or the True Way of Keeping Christmas," in *Works*, 5:251–61. The New

England writer's gloss on Whitefield's journal appears as a postscript in George Whitefield, *Christmas Well Kept, and the Twelve Days Well Spent* (Boston: S. Kneeland and T. Green, 1739), 11.

129. Robert Drew Simpson, ed., *American Methodist Pioneer: The Life and Journals of the Rev. Freeborn Garrettson, 1752–1827* (Rutland, Vt.: Academy Books, 1984), 364.

130. Elmer T. Clark, J. Manning Potts, and Jacob S. Payton, eds., *The Journal and Letters of Francis Asbury* (London: Epworth Press, 1958), 1:584, 2:489.

131. William Augustus White, *A Church Pastor's Christmas Present to His People* (n.p., [1842]), 4. For an indication of the churches' continued difficulty in competing with raucous plebeian forms of Christmas celebration, see Ted Ownby, *Subduing Satan: Religion, Recreation, and Manhood in the Rural South, 1865–1920* (Chapel Hill: University of North Carolina Press, 1990), 23, 45–46.

132. Davies, *Sermons*, 3:563–64.

133. Quoted in Katharine Lambert Richards, *How Christmas Came to the Sunday-Schools* (New York: Dodd, Mead, 1934), 134–35.

134. "Christmas Editorial," *Free Methodist*, 19 December 1888, 1. On the Puritan wish to make Christmas a market day, see Cressy, *Bonfires and Bells*, 45–48.

135. Mactier, diary, 25 December 1859, 25 December 1861, 15 April 1870; "Holidays," *North American Review*, 344.

136. *Suggestions for Christmas Entertainments, Including Decorations, Entertainment and Gifts* (Chicago: David C. Cook, 1883), 17.

137. "Our Festivals," *Ave Maria*, 21 November 1868, 741. I am indebted to Cecelia Richardson for passing a copy of this article along to me.

138. *New York Times*, 26 December 1877, 1.

139. On the burst of Christmas hymnody, see Richards, *How Christmas Came to the Sunday Schools*, 142–43. I have pulled this list from Richards and from the *United Methodist Hymnal* (Nashville: United Methodist Publishing House, 1989), 196–254.

140. "Books for the Season," *Sunday School Advocate*, 18 December 1849, 44; "Our Gift-Books," ibid., 22 January 1853, 61.

141. Mrs. C. A. Halpert, "Festivals and Presents," *Ladies' Repository* 31 (January–June 1871): 43–46. For another critique of the growing "extravagance" of Christmas and wedding presents, see *Philadelphia Public Ledger*, 22 December 1856, 2.

142. *New York Times*, 24 December 1880, 4; "The Observance of Christmas," *American*, 24 December 1887, 154.

143. "Observance of Christmas"; "Our Commercialized Christmas," *World To-Day* 11 (December 1906): 1230; Margaret Deland, "Save Christmas!" *Harper's Bazaar* 46 (December 1912): 593; Nathaniel C. Fowler, Jr., "The Unchristian Christmas," *Outlook*, 9 January 1909, 67–68. See also R. D. Townsend, "Christmas Insincerities," *Outlook*, 16 December 1893, 1123; Agnes Repplier, "The Oppression of Gifts," *Lippincott's Monthly Magazine* 68 (December 1901): 732–36; Edward Bok, "Are We Fair to Our Children at Christmas?" *Ladies' Home Journal* 20 (December 1902): 18; Edward Bok, "The Value of Limitations," ibid., 22 (December 1904): 18; Edward Bok, "The Christmas that Remains," ibid., 18 (December 1900): 20; [Edward Bok], "Complicating Christmas," ibid., 17 (December 1899): 16; and Avis D. Carlson, "Our Barbaric Christmas: A Protest from the Plagued," *North American Review* 231 (January 1931): 66–71.

144. Harriet Beecher Stowe, "Christmas, or the Good Fairy," in *Earthly Care: A Heavenly Discipline* (Philadelphia: Hazard, 1853), reprinted in Rulon, *Keeping Christmas*, 80;

"Religion and Social Service: The Wasteful 'Spasms' of Christmas," *Literary Digest*, 23 December 1922, 30; "Our Commercialized Christmas," 1230.

145. Washington Gladden, "Santa Claus in the Pulpit," *St. Nicholas* 15 (December 1887): 114–17. The story is also included in Washington Gladden, *Santa Claus on a Lark and Other Christmas Stories* (New York: Century, 1890), 157–78.

146. Edwin Markham, "The Grind behind the Holidays," *Cosmopolitan* 42 (December 1906): 143–50; Edwin Markham, "What Christmas Means to Me," *Delineator* 70 (December 1907): 931. See also Florence Kelley, "The Travesty of Christmas," *Charities*, 5 December 1903, 537–40, and "A Dark Side of Christmas," *World's Work* 13 (December 1906): 8264. For more on Markham, see the chapter on Easter below. For another of Markham's caustic Christmas messages on child labor, see Jesse Sidney Goldstein, "The Life of Edwin Markham" (Ph.D. diss., New York University, 1945), 436–37.

147. Walter Rauschenbusch, "The Church and Social Questions," in Mrs. D. B. Wells et al., *Conservation of National Ideals* (New York: Fleming H. Revell, 1911), 116; "The Christmas Curse," *Century* 91 (December 1915): 312–13; Nelle Swartz, "Commercial Organizations Can Aid the Early Shopping Movement," *American City* 13 (November 1915): 406–7. On shopping early, see also Kelley, "Travesty of Christmas," 540; "An Evil of the Holidays," *Ladies' Home Journal* 13 (December 1895): 20; Rheta Childe Dorr, "Christmas from behind the Counter," *Independent*, 5 December 1907, 1340–47; and "Do Your Shopping Early," *Charities and the Commons*, 19 December 1908, 438–40. For comment in the secondary literature, see Waits, *Modern Christmas in America*, 185–87.

148. *New York Times*, 26 December 1896, 3; George P. Hedley, *A Christian Year* (New York: Macmillan, 1934), 23–24.

149. "The Heathenism of Christmas; A Protest against Santa Claus," *Lutheran Observer*, 21 December 1883, excerpted in Shoemaker, *Christmas in Pennsylvania*, 14–16; "Keeping Santa Claus Harmless," *Sunday School Times*, 16 November 1912, 726; "The Right and Wrong of Santa Claus," ibid., 28 November 1908, 606; "Santa Claus Day, or Christmas?" ibid., 20 November 1909, 600; "The Dangers of Santa Claus," ibid., 27 November 1909, 610; James H. Cotter, *Straws from the Manger; or, Thoughts on Christmastide* (Milwaukee: Diederich-Schaefer, 1917), 38; *New York Times*, 29 December 1889, 16; [Paulding], *Book of St. Nicholas*, 220. For earlier reservations about Santa Claus, see "Santa Claus—Deception and Falsehood," *Sunday School Advocate*, 16 January 1844, 57, and Josie Keen, "A Merry Christmas," ibid., 27 December 1873, 24.

150. "The Joy of Christmas—and Afterward," *Sunday School Times*, 7 December 1912, 775; Charles F. Banning, "What's Wrong with Christmas?" *Church Management* 6 (December 1929): 183.

151. J. Harold Gwynne, *The Gospel of Christmas* (Grand Rapids: William B. Eerdmans, 1938), 23, 36.

152. "Christ in Christmas," *Time*, 12 December 1949, 53; "Trend to Spiritual Theme Grows in Retail Christmas Presentations," *Women's Wear Daily*, 1 December 1954, 16. See also Arthur D. Coleman, *Keeping Christmas Christian* (New York: Greenwich, 1957), especially 92–93, 104, 140–53, 247; Lee Voiles, "Put Christ Back into Christmas," *Family Digest* 10 (November 1954): 1–7; and Adrian Cahill Hoar, "Christmas for Christ," *Ave Maria*, 27 November 1954, 15–17.

153. Alice Collins Hamm, "Putting Christ Back into Christmas," *Catholic Digest* 17 (November 1952): 71–75. For several other examples, see the clippings in "Christmas Promotions," Resseguie Collection.

154. On Alternatives, see *To Celebrate: Reshaping Holidays and Rites of Passage* (Ellenwood, Ga.: Alternatives, 1987), 9, and Russell Chandler, "Groups Offer Alternatives to Christmas Commercialism," *Los Angeles Times*, 24 December 1988, sec. I-A, 1, 4.

155. See especially "What Shall We Do about Santa?" in *Whose Birthday Is It, Anyway?* (Ellenwood, Ga.: Alternatives, 1989), 20–22. A similar view of "the injustice and irony" of Santa Claus rewarding the "goodness" of the affluent and punishing the "naughtiness" of the poor was expressed by Elizabeth Phillips, founder of the Santa Claus Association in Philadelphia in 1904. She sought to remedy this not by dislodging Santa Claus, but by collecting money for Christmas presents for poor children and having them distributed in Santa's name. See Rena Caldwell Lewis, "A New Kind of Santa Claus," *Ladies' Home Journal* 23 (November 1906): 24.

NOTES TO CHAPTER FOUR

1. These and subsequent quotations have been transcribed from the movie itself, which is widely available on videocassette. I have also consulted a copy of the screenplay at the Lilly Library, Indiana University. See also Frank J. Prial, "A Step in Time with Irving Berlin," *New York Times*, 13 April 1974, 27.

2. Philip Roth, *Operation Shylock: A Confession* (New York: Simon and Schuster, 1993), 157.

3. *New York Herald*, 16 April 1881, 5. Relevant secondary literature for consideration of Easter in the United States includes: James H. Barnett, "The Easter Festival: A Study in Cultural Change," *American Sociological Review* 14 (1949): 62–70; Theodore Caplow and Margaret Holmes Williamson, "Decoding Middletown's Easter Bunny: A Study in American Iconography," *Semiotica* 32 (1980): 221–32; Gray, *Holidays*, 54–67; Elizabeth Clarke Kieffer, "Easter Customs of Lancaster County," *Papers of the Lancaster Historical Society* 52 (1948): 49–68; Venetia Newall, *An Egg at Easter: A Folklore Study* (Bloomington: Indiana University Press, 1971); and Alfred L. Shoemaker, *Eastertide in Pennsylvania: A Folk Cultural Study* (Kutztown: Pennsylvania Folklife Society, 1960). Both Barnett and Kieffer include commercialization as a theme within their essays; Shoemaker, "concerned exclusively with folk practices," specifically avoids presenting "the story of the gradual commercialization of the Easter festival" (32). Like Shoemaker, Newall and Gray concentrate on folk belief and custom.

4. "Easter Flowers," *Harper's New Monthly Magazine* 27 (July 1863): 189–94.

5. T. J. Jackson Lears, *No Place of Grace: Antimodernism and the Transformation of American Culture, 1880–1920* (New York: Pantheon, 1981), 183–215; Ernest Geldart, ed., *The Art of Garnishing Churches at Christmas and Other Times: A Manual of Directions* (London: Cox Sons, Buckley, 1882), 12. For a helpful secondary work on church decoration, see Peter F. Anson, *Fashions in Church Furnishings, 1840–1940* (London: Faith Press, 1960). For primary works besides Geldart's, see William A. Barrett, *Flowers and Festivals; or, Directions for the Floral Decoration of Churches* (New York: Pott and Amery, 1868); *Church Decoration, A Practical Manual of Appropriate Ornamentation* (New York: E. P. Dutton, 1875); H. E. D., *A Plea for Easter Joys, for Easter Flowers, and Carols* (New York: C. A. Alvord, 1863); E. W. Godwin, *A Handbook of Floral Decoration for Churches* (London: J. Masters and Son, 1865); and *A Plea for the Use of the Fine Arts in the Decoration of Churches* (New York: John F. Trow, 1857).

6. Edward L. Cutts, *An Essay on the Christmas Decoration of Churches: With an Appendix on the Mode of Decorating Churches for Easter, the School Feast, Harvest Thanksgiving, Confirmation, a Marriage, and a Baptism*, 3d ed. (London: Horace Cox, 1868), 12; Geldart, *Art of Garnishing Churches*, 11.

7. Ernest R. Suffling, *Church Festival Decorations: Being Full Directions for Garnishing Churches for Christmas, Easter, Whitsuntide, and Harvest*, 2d ed. (New York: Charles Scribner's Sons, 1907), 74.

8. "Easter Decorations," *Ladies' Floral Cabinet* 14 (April 1885): 100.

9. Henry Dana Ward, diary, 8 April 1855, 23 March 1856, 12 April 1857, Rare Books and Manuscripts, New York Public Library.

10. On this invasion, see Leach, "Transformations in a Culture of Consumption," 325.

11. Anonymous, diary, 1872–73, 13 April 1873, manuscripts, New-York Historical Society.

12. Sarah Anne Todd, diary, 21 April 1867; Merchant, diary, 25 March 1883, 25 April 1886, 10 April 1887; Mrs. George Richards, diary, 1 April 1888, manuscripts, New-York Historical Society. For the initiative of women in church decoration, see, for example, "How Some Churches Looked Last Easter," *Ladies' Home Journal* 21 (March 1904): 32–33, and Reinhold Niebuhr, *Leaves from the Notebook of a Tamed Cynic* (New York: Meridian Books, 1957), 70.

13. Geldart, *Art of Garnishing Churches*, 12, 44; *New York Sun*, 1 April 1861, 2; *New York Herald*, 13 April 1868, 4; Suffling, *Church Festival Decorations*, 85–86.

14. "Easter Flowers," 190; Suffling, *Church Festival Decorations*, 2. On this domestic and sentimental piety, see Douglas, *Feminization of American Culture*, and Colleen McDannell, *The Christian Home in Victorian America, 1840–1900* (Bloomington: Indiana University Press, 1986).

15. "Easter Flowers," 190. On Phelps's novel and "the new domestic heaven," see Douglas, *Feminization of American Culture*, 214–15, 223–26.

16. Ernest Geldart, *A Manual of Church Decoration and Symbolism Containing Directions and Advice to Those Who Desire Worthily to Deck the Church at the Various Seasons of the Year* (Oxford: A. R. Mowbray, 1899), 17–18; *New York Herald*, 16 April 1881, 5; *New York Sun*, 22 April 1878, 3.

17. Veblen, *Theory of the Leisure Class*, 119, 307–9. On the narrow limits of Veblen's model, see Lears, "Beyond Veblen," 73–97.

18. *New York Herald*, 21 April 1867, 4; ibid., 14 April 1873, 4; Suffling, *Church Festival Decorations*, 32–33; *New York Sun*, 22 April 1878, 3. Here I am playing off Lears's argument in *No Place of Grace* about the antimodernism in Anglo-Catholic aesthetics. As Lears suggests, this antimodernist, medievalist stance often had modernist, therapeutic consequences. This was especially evident in the Victorian elaboration of the art of church decoration.

19. Geldart, *Art of Garnishing Churches*, 12, 19; Leach, "Strategists," 104. Leach's conclusions about this "display aesthetic" are offered in expanded and more critical form in his *Land of Desire*. For some of the earliest show-window manuals, all of which feature holiday materials, see J. H. Wilson Marriott, comp., *Nearly Three Hundred Ways to Dress Show Windows: Also Suggestions and Ideas for Store Decoration* (Baltimore: Show Window Publishing, 1889); Pinckney Epstin, *How to Dress Windows and Write Show Cards* (Pittsburgh: Johnston, 1890); Harman, *Window and Store Decorating*; Harman,

Harry Harman's Christmas Pamphlet; and Frank L. Carr, *The Wide-Awake Window Dresser* (New York: Dry Goods Economist, 1894). For another helpful work in the secondary literature, see Leonard S. Marcus, *The American Store Window* (New York: Whitney Library of Design, 1978).

20. *Dry Goods Chronicle*, 26 March 1898, 19; John Wanamaker (Philadelphia), "Easter, 1893," Dry Goods Scrapbook, Bella Landauer Collection.

21. "News from the Cities," *American Advertiser* 4 (April 1890): unpaginated. For other examples, see [Charles A. Tracy, ed.], *The Art of Decorating Show Windows and Interiors*, 3d ed. (Chicago: Merchants Record, 1906), 199–206, 314–15; Cowan, *Window Backgrounds*, 53–59; Alfred G. Bauer, *The Art of Window Dressing for Grocers* (Chicago: Sprague, Warner, [1902]), 30–32; "Robinson Window," *Greeting Card* 8 (March 1936): 28; "Brought Notable Sales Increase," ibid., 8 (February 1936): 10; "Another Easter Is Not Far Away," ibid., 7; "A Distinctive Window," ibid., 7 (February 1934): 8–13; "Lilies, a Cross, Lighted Candles," ibid., 5 (March 1933): 5; and "The Cross Was Illuminated," ibid., 8.

22. Robert A. Childs, *"The Thoughtful Thinker" on Window-Dressing and Advertising Together with Wholesome Advice for Those in Business and Those about to Start* (Syracuse: United States Window Trimmers' Bureau, [1896]), 21; Douglas, *Feminization of American Culture*, 225.

23. [Tracy], *Art of Decorating*, 315. For Wanamaker's Easter displays, see box 11B, F-10, F-23; box 12D, F-2, Wanamaker Collection. On the paintings of Michael de Munkacsy, see box 55, F-14, and box 63, F-3, Wanamaker Collection. See also Leach, *Land of Desire*, 213–14, 222–23. Leach notes that it was Wanamaker's son Rodman who made the decision to exploit these paintings as store attractions.

24. Baum, *Art of Decorating*, unpaginated introduction, 181, 185. On Baum, see Leach, *Land of Desire*, 55–61.

25. This is R. Laurence Moore's conclusion about the varied blendings of Protestant values with commercial amusements and popular literature in the first half of the nineteenth century. See Moore, "Religion, Secularization, and the Shaping of the Culture Industry in Antebellum America," *American Quarterly* 41 (1989): 236. For the expanded version of his argument, see Moore, *Selling God*.

26. George D. Herron, *The Message of Jesus to Men of Wealth* (New York: Fleming H. Revell, 1891), 29–31; Washington Gladden, *Things New and Old in Discourses of Christian Truth and Life* (Columbus, Ohio: A. H. Smythe, 1883), 260; "The Power of Consecrated Wealth: John Wanamaker—What the Rich Can Do," *Christian Recorder*, 15 March 1877, 4–5; Bakhtin, *Rabelais and His World*, 19, 92. On liberal Protestantism and the consumer ethos, see Susan Curtis, *A Consuming Faith: The Social Gospel and Modern American Culture* (Baltimore: Johns Hopkins University Press, 1991).

27. For the Watts hymn within the context of a Victorian Easter service, see Jennie M. Bingham, *Easter Voices* (New York: Hunt and Eaton, 1891), 2. On the consumer culture as a dreamworld, see Williams, *Dream Worlds*. On the new therapeutic gospel, see especially Lears, "From Salvation to Self-Realization." On the wider absorption of religious symbols into modern advertising, see Marchand, *Advertising the American Dream*, 264–84. On contemporary uses of the cross in fashion, see Amy M. Spindler, "Piety on Parade: Fashion Seeks Inspiration," *New York Times*, 5 September 1993, 1, 34.

28. *New York Herald*, 14 April 1873, 4; ibid., 10 April 1871, 4; *New York Times*, 15 April 1897, 12; ibid., 21 April 1889, 13.

29. Francis X. Weiser, *The Easter Book* (New York: Harcourt, Brace, 1954), 159–61; Brand and Hazlitt, *Popular Antiquities of Great Britain*, 1:93; Wright and Lones, *British Calendar Customs*, 1:101; Shoemaker, *Eastertide*, 24; *New York Herald*, 8 April 1855, 1.

30. *New York Herald*, 14 April 1873, 4; ibid., 14 April 1879, 8.

31. *New York Herald*, 26 April 1886, 8; *New York Times*, 7 April 1890, 2.

32. Hower, *History of Macy's*, 170, 451 n. 37; *New York Sun*, 17 April 1878, 4; ibid., 16 April 1878, 4. It is important to underline that my analysis of Easter's commercialization is confined to the United States. It is likely that merchants in Paris and London, where the growth of a modern consumer culture was somewhat ahead of that in the United States and where Easter traditions were far less encumbered by low-church Protestant sentiments, were significantly in advance of their American counterparts. For a hint of this, see McKendrick, Brewer, and Plumb, *Birth of a Consumer Society*, 74.

33. *Dry Goods Economist*, 24 March 1894, 36, 37; *Dry Goods Chronicle*, 26 March 1898, 19; *Dry Goods Economist*, 18 March 1893, 55.

34. Orr, diary, 9 April 1871.

35. Merchant, diary, 16 April 1881, 21 April 1867; Pardee, diary, 25 March 1883; Reynolds, diary, 7 April 1912; "New York Millinery," *Millinery Trade Review* 7 (April 1882): 56.

36. *New York Herald*, 7 April 1890, 3.

37. Anne O'Hare McCormick, quoted in "The Easter Parade," *Time*, 25 April 1949, 19.

38. Rufus Jarman, "Manhattan's Easter Madness," *Saturday Evening Post*, 9 April 1955, 103.

39. Ibid. On Easter Monday parades and costuming, see Shoemaker, *Eastertide*, 43–45. For the woman's outlandish hat, see *New York Times*, 6 April 1953, 14.

40. On the male domination of nineteenth-century parades and public ceremonies as well as the efforts of women to gain a foothold in these rituals, see Ryan, *Women in Public*, 19–57, quotation on 53, and Davis, *Parades and Power*, 47, 149, 157, 190. Taking vital public roles in street festivity was by no means inherently liberating or subversive, but could instead be a dramatic staging of women's domestic entrapment. See Orsi, *Madonna*, especially 123–26, 213–17.

41. Anna Ben Yûsuf, *The Art of Millinery* (New York: Millinery Trade Publishing, 1909), 227.

42. *New York Herald*, 13 April 1925, 3. For representative accounts of Easter parades in the resorts, see *New York Times*, 16 April 1906, 9; John Steevens, "The Charm of Eastertide at Atlantic City," *Harper's Weekly*, 18 April 1908, 20–22; *New York Times*, 20 April 1908, 3; *New York Herald*, 8 April 1912, 4; and *New York Times*, 22 April 1935, 11. On Coney Island and Atlantic City, see respectively John F. Kasson, *Amusing the Million: Coney Island at the Turn of the Century* (New York: Hill and Wang, 1978), and Charles E. Funnell, *By the Beautiful Sea: The Rise and High Times of That Great American Resort* (New York: Alfred A. Knopf, 1975), especially 46, 89. Barnett noted in 1949 of New York's Easter parade: "The pattern appears to be diffusing as an *American* practice." See Barnett, "Easter Festival," 69.

43. *New York Herald*, 16 April 1881, 9. On the varied folk beliefs and customs associated with the Easter egg that undergirded these commercial experiments, see Newall, *Egg at Easter*. Newall takes note of the development of manufactured eggs and

also discusses the history of using embellished Easter eggs as gifts (261–65, 292–300), though her observations are focused on Europe.

44. *New York Times*, 28 March 1882, 2; Kieffer, "Easter Customs," 56–59; *New York Times*, 28 March 1882, 2.

45. Merchant, diary, 25 March 1883, 4 April 1890; Richards, diary, 4 April 1885, 9 April 1887; Pardee, diary, 6 April 1890, 2 April 1893, 14 April 1895, 2 April 1899.

46. Katharine Hillard, "The Easter Hare," *Atlantic Monthly* 65 (May 1890): 665–69; *New York Times*, 5 April 1896, 32. I am indebted to Bonnie Johanna Gisel for the Hillard reference.

47. On the natural dyes, see Gray, *Holidays*, 58, and Kieffer, "Easter Customs," 60; on the Paas Company, see *New York Times*, 3 April 1955, F7.

48. "How Easter Eggs Are Made by the Thousand," *Scientific American*, 14 April 1906, 308–9.

49. L. Prang and Co., "Prang's Easter Publications," 1891; "Net Trade List: Prang's Satin Art Print Tokens and Hand-Painted Goods for Easter," 1893, box 42, series 2, Norcross Greeting Card Collection. On confectioners' rabbits, see F. C. Cassel advertisement, *Confectioners' Journal* 25 (February 1899): 52, and Dena Kleiman, "Where Chocolate Bunnies Come From," *New York Times*, 22 March 1989, C1, C6. On Easter cards and fashion, see *New York Times*, 5 April 1885, 14, and ibid., 28 March 1882, 2.

50. For these trade cards, see cards, box 10, F-1, Warshaw Collection of Business Americana.

51. For samples of Prang's Easter cards, including the one cited, see box 18, series 2, Norcross Greeting Card Collection. For catalogues of Prang's Easter designs from the early 1880s, see box 42, series 2, Norcross Greeting Card Collection.

52. L. Prang and Co., "Prang's Easter Cards of 1885," box 42, series 2, Norcross Greeting Card Collection. For the specific cards cited, see cards, box 8, F-3; box 10, F-2, Warshaw Collection of Business Americana; and box 18, series 2, Norcross Greeting Card Collection.

53. David C. Cook Publishing Company, "Easter Annual," 1886, Religion, box 6, Warshaw Collection of Business Americana. For other Cook catalogues, see Churches, box 3, Warshaw Collection of Business Americana. The notion of "consumption communities" is developed in Boorstin, *Americans*, part 2. For examples of Easter gifts in late-nineteenth-century Sunday schools, see *New York Times*, 18 April 1892; Kieffer, "Easter Customs," 61; and Shoemaker, *Eastertide*, 38. On Sunday school rewards in general, see Anne M. Boylan, *Sunday School: The Formation of an American Institution, 1790–1880* (New Haven: Yale University Press, 1988), 44–45, 153–60.

54. Box 18, series 2, Norcross Greeting Card Collection; cards, box 10, F-1, Warshaw Collection of Business Americana.

55. "Easter among the Confectioners," *Confectioners' Journal* 23 (May 1897): 54.

56. *New York Times*, 23 April 1946, 25; ibid., 19 April 1930, 9; ibid., 2 April 1956, 14; Raymond Kresensky, "Easter Parade," *Christian Century*, 23 March 1932, 384–85; Dorothy Lee Richardson, "Easter Sunday, Fifth Avenue," ibid., 28 April 1954, 511.

57. Edwin Markham, "The Blight on the Easter Lilies," *Cosmopolitan* 42 (April 1907): 667–68. On Markham, see Louis Filler, *The Unknown Edwin Markham: His Mystery and Its Significance* (Yellow Springs, Ohio: Antioch Press, 1966); George Truman Carl, *Edwin Markham: The Poet for Preachers* (New York: Vantage Press, 1977); and

David G. Downey, *Modern Poets and Christian Teaching: Richard Watson Gilder, Edwin Markham, Edward Rowland Sill* (New York: Eaton and Mains, 1906). Markham's essays on child labor were collected in *Children in Bondage* (New York: Hearst's International, 1914).

58. Markham, "Blight," 670–73; Charlotte Rankin Aiken, *Millinery* (New York: Ronald Press, 1922), ix, 12–13. On the exploitation of immigrant laborers in the artificial-flower industry, see Orsi, *Madonna*, 28.

59. Markham, "Blight," 669.

60. *New York Times*, 28 March 1932, 1; Jarman, "Manhattan's Easter Madness," 104; *New York Times*, 11 April 1966, 4.

61. *New York Times*, 22 March 1932, 23; J. E. Twitchell, "Easter Week," *Homiletic Review* 23 (April 1892): 377.

62. *New York Times*, 6 April 1935, 17; ibid., 8 April 1935, 21; "'Commercialized Easter' Is Assailed," *Literary Digest*, 20 April 1935, 26.

63. *New York Times*, 6 April 1935, 17; ibid., 8 April 1935, 18.

64. *New York Times*, 14 April 1952, 1, 14; "Easter Parade Turns Pro," *Life*, 28 April 1952, 49–50; *New York Times*, 14 April 1952, 28, 26.

65. *New York Times*, 19 April 1952, 8; ibid., 23 April 1952, 21.

66. *New York Times*, 6 April 1953, 28; ibid., 14 April 1960, 32; ibid., 18 April 1960, 1. See also "No More Clowns," *New Yorker*, 4 April 1953, 25–26; *New York Times*, 1 October 1952, 35; ibid., 4 March 1953, 36; and ibid., 19 March 1953, 31.

67. Charles Colson, "Beware of the Easter Bunny," *Christianity Today*, 21 March 1986, 72; *To Celebrate*, 103.

68. *New York Times*, 28 March 1880, 2; "Proper Observance of Easter," *Concert Quarterly* 1 (March 1883): 1; *New York Times*, 18 March 1894, 18; Markham, "Blight," 668; Filler, *Unknown Edwin Markham*, 140.

69. E. S. Martin, "New York's Easter Parade," *Harper's Weekly*, 22 April 1905, 567; William C. Doane, *The Book of Easter* (New York: Macmillan, 1910), vii.

70. Samuel Pickering, Jr., "Easter Sunday: A Reminiscence," *Southwest Review* 70 (1985): 127–29.

NOTES TO CHAPTER FIVE

1. "Mother's Day," *Greeting Card* 3 (May 1931): 2; *Greeting Cards: When and How to Use Them* (New York: Greeting Card Association, 1926), 20; Ernest Dudley Chase, *The Romance of Greeting Cards* (Cambridge, Mass.: Harvard University Press, 1926), 98.

2. Anna Jarvis to James F. Holt, 1 May 1941, Anna Jarvis Papers, West Virginia and Regional History Collection, West Virginia University Library, Morgantown; Jarvis to John McCall, 4 February 1933, ibid.; Jarvis, untitled paper, [1931?], ibid.; Jarvis, "Trade Vandals," [1930?], ibid.; Jarvis to unidentified correspondent, [1923?], ibid.; Jarvis, "Charity Charlatans," [1930?], ibid. The best scholarly treatment of Mother's Day is Kathleen W. Jones, "Mother's Day: The Creation, Promotion, and Meaning of a New Holiday in the Progressive Era," *Texas Studies in Literature and Language* 22 (1980): 175–96. Jones concentrates on the role of the Sunday schools in forwarding Mother's Day (which I agree was important), but also suggests that "business interests" were "slow to capitalize" on it and that "commercial interests did not significantly influence

the sweeping acceptance of the day during the Progressive era" (180). For brief biographical treatments of Anna Jarvis and her mother, respectively, see James P. Johnson, "How Mother Got Her Day," *American Heritage* 30 (1979): 15–21, and James P. Johnson, "Death, Grief, and Motherhood: The Woman Who Inspired Mother's Day," *West Virginia History* 39 (1978): 187–94. Also useful is Howard H. Wolfe's local history of Andrews Methodist Episcopal Church, *Mothers Day and the Mothers Day Church* (Kingsport, Tenn.: Kingsport Press, 1962). For a detailed analysis of an international parallel, see Karin Hausen, "Mothers, Sons, and the Sale of Symbols and Goods: The 'German Mother's Day,' 1923–33," in *Interest and Emotion: Essays on the Study of Family and Kinship*, ed. Hans Medick and David Warren Sabean (Cambridge: Cambridge University Press, 1984), 371–413. Though the German version of the holiday took on distinctive social and political significance in Weimar culture, the German florists directly appropriated their campaign from their American counterparts, who, in effect, had already rehearsed the strategies and slogans that the German trade journals would employ in the 1920s and 1930s.

3. James Reeves to Jarvis, 24 August 1891, Jarvis Papers; Reeves to Anna Jarvis (the elder), 27 August 1891, ibid.; Reeves to Jarvis, 27 August 1891, ibid. Johnson, in "How Mother Got Her Day," indicates that Jarvis did not leave home for Chattanooga, but reluctantly yielded to her mother's pressure to stay in Grafton (16). For evidence to the contrary, see the letter signaling her resignation and departure from the Grafton public school, B. F. Martin to Reeves, 12 September 1891, Jarvis Papers. In the same collection there is also an undated, unsigned biographical note on James Reeves that indicates Jarvis was coming from Reeves's "Chattanooga, Tenn. home" when she "came to Philadelphia." On the whole, I see few signs of the daughter's ambivalence toward her mother that Johnson stresses.

4. Jarvis to Jarvis (the elder), 13 July 1903, Jarvis Papers. For this advertising theme, see, for example, *Florists' Exchange*, 29 April 1916, 1086–87; *American Florist*, 1 May 1920, 787, 789; and *Florists' Review*, 4 May 1922, 32.

5. Jarvis (the elder) to Jarvis, 29 September 1898, Jarvis Papers; Jarvis to Jarvis (the elder), 13 July 1903, ibid; Jarvis, "Mother's Day Work," [1930?], ibid.

6. Anna Jarvis, "Recollections of Anna M. Jarvis," [1905], unpaginated, Jarvis Papers.

7. Ibid.

8. See Wolfe, *Mothers Day*, 232.

9. Jarvis, "Recollections," unpaginated.

10. Ibid.

11. For "O, How Happy Are They Who Their Savior Obey," see William Walker, *The Southern Harmony, and Musical Companion*, ed. Glenn C. Wilcox (Lexington: University of Kentucky Press, 1987), 127. For "Beulah Land," see Ira D. Sankey et al., *Gospel Hymns Nos. 1 to 6 Complete*, ed. H. Wiley Hitchcock (New York: Da Capo Press, 1972), 436. For "Jesus, Lover of My Soul" and "Nearer, My God, to Thee," see *United Methodist Hymnal*, 479, 528.

12. Jarvis, "Recollections," unpaginated.

13. Lillie Maxwell to Jarvis, 11 October 1905, Jarvis Papers; Jarvis, "Recollections," unpaginated.

14. On these activities, see L. L. Loar to Jarvis, 25 March 1907, Jarvis Papers; Loar to Jarvis, 29 June 1907, ibid.; Loar to Jarvis, 8 August 1907, ibid.; and Clay V. Miller to Jarvis, 24 July 1907, ibid.

15. See Marion Lawrance, *Special Days in the Sunday Schools* (New York: Revell, 1916); Jones, "Mother's Day," 181; George Richard Crooks, *Origin and Establishment of Children's Day* (n.p., 1885); Harry S. Henck, "The First Children's Day—1866," *Christian Advocate*, 8 May 1947, 584; "Children's Day," *Christian Recorder*, 10 May 1883, 2; and "Results of Children's Day," ibid., 9 August 1883, 2.

16. Mother's Day program for 1924 in "Circulars, Clippings, etc., Relating to Anna Jarvis, Originator of Mother's Day," Rare Books and Special Collections, Library of Congress, Washington, D.C.; Jarvis, untitled press release, [1930?], Jarvis Papers. See also Daniel A. Poling, "The Name of Woman," *Homiletic Review* 93 (May 1927): 403. On Memorial Day, see W. Lloyd Warner, *The Family of God: A Symbolic Study of Christian Life in America* (New Haven: Yale University Press, 1961), 216–59; Albanese, "Requiem for Memorial Day"; Cherry, "Two American Sacred Ceremonies"; Ryan, *Women in Public*, 49–50; and Gaines M. Foster, *Ghosts of the Confederacy: Defeat, the Lost Cause, and the Emergence of the New South, 1865–1913* (New York: Oxford University Press, 1987), 36–46. See also *Confederate Memorial Day at Charleston, S.C.* (Charleston: William G. Mazyck, 1871), 3–4, 25. The lines of consecration around Memorial Day were drawn with the same juxtaposition of religious solemnity and commercial bustle:

> Hushed be the clamor of the mart;
> Stilled as when stricken peoples pray.

Confederate Memorial Day, 4.

17. See Deborah Pickman Clifford, *Mine Eyes Have Seen the Glory: A Biography of Julia Ward Howe* (Boston: Little, Brown, 1979), 187, 207, and Julia Ward Howe, "How the Fourth of July Should Be Celebrated," *Forum* 15 (July 1893): 574. Though connecting Mother's Day with Howe's proposal has been fairly common in recent years among peace activists and liberal Protestants, the historical connections are at best vague. In such contexts, Howe obviously represents a more usable past than Jarvis.

18. On these activities, see Wolfe, *Mothers Day*, 185–87.

19. Anna Jarvis, "Announcement—Celebration of Mother's Day," in National Education Association of the United States, *Proceedings of the Seventy-Second Annual Meeting* (Washington, D.C.: National Education Association, 1934), 157–58.

20. See *Philadelphia Inquirer*, 20 May 1908, 8.

21. For these endorsements and the effusion of the *Congregationalist*, see the printed brochure "Mother's Day, Second Sunday in May," [1915?], Jarvis Papers.

22. For an assessment of the constellation of social and cultural issues from which Mother's Day drew energy, see Jones, "Mother's Day."

23. "Current Motherhood," *Homiletic Review* 73 (May 1917): 372–73. In fairness, the churches were not uncritical supporters of Jarvis's proposal. The liturgically minded pointed out its occasional direct conflict with the movable feast of Pentecost. Others, wanting a more muscular Christianity, saw the holiday as too effeminate and maudlin, and still others saw the de facto Protestant calendar as already too crowded with special days and appeals. The popularity of the holiday in the churches, however, outstripped these reservations.

24. See, for example, Thomas F. Coakley, "A Catholic Mothers' Day," *America*, 28 April 1934, 59–60, and Thomas F. Coakley, "Make Mothers' Day Catholic," ibid., May 6, 1933, 110–11.

25. See Warner, *Family of God*, 75–79. By some accounts Mother's Day joined Christmas and Easter as one of the three banner days for church attendance among

American Protestants. See, for example, George E. Sweazey, *The Keeper of the Door* (St. Louis: Bethany Press, 1946), 7, and Wolfe, *Mothers Day*, 227.

26. Jarvis to W. C. Murphy, 10 October 1921, Jarvis Papers.

27. See, for example, *American Florist*, 3 May 1913, 823, and *Florists' Exchange*, 2 May 1914, 1110.

28. See, for example, James Myers, "A Litany for Mother's Day," *Christian Advocate*, 3 May 1934, 419; F. W. Peakes, "A Mother's Throne," *Homiletic Review* 89 (May 1925): 403; and Walter Rauschenbusch, "A Prayer for All Mothers," *Homiletic Review* 71 (May 1916): 385–86.

29. *New York Times*, 13 May 1968, 1; ibid., 8 May 1970, 44; ibid., 1 May 1971, 30; ibid., 16 May 1978, 70; "Peace Restored to Mother's Day," *Sojourners* 10 (May 1981): 8.

30. Coakley, "Make Mothers' Day Catholic," 110.

31. *Florists' Review*, 24 April 1913, 11. For other examples of florists' claims to have made the holiday, see *Florists' Exchange*, 3 May 1930, 11; *American Florist*, 30 April 1921, 705; *Florists' Review*, 29 April 1920, 17–18; ibid., 23 April 1914, 13; and ibid., 12 May 1910, 5. Of the three leading florist trade journals, *Florists' Review* was the most aggressive in the commercial promotion of Mother's Day and in claiming it as the trade's own creation; *American Florist* was a close second; *Florists' Exchange* was slightly more restrained. The last's editors, having a fair amount of direct contact with Jarvis, were somewhat more considerate of her views.

32. Roland Green, *A Treatise on the Cultivation of Ornamental Flowers* (Boston: G. Thorburn and Son, 1828), 3–5; Thomas Bridgeman, *The Florists' Guide; Containing Practical Directions for the Cultivation of Annual, Biennial, and Perennial Flowering Plants* (New York: W. Mitchell, 1835), 93–98. See also Joseph Breck, *The Flower-Garden; or, Breck's Book of Flowers* (Boston: John P. Jewet, 1851), 13–16.

33. See Robert Kift and T. Austin Shaw, "The Progress of the Floricultural Press," in *The S.A.F. and O.H. Annual: The Official 1922 Yearbook* (New York: A. T. De La Mare, 1923), 177–78. By the early 1920s, the industry had added six more trade papers: *Southern Florist*; *Horticulture*; *F.T.D. News*; *Progressive Florist*; *Western Florist, Nurseryman, and Seedsman*; and *Weekly Florist*.

34. Peter Henderson, *Practical Floriculture: A Guide to the Successful Cultivation of Florists' Plants, for the Amateur and Professional Florist*, 2d ed. (New York: Judd, 1874), v, 102, 189; ibid., 4th ed. (New York: Judd, 1887), 239. On Henderson, see Alfred Henderson, *Peter Henderson, Gardener-Author-Merchant: A Memoir* (New York: McIlroy and Emmet, 1890).

35. Alfred Henderson, "American Horticulture," in *One Hundred Years of American Commerce*, ed. Chauncey M. Depew (New York: D. O. Haynes, 1895), 1:252.

36. Emerson, *Essays: Second Series*, 93.

37. On the Victorian language of flowers, see Beverly Seaton, "Considering the Lilies: Ruskin's 'Proserpina' and Other Victorian Flower Books," *Victorian Studies* 28 (1985): 255–82, and Sabine Haass, "'Speaking Flowers and Floral Emblems': The Victorian Language of Flowers," in *Word and Visual Imagination: Studies in the Interaction of English Literature and the Visual Arts*, ed. Karl Josef Höltgen, Peter M. Daly, and Wolfgang Lottes (Erlangen, Germany: Universität-Bibliothek Erlangen-Nürnberg, 1988), 241–67. For primary works, see, for example, Catharine H. Waterman, *Flora's Lexicon: An Interpretation of the Language and Sentiment of Flowers* (Boston: Crosby, Nichols, Lee, 1860); Barrett, *Flowers and Festivals*; and Edwin Ruston, *Floral Talks* (New

York: W. N. Swett, 1892). Also helpful are floral periodicals such as *Vick's Monthly Magazine* and *Ladies' Floral Cabinet and Pictorial Home Companion*. For the retailers' booklets, see "Whispers from Flowerdom," 1905; "The Boudoir Language of Flowers," 1885; and "Language of Flowers," [1890?], in Florists, box 1, Warshaw Collection of Business Americana. On the "Say It with Flowers" campaign, see *The S.A.F. and O.H. Annual: The Official 1923 Yearbook* (New York: A. T. De La Mare, 1924), 51–52, and *Weekly Florist*, 12 May 1927, 5–6.

38. Henderson, *Practical Floriculture*, 2d ed., 105–6, 174, 194–95; William Scott, *The Florists' Manual* (Chicago: Florists' Publishing, 1899), 181; Fritz Bahr, *Fritz Bahr's Commercial Floriculture: A Practical Manual for the Retail Grower* (New York: A. T. De La Mare, 1922), 157–80; Robert Kift, *The Retail Flower Shop* (New York: A. T. De La Mare, 1930), 61–67, 205–321; "Flower Day Dates This Year and Next," in *S.A.F. and O.H. Annual*, 116; *American Florist*, 25 April 1914, 725. On the expansion of the Easter market during these years, Kift tellingly comments: "It may seem strange to many but at the time of my branching out into business for myself in Philadelphia, March 1, 1876, there was no gift giving demand for plants or cut flowers at this season except for church decoration, and even this was quite limited" (61).

39. *American Florist*, 3 May 1919, 738. On the widening of the floral market at Mother's Day, see, for example, *Florists' Review*, 12 May 1910, 5–6; ibid., 4 May 1911, 9; ibid., 23 April 1914, 13–15; and *Florists' Exchange*, 3 May 1913, 1086–88. On alarm at the surge of competition in the 1920s, see *Florists' Exchange*, 20 May 1922, 1293; ibid., 17 February 1923, 456–58; ibid., 14 May 1927, 138A; *Southern Florist*, 14 May 1926, 7, 32–36; and Hilmer V. Swenson, "The Problem of Mother's Day," *F.T.D. News* 2 (April 1921): 13–14.

40. *Florists' Review*, 14 May 1908, 4; *American Florist*, 23 May 1908, 894.

41. *American Florist*, 24 April 1915, 738; *Southern Florist*, 1 May 1920, 9.

42. *American Florist*, 3 May 1919, 737; ibid., 3 May 1913, 823; *Southern Florist*, 23 April 1921, 9; *Florists' Review*, 1 May 1919, 17.

43. For poems, see *Florists' Review*, 29 April 1920, 18; ibid., 3 May 1923, 27–29; *Florists' Exchange*, 3 May 1913, 1088; ibid., 26 May 1923, 1515; ibid., 7 May 1921, 1095; and ibid., 3 May 1924, 1371. For windows, see *Florists' Review*, 3 May 1923, 27–29, and Kift, *Retail Flower Shop*, 242–45.

44. On the magazine advertising, see *Florists' Exchange*, 5 May 1917, 1038; ibid., 9 February 1918, 262; ibid., 2 February 1918, 190; ibid., 27 April 1918, 868; *Southern Florist*, 12 May 1917, 5; and *Florists' Review*, 25 April 1918, 7–9. For the theater slides, see *Florists' Review*, 23 April 1914, 16, and *Florists' Exchange*, 18 April 1914, 984.

45. See, for example, *Florists' Review*, 4 May 1922, 32; *Florists' Exchange*, 5 May 1928, 43; and any of the Mother's Day issues of *F.T.D. News*.

46. Marc Williams, *Flowers-by-Wire: The Story of the Florists' Telegraph Delivery Association* (Detroit: Mercury House, 1960), 154.

47. On the importance of repetition, see, for example, *American Florist*, 3 May 1919, 737, and *S.A.F. and O.H. Annual*, 52–53.

48. *Florists' Review*, 28 April 1910, 5. See also ibid., 14 May 1908, 4; ibid., 1 May 1919, 17–18; and *Florists' Exchange*, 3 May 1919, 907.

49. *Florists' Review*, 28 April 1910, 5; ibid., 27 April 1911, 8; *American Florist*, 1 May 1920, 786. See also ibid., 30 April 1921, 705, and *Florists' Exchange*, 29 April 1922, 1099–1101.

50. *Florists' Exchange*, 28 August 1915, 489; ibid., 11 May 1918, 969; *American Florist*, 30 April 1921, 705; *Florists' Review*, 1 May 1919, 18. See also *American Florist*, 4 May 1912, 866; ibid., 26 April 1919, 689; and ibid., 1 May 1920, 786.

51. *Florists' Exchange*, 28 April 1917, 993.

52. On Shaw, see *Florists' Exchange*, 11 June 1921, 1383, and ibid., 25 June 1921, 1472–73. I am thinking here particularly of the retelling of Jarvis's story each year by the New York–based Mother's Day Council as part of its holiday promotions and press releases. The Father's Day Council does the same thing with Sonora Dodd's story (see the section on Father's Day below). I have become especially aware of the promotional uses of scholarly accounts of Jarvis's campaign from a handful of newspaper accounts of my own research. On such promotions involving Grandparents' Day and its founder, see *Grandparents Day and Marian McQuade* (Richmond, W.Va.: West Virginia Press Club, [1982]), 23, 27, 70–71, 98, 118–19. On Patricia Bay Haroski and Bosses' Day, see *Industry Week*, 16 October 1989, 5. On Mary Barrett and Professional Secretaries' Day, see "Secretaries Day Fact Sheet—1992," Hallmark Cards, Inc., Kansas City, Missouri.

53. *Florists' Exchange*, 3 May 1913, 1089; ibid., 3 May 1919, 907; ibid., 13 May 1922, 1210; ibid., 22 May 1920, 1199.

54. *Florists' Exchange*, 20 May 1916, 1275; ibid., 20 May 1916, 1234; *Florists' Review*, 1 May 1919, 17; *Florists' Exchange*, 13 May 1922, 1210; *American Florist*, 22 April 1916, 722.

55. Jarvis, "Charity Charlatans"; Jarvis, "Mother's Day Work"; Jarvis, "Second Sunday in May," [1930?], Jarvis Papers.

56. On these connections, see Wolfe, *Mothers Day*, 195–96, and Jones, "Mother's Day," 177. On Wanamaker's patronage of the holiday, see the Mother's Day file in box 87, F-1, Wanamaker Collection.

57. On her role as "literary and advertising editor" at Fidelity Mutual, see Bette Marsh, "Civic Group to Honor Mother's Day Founder," *Philadelphia Daily News*, 6 May 1949, 4.

58. For evidence of this early cooperation, see *Florists' Exchange*, 2 May 1914, 1110; ibid., 15 May 1915, 1140, 1142; *American Florist*, 6 May 1911, 786; ibid., 4 May 1912, 866; and ibid., 29 April 1916, 769.

59. Jarvis, untitled paper, [1930?], Jarvis Papers; Jarvis to Ben W. Olcott, 15 February 1921, ibid.

60. For early signs of strain, see *Florists' Exchange*, 10 May 1913, 1142; ibid., 1 May 1915, 1032; and *Florists' Review*, 25 April 1912, 9. The final break in 1920 was widely covered in the trade press. See *American Florist*, 15 May 1920, 885–86; *Southern Florist*, 15 May 1920, 3–5; *Horticulture*, 8 May 1920, 372; ibid., 15 May 1920, 386–90; and *Florists' Exchange*, 15 May 1920, 1145. For a look back on the troubled relationship between Jarvis and the trade upon her death, see *Florists' Exchange*, 4 December 1948, 15. Jarvis's "official" Mother's Day program for 1924 carried the abrupt line "Flowers are not used." See "Circulars, Clippings, etc.," and Anna Jarvis, "Scrapbook," Historical Society of Pennsylvania, Philadelphia.

61. *Florists' Review*, 18 May 1922, 39; *American Florist*, 30 April 1921, 705. For the view that controversy was good for publicity, see *Florists' Exchange*, 14 May 1921, 1160; ibid., 27 April 1929, 11; *Horticulture*, 8 May 1920, 372; and *Florists' Review*, 19 May 1921, 29.

62. Jarvis to Howe, 1 November 1934, Jarvis Papers; Jarvis to unidentified correspondent, [1923?], ibid.; Jarvis, "Anti*Mother," [1930?], ibid.

63. Jarvis, "Charity Charlatans"; Jarvis to Clay V. Miller, 6 May 1941, Clay V. Miller Papers, West Virginia and Regional History Collection.

64. *Florists' Exchange*, 4 December 1948, 15; Jarvis, "Second Sunday in May."

65. *Florists' Exchange*, 4 December 1948, 15; Jarvis, "Trade Vandals."

66. Jarvis, "Mother's Day Work." The phrase "commercial grip" is taken from a sympathetic paraphrase of Jarvis's views by J. Edgar Williams, a Quaker, in his *White Carnation and Mother's Day* (Detroit: Northwestern Printing, 1950), 12.

67. Myers, "Litany for Mother's Day," 419. This litany from the 1930s, penned by a leader within the Federal Council of Churches, may have become a familiar liturgical formula for the holiday in mainstream Protestantism. W. Lloyd Warner recorded its use in Newburyport, Mass., in the 1950s. See Warner, *Family of God*, 76–77.

68. Jarvis, "Announcement," 157.

69. *Grafton News*, 8 October 1951, 4. There are also photographs of her Philadelphia home at the International Mother's Day Shrine, Grafton, W.Va.

70. Jarvis, untitled paper, [1930?], Jarvis Papers.

71. See, for example, the Mother's Day program for 1927 in Jarvis, "Scrapbook," 4, and "Mother's Day Programme" for 1909 in Wolfe, *Mothers Day*, 213–16.

72. Laura A. Athearn, "Keeping Mother's Day in the Home," *Christian Advocate*, 7 May 1942, 20–21.

73. *Florists' Review*, 12 May 1921, 32. See also ibid., 19 May 1921, 29; *Florists' Exchange*, 14 May 1921, 1160, 1175; and ibid., 20 May 1922, 1288. These trade reports show that the suggestion was picked up by newspapers in Boston, Denver, and New York.

74. *Florists' Exchange*, 22 May 1920, 1199. For a textbook example of the holiday's maintenance of boundaries around home and motherhood, see Sweazey, *Keeper of the Door*, 13–27. For additional examples of the religious ruing of commercialism, see "Mother's Day," *Homiletic Review* 95 (May 1928): 365; "What Motherhood Means," *Christian Advocate*, 7 May 1953, 588; "A Home or Family Day," *Mennonite*, 28 May 1940, 1; Martin B. Hellriegl, "The Apostolate: Towards a Living Parish," *Worship* 30 (1956): 571; Sweazey, *Keeper of the Door*, 8; Thomas F. Coakley, "How a Parish Can Celebrate Mother's Day," *America*, 26 April 1930, 64; *Florists' Exchange*, 22 May 1920, 1202; and ibid., 20 May 1922, 1287.

75. See Crooks, *Origin and Establishment*, unpaginated; *The New Children's Day Book* (New York: Methodist Book Concern, [1937]), 5–7, 86–87; Jones, "Mother's Day," 181–83; "Children's Day," *Sunday-School Advocate*, 10 June 1876, 147; "Children's Day, June 11, 1893," *Christian Recorder*, 8 June 1893, 7; and C. S. Smith, "To Whom Shall the Children's Day Money Be Sent?" ibid., 24 July 1882, 2.

76. James F. White, *Introduction to Christian Worship* (Nashville: Abingdon, 1980), 61–62.

77. *Florists' Review*, 28 April 1920, 5.

78. See Jesse Halsey, "Suggestions for Mothers' Day," *Homiletic Review* 71 (May 1916): 381–82, and Jones, "Mother's Day," 181.

79. Henck, "First Children's Day," 584.

80. *Florists' Review*, 25 April 1912, 9–11; ibid., 24 April 1913, 11; ibid., 29 April 1920, 18; *Florists' Exchange*, 10 May 1913, 1142; ibid., 17 May 1913, 1186.

81. See, for example, Susan Tracy Rice, comp., *Mothers' Day: Its History, Origin, Celebration, Spirit, and Significance as Related in Prose and Verse* (New York: Dodd, Mead, 1915), 362.

82. Hallmark Mother's Day poster, 1992, Inland Center, San Bernardino, Calif.

83. Statistic from "1992 Mother's Day Section," Mother's Day Council, New York, N.Y.

84. Susan Bergman, "Presents," *North American Review* 277 (March–April 1992): 40.

85. This is her oft-repeated memory of what she told the Reverend Henry Rasmus. See *Spokesman-Review*, 18 June 1950, in the clipping file on Dodd at the Northwest Room, Spokane Public Library. I have reconstructed Dodd's story from early newspaper accounts in the *Spokesman-Review* and from the local clipping files supplied by the Spokane Public Library and the Eastern Washington State Historical Society. I have also had exchanges with her granddaughter Barbara Dodd Hillerman and a niece, Helen Dodd Brown, but no personal papers survive, so one has to rely almost entirely on newspaper accounts (and the snippets of interviews contained in them). For material on her church membership, I am indebted to an information sheet provided to me by the Central United Methodist Church in Spokane. Dodd switched her membership to the First Presbyterian Church in 1941. Two anniversary compilations on the holiday are helpful: Grace Willhoite Hitchcock, comp., *Father's Day Silver Anniversary, 1935* (Spokane: Lighthouse Publishing, 1935), and *Father's Day: 75th Anniversary Commemorative, 1910–1985* (New York: Father's Day Council, [1985]). For a social and economic history of Spokane in these decades, see John Fahey, *The Inland Empire: Unfolding Years, 1879–1929* (Seattle: University of Washington Press, 1986).

86. The petition is reprinted in Hitchcock, *Fathers' Day*, unpaginated.

87. Dodd's granddaughter Barbara Hillerman made particular note of her grandmother's support of the WCTU in conversations with me. In stories that Hillerman's father remembered about his mother, her adamant commitment to temperance was a serious point of contention between mother and son.

88. "This Man Father," in Hitchcock, *Fathers' Day*, unpaginated; Rene Albourne de Pender, "The Father Mountain," in ibid.; *Spokesman-Review*, 18 June 1916, D2.

89. Conrad Bluhm, "Fathers' Day," in Hitchcock, *Fathers' Day*, unpaginated. A somewhat fuller version of Bluhm's holiday message was also reprinted in "Fathers' Day Program," 16 June 1912, Centenary Presbyterian Church, and in local YMCA newsletters in the 1910s, copies of which Barbara Dodd Hillerman provided to me. (His concordance numbers are found in the "Fathers' Day Program.") For early Father's Day messages, see *Spokesman-Review*, 21 June 1915, 6; ibid., 18 June 1917, 2; and ibid., 17 June 1917, D2. For these sermonic themes beyond Spokane, see *New York Times*, 22 June 1925, 18, and ibid., 22 June 1936, 17. For accounts of the wider debates on masculinization, see, for example, Gail Bederman, "'The Women Have Had Charge of the Church Work Long Enough': The Men and Religion Forward Movement of 1911–1912 and the Masculinization of Middle-Class Protestantism," *American Quarterly* 41 (1989): 432–61; Betty A. DeBerg, *Ungodly Women: Gender and the First Wave of American Fundamentalism* (Minneapolis: Fortress Press, 1990), 75–98; and Margaret Lamberts Bendroth, *Fundamentalism and Gender, 1875 to the Present* (New Haven: Yale University Press, 1993).

90. "Fathers' Day Program," unpaginated.

91. I found nothing on Father's Day in the *Spokesman-Review* from 1919 to 1925

and only scattered mention of it between 1926 and 1930. In our conversations Barbara Hillerman has emphasized the independence of her grandmother, her go-getter flair for the dramatic, and her keen desire to make her own mark in the world. Her art studies in Chicago and her design work in California in the 1920s are good indications of this; even with her marriage to a Spokane insurance man, John Bruce Dodd, and even with her one son, she moved with considerable autonomy.

92. *Spokesman-Review*, 17 June 1934, 11B; ibid., 21 June 1937, 6.

93. See, for example, *Spokesman-Review*, 17 June 1939, 6, and ibid., 15 June 1935, 12.

94. *New York Times*, 28 May 1911, 1.

95. *Spokesman-Review*, 17 June 1927, 6; ibid., 16 June 1935, 6; Chase, *Romance of Greeting Cards*, 99; Robert A. Fremont, ed., *Favorite Songs of the Nineties* (New York: Dover Publications, 1973), 79–81.

96. *New York Times*, 14 June 1914, sect. 2, 14.

97. *Spokesman-Review*, 19 June 1938, 4; *New York Times*, 19 June 1938, sect. 4, 2.

98. *New York Times*, 21 June 1931, 21; ibid., 6 June 1925, 14; Chase, *Romance of Greeting Cards*, 102; *New York Times*, 17 June 1928, sect. 2, 1.

99. For the cartoons, see *Spokesman-Review*, 18 June 1911, 1; ibid., 20 June 1915, 1; and ibid., 20 June 1937, 1. For the commentary on Father paying the bills, see *New York Times*, 19 June 1938, sect. 4, 2; ibid., 17 June 1928, sect. 2, 1; and ibid., 19 June 1927, sect. 2, 1.

100. On similar hierarchical negotiations in Christmas gifts, see Waits, *Modern Christmas in America*, 114–16.

101. Jarvis, "Anti*Mother," unpaginated; "Father on Mother's Day," *Christian Advocate*, 10 May 1951, 607; *New York Times*, 17 June 1928, sect. 2, 1; ibid., 19 June 1927, sect. 2, 1.

102. Harris, *Humbug*, especially 61–89; *Spokesman-Review*, 19 June 1927, A4. See also *New York Times*, 16 June 1929, sect. 2, 6.

103. *Spokesman-Review*, 16 June 1938, 2; ibid., 10 June 1934, 3; Theodor W. Adorno, *The Culture Industry: Selected Essays on Mass Culture*, ed. J. M. Bernstein (London: Routledge, 1991), 11. This particular quotation is from *Dialectic of Enlightenment*, which Adorno wrote with Max Horkheimer.

104. On these activities, see *Spokesman-Review*, 20 June 1910, 7; ibid., 20 June 1926, B2; ibid., 11 June 1939, 10A; and ibid., 19 June 1949, 8.

105. See *Spokesman-Review*, 19 June 1910, B5; ibid., 18 June 1911, B5; ibid., 14 June 1929, 2; ibid., 15 June 1929, 2; ibid., 17 June 1931, 2; ibid., 14 June 1933, 10; and ibid., 14 June 1936, 18. The early show window was described from memory by Graham's advertising manager in ibid., 11 June 1939, 10A.

106. On Meek's claim, see *New York Times*, 18 June 1932, 3, and *Spokesman-Review*, 17 June 1973, clipping file, Spokane Public Library.

107. See *Florists' Exchange*, 11 June 1921, 1387; *New York Times*, 5 June 1925, 3; ibid., 16 June 1929, sect. 2, 6; ibid., 18 June 1932, 3; ibid., 25 April 1934, 39; and *Men's Wear*, 22 June 1938, 62. See also "An Appreciation of Father," *Greeting Card* 7 (May 1935): 26–27.

108. On the early Father's Day activities of the Associated Men's Wear Retailers, see *New York Times*, 6 June 1934, 30; ibid., 21 March 1935, 40; ibid., 9 May 1935, 38;

ibid., 30 May 1935, 15; ibid., 19 June 1936, 37; ibid., 9 April 1937, 40; ibid., 19 June 1937, 28; and ibid., 21 June 1937, 12. On the realization of Father's Day as a "second Christmas," see *Father's Day: 75th Anniversary Commemorative*, 56. I am indebted to John Fleckner of the Smithsonian Institution for pointing me to this commemorative volume and to this passage. The Father's Day Council now posits that more than 90 percent of American fathers are recognized in some fashion on the day. This statistic appears in "Father's Day June 16: In the Spirit of Giving," a multipage press release and gift guide put out by the Father's Day Council. It is sent to five thousand newspapers. How such numbers were derived is not indicated; they should obviously be read within their promotional context. For one sampling of holiday marketing surveys, see Judith Waldrop, "Marketing Motherhood," *American Demographics* 12 (May 1990): 4.

109. On the council's organization, allies, and membership, see *New York Times*, 10 June 1938, 39; ibid., 18 June 1938, 17; ibid., 30 March 1938, 38; ibid., 2 April 1938, 20; ibid., 13 April 1938, 40; and ibid., 19 April 1938, 30.

110. On Macy's sports event, see *New York Times*, 5 June 1941, 30; ibid., 10 June 1941, 31; ibid., 15 June 1941, sect. 5, 8; and ibid., 16 June 1941, 19. On the council, see ibid., 19 May 1939, 40; ibid., 26 June 1939, 30; ibid., 10 June 1940, 12; ibid., 21 July 1941, 24; ibid., 18 September 1947, 43; ibid., 15 September 1949, 40; and ibid., 11 June 1950, sect. 3, 1. For a clear sense of this dual mission, see the council's account of its own history and purpose, *Father's Day: 75th Anniversary Commemorative*.

111. I obtained copies of two different press-release packets for 1992 from the Father's Day Council; Dodd's story appears in both. It appears in similar form in *Father's Day: 75th Anniversary Commemorative*, 4–5. On Dodd's view of the council and gift giving, see the files of clippings on Dodd and Father's Day at the Spokane Public Library and Eastern Washington State Historical Society. The Dodd quotations are in the following: Thomas J. Goldthwaite, "Father's Day Spurs Buying," *Spokesman-Review*, 15 June 1968, clipping file, Spokane Public Library; *New York Times*, 18 June 1972, 52; and *Spokane Daily Chronicle*, 13 June 1975, 1. The statistic on sales volume is from *New York Times*, 17 June 1972, 37.

112. For this secular, leisure-centered version of the holiday, see *New York Times*, 22 June 1936, 21; ibid., 18 June 1928, 18; and ibid., 18 June 1932, 3. For this greeting card, see Chase, *Romance of Greeting Cards*, 101.

113. For more on Candy Day and Friendship Day, see Leigh Eric Schmidt, "The Commercialization of the Calendar: American Holidays and the Culture of Consumption, 1870–1930," *Journal of American History* 78 (1991): 913–15, and the epilogue. On the toy industry's claiming of Children's Day in the 1920s, see Miriam Formanek-Brunell, *Made to Play House: Dolls and the Commercialization of American Girlhood, 1830–1930* (New Haven: Yale University Press, 1993), 173–79. For earlier department-store versions of Children's Day, see, for example, Robert W. Twyman, *History of Marshall Field and Co., 1852–1906* (Philadelphia: University of Pennsylvania Press, 1954), 148–49, and *Dry Goods Reporter*, 17 October 1903, 72–73. On the debate about moving Thanksgiving, see Diana Karter Appelbaum, *Thanksgiving: An American Holiday, an American History* (New York: Facts on File Publications, 1984), 234–42.

114. *Advisory Commission on National Commemorative Events* (Washington, D.C.: G.P.O., 1990), 6; E. N. Ferdon, "What Is the Value of Calendar Advertising?" in *Library of Advertising: Show Window Display and Specialty Advertising*, comp. A. P. Johnson (Chi-

cago: Cree Publishing, 1911), 250. The use of calendars for advertising was also evident in some holiday trade cards of the 1870s and 1880s. For indications of the proliferation of promotional days, see Laurence Urdang and Christine N. Donohue, eds., *Holidays and Anniversaries of the World* (Detroit: Gale Research, 1985), and *Chase's Annual Events: Special Days, Weeks, and Months in 1990* (Chicago: Contemporary Books, 1989).

NOTES TO EPILOGUE

1. William S. Walsh, *Curiosities of Popular Customs and of Rites, Ceremonies, Observances, and Miscellaneous Antiquities* (Philadelphia: J. B. Lippincott, 1898), 62; Robert Chambers, *The Book of Days* (1863–64; reprint, London: Chambers, 1886), 1:460–62. On Melville's setting and publishing of *The Confidence-Man* on 1 April, see Jean-Christophe Agnew, *Worlds Apart: The Market and the Theater in Anglo-American Thought, 1550–1750* (Cambridge: Cambridge University Press, 1986), 196, 203, and Herman Melville, *The Writings of Herman Melville*, vol. 10, *The Confidence-Man: His Masquerade* (Evanston: Northwestern University Press and Newberry Library, 1984), 3, 255–56, 316. William Mactier's diary entry for the holiday in 1847 was indicative of the custom's prevalence: "All Fools Day—I am not conscious of having been fooled to day though the effort was made repeatedly to catch me napping." See Mactier, diary, 1847–73, 1 April 1847.

2. The sign "NO TRUST" hangs outside the barber's shop in Melville's *Confidence-Man* (5). For a discussion of its plebeian sources, see David S. Reynolds, *Beneath the American Renaissance: The Subversive Imagination in the Age of Emerson and Melville* (Cambridge, Mass.: Harvard University Press, 1988), 441–42.

3. See Greg Phillips, "Love, and Other Ills," *Princeton Alumni Weekly*, 24 March 1993, 15.

4. *Weekly Florist*, 21 May 1925, 1–2.

5. See *S.A.F. and O.H. Annual*, 59; *Florists' Exchange*, 20 May 1911, 1037; Ernest A. Densch, "Mother's Day Surrounded by Two Lesser Events," *F.T.D. News* 10 (May 1925): 74; and *American Florist*, 29 April 1916, 769.

6. Chase, *Romance of Greeting Cards*, 108–9; Ernest Dudley Chase, *The Greeting Card Industry* (n.p.: Bellman, 1946), 13; Stern, *Very Best from Hallmark*, 9; *Florists' Exchange*, 23 July 1921, 196; ibid., 28 May 1921, 1266; ibid., 25 June 1921, 1472–73.

7. *Confectioners Gazette*, 10 September 1916, 17, 20; *Confectioners Gazette*, 10 October 1916, 17; *Candy*, 1 October 1929, 3; "Can Candy Day Be Put Over?" *Candy Factory* 3 (November 1923): 18–19; "Candy Day Boosts Sales," ibid., 50.

8. V. L. Price, "What Are You Going to Do on Candy Day?" *Candy Factory* 3 (August 1923): 18–19; Price, "Make the Holidays Pay"; V. L. Price, "Making the Holidays Pay," *Candy Factory* 4 (June 1924): 20, 108, 110, 112.

9. George Eastman, *Do We Need Calendar Reform?* (n.p., [1927]), 18–19, 32–33; George Eastman, "The Importance of Calendar Reform to the Business World," *Bulletin of the Pan American Union* 61 (July 1927): 655–66. See also Moses B. Cotsworth, *The Rational Almanac* (York, England: n.p., [1902]), 437–42; Alexander Philip, *The Reform of the Calendar* (London: Kegan Paul, 1914), 107–15; Jerome S. Schwartz, "Adver-Timing," *Journal of Calendar Reform* 11 (first quarter 1941): 30–32; and "Anchoring Easter—Pro and Con," *Nation's Business* 60 (June 1972): 26–28. The ecumenical hope to have a common date for Easter across the Orthodox–Roman Catholic–Protestant

spectrum has long undergirded what Christian support there is for a fixed date. See "A Common Date for Easter?" *Christian Century*, 26 March 1975, 299–300. This ecumenical push for unity clearly plays into the hands of those advocating a fixed date on secular grounds. See Philip H. Pfatteicher, "A Fixed Date for Easter?" *Christian Century*, 22–29 March 1989, 300–301.

10. Hall, *When You Care Enough*, ix, xi, 253, 256.

11. Teresa Watanabe, "Japanese Parade for St. Patrick, Whoever He Was," *Los Angeles Times*, 16 March 1993, H6; Clifford, *Predicament of Culture*, 16–17; Greenblatt, *Marvelous Possessions*, 3–5. On the globalization of Christmas, including its becoming indigenous in Japan, see Miller, *Unwrapping Christmas*, 4–5, 22, 105–33.

12. See the fine discussion of these tensions in Molly O'Neill, "When Holiday Styles Are Generations Apart," *New York Times*, 21 December 1993, sect. A, 1, sect. B, 6.

13. John B. Peaslee, *Trees and Tree-Planting with Exercises and Directions for the Celebration of Arbor Day* (Cincinnati: Ohio State Forestry Association, 1884), 7–8, 13–14, 32–33, 51.

14. Robert W. Furnas, comp., *Arbor Day* (Lincoln, Nebr.: State Journal Co., 1888), 103, 113. See also B. G. Northrop, "Arbor Day—Progress of the Tree Planting Movement," *Transactions and Reports of the Nebraska State Historical Society* 4 (1892): 106–10. On bird protection, see Frank Graham, Jr., *The Audubon Ark: A History of the National Audubon Society* (Austin: University of Texas Press, 1992), especially 24–26, and Robin W. Doughty, *Feather Fashions and Bird Preservation: A Study in Nature Protection* (Berkeley and Los Angeles: University of California Press, 1975), especially 32–33, 103, 127, 153, 157, quotation on vii. I have looked at the issues of ecological ritual in more detail in "From Arbor Day to the Environmental Sabbath: Nature, Liturgy, and American Protestantism," *Harvard Theological Review* 84 (1991): 299–323.

15. For good descriptive accounts of Earth Day rites, see "A Giant Step—Or a Springtime Skip," *Newsweek*, 4 May 1970, 26–28, and "A Memento Mori to the Earth," *Time*, 4 May 1970, 16–18. On recycling, see Garrett De Bell, *The Environmental Handbook Prepared for the First National Environmental Teach-In* (New York: Ballantine Books, 1970), 214–18.

16. Charlayne Hunter, "Spirit of Kwanza: A Time of Giving," *New York Times*, 24 December 1971, 28; Maulana Karenga, *The African American Holiday of Kwanzaa: A Celebration of Family, Community, and Culture* (Los Angeles: University of Sankore Press, 1989), 32–34; Douglas Martin, "Will Success Spoil Kwanzaa?" *New York Times*, 26 December 1993, sect. E, 4. See also George White, "The Kwanzaa Bonanza," *Los Angeles Times*, 30 December 1992, sect. D, 1–2, and Lena Williams, "In Blacks' Homes, the Christmas and Kwanzaa Spirits Meet," *New York Times*, 20 December 1990, sect. C, 6.

17. *American Florist*, 25 April 1914, 725–26. For a contemporary statement of this business perspective, see Archie Anderson and Mitchell Koss, "Is Christmas an Ad Illusion?" *Advertising Age*, 25 December 1978, 18.

18. The "social carnival" description of New Year's is from "Holidays," *North American Review*, 357.

19. *New York Times*, 25 October 1992, sect. 13, 2; "Adult Halloween Revelers Seek Fun and Fantasy for 1991 Halloween Costumes," news release, Hallmark Cards, Inc., 1991; Carin Rubenstein, "Halloween: A Big Boom in Boos," *New York Times*, 27 October 1994, sect. C, 1, 12. See also Kate Fitzgerald, "Hallmark Targets Boo-rish Adults," *Advertising Age*, 9 October 1989, 14, and Bruce Serlen, "What's New in Halloween

Marketing," *New York Times*, 23 October 1988, sect. 3, 15. For early Halloween novelties, see "Hallowe'en Novelties Appear," *Confectioners' Review* 6 (October 1907): 55; "Hallowe'en Lines for 1909," *Playthings* 7 (March 1909): 70–71; and *Dennison's Bogie Book*, 13th Annual Edition (Framingham, Mass.: Dennison, 1915).

NOTES TO ACKNOWLEDGMENTS

1. Quoted in Pamela Wells' review of Vicki Hearne, *Animal Happiness*, in *New York Times Book Review*, 13 March 1994, 11. For this "confessional" turn in ethnography and the dissolution of subject-object dichotomies, see, for example, Ruth Behar, *Translated Woman: Crossing the Border with Esperanza's Story* (Boston: Beacon Press, 1993). For the Updike epigraph, see John Updike, *A Month of Sundays* (New York: Alfred A. Knopf, 1975), 3.

2. Bakhtin, *Rabelais and His World*, especially 33–37, 278–302.

3. See ibid., 33, 37, 52–53, 106; Stallybrass and White, *Politics and Poetics of Transgression*, 171–90; and Douglas, *Feminization of American Culture*.

4. See Janice Radway, *Reading the Romance: Women, Patriarchy, and Popular Literature* (Chapel Hill: University of North Carolina Press, 1984), and Hall, *When You Care Enough*, 69.

5. Edna St. Vincent Millay, *Collected Sonnets* (New York: Harper and Row, 1988), 68.

6. Nietzsche, quoted in Dominick LaCapra, *Rethinking Intellectual History: Texts, Contexts, Language* (Ithaca: Cornell University Press, 1983), 291. The textualization of festival is built into this Rabelaisian, Bakhtinian tradition. For a critical discussion, see Stallybrass and White, *Politics and Poetics*, especially 59–79, 171–90; Clair Wills, "Upsetting the Public: Carnival, Hysteria, and Women's Texts," in *Bakhtin and Cultural Theory*, ed. Ken Hirschkop and David Shepherd (Manchester, England: Manchester University Press, 1989), 130–51; and Tony Tanner, "Games American Writers Play: Ceremony, Complicity, Contestation, and Carnival," in *The Salmagundi Reader*, ed. Robert Boyers and Peggy Boyers (Bloomington: Indiana University Press, 1983), 592–622.

INDEX